The Rise of HR

WISDOM FROM 73 THOUGHT LEADERS

EDITORS

Dave Ulrich, Bill Schiemann, GPHR *and* Libby Sartain, SPHR

FOREWORD

Amy Schabacker Dufrane, SPHR

PREFACE

Jorge Jauregui Morales, HRMP

HR
CERTIFICATION
INSTITUTE™

Copyright © 2015, HR Certification Institute
1725 Duke Street, Suite 700, Alexandria, VA 22314

ISBN 978-1-329-01831-0

www.hrci.org
www.riseofhr.com

Every contributor to this remarkable volume has graciously donated ideas and time to the over 1 million global HR professionals who want to make a difference.

HR LEADERSHIP FOR THE FUTURE WORKPLACE

Amy Schabacker Dufrane

First, on behalf of our more than 140,000 certificants and the HR Certification Institute (HRCI) board and staff, I would like to thank **Dr. Dave Ulrich**, **Dr. Bill Schiemann, GPHR**, and **Libby Sartain, SPHR**, for contributing hundreds of hours of their personal time to ensuring that this book illuminates the value and impact that HR professionals bring to organizations every day.

As the industry's foremost voice for human resources certification, HRCI has brought together the world's leading HR experts to share insights on our profession through this inaugural Institute-sponsored publication that is being distributed globally in an effort to advance the HR profession.

Seventy-three human resources thought leaders from across the globe volunteered to contribute their expertise to this compilation of wisdom regarding the HR profession. Together, their contributions offer a comprehensive look into the critical issues transforming human resources—one of the fastest-growing professions in the workplace and one that is being influenced by many factors, including technological developments and globalization.

The human resources profession sits at the center of some of the most important decisions in any business and is rapidly expanding its influence in the workplace. In the United States alone, economists predict double-digit growth for human resources managers this decade, as business operations increase in volume, complexity, and variety. Organizations across the globe recognize the contributions of HR as a means to elevate acceptable business practices to exceptional business performance.

HRCI is approaching 40 years of certifying human resources professionals. Turning 40 affords us the chance to reflect on the lessons of youth and apply them to the future. During the first four decades of our organizational journey, we have faced numerous opportunities and tests of character. From these experiences, we have gained valuable knowledge about how to create still more opportunities and how to rise to meet oncoming challenges. Most importantly, we at HRCI feel privileged to have served—and to continue to serve—the HR field by helping to spread, scale, and support best practices and professional standards.

As HRCI looks ahead to the next 40 years and beyond, we recognize that HR professionals will play increasingly critical leadership roles within their organizations, further underscoring the need for strong leadership in our field.

As the world's leading provider of certification for human resources professionals, HRCI has a lengthy record of propelling the HR profession to new heights. The organization began certifying HR professionals in 1976 and has evolved into providing new opportunities for ongoing career enhancement for the human resources professional. Among other HR credentials conferred by HRCI, the PHR®, SPHR®, GPHR®, HRMP®, HRBP®, and CA® are the world's most recognized HR certifications. To date, nearly 140,000 professionals in 100 countries have earned these credentials through HRCI.

It is both an honor and a pleasure to present the impressive collection of insights, observations, and provocations about the future of human resources presented in this book. Without the leadership of Dave, Bill, and Libby, the astute contributions of Virginia Lyon, PHR, and the both highly committed and competent staff of the HR Certification Institute, this publication would not exist.

Thank you!

PREFACE

JORGE JAUREGUI MORALES

President, World Federation of People Management Associations (WFPMA)

These are exciting and frightening times for professionals in HR and in other human capital roles. We are all challenged globally to respond to the rapidly changing world around us. I am privileged to serve as president of the World Federation of People Management Associations, representing more than 90 national human resource associations and more than 600,000 people management professionals. In this role, I see many global trends that will reshape our professional and personal world. These trends are influencing, and will continue to influence, the role of HR and human capital practices in organizations, whether they are private sector, government, NGOs, or nonprofits.

For example, leaders in almost every country are facing shifting demographic trends, including five generations simultaneously in the workforce for the first time, the ever-expanding roles of women and minorities in organizations, and an aging population in many industries and locales. These undeniable trends are occurring amid geopolitical shifts, unprecedented economic challenges in many regions, and unstoppable acceleration in technological innovation. And, no part of the world today can survive without increasing innovation, collaboration, and productivity.

Change is everywhere and all the time. For HR professionals and leaders who manage or shape human capital, whatever game you are playing will be changed not once, but many times over the next decade.

This is the crucial setting in which the HR Certification Institute (HRCI) saw the need to pull together HR thought leaders from around the world from associations, universities, consulting, government, and business to discuss these challenges. I participated in the first such event in Chicago last November where the goal was to model collaboration, innovation, and global insights on human resource issues. The result of that discussion was an invitation to more than 80 global leaders to contribute their thinking to a truly remarkable anthology. Dave Ulrich, Bill Schiemann, and Libby Sartain, who moderated the event, have pulled together 73 of these leaders to answer a simple question: ***What do HR professionals need to know or do to be effective in today's and tomorrow's business world?***

This book contains essays from these thought leaders that provide fascinating and unique insights into the role of HR in today's changing business environment. The contributors to this book address questions that will shape tomorrow's HR: What will customers and investors expect of our organizations, and how will HR leaders help grow value for these external stakeholders? What can HR do to deliver and optimize talent? How can HR professionals build organizations with capabilities in innovation, collaboration, culture, and execution? How can changing technology and advanced analytics be applied to human capital management? How will the HR function be governed in the future? What competencies will be critical to success as an HR professional tomorrow?

These topics—and many more—provide rich reading and a head start for those who aspire to be tomorrow's leaders and who desire to add value through HR. What's exciting about the organization of the book is the ability for readers to move around to topics that may be of the most interest to them. Also, in asking for essays, Dave, Bill, and Libby limited lengthy dissertations and instead focused authors on key points—making this an enjoyable read. They also added a useful overall introduction, conclusion, and section introductions that help frame the book's contents.

What is equally impressive to me is that these thought leaders have collaborated in an unheard of way to share their global insights. No one has been paid, and everyone who has contributed has done so because of their personal commitment to the profession. HRCI has graciously spearheaded this event and is willing to help distribute this work for free. With them, I envision up to 1 million HR professionals worldwide accessing this book. What a remarkable statement about how we can further this great profession.

Regardless of your current role or life stage, this anthology will provide new insights, but it is up to you to translate those insights into practice in your organization. Also, as the world shrinks and our reachable networks increase, I hope that you will share these insights with your colleagues, enabling these ideas to reach the far corners of the globe. Let us join together in the rise of HR.

J. Jauregui Morales, HRMP
February 2015

CONTENTS

2 ORGANIZATION

3 TALENT SUPPLY

4 TALENT OPTIMIZATION

5 INFORMATION & ANALYTICS

6 HR GOVERNANCE

7 HR PROFESSIONALS

CONCLUSION

INTRODUCTION

ADVOCATES OF THE HR PROFESSION

Dave Ulrich, William A. Schiemann and Libby Sartain

We are advocates of the HR profession. For the most part, we like HR professionals (probably more than 1 million people worldwide), but liking the people in HR does not sustain our HR activism. We strongly believe—and, importantly, can quantify—that working in HR today delivers outcomes that matter to many stakeholders. When HR professionals do their work well, good things happen to:

- Employees who have both higher work productivity and personal well-being
- Organizations that deliver on business goals and create cultures that endure
- Customers who receive products or services that matter to them
- Investors (debt or equity) who have greater confidence in future earnings
- Communities (cities, regulators, society) where citizens needs are better met

In a world of increased volatility, uncertainty, complexity, and ambiguity (VUCA), HR issues matter more than ever.

GREAT (AND RISKY) TIME TO BE IN HR

The increased relevance of HR functions, practices, and professionals to stakeholder outcomes makes this both a great and a risky time to be in HR. The good news is that HR professionals have more opportunity to influence business success. The

Conference Board's 2014 survey of global CEO challenges ranked human capital issues as the number one challenge.[1] We have also found that the leadership profile of successful CEOs matches the leadership profile of effective CHROs,[2] and that HR issues are increasingly a part of firm valuation by thoughtful investors.[3] Estimates are that about one-third of the issues discussed at the board level are HR related (e.g., succession planning, talent review, executive compensation, governance, strategy execution, ethics, and culture).

But it is also a risky time to be in HR because the performance bar is higher. HR professionals are under more scrutiny than ever to respond as their role takes on a higher profile. When understudies become the leads in a play, when backup players enter a game, or when employees become owners of a company, opportunities for both success and failure increase. Likewise, as HR professionals shift from policy administration, employee transactions, and functional excellence to business outcomes, they will have more and unique opportunities available to have influence.

Indeed, HR is at a crossroads. We believe that HR can rise to this occasion and meet these higher expectations. As the role and function of HR continue to evolve, the business world's perspectives on the field will need to evolve with them. To respond to the new HR opportunities, many HR legacy mindsets that may have been true in the past need to evolve to modern realities, including:

HISTORICAL MYTH	MODERN REALITY
HR professionals go into HR because they like people.	HR is not just about liking people, but about understanding and solving people-related problems in organizations. In fact, HR often requires tough people choices to assure business results.
HR professionals don't believe in or rely on numbers.	HR has relied on data for years; now more than ever predictive analytics guide HR decision-making.
HR professionals want to get "to the table" where business decisions are made.	HR professionals are now invited to the table; the challenge is knowing what to contribute to stay.
HR's customers are the employees in the company.	HR's customers are the customers of the company; HR work helps both internal employees and external customers.

HR's measures of success come from delivering the practices related to HR (e.g., staffing, training, compensation, etc.).	HR is about delivering business results; the scorecard of HR is the business's scorecard.
HR is responsible for the organization's talent, leadership, and capability.	Line managers are the primary owners of talent, leadership, and culture; HR professionals are architects who design blueprints and inform choices.
HR's primary role is to keep the organization compliant with laws and regulations.	Good HR leaders help the organization make good business decisions that match the risk tolerance (or appetite) of the organization.

WHY THIS BOOK AND WHY NOW: RISING TO THE OPPORTUNITIES FOR HR

As the bar on HR has been raised, many thoughtful groups are working to shape the future of HR. John W. Boudreau and his colleagues (sponsored by SHRM, PwC, and NAHR) are focusing on expectations of HR constituencies, HR and performance, talent pipeline for HR professionals, and rewiring of the modern world. Pat Wright and his colleagues (with NAHR sponsorship) are studying the role of the CHRO, with a particular focus on senior leader succession. Professional HR organizations such as CIPD, AHRI, NHRDN, and others are exploring innovative ways to respond to the opportunities.

To complement and rapidly advance this work, HRCI decided to use the wisdom of crowds to gather perspectives on the state of the field, the future of HR, and the ways HR can rise to the increased opportunities. To do so, HRCI invited about 75 HR "thought leaders"[4] from all areas of HR to offer their insights on a relatively simple question: What do HR professionals need to know or do to be effective in today's and tomorrow's business world?

While this question sounds simple, answering it is not easy. It requires granular thinking about HR across numerous variables: from industry (e.g., public versus private sector) to firm size (e.g., large global firms versus small startup ventures) to the global reach of an organization's operations. The answer to this question also requires mature thinking about a wide range of HR functions, from doing administrative processes more efficiently and providing HR functional expertise to offering integrated HR solutions to multiple stakeholders and managing the paradoxes inherent in modern organizations. Managing HR at the crossroads means making these transitions by requiring that HR professionals both master new ideas and no longer do some of the practices of the past.

We also believe that the "content" of what HR professionals must learn has to be shaped by the "process" of doing HR. How HR works together within the HR profession and between HR and its constituents (e.g., leaders, employees, customers, investors, communities) reflects the modern adaptable, networked organization. HR as a profession should model what we ask organization leaders and employees to do, including:

- *Collaboration* – We appreciate that competition can lead to progress. But in today's business world, those who compete most effectively over time need to learn to collaborate and work together. Traditional "command and control" leadership styles are being replaced by "coach and collaborate" approaches that make the whole greater than its parts.
- *Innovation* – We should focus more on what can be than what has been, which requires innovation. Innovation can and will occur in HR services, business models, and mindsets. We should look for new, creative, and pioneering solutions to business problems.
- *Application* – We realize that activity for the sake of activity is not helpful. HR practices, governance, and competencies should result in favorable stakeholder outcomes. We want to see more ideas with impact, where academic theory and research inform practice and where practice guides research.
- *Globalization* – In our digitally wired, global world, ideas move quickly— instantly even—from one part of the world to another. HR work should be adaptive to unique global contexts so that learning can occur through diversity of thought.

As editors of this volume, we strongly believe that the opportunities facing HR will be realized when HR content informs, and HR processes model, the modern and ever-evolving organization.

HOW TO READ AND USE THE BOOK

As discussed, we asked a number of thought leaders to share their insights on how HR professionals can be effective. We did not have a preconceived framework for how these thought leaders would answer this question, but we hoped we would access a broad cross-section of ideas. We have been delighted by the thoughtfulness with which they approached the question and both the breadth and quality of their responses. We are especially pleased that many of the thought leaders were also willing to prepare a short video clip to go along with their essay to make their ideas even more accessible.

When we met with thought leaders and reviewed their essays, we distilled their ideas and placed their essays into seven sections. **Figure 1** shows the flow of these ideas and **Table 1** offers the details behind each of the seven sections. Each section represents a body of knowledge or insights that HR professionals should be aware of in order to respond to the opportunities they face.

HRCI (and other partners) have sponsored and underwritten this project. HRCI plans to share this book with its 140,000 certificants. We believe that with other HR associations joining this effort and with the book being forwarded to aspiring HR professionals, these ideas could touch more than 1 million HR professionals and others in related professions.

As an HR professional who wants to get better, we encourage you to look at sections, articles, and authors and to read, watch, and learn from these thoughtful HR leaders. We hope the ideas captured in this book will lead to experimentation and adaptation. We hope that the HR field will rise to the promises and opportunities available to us. We hope that the next generation of HR professionals will also be advocates for the HR profession and continue to evolve it to deliver sustainable value.

FIGURE 1. LOGIC AND FLOW OF HR INSIGHTS

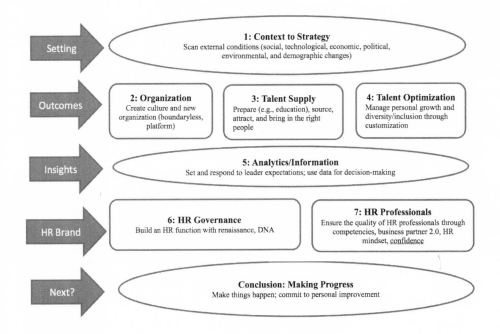

TABLE 1. OVERVIEW OF KEY QUESTIONS AND FINDINGS

SECTION	HR CHALLENGE	MAJOR FINDING
Setting: What is the context for doing the right HR work?		
1 Context to strategy	How does HR respond to external trends and help inform strategic choices?	View HR from the outside in; link HR to external outcomes
Outcomes: What are the outcomes for HR work? When we come to the table, what do we talk about?		
2 Organization	How does HR build the right organizational capabilities, workplace, or systems that make the whole greater than the individual parts?	Create a competitive organization through organization diagnosis
3 Talent Supply	How does HR ensure a supply of the right talent into the organization by managing the flow of talent?	Redefine the workforce now and in the future

4 Talent Optimization	How does HR ensure selection, acculturation, development, performance, and retention of talent, whether employees or other forms of labor?	Ensure personal development and growth of employees by eliminating one size fits all for a diverse and global workforce

Insights: How can information be used to improve HR decision-making and impact?

5 Analytics/ information	How does HR provide unique insights through analytics and information?	Use data to make decisions that have impact and build a narrative

HR Brand: What is the HR brand for delivering value?

6 HR Governance	How does the HR department reinvent itself to have a new DNA and renaissance going forward?	Create a new DNA and a renaissance for how to govern HR

7 HR Professionals	How do HR professionals continue to learn and grow for the future?	Manage yourself and commit to personal improvement

Conclusion and Making Progress: How can HR professionals and departments implement and sustain their future success to really make progress?

About Dave Ulrich

Dave Ulrich is the Rensis Likert Professor of Business at the Ross School, University of Michigan, and a partner at the RBL Group, a consulting firm focused on helping organizations and leaders deliver value. He studies how organizations build capabilities of leadership, speed, learning, accountability, and talent through leveraging human resources. He has also helped generate award-winning databases that assess alignment between strategies, organizational capabilities, HR practices, HR competencies, and customer and investor results. Ulrich has published more than 200 articles and book chapters and more than 25 books. He edited Human Resource Management from 1990 to 1999, served on the editorial boards of four journals, on the board of directors for Herman Miller, on the board of trustees at Southern Virginia University, and is a Fellow in the National Academy of Human Resources (NAHR). Ulrich has consulted and done research with over half of the Fortune 200 and received numerous honors for his research and thought leadership. In 2014, he was ranked the No. 1 speaker in management and business by Speaking.com. In 2011, he was ranked the No. 1 most influential thought leader in HR by HR Magazine. The following year, the magazine honored him with a Lifetime Achievement Award for being "the father of modern human resources."

About William A. Schiemann

Bill Schiemann, PhD, GPHR, is founder and CEO of Metrus Group, specializing in strategic performance measurement, organizational change, and employee alignment. He and his firm are known for their pioneering work in the creation of the People Equity (ACE) talent optimization framework, strategic performance metrics, and balanced scorecards. Schiemann has consulted extensively with corporations on the development and implementation of business and people strategies; HR measurement; strategic employee surveys; internal value assessments; and creating high-performance cultures. He also founded the Metrus Institute, which supports research and publications in the human capital arena. Schiemann is a thought leader in the human resources field, having written scores of articles and six books in the human capital area, most recently the SHRM-published book, "Hidden Drivers of Success: Leveraging Employee Insights for Strategic Advantage" (2013). He currently serves on the board of directors of the HR Certification Institute (HRCI) and is the past chair of the SHRM Foundation board of directors. He has been named a Fellow and Scholar by the Society of Industrial and Organizational Psychology.

About Libby Sartain

After a distinguished 30+ year career in human resources, Libby Sartain is now an active business advisor, board member, and volunteer. As head of HR at Yahoo! Inc. and Southwest Airlines, Sartain led significant business transformation initiatives and guided global human resources efforts focusing on attracting, retaining, and developing employees. Both Yahoo! and Southwest were listed in Fortune's "100 Best Companies to Work For in America" and in the Fortune 500 during her tenure. Sartain serves on the board of directors of ManpowerGroup and AARP. She was on the board of Peet's Coffee & Tea Inc. from 2007 to 2012. She is on the board of the SHRM Foundation and is a trustee for the National Academy of Human Resources Foundation. She advises several startups and Fortune 500 organizations on HR, employer branding, and talent management. Sartain served as chairman of the board of the Society for Human Resource Management in 2001 and was named Fellow of the National Academy of Human Resources in 1998. The co-author of several books, she was named one of the 25 most powerful women in HR by Human Resources Executive in 2005. She holds an MBA from the University of North Texas and a BBA from Southern Methodist University.

---

[1] The Conference Board CEO Challenge 2014. (www.ceochallenge.org)

[2] Dave Ulrich and Ellie Filler, "CEOs and CHROs: Crucial Allies and Potential Successors," published by the Korn Ferry Institute, 2014; also to be published in Leader to Leader.

[3] Dave Ulrich, "Leadership Capital Index" (forthcoming 2015); Laurie Bassi, David Creelman, and Andrew Lambert, "The Smarter Annual Report: How Companies Are Integrating Financial and Human Capital Reporting," Creelman Lambert and McBassi & Company, 2014.

[4] We clearly acknowledge that the list of "thought leaders" who have participated in this anthology is far from exhaustive. Many, many, many insightful HR leaders are doing outstanding work. We tried to cull individuals from universities, professional associations, consulting firms, the public sector, and the private sector who have unique experiences and points of view to inform next-generation HR professionals. We invited these targeted individuals from around the world to capture a global perspective, but we clearly recognize that there are many more thoughtful HR professionals who could offer valuable insights to the question we posed.

1 CONTEXT TO STRATEGY

CONTEXT TO STRATEGY

Introduction

No one can deny that our world is changing, FAST. Technology has enabled information to flow rapidly around the world and to dramatically change when, where, and how we live and work. We inhabit global villages where events in any one part of the world quickly become news and actionable everywhere. Global changes affect all aspects of our personal and professional lives.

This section of essays shares how HR professionals need to be increasingly aware of global business and social trends because they create the context and set the criteria for doing effective HR work. Each of the essays in this section connects changes in the outside world to responses inside a company. Each essentially offers the logic of the entire anthology: external business and social conditions are changing the expectations of how work is done and thus setting new standards for HR. Collectively, these essays capture the content for the evolution and future of effective HR work.

In the past half-century or so, the HR profession has evolved through three general waves (see **Figure 1**), and a fourth (highlighted by these essays) is emerging. Each wave follows a similar curve through time, from startup through learning, growth, and then stability. Note that each wave continues today and builds on the previous waves.

FIGURE 1. EVOLUTION OF HR WORK IN WAVES

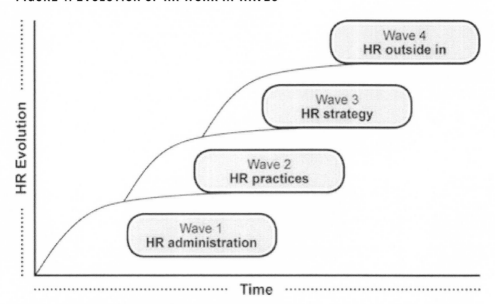

Wave 1 emphasized the administrative work of HR, where HR personnel focused on terms and conditions of work, delivery of HR services, and regulatory compliance. HR was predominantly what we would describe as an "administrative and transactional utility." So long as HR consistently and cost-efficiently delivered the basics— employees were paid, pensions where administered, attendance was monitored, and employees were recruited—HR was seen as doing its job (e.g., cost per hire per employee would be a standard for HR).

Wave 2 emphasized the design of innovative HR practices in sourcing, compensation or rewards, learning, communication, and so forth. While each of these HR practice areas innovated in terms of what and how things were done, they also interacted with one another to provide a consistent approach to HR. HR effectiveness in Wave 2 derives from innovating and integrating HR practices, and HR credibility derives from delivering best practices (e.g., HR innovation and integration would be a standard for HR).

Wave 3 has focused on the connection of individual and integrated HR practices with business success through strategic HR. For the last 15 to 20 years, HR has worked to link its work to the strategy or purposes of a business. In this wave, HR professionals turned strategies into HR priorities to deliver on strategic promises (e.g., implementation of strategy would be a standard for HR).

Wave 4 uses HR practices to derive and respond to external business conditions. We call this wave "HR from the outside in." Outside-in HR goes beyond strategy to align its work with business contexts and stakeholders. We acknowledge that the three earlier waves represent HR work that still has to be done well—HR administration must be flawless; HR practices must be innovative and integrated; and HR must turn strategic aspirations into HR actions (increased investor, customer, and community value would be the standard for HR).

The essays in this section highlight how to respond to this outside-in focus by understanding and relating to general business conditions so that investor, customer, and community value are created.

SIX GENERAL BUSINESS CONDITIONS AND THE HR RESPONSE

When informed HR professionals tell us about their business, they often have a relatively long list of general trends that affect them. The essays in this section offer more rigorous typologies that go beyond general lists. Wayne F. Cascio's essay does an exceptional job at building the case for environmental scanning, and he offers an approach to accomplish this scanning by looking at six contexts that will shape work. Seth Kahan also offers insights on 12 predictions for the future of work that will shape HR. Robert Ployhart makes a clear case for HR being at the center of responding to key external business trends, and he lays out five of them. Ian Ziskin examines five trends and offers 11 implications of these trends for HR. As we look across these wonderful essays, we can organize and prioritize these contextual trends into six categories, each of which operates both independently and collectively in shaping the future of HR.

- *Social* – Personal lifestyles are changing with respect to families, urbanization, ethics, religion, and expectations of well-being. For example, Chee Wei Kwan's essay offers unique insights into Asian economic growth, social conditions, and organizational implications. Ian Ziskin's deep example of mass customization is a social trend that will shift how HR responds. Many essays point to the globalization of society as a major driver of business performance.

- *Technology* – New devices and concepts enable access and transparency not only through information but also in relationships, and they can destroy whole industries while bringing new ones to life. Almost every essay refers to digital, information, and technological shifts. Josh Bersin's essay shows how the digital workplace will dramatically shift HR to help employees scientifically access information to make better decisions.
- *Economics* – Economic cycles shape consumer and government confidence. Freer flow of capital across economic boundaries leads to more granular, or precise, thinking about investments and risk-taking, and gives rise to some industries. The growth of the Asian economy in Kwan's essay is an example of this new economy.
- *Politics* – Regulatory shifts change the expectations of government in corporate and personal lives; political unrest often signals a loss of confidence in government institutions. Charles G. Tharp offers unique insights into the legislative and public policy process and how it shapes an HR agenda. Neil Reichenberg and Fagan Stackhouse offer unique insights about accomplishing HR work from the public-sector perspective and they show how public-sector work shapes the economy of an entire country.
- *Environment* – The earth's resources that provide energy for growth are limited and need to be managed responsibly; in addition, social responsibility shapes how people behave. Holly Burkett's essay on sustainability and Clarissa Peterson's insights on ethics give us perspectives on the social responsibility that shapes HR work.
- *Demographics* – Changing birth rates, education, and income levels affect employee and consumer behavior. Effective HR professionals are aware of and sensitive to these external conditions, which determine how their organizations position themselves for the future. The demographic profile of the future workforce is mentioned in nearly every essay, as HR must manage talent in the future.

These exceptional essays call for HR professionals not only to recognize and understand these trends but to build HR services that respond. These services address many of the issues discussed throughout this book, including more awareness of managing talent, building the organization, using information and analytics to make decisions, governing the HR department and processes, and informing HR professionals.

The mega message of these essays is for HR professionals to move beyond Wave 1 (administrative expertise), Wave 2 (functional excellence), and Wave 3 (strategic

HR) and to capture the value of Wave 4 (outside in). While most might acknowledge that the idea of "outside in" has merit, these essays go beyond the idea to offer ways for HR professionals to access very specific business contexts, and give marvelous guidance about how to shape organizational actions against these external factors.

These essays capture the future of business, work, and HR. When HR professionals grasp external expectations, they create appropriate internal actions. When HR professionals appreciate these trends and their implications, they come to business discussions ready to turn context into strategy, which goes beyond strategic HR where they help implement strategies that others create. When HR professionals understand the context, they can create tailored HR practices that will serve external investors, customers, and communities as well as internal employees and organizational cultures. These contextual factors set criteria that guide actions and increase HR value.

HR'S ROLE IN THE DIGITAL WORKPLACE: A TIME FOR REINVENTION

Josh Bersin

The human resources profession is at a crossroads. Over the last few years digital and internet technologies have radically changed the way we work, requiring a tremendous change in all areas of human resources. Our latest global research[1] shows that business and HR leaders have three major challenges: (1) building and strengthening the new and changing leadership pipeline; (2) finding ways to re-engage employees and build a strong global culture in a world of never-ending work; and (3) reskilling the HR function itself, which often feels behind.

If we consider HR's job as the steward of the "people processes" in a company, we have to recognize that almost every part of management, capability building, recruiting, and communication has been radically changed by technology.

- *The overwhelmed employee.* Today the barriers between work and life have gone away. More than two-thirds of our research respondents tell us they are "overwhelmed by work." A National Journal poll found that more than 40 percent of all workers today believe it is impossible to get ahead in their career without significantly sacrificing time with their family and personal life.[2] Companies are struggling to deal with this issue and know we need to simplify, help people focus, and reduce complexity—but how we create this "new organization" is still a work in process.

- *Transparency of all people data.* Almost all HR-related information is now freely shared on the internet. Glassdoor holds unfiltered feedback about an organization's CEO, culture, and benefits; LinkedIn is an open recruiting tool that lets recruiters find and contact more than 500 million professionals at almost no cost; and a flurry of new tools are now enabling employees to share their salaries, rate their managers, and talk about what it's like to work at their company. Should we still have secret talent reviews and performance ratings? More and more people resent this. They expect transparency in HR practices as well as from leadership.

- *Accelerated expectations for careers.* Only 30 years ago, when I entered the workforce, we expected our employers to give us lifetime careers. Today this expectation has all but disappeared, and young employees change jobs every 12 to 24 months readily. In his new book The Alliance, Reid Hoffman, chairman and founder of LinkedIn, writes that we have entered a world where workers are like professional athletes. They work for a company and contribute for a while, but when needs change, they move to another team, taking their skills and expertise with them. So the concept of a "job" has changed and organizations have to manage their teams in a world of a rapidly changing, mobile, contingent working economy. Companies now have to move beyond "succession management" to putting in place what we call programs for "facilitated talent mobility." But how?

- *New models of leadership.* One of the most important roles HR plays is the development and support of the leadership pipeline. But leadership styles and needs today are radically different from the traditional models pioneered by GE and IBM in the last few decades. Leaders must be agile, globally aware, innovative, and highly collaborative. While the top-down hierarchical structure still exists in most companies, more and more research shows that it is empowerment and agility that drives success in today's economy.

- *The enormous power of data and science.* Finally, HR must come to grips with the fact that data and science are going to transform much of what we do. Many of the "gut feel" decisions made by management (and HR) are soon to be replaced by data-driven decisions: who to hire, who to promote, what career paths to facilitate, how much to pay people—and even where to locate a facility, how big an office someone needs, and what type of food we should serve in the cafeteria. All these decisions, many of which were made by HR working with leadership, can now be informed by data and science, making the "datafication of HR"[3] a new and urgent priority.

How do all these changes impact our profession and the organizations we build in HR? I suggest the changes are profound, important, and exciting.

1. Educate yourself and reinvent traditional practices. First, HR teams must become more educated and professionally conversant in the digital world of business. Today's organizations are flooded with new tools and technologies for work, new ways of working, and a deluge of multigenerational work issues. Old-fashioned HR practices, many of which were developed around the turn of the century, simply have to be reengineered.

Take programs like performance management (only 8 percent of the companies we surveyed believe the time they put into performance management is worth the effort), which is shifting radically away from forced ranking and rating toward an agile, open coaching and development process. Look at succession management, which is only used by 30 percent or fewer of top executives and fewer than 15 percent of leaders at lower levels. These traditional practices, which were designed to operate in top-down hierarchies of the past, simply do not work well today. We need to reinvent them.

Should compensation be fair and equal or do some people really deserve to make 10 times the rewards of others? Research shows that the latter is true today—the traditional "bell curve" of performance is not even valid,[4] so perhaps our compensation models need to be changed as well.

2. Become facile with technology, data, and research. The HR organization of today is highly enabled and empowered by technology. This means HR professionals must be familiar with software, data, analytics, mobile tools, and all the vendors building innovative solutions.

The days of "HR technology" sitting in the basement running PeopleSoft are over. Today mobile collaboration tools, mobile recruiting tools, and predictive analytics tools are among the most important parts of the HR ecosystem. People in the HR function must feel comfortable with technology and be willing to learn and look at data. One CHRO told me, "I am no longer hiring anyone into HR who does not have at least a working set of expertise in statistics." We in HR must be vigilant of new technology and constantly research and study how it impacts the workplace and all our management practices.

3. *Turn ourselves outward into the business.* Finally, as we reinvent what we do and what we know, we have to reinvent where we spend our time. Technology is now making more and more of the "generalist" function available to people online or through a service center (e.g., managing my benefits, viewing vacation days, etc.). Self-service cloud-based HR technology is what we call a "system of engagement,"[3] meaning it is now designed to let individual employees and managers serve themselves.

This means that HR teams must become business advisors, consultants, and expert specialists in their domain. Our job is no longer to be a "generalist" waiting for someone to help, but rather a trusted business advisor, trained with excellent skills and connected to what we call "networks of expertise" (not just centers of expertise). Specialists (recruiting, OD, employee relations, compensation) can and should be more embedded and assigned to the business, so they must be networked and share information and skills with one another.

The HR professional of today is more likely to be a talent expert, a technology expert, and a consultant—and less likely to be an OD professional who likes to train and help people. This is not to say that HR skills are not needed. Today more than ever, HR professionals must focus on three categories of skills: how to recruit, develop, and manage people; how to organize, enable, and improve the organization; and how to manage, leverage, and exploit data and technology. I believe HR is a "craft" and these skills are learned over time, through apprenticeship, and through study and research. If we think about the talent and technologies now impacting HR, these are difficult roles to fill, so the bar has been raised for everyone in our profession.

And there is no question that the digital transformation of business will continue to accelerate. How we work, what we do, and how computers and data inform and aid our jobs will continue to change over time. Human resources professionals, as the stewards and experts in people and change practices in the organization, must reinvent ourselves so we stay relevant, valued, and strategic in the organization of the future.

About Josh Bersin

Josh Bersin is principal of Bersin by Deloitte, part of Deloitte Consulting LLP. He founded Bersin by Deloitte in 2001 to provide research and advisory services focused on corporate learning and is responsible for its long-term strategy and market eminence. Bersin is a frequent speaker at industry events and has been quoted on talent management topics in key media, including Harvard Business Review, The Wall Street Journal, Bloomberg, The Financial Times, BBC Radio, CBS Radio, and National Public Radio. He is a popular blogger for Forbes.com and has been a columnist since 2007 for Chief Learning Officer magazine. He spent 25 years in product development, product management, marketing, and sales of e-learning and other enterprise technologies at companies including DigitalThink (now Convergys), Arista Knowledge Systems, Sybase, and IBM. He holds a BS in engineering from Cornell University, an MS in engineering from Stanford University, and an MBA from the Haas School of Business at the University of California, Berkeley.

---

[1] Deloitte, "Global Human Capital Trends 2014," Deloitte University Press. (http://dupress.com/periodical/trends/global-human-capital-trends-2014/)

[2] "New Allstate/National Journal Heartland Monitor Poll Finds Narrow Majority of Americans See Work/Life Balance as Attainable," National Journal, 2014. (http://www.nationaljournal.com/pressroom/new-allstate-national-journal-heartland-monitor-poll-finds-narrow-majority-of-americans-see-work-life-balance-as-attainable-20141114)

[3] Josh Bersin, "The Datafication of Human Resources," Forbes, 19 July 2013. (http://www.forbes.com/sites/joshbersin/2013/07/19/the-datafication-of-human-resources/)

[4] John Bersin, "The Myth of the Bell Curve: Look for the Hyper-Performers," Forbes, 19 February 2014. (http://www.forbes.com/sites/joshbersin/2014/02/19/the-myth-of-the-bell-curve-look-for-the-hyper-performers/)

[5] Josh Bersin, "The Move From Systems of Record to Systems of Engagement," Forbes, 16 August 2012. (http://www.forbes.com/sites/joshbersin/2012/08/16/the-move-from-systems-of-record-to-systems-of-engagement/)

THE CASE FOR CHANGE CAPABILITY: HOW HR CAN STEP UP AND STAND OUT AS A STRATEGIC CHANGE LEADER

Holly Burkett

"If the rate of change on the outside exceeds the rate of change on the inside, the end is near." – Jack Welch

Today's business landscape is characterized by a new "normal" of fast-paced change related to advancing technology, skill shortages, economic flux, competitive pressures, the global competition for talent, and demographic shifts, to name a few. VUCA is an acronym originally used by the military to describe the volatile, uncertain, complex, and ambiguous context of these conditions. The rising pressure of a VUCA world is rampant, with one out of four organizations experiencing major change initiatives every eight weeks, or more, during the past year.[1]

Given this turbulent landscape, change leadership and an organization's change capability need to be constantly evolving. In fact, the ability to manage unpredictable change demands is commonly cited as the biggest factor separating high- and low-performing organizations. While there is no shortage of literature about how to manage change, studies show that attending to change issues remains an elusive leadership practice. Some experts cite mismanagement of change as the number one factor in the firing of 31 percent of CEOs.[2]

WHY IS CHANGE CAPABILITY SO IMPORTANT?

Managing change and cultural transformation is among the top five challenges facing HR professionals—and the one area in which HR is most likely to partner.[3] Yet few business leaders rate their organizations as highly effective at managing change (17 percent). Most work for an organization with no change strategy in place (83 percent), and most have no designated person to lead change efforts (66 percent). In those organizations with designated change managers, only 3 percent believe change management is sufficiently recognized and funded.[4]

One of the biggest barriers to leaders' ability to maintain and sustain change efforts is the "change fatigue" generated by competing priorities in an environment that is unlike anything they or their predecessors have previously encountered. As one HR executive from a global chemicals company put it: "The pace of organizational change is so great, executives are struggling to keep their leadership focus. But the real challenge is developing and maintaining a leadership pipeline while the world around us changes every three months."[5]

Change management is no longer focused simply on operational improvements, cost efficiencies, or process reengineering. The complexities of perpetual change are an interwoven part of every organization's DNA. Change capability plays into everything that leaders, HR professionals, and employees do every day, regardless of hierarchy or rank.

WHAT CAN HR DO?

Building and providing strategic change leadership in the midst of explosive change patterns can seem much like trying to change tires on a moving car. While the effort might seem daunting, the key is to progressively focus on core elements that will strengthen both individual and organizational change capabilities.

Understand the nature of change. Identifying the type, scale, magnitude, and duration of the change your organization is experiencing helps define the change strategy needed. Largely unpredictable and messy, transformational change (restructures, mergers, acquisitions) requires special capabilities beyond prevailing "one size fits all" change management approaches. Transformational change is best managed as an iterative process as opposed to a single isolated event. Getting the process right means attending to the following elements.

- *Structural elements* define how the change strategy will be operationalized. This includes the use of specific change methodologies, communication planning, project management, monitoring and measuring change outcomes, and structured follow-up. Follow-up is an area that is often underestimated by leaders who may jump too quickly from one change effort to another. HR professionals can add value by emphasizing that change requires time to be sustainable.
- *Cultural elements* represent organizational norms and values in such areas as communication, decision-making, measuring success, and rewarding achievement. Cultural integration is a critical success factor with any transformational change effort. HR can facilitate cultural integration through enabling mechanisms (employee networks, performance management systems) that support the objectives of the new culture. Building support for culture change also means helping leaders to "walk the talk" and role model desired actions in real time.
- *Human elements* are at the heart of successful change and are often the most challenging to manage. HR can help organizational members successfully navigate change by recognizing that:
  - Motivation increases when individuals are confident they can meet change expectations.
  - Resistance may be more related to performance anxiety than negative attitudes.
  - Change expectations should allow for a learning curve after change is introduced.
  - Additional resource support provided right after a change can minimize performance declines and ramp up proficiency.
  - The more individuals are involved in the change process, the more engaged they will be.
  - Change volatility saps motivation, erodes confidence, and depletes any reservoir of goodwill.

Understand the business context. By maintaining a line of sight on the business context where change actions will occur, HR can help leaders get ahead of the curve, not stuck behind it. Marcus Buckingham equates this kind of leadership savvy to the difference between checkers and chess. In checkers the pieces all move the same way, whereas in chess all the pieces move differently. As in the game of chess, the success of any significant change movement is directly related to how well the component pieces, downstream impacts, and cascading sub-changes are addressed and managed. HR can use its consultative role to educate leaders about how each piece of change fits with current organizational structures, systems, and processes—and how each piece is moving and contributing toward the overall game plan.

Make change capacity a strategic readiness issue. An integrated, well-planned change strategy is meaningless if an organization lacks the capacity to execute it. In reality, capacity is finite; people can only do so much and there are only so many people. Capacity becomes a strategic issue when leaders demand that there be more capacity than there actually is or can be, or when they add major change on top of normal operating requirements and don't take anything off the plate to allow for added burdens.

HR professionals must level leaders' expectations of change. All change requires an expenditure of physical, emotional, and cognitive resources that should be prioritized like any other organizational asset. One way to prioritize change tasks and resources is to assess the capacity gaps among the key jobs, employees, and/or business units targeted by change:

- ***High-priority jobs*** may include those that are mission critical, hard to fill, highly paid, revenue generating, close to the customer, or filled by executive search.
- ***High-priority employees*** may include those who are high performers, innovators, leaders or potential successors, hard-to-replace individuals, revenue generators, diverse employees, and/or high-value employees who may be at risk of leaving.
- ***High-priority business*** units may include those that represent high profit/margin, high growth, or high criticality to business performance.

Grow and leverage change capability. While change capacity relates to the ability of individuals and organizations to accommodate new change demands, change capability is a feature, ability, or competence that can be developed or improved. Organizations with leaders who demonstrate high change capability are three and a half times more likely than organizations with low capability to have a strong bench of prospective leaders ready to step into higher-level roles when needed. Findings suggest that organizations should focus more energy on talent development here. For instance, the presence of a designated change management team is strongly linked to both learning and change management effectiveness, but most organizations don't have teams in place.

Available resources, however, are not enough. Resources are only an asset if they are capable and competent. Building change competencies includes providing relevant training. It also means the integrated use of tools to assess change competencies during recruiting, performance management, and talent development, including succession planning. In general, HR's strategic role is to:

1. Hire for resilience.
2. Create a culture of change readiness.
3. Train for and reward change capability.

Anticipate and manage risks associated with change. The path of true change is rarely smooth. Strategic change capabilities can be improved by properly managing risks as they occur, having better risk controls in place, and practicing due diligence. Common risks associated with transformational change include staff attrition, changes in leadership, flawed communications, resource constraints, employee resistance, lack of follow-through, scope creep, and poor accountabilities.

Executives need information about risks to determine whether to continue or alter the course of a change project and whether to continue allocating resources toward its progress. Risk assessment typically involves ranking a risk based upon its severity of consequence and its probability of occurrence. Critical risks that could adversely impact change goals should be given maximum importance, and risk response strategies should be formulated to deal with them.

Manage change turbulence. Change fatigue is a major risk to successful change. Multiple, change-after-change demands have become standard for most organizations, and studies show that demands are on the rise. For instance, a large proportion (45 percent) of respondents in a recent survey by ATD and i4cp said that the number of changes their organizations encounter in a year is more now than it was just two years ago. In essence, many people in today's organizations spend their time "underwater," gasping for breath between one change and the next. Change turbulence drains support regardless of how well planned or executed the change may be and regardless of how motivated and capable the workforce may be.[6]

HR can help organizations manage the churn of constant change by sensitizing leaders to its impact on employee motivation and their overall capacity to achieve performance results. Best practices for managing change turbulence include adopting a vetting process where proposals for significant change are subjected to a rigorous "war room" screening by key stakeholders and then prioritized according to their centrality to the business strategy, financial impact, and probability of success.

Know when to adapt or change course. High-impact HR functions are adaptive, resilient, and responsive to changing needs. Responsiveness means ensuring that HR models and practices are strategically aligned to the business and are adding value to their operational and functional counterparts. It also means taking corrective or innovative action to improve the total flow of processes and to replace archaic systems that are poorly aligned, too complicated, or too isolated with technology-enabled, adaptive structures. In this regard, it is also important for HR professionals to monitor their own aversion to change so that their human capital strategies and core functions are actively driving high performance and operational excellence.

Monitor and measure change investments. While leaders often envision change as a driver of revenue growth, innovation, cost savings, or talent development, an abundance of research suggests that most change initiatives fail at the alarming rate of 70 percent—or up to 75 percent if the ability to sustain change is included.[7] Given this dismal record, it's not surprising that most organizations do not measure the effectiveness of their change efforts. Those who do say leaders' satisfaction is the preferred method of gauging success.

Research reveals that CEOs and business leaders want metrics showing the business impact of change programs.[8] HR professionals must be accountable for consistently measuring the payback of change efforts so that decision-makers have credible data for determining whether to continue their investment.

When developing and analyzing metrics, it is often helpful to provide a macro and micro perspective. Macro-level metrics represent the performance of the entire organization or a function in a variety of categories and are typically reflected as strategic measures shown in a company scorecard or executive dashboard. For the

HR function, macro-level measures may include such categories as turnover or cost-per-hire. Micro-level metrics are those measures (satisfaction, learning, on-the-job application, business results) used to track the success of a specific project, program, or initiative.

Because the fundamental purpose of most change projects is to improve performance, the value of major change efforts can be evaluated by determining the extent to which a project influenced measures related to job performance (proficiency) as well as business performance (productivity, quality, cost, time). If HR expects to be perceived as a true business partner, HR professionals must become more adept at showing how HR practices contribute to business results.[9]

PUTTING IT ALL TOGETHER

While there is no shortcut or one best approach to building change capabilities, the emerging profile of a strategic change leader (**Figure 1**) includes the following characteristics:

- Understands the complexities of change
- Shows the business acumen to analyze the context of change
- Demonstrates the ability to assess, manage, and take risks
- Is sensitive to the impact of change turbulence
- Actively recruits, develops, and rewards change capability
- Fosters adaptability and customer-centric responsiveness
- Can measure the business impact of change projects

FIGURE 1. ELEMENTS OF STRATEGIC CHANGE LEADERSHIP

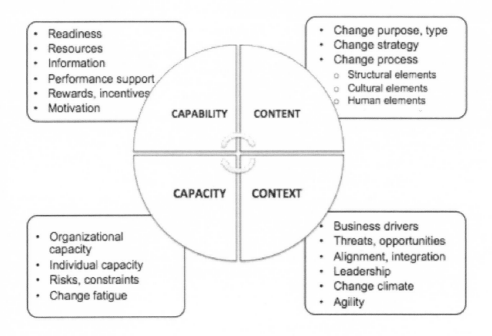

- Readiness
- Resources
- Information
- Performance support
- Rewards, incentives
- Motivation

CAPABILITY

- Change purpose, type
- Change strategy
- Change process
  - Structural elements
  - Cultural elements
  - Human elements

CONTENT

CAPACITY

- Organizational capacity
- Individual capacity
- Risks, constraints
- Change fatigue

CONTEXT

- Business drivers
- Threats, opportunities
- Alignment, integration
- Leadership
- Change climate
- Agility

FINAL THOUGHTS

Managing change and organizational transformation is clearly a universal trend and a critical challenge for HR. The lackluster state of change leadership today shows that the world needs better change leaders. The pressures for change are real, change is here to stay, and organizations are looking for leadership from HR. As HR professionals, we have a responsibility to heed the call by helping leaders and managers gain the confidence, capabilities, and insights needed to thrive amid the complexities of a fast-paced global marketplace. We also have a responsibility to step up and embrace our role as change agents. Only by transforming our own skills and capabilities can we take bigger leaps into the future and deliver on the promise and opportunity of dynamic change.[10]

About Holly Burket

Holly Burkett, PhD, SPHR, CPT, is principal of Evaluation Works, a performance consultancy in Davis, CA. For more than 20 years, she has helped multinational clients achieve strategic impact with diverse human resource development (HRD) initiatives focused on talent development, workplace learning, and organizational change. Formerly with Apple Computer, she works with organizations to ensure that HRD solutions are designed to add and create measurable value. A certified ROI professional, she is a recognized evaluation expert with the Office of Performance Review and an elected member of ISPI's Certification and Governance Committee (CAGC). She has served as a volunteer item writer/forms reviewer for HRCI's certification exams for nearly 10 years. Burkett is also a member of a "Measures and Metrics" taskforce, which, under the auspices of the American National Standards Institute (ANSI), is working to develop national HR standards. She is a frequent conference presenter, international workshop leader, and author on human capital and performance improvement topics, and serves as adjunct faculty with the HRD Graduate Studies program at Drexel University. She holds a PhD in human capital development.

---

[1] ATD/i4cp, "Change Agents: The Role of Organizational Learning in Change Management" (Alexandria, VA: ASTD Press, 2014).

[2] D. Herold and D. Fedor, "Change the Way You Lead Change" (Stanford, CA: Stanford University Press, 2008).

[3] "Future Insights: The Top Trends for 2014 According to SHRM's HR Subject Matter Expert Panels," SHRM Research, 2014. (www.shrm.org/research)

[4] ATD/i4cp, Change Agents, 2014.

[5] HfS Research, "Human Resources Transformation: Is it Driving Performance?" (Delaware: Pricewaterhouse Coopers, May 2012).

[6] Herold and Fedor, "Change the Way You Lead Change," 2008.

[7] "Only One-Quarter of Employers Are Sustaining Gains From Change Management Initiatives, Towers Watson Survey Finds," Towers Watson, August 29, 2013. (www.towerswatson.com/en/Press/2013/08/Only-One-Quarter-of-Employers-Are-Sustaining-Gains-From-Change-Management)

[8] C. Mitchell, R. Ray, and B. van Ark, "The Conference Board CEO Challenge 2014: People and Performance," 2014.

[9] Dave Ulrich, "Measuring Human Resources: An Overview of Practice and a Prescription," Human Resource Management, Vol 36, No 3, Fall 1997, pages 303–320.

[10] Additional sources informing this essay include: J. Hollolon, "New Study: The Top 10 Best Practices of High-Impact HR Organizations," TLNT, ERE Media, Inc., January 2011; D. Leonard and C. Coltea, "Most Change Initiatives Fail—But They Don't Have To," Gallup Business Journal, May 24, 2013. (http://businessjournal.gallup.com/content/162707/change-initiatives-fail-don.aspx); J. Phillips and P. Phillips, Investing in Your Company's Human Capital, AMACOM, 2005.

ENVIRONMENTAL SCANNING: AN EMERGING CHALLENGE FOR HR PROFESSIONALS

Wayne F. Cascio

Consider an intriguing question: "What do HR professionals need to know or do to be effective in today's and tomorrow's business world?" There certainly are myriad possible answers, each posing its own challenges. But I believe that environmental scanning is particularly critical. Let's begin by acknowledging that organizations operate in multiple environments: political, economic, sociocultural, technological, legal, and environmental (PESTLE). **Figure 1** shows each of these.

FIGURE 1. ORGANIZATIONS OPERATE IN MULTIPLE DYNAMIC ENVIRONMENTS

It is no exaggeration to say that the business world is dynamic, complex, and fast moving. "Change or die" is a well-known slogan that often appears in business advertising. The real challenge, however, is not to change for the sake of changing, but to change in ways that will ensure the survival and growth of your organization. To do that well, it is necessary to sift through numerous developments in the six environments shown in **Figure 1**, filtering out those that are unlikely to have significant impact on your organization. Consider some key issues in each of these six environments:

Political – regulatory developments, government policies related to issues that affect your industry, taxation schemes, government grants and fiscal incentives, political stability, strikes, the role of governments in different countries, war

Economic – interest rates, currency exchange rates, the state of economies, prices, inflation, the distribution of wealth in a society, the effects of globalization, vertical and horizontal integration in one's industry, industry trends and changes

Sociocultural – demographic changes, lifestyle developments (e.g., the movement toward "wellness" and healthy living), differing wants and needs of generations in the workplace and outside of it, education and expectations of higher education

Technological – product technologies (e.g., smartphones, virtual reality, robotics), communication technologies (e.g., the internet, Skype, FaceTime, email, text messages, social media), operational technologies (e.g., global distribution systems, global supply chains, mass customization)

Legal – both statutory as well as developments in case law (e.g., immigration, health care, water, cyber law, privacy, product liability, patent law, intellectual property, civil rights)

Environmental – climate change, global sustainability with respect to the use of natural resources (including air, water, and land), mining, hydraulic fracturing, fossil fuels, clean energy, alternative energy sources

With respect to each of these areas, there are two key questions to address. First, which factors are likely to have the greatest impact on the ability of an organization to achieve its short- and long-term objectives? Second, how might these effects change over the short and long term? From the perspective of HR, the key challenge is to identify and then prioritize the people- and organization-related implications of these developments.

In a recent study by the Economist Intelligence Unit,[1] 636 C-level executives identified the top five challenges facing their organizations over the next five to 10 years. The top five were: people management (28 percent), innovation (20 percent), government regulation (18 percent), disruptive technological change (18 percent), and environmental issues (16 percent).

If you think this is just an academic exercise, think again. Here are just a few examples of companies or industries that failed to detect or anticipate key developments that ultimately proved to be their undoing:

• Kodak – the rise of digital photography
• Nokia – the popularity of smartphones
• Sony – the rise of LCD TVs and how consumers purchase, listen to, and share music
• Motorola – digital wireless phones
• Music stores
• Video stores
• Travel agencies

At the same time, there are a number of advantages associated with being a first mover or a fast follower. Here are some examples:

• iPod, iTunes, iPhone, iPad
• Smartphones
• Facebook, Twitter, Instagram
• Big-screen TVs
• Robotics
• Numerically controlled machines
• Hybrid-powered autos
• The fashion industry ("fast fashion")

Environmental scanning is an ongoing challenge for all organizations, because all organizations have a constant need for information on current and emerging trends.

With respect to HR strategy per se, as noted earlier, the key questions are "What are the people- and organization-related implications of these trends?" and "How might these trends affect our ability to achieve our strategic and operating objectives?"

It is important to emphasize that environmental scanning is not the province of a few people or a small department. Rather, it represents a great opportunity for HR to champion this initiative. To do that, it is necessary to capture the diversity of the entire organization. That includes input across generations, genders, ethnicities, organizational levels, functional areas, and geographies. Environmental scanning networks make that possible.

ENVIRONMENTAL SCANNING NETWORKS

Environmental scanning networks are similar to the diversity networks found in many large organizations. Members volunteer to serve and may meet during work time for quarterly meetings. Large organizations might even have environmental scanning networks in each separate location or region in which they operate. The charge for each network is as follows:

- What's new in the political, economic, social, technological, legal/regulatory, and environmental realms?
- What are the implications for the ways we manage our people?
- How might this affect our organization's long- and short-term strategic objectives?

The next task is to integrate information across the networks. To do that, one approach is to collect summary results from each environmental scanning network on a quarterly basis, and then send those results to a central screening committee that reflects the composition of the workforce. The task of the screening committee is to evaluate reports and identify the most pressing trends or actions within them. The screening committee then presents those trends or actions to senior decision-makers for further analysis and action.

Environmental scanning need not always be so formal. At the level of the HR function (if an organization is large enough to have one), the CHRO would need to champion this approach and actively seek input from the HR professionals who report to him or her. The activity itself is extremely important, because HR strategies need to be aligned closely with broader business strategies. To do that effectively and proactively, for example, with respect to social media and mobile computing platforms, HR professionals need to identify and understand the organization- and people-related implications of emerging trends.

At this point, readers might quite understandably be asking, "As an employee or manager, why should I join one of these networks? What is in it for me?" To provide an incentive for participation, and to reinforce network members for their contributions, there needs to be formal recognition of the members of environmental scanning networks who have identified the most significant trends and their implications. In short, it is important to award prizes (monetary, merchandise, or other forms of recognition) to members of these networks. Doing so will motivate them to contribute and also promote an organizational culture of continuous learning—championed by HR and reflecting the full diversity of the broader workforce.

Don't underestimate the power of recognition. Yum Brands CEO David Novak sure doesn't. He has made recognition a signature feature of his leadership style: "One of the things a leader has to do is cast the right shadow, and one of the things I'm most proud of is that our culture is one that really does have fun celebrating the achievements of others. We constantly invest in our culture."[2] Environmental scanning networks represent a great opportunity for HR to seize the leadership of a critical initiative, and to use recognition to keep it going.

About Wayne F. Cascio

Wayne F. Cascio is a distinguished professor at the University of Colorado Denver and holds the Robert H. Reynolds Chair in Global Leadership at the University of Colorado Denver. He has served as president of the Society for Industrial and Organizational Psychology (1992–1993), chair of the SHRM Foundation (2007), and as a member of the Academy of Management's board of governors (2003–2006). A prolific writer in the field, Cascio has authored or edited 27 books, including "Short Introduction to Strategic Human Resource Management" (with John W. Boudreau, 2012), "Investing in People" (with John W. Boudreau, second edition, 2011), and "Managing Human Resources" (tenth edition, 2015). His work is featured regularly in the national business media. Cascio also holds many distinguished awards, including the Distinguished Career Award from the HR Division of the Academy of Management (1999), the Michael R. Losey Human Resources Research Award from the Society for Human Resource Management (2010), and the Distinguished Scientific Contributions Award from the Society for Industrial and Organizational Psychology (2013). The Journal of Management has also named him one of the most influential scholars in management in the past 25 years. From 2011 to 2013, he served as chair of the U.S. Technical Advisory Group that is developing international standards for the HR profession, and he represented the United States to the International Organization for Standards. Currently he serves as chair of the SHRM Certification Commission. He holds a BA from Holy Cross College, an MA from Emory University, and a PhD in industrial/organizational psychology from the University of Rochester.

---

[1] Economist Intelligence Unit, "What's Next: Future Global Trends Affecting Your Organization"(Alexandria, VA: SHRM Foundation, 2014).

[2] Geoff Colvin, "Great job! How Yum Brands Uses Recognition to Build Teams and Get Results," Fortune, 12 August 2013. (http://fortune.com/2013/07/25/great-job-how-yum-brands-usesrecognition-to-build-teams-and-get-results/)

TWELVE PREDICTIONS FOR A NEW WORLD

Seth Kahan

Below are 12 significant and powerful changes that will impact the world of work over the next five to 10 years. HR professionals need to take these into consideration to be effective in both today's and tomorrow's business worlds.

Society is undergoing massive shifts that are difficult to imagine. We are all familiar with change and its increasing presence. It is now clear that this change will continue to not only increase but also become more powerful and complex. In the recent past we have mostly experienced episodic change: episodes of turmoil followed by periods of stabilization in which we could adjust, learn the new skills, become proficient in the new processes, and stabilize. For example, when a new tool came out, like the fax machine or typewriter, at first it would be challenging but soon everyone would have mastered basic functions and how to take advantage of them for their work.

Then came continuous change—change that did not stop. We have had to learn how to incorporate moving targets, dynamic relationships, and fluid protocols in every aspect of work. While we used to have five-year strategies, executives now talk of ongoing strategy in real time. We have become accustomed to one change initiative after the next, though we often complain about the lack of a chance to let things settle.

Today we are experiencing exponential overlapping change. It is exponential because the speed is increasingly faster, and it is overlapping because every change impacts the other changes, each rippling out to touch others in ways that create cross-currents and interference patterns. We may yearn for the day when we can sit back and once again feel that we are in control, but alas that day is never coming. Instead, we need to build our tolerance for complex adaptive systems that never stop and never cease to influence the ways we work.

Exponential change is difficult to comprehend. It goes on for a long time with no apparent rise. It feels flat, like nothing is happening. Then it begins to accelerate, slow at first and then faster. The speed continues to increase until it achieves a vertical climb that is extremely rapid and powerful.

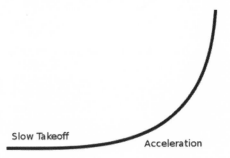

Slow Takeoff

Acceleration

Think about communication as an example. For tens of thousands of years, we had oral communication. Nothing changed until we began to write. Writing was the most advanced form of communication for about 6,000 years. Then there was block printing, which was born in Asia around 200 AD. That continued as the biggest breakthrough until movable type—the printing press—in the 15th century. The press took less than 300 years to propagate across most of the world. And so it goes. Today new technologies come out in parallel. Advances include simultaneous wireless breakthroughs like LTE Advanced, last-mile copper network acceleration, and 5G.

Why is this increasing change important for HR professionals? Because talent development and acquisition is the critical differentiator for strategic achievement. Further, knowledge is enabled by and embedded in every aspect of the work environment.

In that vein, here are 12 disruptions that every HR professional will need to understand, prepare for, and be ready to deliver against:

1. We will need both "dots" and "dot connectors." Because the market will continue to grow more complex and nuanced, there will simultaneously be an increased need for two types of workers: those who are highly specialized (the dots) and those who can connect multiple specialties, bridging their value streams to realize ever greater influence and impact (the dot connectors). Each requires the other for maximum value realization.

2. *Technology and innovation will accelerate exponentially.* This will be seen in three areas: smart objects, artificial intelligence, and new HR tools and applications.

Smart objects – All staff members will need to understand the "Internet of Things"—connected and communicating objects that collect data and aggregate it.

Artificial intelligence – Software, which already runs a great deal, will insinuate itself into every aspect of work, requiring professionals to understand programming as pervasively as the ways we have required workers to keyboard today. Everyone will interface with smart systems continuously.

New HR tools and applications – HR workers will use more and more advanced technology to understand and deliver their work. This will include everything from more advanced employee cost calculators that take into account knowledge and expertise to assessment design, strategy development, and outcome bench-marking tools.

3. *Multiculturalism will take on new meaning as value is derived from a more diverse cultural ecology of frameworks and mindsets.* The developing world will come more fully online in the next five to 20 years at an increasing rate. New ways of working that connect people in new parts of the world will be required. There will be deeper penetration where now there is only shallow connectivity. As a result, we will need workers who understand the nuances and potential of developing-world penetration as well as those who can integrate the differing mindsets and leverage the value they offer.

4. *The business world will increasingly convert from an "old boys' network" to a true meritocracy.* We will see dramatic progress in the next five years due to technology leveling the playing field, providing opportunity to anyone who can find it, and delivering better measurable outcomes.

5. Economic parity for women will be achieved in the United States within five years and on a global scale within 10 years. Diversity will take on new value and be mined for its ability to yield growth. There will be correspondingly significant changes in leadership and culture. This will include increased economic performance and greater mission impact.

6. While the rich will get richer, so will the poor. The number of people living at subsistence levels will dramatically decline. This is already happening today, with the number of people living on less than $1.25 per day dropping from just under 2 billion in 1990 to under 1 billion in 2010. This means the overall standard of living is rising on a global scale, which will have marked impact on both priorities and economies.

7. Knowledge execution will become the most valuable core asset in the world. The ability to execute on knowledge will trump profitability, which will trump politics. Nation states and their governments will continue to be important—but not as influential in international relations and global engagement as corporations. Corporations will continue to grow but be fundamentally transformed by knowledge and the capacity to execute on that knowledge.

8. There will be a blending of nonprofits and the private sector, opening up new markets and opportunities for mission-driven organizations and priorities. The false distinction between nonprofits and the private sector will mostly dissolve in the next 10 years, with mission impact becoming the final focus.

9. Terrorism will be largely disrupted, contained, and eradicated within 10 years. New technologies will make it possible to quickly isolate individuals and events, enabling immediate retaliation. We will finally start destroying terrorists faster than we are fostering them, which will lead to inevitable extermination. While the world will never be fully free of terrorism, it will diminish to the point of negligibility and an inability to disrupt millions of people.

10. Customer service will take giant leaps forward. Just as social benefit has become a requirement for doing business, there will be a similar expectation for customer service. Organizations that today do not have to make customer service an asset will be forced to develop this competency and do so with excellence. This will be due to customers wielding big data, which will follow the drop in cost of processing power and rise in access to information.

11. *Management will transform twice in the next 10 years.* Management 2.0 will arrive within five years on a grand scale, completely changing today's hierarchical leadership protocols to decentralized, self-organizing, and rapid prototyping because of its ability to stabilize and dramatically grow organizational profit. Management 3.0 will arrive within 10 years, humanizing corporations and fostering corporate cultures that are inspiring, innovative, and creative. This will come not as a result of altruism or good intentions but by necessity, as work will be fully integrated with life. Organizations that have adopted Management 3.0 will thrive and excel visibly and undeniably in every bottom line that is being measured, including wealth, social benefit, and ecological.

12. *If work today is 50 percent integrated with life, it will become 95 percent integrated within five years.* The integration of work and life that began with the internet—and has been accelerated through wireless technology and smartphones—will continue to accelerate, making it possible for work to be done anywhere, anytime, by anyone. The tradeoff between doing work everywhere and being able to have a life will reach optimum resolution without being limited by technology.

These 12 changes—and others that result from the same forces—will make for a very different world in the coming decade. Because the pace of change will pick up, becoming more complex and disruptive, an entirely new mindset will dominate the workforce.

HR will be called upon to play an increasingly important role to midwife workers and the business environment for the best possible outcomes. It will be a dramatic challenge and a profound opportunity that will call into question many sacred cows as new value is unearthed.

Because talent development and acquisition is the critical differentiator for strategic achievement, HR will be accountable for market success in *every sector.* Therefore, each of us must take on the mantle of responsibility, develop ourselves and our field to our greatest capacity, and engage fully. This is our call to action. This is our time.

About Seth Kahan

Seth Kahan is a leadership and performance improvement authority specializing in change leadership. He has been designated a thought leader and "Exemplar in Change Leadership" by the Society for the Advancement of Consulting, and has been called a "visionary" by the Center for Association Leadership. Kahan has worked hand-in-hand with more than 125 leaders and executives since 1996—from Jim Wolfensohn, president of the World Bank; to Chris McEntee, executive director and CEO of the American Geophysical Union; to Tony Cancelosi, CEO of Columbia Lighthouse for the Blind. He has also been involved in a $20 million initiative with Royal Dutch Shell. Stories from his work are highlighted in his most recent book, "Getting Innovation Right," and on his two websites, VisionaryLeadership.com and AssociationTransformation.com.

WHAT HR NEEDS TO DO TO HELP DEVELOP GLOBAL ASIAN TALENT

Chee Wei Kwan

The last 20 years have witnessed an unprecedented shift of global economic growth from West to East. The Organisation for Economic Co-operation and Development (OECD) projects that Asia will grow at almost 7 percent over the next five years,[1] and analysts predict that the region could become the world's largest economy (by GDP contribution) by 2030.[2] This growth is leading global organizations to anticipate that Asia will drive the top-line revenue over the next decade owing to incremental business from the region.

While the pace of economic activity in Asia continues to attract multinationals from the West, the trend of business heavyweights in the region—or firms from emerging markets growing through their Asian operations—is also on a rapid rise. McKinsey Global Institute forecasts that by 2025, the emerging world will account for more than 45 percent of the Fortune Global 500, and about half of this will be from Greater China. It also points out that "it is only a matter of time before the most successful companies in the emerging world set their sights on international expansion."[3] China's Lenovo, Haier Group, and Huawei Technologies, and India's Tata companies, HCL Technologies, and Aditya Birla are already contemporary examples.

The regional (Asia and/or ASEAN) HR function needs to play a critical role in helping support business with the talent needed to drive growth in Asia. In fact, while regional HR teams implement talent practices in Asia to match global standards, business heads are expecting HR to create a cadre of "global Asian leaders." This essay attempts to unpack the definition of "global" leader, highlight key characteristics that leaders need to be successful in global roles, and explain the "hats" that regional HR needs to wear to create a robust global Asian leadership pipeline.

WHO IS A "GLOBAL ASIAN LEADER"—AND WHY IS THIS ROLE CRITICAL?

As business crosses borders, the need for talent and leaders who can do likewise has intensified, leading to increased interest in the topic of global leadership. In framing global leadership, Beechler and Javidan's definition is often quoted:

Global leadership is the process of influencing individuals, groups, and organisations (inside and outside the boundaries of the global organisation) representing diverse cultural/political/institutional systems to contribute towards the achievement of the global organisation's goals.[4]

Building on this and other definitions, some have proposed that the extent of global leadership—or its differentiation from local leadership—be assessed through the dimensions of:[5]

- *Complexity* – Global business leaders deal with more—and different— competitors, customers, governments, and stakeholders. Moreover, today's world is also an ambiguous one. Particularly for leaders managing multiple markets in Asia, the region is more VUCA (volatile, uncertain, complex, and ambiguous) than the developed markets.
- *Boundaries* – A global business consists of a variety of boundaries. Externally, boundaries exist between the organization and its stakeholders, multiplied across different country markets. Internally, one critical boundary is that between headquarters (HQ) and local affiliates.
- *Physical (and cultural) relocation* – In order to engage with key stakeholders situated around the world, global business leaders usually experience physical relocation, which can range from short-term international assignments to long-term expatriation and extreme international business travel.

While most businesses see Asia as a long-term prospect and are investing in physical infrastructure and economic assets, they are also beginning to realize that the most critical lever that—according to global consultancies—could make the Asian growth dream a reality is Asian leadership talent. However, global Asian leaders are in short supply. According to a 2012 McKinsey survey,[6] just 2 percent of the top 200 employees in global companies are located in Asian emerging markets. One key factor contributing to this lack of senior talent stationed in Asia is a weak local leadership pipeline.

WHAT DOES HR NEED TO DO DIFFERENTLY TO DELIVER ON THE GLOBAL ASIAN LEADERSHIP AGENDA?

Regional HR teams in Asia suddenly finds themselves in the spotlight for multinational companies seeking growth. While these businesses want HR to upgrade talent systems and processes and bring them to global level, they also want HR to facilitate a constant "supply" of global Asian leaders. To fulfill businesses expectation, there are three action steps that HR may want to take, each explored below.

1. Understand key attributes of successful global leaders. Researchers have suggested critical traits and abilities—including cosmopolitanism, cognitive complexity, mental inquisitiveness, honesty, humility, and personal resiliency—that make for an effective global leader.[7] A 2012 survey-study of 420 global leaders suggests an additional two key factors: an individual's tolerance of ambiguity and their cultural flexibility.[8] Similarly, at Human Capital Leadership Institute (HCLI), we highlight three qualities that individual leaders need in order to excel in a global leadership role influenced by a complex, boundaryless business environment:[9]

- *Comfort with discomfort* – Successful global leaders seem to not just tolerate discomfort but embrace it. They do not let ambiguity cripple them. Instead, they recognize the need to act decisively even without possessing complete knowledge of the situation. They realize that learning from a poor decision is better than not making any decision at all.
- *Judicious relationship building* – Relationship building is important for driving business growth. But it is more important to discern the right partners. In an extreme example, associating with partners that engage in corrupt practices can undermine one's reputation in a new market. Similarly, it is important to identify and build relationships with internal partners on both sides of the HQ/

local affiliate divide, in order to holistically champion the global organization's goals.

- *Authentic adaptation* – Global leaders need to appreciate diversity across different countries and cultures. While cross-border leaders should learn to adapt their behaviors accordingly, they should also stay authentic to their cultural roots. Completely assimilating into another culture robs global leaders of their unique differentiators and value to their organizations. As one Singaporean executive working in a Chinese bank explained, his more direct management style, relative to his Chinese peers, helped his bank win its first renminbi bond mandate from a global European motor company.[10]

2. Reinvent the role of regional HR to facilitate global Asian talent development. HCLI research indicates that in order to develop global Asian leaders, regional HR teams must ensure that they are perceived within the organization as playing four business-critical roles:[11]

- *Trusted Advisor* – Ensure Asia's talent agenda remains top-of-mind for key internal stakeholders. Regional HR must speak the language that business "appreciates"; understand key metrics critical to business; partner with stakeholders to be a part of the annual planning exercise; and tie business plans to the leadership agenda.
- *Passionate Advocate* – Create opportunities for Asian talent to get the experience required to step into global leadership roles. Regional HR needs to collaborate closely with business to identify, create, and staff key regional and global roles with Asian leaders to ensure the right set of experiences.
- *Innovative Marketer* – Position global roles for Asian leaders as both attractive and career advancing. Regional HR needs to position global roles in a compelling manner for Asian leaders to overcome their mobility concerns. HR also needs to better prepare outgoing global leaders for repatriation, which is often one of the biggest concerns Asian leaders have as they take on international roles.
- *Astute Facilitator* – Continually help talent develop the necessary skill sets, such as being comfortable with discomfort, creating internal and external networks, and being able to adapt authentically to succeed in a global role.

The above roles are diverse and cover multiple HR functions, including talent attraction, recruiting development, and engagement. Excelling at them all is no easy task. Regional

HR teams in Asia therefore need to ensure that they can deliver in each aspect. Here are a few examples of action steps regional HR may consider as they play the above mentioned roles:

- Collaborate actively with regional and global business leaders to unpack the regional business strategy and map out key opportunities/positions that may open up in the region so that they can plan possible leadership opportunities for local talent.
- Try to "influence" business leaders to conduct at least a few global meetings in Asia. This will give HR an opportunity to showcase local talent and offer a possible window for local talent to interact with global leaders.
- Push regional business leaders to staff their local talent on global projects with or without the need for physical relocation. This will help build necessary skills for future global roles and help local talent build their "network" within the organization.

3. Appreciate diversity in Asian leadership. Regional HR needs to appreciate and even educate global business and HR on the nuances of different leadership styles prevalent in the region and the influence of culture, context, and local environment on leaders in different Asian countries. For instance, what makes a Singaporean leader highly ethical and a superb administer? Why is a Chinese leader very competitive? What makes an Indonesian leader extra polite? What drives an Indian leader to innovate at the grassroots? Or, why is a Japanese leader driven by methodical problem-solving?

HR needs to understand and appreciate why these leaders behave in a particular manner, and more importantly what drives their behavior. Appreciation of such nuances will help HR to prepare leaders for cross-country or pan-region roles and set up incoming leaders (from outside Asia stepping into Asian roles) for success in Asia.

For instance, **Figure 1** highlights how Singaporean and Indonesian leaders compare on key attributes of global leadership success.

FIGURE 1. WHERE SINGAPOREAN AND INDONESIAN EMERGING LEADERS STAND[12]

	The World of Global Business Leaders	Traits and Abilities of Effective Global Business Leaders	How does Southeast Asian Leaders Compare?	
			Singapore	Indonesia
1	At the macro level: VUCA	Comfort with discomfort	Great administrators but not VUCA navigators	Adept VUCA navigators
2	At the organizational level: Bridging boundaries through interpersonal links	Judicious relationship building	Quiet workers but not passionate advocates	Polite collaborators but not tough performers
3	At the team level: Relationship to diversity, particularly of the cultural kind	Authentic adaptation	Familiar with diversity but not personally invested	Comfortable with diversity but only within Indonesia

CONCLUSION

As Asia assumes unprecedented importance in the global business strategies of most global enterprises, it is imperative that the region's leadership talent grows exponentially not only for on-the-ground execution, but also to help global organizations better understand the region.

FIGURE 2. MEETING ASIA'S GROWTH DEMANDS

Roles Regional HR Should Play in Building Global Asian Leaders

1. Trusted Advisor
2. Passionate Advocate
3. Innovative Marketer
4. Astute Facilitator

Competencies Leaders Must Have to Succeed in a Global Leadership Role

1. Comfort with discomfort
2. Judicious relationship building
3. Authentic adaptation

To Meet Asia's Growth Demands

Analysts predict that Asia could become the world's largest economy by 2030

As **Figure 2** suggests, local talent needs to not only develop a deep understanding of diversity but learn to thrive in it. Asian leaders aspiring to global careers need to develop a level of comfort with the VUCA environment. They need to step out of their comfort zone to develop relationships not only within their organizations but also with outside stakeholders, including vendors, suppliers, and clients. Most importantly, they need to learn to assimilate "honestly" without losing their cultural roots.

Regional HR needs to play the critical role of being the "ears on ground" for global HR, helping those at HQ to better understand Asian talent nuances, capabilities, and development needs. In their efforts to create more global Asian talent, regional

CHROs need to simultaneously and skillfully manage multiple tasks—including elevate the maturity of existing HR operations to match global standards, partner with business leaders to create more global opportunities for Asian talent, accelerate talent development, and fire up the global aspirations of local leaders.

As the Asia business agenda becomes more central in global organizations, there is incremental pressure on HR to achieve all of this, and at an accelerated pace.

About Chee Wei Kwan

Chee Wei Kwan joined the Human Capital Leadership Institute (HCLI) as the executive director in 2010 and is currently CEO of the Institute. Previously, he was the chief human resources officer at IMC Corp Limited, where he was responsible for all HR matters spanning all operations across the IMC Corp group of companies. Prior to that, he gained his HR consulting experience at Watson Wyatt, where he served as the regional director for the Human Capital Group, Asia Pacific. He also served as managing director for South East Asia at SHL from 1997 to 2000. Kwan has worked extensively across the Asia Pacific region with clients on various operational and strategic HR issues, including recruitment and selection, competency modeling and development, performance management, promotion, and career and succession planning. He started his career as an organizational psychologist in the Singapore Ministry of Defense, leading many signature leadership and organization development projects during his 10-year tenure. Kwan holds a BS in psychology from Leeds University and an MBA from the University of Leicester.

---

[1] "Economic Outlook for Southeast Asia, China, and India 2014: Beyond the Middle-Income Trap," Organisation for Economic Co-operation, 2014. (http://www.oecd.org/site/seao/Pocket%20Edition%20SAEO2014.pdf)

[2] Tabassum Zakaria, "U.S. Intelligence Sees Asia's Global Power Rising by 2030," Reuters, December 10, 2012. (http://www.reuters.com/article/2012/12/10/us-usa-intelligence-idUSBRE8B90HY20121210)

[3] McKinsey Global Institute, "Urban World: The Shifting Global Business Landscape," October 2013. (http://www.mckinsey.com/insights/urbanization/urban_world_the_shifting_global_business_landscape)

[4] M.E. Mendenhall, B.S. Reiche, A. Bird, and J.S. Osland, "Defining the "Global" in Global Leadership," Journal of World Business, 47(4), 2012, pages 493–503.

[5] Ibid.

[6] Martin Dewhurst, Jonathan Harris, and Suzanne Heywood, "The Global Company's Challenge," McKinsey Quarterly, June 2012. (http://www.mckinsey.com/insights/organization/the_global_companys_challenge)

[7] R.M. Steers, C. Sanchez-Runde, and L. Nardon, "Leadership in a Global Context: New Directions in Research and Theory Development," Journal of World Business, 47(4), 2012, pages 479–482.

[8] Paula Caligiuri and I. Tarique, "Dynamic Cross-Cultural Competencies and Global Leadership Effectiveness," Journal of World Business, 47(4), 2012, pages 612–622.

[9] M. Ramakrishnan, I. Nguyen, and R. Siow, "Leading Across Borders: Playing Global, Staying Asian," HQ Asia, 4, 2012, pages 48–53. (http://hqasia.org/article/leading-across-borders-playing-global-staying-asian)

[10] D. Wong, "Learning to Adapt and Staying Authentic," HQ Asia, 4, 2012, pages 58–61. (http://hqasia.org/article/learning-adapt-and-staying-authentic)

[11] Puri Sunil, "The Many Hats of HR—The Four-Step Guide to Building Global Asian Leaders," HQ Asia, 2014, pages 68–75.

[12] HCLI research.

ETHICS: THE PRICE OF ADMISSION IN HIGH-PERFORMING ORGANIZATIONS

Clarissa Peterson

Somewhere right now, a human resource leader is tending to an ethical issue within their business. The matter probably isn't a calamity. More frequently than not, it's a minor affair, a second-guessing of a decision, or a misstep to be discussed, dealt with, and filed away as a teachable moment in professional judgment.

It's precisely these types of matters, of apparent inconsequence, that help organizations shape their ethical code.

High-performing organizations understand the value of ethics within the chain of command and extend those principles to their stakeholders, which include employees, customers, and suppliers. As growing numbers of organizations become global enterprises, entering markets with vastly differing ethical codes, the human resources profession must take leadership in ensuring those norms are upheld.

Ethics as a discipline is a notion dating back to antiquity, when scholars of the classical period began to study the impact of human behavior. And while business ethics as a practice has influenced commerce since ancient times, corporate ethics as we know and express the concept today is a fairly new idea. The definitions date back barely two generations, when the business world began to form groups to support the concept and business schools began offering ethics courses on a broad scale.

As chief human resources and chief ethics officer for a major government contracting organization with operations across the globe, I'm responsible for making sure our employees in all locations understand our commitment to ethics and carry out our business accordingly. And I have to make sure those codes translate across cultural realities.

My organization employs great numbers of researchers, people who are quantitatively focused by design. They love data and evidence that help explain human behavior, much like the classical scholars who first studied ethics. When our organization does training, in the United States or abroad, I frequently ask: "By a show of hands, how many of you in the room had a mother?"

The query is often met with bewilderment, until I begin to explain the logic behind the question. A mother—or a father, or another authority figure—taught them a code of behavior. Parents have shared a code of conduct to get by in the world, to make choices between right and wrong. There are lessons about sharing toys and telling the truth. Someone has taught you a code of behavior, no matter where you come from in the world.

These childhood rules are the fundamentals of business ethics. When I think about ethics, I tell people it's about doing the right thing, especially when no one is watching. And what is the right thing in the context of our company? It is understanding our code of conduct and applying that code—even when it's difficult to do so.

EMBEDDING ETHICS INTO BUSINESS

Creating a framework for ethics within an organization often requires us to challenge longstanding customs. Within the scope of my organization's work—which includes research, technical assistance, and implementation of projects in emerging nations around the world—there's a concept known as facilitating payments. To conduct business, a vendor or another stakeholder might expect financial consideration to get things done. Justification for these payments might sound like this: "I work in this country, and this is part of the way we do things here."

At Abt Associates, we've made it clear that these payments are prohibited in every location where we operate, even if the prohibition conflicts with the culture in these locales.

Federal law, in fact, prohibits American individuals and companies from seeking advantage from a foreign public official through payments or rewards. Legislation passed during the Carter administration and updated as recently as 1998 makes it clear that such practices are illegal.

As HR leaders in ethical and compliant organizations, we must ensure that our employees, who work for companies with a different ethical code, understand such norms. Our role as HR professionals is to enforce the concept that ethics doesn't mean yielding to a situational issue, such as facilitating payments. Ethics are global, so doing the right thing means adhering to your company's standards regarding that behavior no matter the geography, situation, or perceived pressure.

A commitment to ethics also means that employees within an organization commit to making the right decisions even when no one in authority is there to say, "Good job."

For HR professionals, that means helping people translate the ethical realities of the companies that they work for into the cultural realities in which they live and work. Through effective recruiting and training, we can bridge that gap, equipping our teams with the language and coaching that prepare them for ethical challenges.

At my organization, when we onboard new talent—from junior staff to the C-suite— we ask questions about situations they've encountered. We want to understand how they handle pressure and whether their decisions reflect good ethical practices.

The same degree of vetting goes for companies we're looking to acquire. As the acquisitive party, we want to know about the target company's code of conduct and how employees demonstrate ethics at the company before closing the deal. We ask situational, open-ended questions to help us assess how a company would address a potential ethical dilemma.

COMPASS FOR BEHAVIOR

Given my organization's role and practice areas, we are not a profit maximizing company. Rather, our mission is to use research to improve the quality of life of people worldwide. Therefore, the business we seek and the projects we undertake are geared toward making an impact.

We are seeing an increase in media reports of business and government leaders displaying unethical behavior. In these cases, unethical and sometimes illegal practices by a few have the potential to tarnish the organization as a whole.

As companies expand globally, regardless of their mission, the ethical choices of their employees are increasingly important. That behavior not only drives performance, contributing to the bottom line, but also has a direct impact on the communities where the organization operates.

So imagine if we stripped ethics from the value proposition of a multinational organization. Consider the impact on the bottom line. Hasty, ill-advised decisions are made in the name of competition. Public opinion turns when the decisions backfire. The financial health of those organizations begins to decline. In the most extreme cases, the impact on communities or even their natural resources is disastrous.

Luckily, there's an emerging ethical consciousness around poor decision-making and its impact on high-performing organizations. Increasingly, companies understand that one regretful decision can impact many others in an organization. These skills are absolutely critical to running a successful business.

The focus on ethics begins at the top. Within my organization, the CEO is present at major professional development events. We underscore ethics by making it standalone content for our professional development for managers, as opposed to a passage within a chapter on training. We strive to give the topic its proper importance, making sure conversations about ethics are two-way discussions.

We also leverage technology, bringing mandatory e-learning courses in ethics and compliance to employees across the globe. As organizations continue to expand

and as companies enter new markets, we must continue to rethink how we support employees as they wrestle with ethical dilemmas in new territories.

ETHICS LESSONS FROM HRCI

I've been working in HR for more than two decades, and have the privilege of serving our profession as the board chair of the Human Resources Certification Institute. The issues that come across my desk, the desks of my HRCI colleagues, and others senior HR leaders are dramatically different than they were 25 years ago. Technology has revolutionized the workplace, as our colleagues have relationships with counterparts around the world. Job descriptions reflect new realities in a truly global economy.

Such demands brought on by the changing economy make it imperative that HR practitioners serve as champions of ethics. Additionally, we have to embed the following skills among our HR colleagues:

- Be students of the HR profession, understanding its unique responsibilities within teams and the currency it carries within the business.
- Understand how current business developments impact the day-to-day realities of your organization.
- Be fluent in long-term trends that will affect your business over time.
- It's incumbent upon us to stay a step ahead of these challenges as HR professionals, acquiring knowledge and sharing that information with colleagues. Organizations look to HR to lead such efforts.

We have to understand how business realities not only impact people but could create unintended ethical challenges. For instance, in a for-profit organization, if there is a slump in the economy or another action that creates a dip in earnings, could our people be more ethically challenged? Would there be temptation to skirt the rules? Possibly. It's precisely at these times that HR has to remind our talent to do the right thing, even when things don't seem like they're going well.

Staying focused on the ethical tenets of the organization can be difficult work. But as ethically focused organizations, even when faced with a slumping economy, headwinds from the competition, or other challenges, these are reminders of the importance of respecting our codes of conduct.

Ethics can't be applied through the filter of situation, whim, or convenience. Rather, high-performing organizations and their HR leaders know that good behavior is the price of admission in the global economy.

About Clarissa Peterson

Clarissa Peterson is an HR executive with more than 20 years of experience. Currently, she is chief human resources officer and ethics officer for Abt Associates, a mission-driven, global leader in research and program implementation in the fields of health, social and environmental policy, and international development. Peterson is responsible for the alignment of Abt Associates' global strategy with its people, their overall employment experience, and their engagement and development. She is also a member of the company's Management Advisory Group. From 2000 to 2005, she served as the company's vice president of human resources. Prior to joining Abt Associates, Peterson was chief people officer for DLA Piper, one of the world's largest law firms, and served on the global integration team for the DLA Piper Rudnick Gray Cary merger, the largest law firm merger in history. She also has led human resources teams in telecommunications and consumer product companies, and co-authored the 2009 book "Maximizing Your HR Efforts." Peterson is an active member of the Human Resource Association of the National Capital Area (HRA-NCA), the National Association of African Americans in Human Resources (NAAAHR) and WorldatWork. She also holds the Global Professional in Human Resources (GPHR) and Senior Professional in Human Resources (SPHR) designations. She earned her BS at the University of Maryland, University College.

THE RELUCTANT HR CHAMPION?

Robert Ployhart

Dave Ulrich's 1997 book, "Human Resource Champions,"[1] helped capture the role of HR professionals for the modern world. It shifted the view of HR as a compliance function to HR as strategically valuable. In turn, many HR leaders blossomed from administrators to strategic partners. Although there is still a long way to go, the HR function and HR leaders have generally become more strategically valuable over the last 20 years. Yet questions remain. Is HR as strategic as it should be? Are HR professionals as effective as they could be? And most importantly, what do HR professionals need to know and do in order to be effective in today's and tomorrow's business world?

There has never been a time in history when HR has been more important to business. Indeed, a number of social, economic, and political factors have converged to make HR the most important function in many organizations today. As a result, HR is being thrust into the spotlight—and this is the moment for HR to step forward and realize its strategic destiny. Will HR professionals embrace the lead role with courage and conviction? Or will they remain within the shadowy margins, clinging to a past that is comfortable and reassuring? Will they be reluctant champions of the HR profession?

For HR professionals to achieve their potential, they need to redefine their role and understand how they fit within this brave new world. The trends shaping the future require fundamental shifts in both the way HR professionals view themselves and the competencies they must master in order to add value. In this new world, HR professionals are no longer compliance officers or strategic advisors. Instead, they coordinate and align talent, data, and strategy in a profitable manner while balancing the interests of relevant stakeholders.

TRENDS SHAPING THE FUTURE OF HR

Several macro trends are already in play that are shaping the future of business. What makes the present situation so unique is the number of distinct trends that are quickly converging. While these trends are interrelated, each has its own implications:

- *Globalization* – The "Great Recession" made it painfully clear that no firm is an island. Economic problems (or opportunities) that afflict other parts of the world are not isolated. With greater connectivity comes greater complexity and greater risk. The U.S. military calls this a VUCA world, for volatile, uncertain, complex, and ambiguous. How can HR help organizations survive and even thrive in a VUCA world?
- *Demographics* – Baby Boomers will sooner or later have to retire, although the manner in which they will retire is unclear. Some Baby Boomers may continue working on a part-time basis, while others may venture into freelance consulting. Firms will struggle with the large numbers of people exiting the workforce and with the loss of the knowledge they will take with them. At the same time, workforces in developing countries are growing rapidly—but most of these workers lack the requisite skills. In both developed and developing countries, newer workers are also much more diverse (by gender, ethnicity, etc.) than Baby Boomers. How can HR manage this diversity?
- *Mobile technology* – There is more technology in a smartphone than in the computers used in the Apollo 11 moon landing. We have moved from the "static internet" (desktop devices) to the "mobile internet" (smartphones) to the "Internet of Things" (devices such as parking meters, street signs, and household appliances that are connected to the internet). Technology flattens hierarchies, provides more access to information to more people, and enhances transparency. Technology also divides the world into those that have the technology and those that do not. As we become more connected, it also becomes easier for fewer people to cause greater damage (think hacking but on a grander scale). How should HR balance the opportunities and threats that technology creates?

- *Data and information* – IBM CEO Ginni Rometty has said that data will be the most important "natural" resource in the near future. People and things generate massive amounts of data. This data contains information that is useful for making powerful predictions and decisions. However, the same information can be used to ruin people and organizations. Employees and potential employees create millions of data points every day. Consequently, "big data" is fundamentally an HR issue. So how can this data be used for good and not evil?
- *Competition* – The days of "sustainable" competitive advantage are over for most firms. Today, one can only hope for a series of short-term competitive advantages. Industry boundaries are disappearing and time horizons are shortening. With fewer external resources, firms are turning inward to search for efficiencies. How can HR help firms make do with less and grow with shrinking resources?

Sitting at the intersection of all these trends is HR. The HR function continually touches every part of the organization and also spans the boundary between internal and external stakeholders. The HR leader has a difficult job, with success not defined in terms of winning but in terms of maintaining balance. It is a zero-sum game—and it's going to be like that for the foreseeable future. The old HR will not be successful in this environment, and HR professionals who are reluctant to make the mental transformation to think of their roles and their function differently will fade away. HR could own the future of business—but it will take a new kind of HR leader to do it.

THE NEW HR LEADER

A useful analogy of the new HR leader is that of a conductor of a large orchestra (in various ways, this analogy has been used by Frank Barrett, Peter Drucker, Lee Faller, and Karl Weick, among others). The conductor's main job is to coordinate the individual elements (musicians, instruments) so that the overall sound is pleasing. The conductor is not an expert in most of the instruments, but is only generally familiar with them. He or she must balance several tensions or paradoxes. One tension is between the motivations and incentives of individually gifted musicians versus the orchestra as a whole. A second tension is between musicians or sections that are strong or vital to a piece versus those that are supporting. A third tension is balancing the flow, timing, and tempo of individual sections to create a harmonious temporal experience. Last but not least, the conductor must balance the needs of patrons, musicians, and owners, and do so in a manner that is enjoyable to all.

HR leaders need to be conductors of the organizational orchestra. In the past, they brought content expertise to assist business lines (e.g., knowledge of staffing practices, understanding of compensation systems). This would be similar to the conductor having deep knowledge of each instrument, where each instrument is like an HR practice. However, the actual playing of the instrument was left to the musician (i.e., the line manager).

In contrast, new HR leaders add value by coordinating the orchestra rather than having deep expertise with each of the instruments. The new HR leader needs to be comfortable balancing the various tensions (individual versus firm, star versus supporting players, timing, and flow) without having the benefit of knowing how to play any particular instrument. This HR leader lets the musicians do what they do best—maximize the performance of their instruments—while the conductor does what he or she does best—maximize the coordination of the musicians in a manner that creates value through intangible resources.

What makes this new HR identity so scary is that the HR leader moves away from what has historically made him/her unique—HR practices—and adopts a role that relies more on coordinating three key elements: talent, data, and strategy. HR leaders own the coordination of these elements. Indeed, they are the leaders that most understand how to create, implement, and develop competitive advantage in the modern economy.

ELEMENTS OF THE NEW HR

There are three key elements underlying the new HR. The first is talent. Understanding how to accumulate, develop, maintain, and divest of talent, both individually and collectively, remains a critical element in the new HR. Although this was true of the old HR, the new HR must address these issues within a very different environment. For example, globalization changes where talent is located, and technology changes how talent is sourced. The management of individual talent also differs significantly from talent as a collection of interdependent individuals.

The second element is data. Big data is largely HR data, and HR leaders will need to be comfortable working with data analysts who may have little knowledge or appreciation of the "human" nature of their numbers. Predictive modeling makes it possible to conduct all kinds of decision analytics. These analytics will fall under Title VII regulations and related legislative guidelines. HR leaders will need to know how to work with data in a legally appropriate, ethical, and professional manner.

The third element is strategy. To argue that HR managers need to think strategically is certainly not new. What is new is that a firm's differentiation strategy is increasingly based on people and how they are organized. That is, employees don't just help implement the strategy—they are the strategy. In turn, HR managers need to embrace new methods for demonstrating the strategic value of talent.[2]

ORCHESTRATING ALIGNMENT

It is the HR leader's job to understand how to leverage and orchestrate these three key elements to generate profitability and value for stakeholders. Some might say, "We already do this." For example, doesn't workforce planning consist of people, data, and strategy? My answer is no. Workforce planning is important but not the right strategic solution because it is based on predictions about a future that is probably not going to exist. In contrast, orchestrating people, data, and strategy enables real-time planning that is flexible and agile.

Orchestrating people, data, and strategy requires an ability to coordinate alignment across different levels of the organizational hierarchy. Most prior HR training has focused on teaching the skills needed to create talent pipelines (or supply chains) that may exist at the individual or firm level. Yet in the new economy, it is not enough to create alignment horizontally. In the search for doing more with less, HR leaders must learn to orchestrate alignment vertically as well. Vertical alignment occurs by ensuring alignment between individuals, teams, strategic business units, and the entire firm. Simply getting good people doesn't ensure better firm performance if those people can't work together or are underutilized. The orchestration of talent across levels creates synergies where the whole is greater than the sum of the parts, but it requires the use of data to understand the required talent configurations that most strongly contribute to strategy execution.[3]

The future should be an exciting time for HR, but will HR leaders cling to the comfort of practices and compliance—or will they embrace the spotlight by orchestrating talent, data, and strategy? Will HR leaders be the champions of a VUCA world—even if reluctantly?

About Robert Ployhart

Robert Ployhart is the Bank of America Professor of Business Administration at the University of South Carolina's Darla Moore School of Business. An internationally recognized expert in human resources, his expertise relates to the acquisition, development, and maintenance of human capital. His more specific areas of focus are recruitment, personnel selection, staffing-related legal issues, employee and leadership development, and organizational strategy. Ployhart has published more than 100 scientific articles and chapters, two books, and holds two copyrights. He has received many scholarly and teaching awards and is a Fellow of the American Psychological Association, the Association for Psychological Science, and the Society for Industrial and Organizational Psychology. Ployhart has worked with numerous private and public organizations to create selection and psychological assessments (e.g., tests, assessment and development centers, interviews, simulations, situational judgment tests), develop culture and climate surveys, develop leadership programs and performance management processes, create training programs, and provide statistical/legal support. He has also consulted and advised organizations on human resource policy and strategy. He received his PhD in industrial/organizational psychology from Michigan State University.

---

[1] Dave Ulrich, "Human Resource Champions" (Boston, MA: Harvard Business School Press, 1997).

[2] I.S. Fulmer and R.E. Ployhart, "Our Most Important Asset: A Multidisciplinary/Multilevel Review of Human Capital Valuation for Research and Practice," Journal of Management, 40, 2014, pages 161–192.

[3] R.E. Ployhart, A.J. Nyberg, G. Reilly, and M.A. Maltarich, "Human Capital Is Dead: Long Live Human Capital Resources!" Journal of Management, 40, 2014, pages 371–398.

KNOWING THE INTERNAL AND EXTERNAL PUBLIC-SECTOR ENVIRONMENT: APPLYING HR COMPETENCIES FOR RESULTS

Fagan Stackhouse and Neil Reichenberg

This essay enunciates the trends and challenges faced by public-sector HR professionals and what makes addressing them so complex. We describe six competencies that can help solve many of these challenges, then suggest several creative, flexible, and permanent processes and systems designed to help attract and retain a talented, engaged workforce that believes in the value of government. For each, success is largely determined by proactive efforts led by HR professionals, in partnership with the organization's leadership.

In 2014, the International Public Management Association for Human Resources (IPMA-HR) surveyed members of the association who are HR directors to determine their top HR challenges. In this same year, the Center for State and Local Government Excellence also surveyed 298 IPMA-HR members. The resulting publication, "2014 State and Local Government Workforce Trends," highlighted a number of important HR issues. The top issues identified were:

- Addressing talent management issues, ranging from recruiting and retaining well-qualified employees to staff development to managing workloads with reduced staff

- Reducing health care costs and implementing and complying with the Affordable Care Act
- Solving the issues of competitive pay and compensation packages
- Public perception of government workers and justifying services provided to citizens
- Impact of technology on the workforce

Taking action to engage the workforce, establish talent management programs, seek competitive pay, reduce benefits costs, and transition to a more technological world fills the public-sector HR professional's plate—and then some. Indeed, the public-sector environment is unique and in many ways more complex and challenging than the private sector. Factors contributing to this complexity include:

- *Transparency* – The public sector is required to be open and transparent about its policies, practices, and compensation.
- *Citizen involvement* – Many governments have citizens who expect high levels of service but do not want to pay more taxes.
- *Spending/staffing reductions* – State and local governments have balanced budget requirements. During the recession, governments experienced significant cutbacks, many of which have not been restored. Unlike in the private sector, staffing levels are below pre-recession levels. The public sector has lost more than 700,000 jobs since the great recession—and even where there is hiring, the number of new positions is low. IPMA-HR's eleventh annual employment outlook survey, conducted in January 2015 and with more than 1,100 responses, found that among governments that plan to add new positions, 50 percent indicated it would be less than 1 percent of the current workforce, with another 22 percent saying that it would be between 1 percent and 2 percent.
- *Political leadership* – Elected government officials are often concerned with constituent service and reelection, which may lead to short-term thinking rather than a focus on the long term.
- *Anti-government sentiment* – The United States is in an anti-government period. Large segments of the public believe that government does not provide the needed solutions and that government employees are not as productive as their public-sector counterparts and receive overly generous benefits—especially retirement benefits. Such rhetoric creates citizen anger and diminished morale among government employees. In 2014, the Partnership for Public Service reported that federal employee job satisfaction had fallen for four consecutive years to a score

of 56.9 on a scale of 100. This is the lowest overall score since the rankings were first launched in 2003. By contrast, according to the Hay Group, private-sector employee satisfaction improved by 1.3 points in 2014 to a score of 72.

- *Unionization* – In states that allow collective bargaining, the public sector tends to be heavily unionized. In 2014, according to the Bureau of Labor Statistics, 11.1 percent of wage and salary workers belonged to unions. Public-sector workers had a union membership rate of 35.7 percent, more than five times higher than that of private-sector workers, where the rate of unionization is 6.6 percent. In some governments, as much as 90 percent of the workforce is unionized. For example, one large county in the Pacific Northwest has more than 100 bargaining units and 81 contracts.

- *Demographics* – According to the Bureau of Labor Statistics, the percentage of government employees who are at least 50 years old ranges from 37 percent to 43 percent; in the private sector, it is 28 percent. By comparison, 23 percent of private-sector employees are under age 30, while in the public sector it ranges from 8 percent to 12 percent. As a result, there is a growing need for the public sector to focus on succession planning as part of its overall workforce planning efforts. Despite the need for succession planning, only 27 percent of the respondents to the 2014 IPMA-HR talent management survey indicated that their organizations have succession plans in place. The top barriers to succession planning identified by survey respondents include management being more focused on day-to-day business, lack of sufficient time to make succession planning a priority, lack of resources, fears within the organization that succession planning will result in favoritism and pre-selection, and lack of commitment by top leadership.

Public-sector HR professionals should seek to understand their unique environment and put forth significant learning efforts to acquire competencies that will allow them to work confidently and effectively in their respective arenas, whether it is federal, state, or local.

SIX COMPETENCIES FOR PUBLIC-SECTOR HR PROFESSIONALS

Applying the six HR competency domains offered by Dave Ulrich in his book "HR From the Outside In" can help us meet and address the challenges and complexities facing the public sector. While other similar and effective approaches can also provide competency development for performing our HR jobs, Ulrich's is an excellent model. The six competencies (shared below), along with 20 supporting competency factors, provide a clear path for HR's development and sustainability. These six competencies offer public-sector HR professionals a sufficiently broad range of tools to tackle the intricacies and unstable political environments that they encounter on a daily basis:

1. *Strategic Positioner* – The ability to position your organization to anticipate and match external implications
2. *Credible Activist* – The combination of credibility and activism that enables HR professionals to establish trusting relationships with line managers and other colleagues
3. *Capability Builder* – Helping make organizations more efficient by reengineering work, clarifying roles and responsibilities through organizational design choices, aligning and integrating systems through audits, and delivering the right capabilities
4. *Change Champion* – The ability to turn change theory into practice at individual (personal), initiative (specific projects), and institutional (culture and work environment) levels
5. *HR Innovator and Integrator* – Ensuring that the organization has the talent and leadership it needs for current and future success by designing innovative and integrated HR practices and using analytics to obtain and sustain top talent
6. *Technology Proponent* – Playing an active role in using new and existing technologies to address issues and add materially to the business

How might public-sector HR professionals use these competencies to address the complexities and challenges mentioned earlier?

Government transparency (of policies, practices, compensation, and individual performance) requires Strategic Positioners whose efforts include:

- Understanding the political environment and how it changes, while also realizing that no top-level HR professionals are protected from public view or scrutiny
- Proactively and professionally creating policies and HR practices that are sustainable regardless of political direction
- Creating community visibility with the media, citizens, and special interest groups, and identifying and respectfully addressing their needs

- Designing all work so that it can be held to the highest level of openness, scrutiny, and public review
- Becoming strategic and communicating the HR strategies for all functional areas before policy boards, governing bodies, administrations, and employees
- Knowing that all compensation data may be of public interest and concern and therefore being willing to share it

Citizen involvement is becoming more commonplace. Being a Credible Activist is essential to demonstrating that you are willing to work with them by:

- Earning their trust by sharing results
- Being proactive and shaping HR functions so that they stand strong against outside reviews
- Collaboratively crafting strategic agendas and using influence to ensure priority initiatives are included in action plans

Political leaders often seek quick fixes to complicated problems and show less interest in addressing root causes. Change Champions can ensure that sustainable and meaningful change occurs by:

- Initiating change that helps political leaders more clearly define their issues
- Building change processes that articulate when and how change occurs through system changes
- Sustaining change by engaging others in these processes and addressing small portions of larger issues first
- Making efforts to put forth policies and procedures that establish behaviors, processes, and metrics to further sustain the changes

Spending and staff reductions in many ways limit public-sector opportunities. This requires HR professionals to seek dollars that will better leverage results. Being a Technology Proponent will not fully make up for these reductions, but it can create greater efficiency by:

- Improving the utility of HR operations
- Providing more cost efficiencies and data/analytics to make effective and sound decisions

- Using social media to recruit talent and brand the organization
- Connecting and effectively communicating throughout the organization and the larger community

Anti-government sentiment significantly impacts talent management, employee engagement, and other initiatives and programs that typically contribute to positive employee involvement. Although a combination of other competencies would prove helpful, the HR Innovator and Integrator provides excellent opportunities to address this sentiment by:

- Shaping organizational and communication practices to define and clarify the roles, responsibilities, and rules of a successful organization
- Identifying and improving work processes
- Designing more effective measurement systems that help drive performance throughout the organization
- Continuing to build talent through workforce planning and individual development plans
- Creating analytics that help make the case for our work and that align with the organization's mission, strategy, and outcomes

Unionization offers a unique opportunity to create more meaningful work environments. The Credible Activist can:

- Create cultural and engagement surveys that help employees find meaning and purpose in their work and discover what matters most to them
- Help define individual value propositions for employees based on these results

Recognizing that more has to be done—and figuring out how it could and should be done—is what is most critical. The tools available are extraordinary. Developing a strategy to move in this direction can be a challenging but rewarding journey for the public-sector HR professional.

About Fagan Stackhouse

Fagan Stackhouse has worked in the public human resources field for more than 40 years in local jurisdictions in North Carolina, Michigan, Wisconsin, Virginia, and now South Carolina. He is currently serving as the human resources director for Charleston County. As a dedicated member of the International Public Management Association for Human Resources (IPMA-HR), he served in the capacity of president. He also served as president of the IPMA Certification Council; represented the Association internationally; and has served as trainer/facilitator for IPMA-HR in Canada, China, Iraq, Sri Lanka, Thailand, and throughout the United States. He is the recipient of numerous awards, including the Virginia IPMA Chapter Award for Outstanding Service, the IPMA-HR Honorary Life Member Award, the Edwin L. Swain Award for distinguished human resources career (Southern Region), and the Warner W. Stockberger Achievement Award (national) for a lifetime of outstanding contributions toward improvements for public human resources. Stackhouse holds a BA in political science and an MA in public administration from UNC-Chapel Hill.

About Neil Reichenberg

Neil Reichenberg is executive director of the International Public Management Association for Human Resources (IPMA-HR), where he is responsible for its overall management. He joined IPMA-HR in 1980 and has served as executive director since 2006. Previously, he worked for a law firm specializing in labor and employment law. Reichenberg speaks and writes on human resource and employment issues and has given presentations at international conferences in numerous countries and at United Nations meetings. He has also testified before the United States Congress. Reichenberg is a graduate of the University of Maryland and New York Law School and a member of the bar in the District of Columbia and New York. He is also a member of the American Society of Association Executives, which awarded him the designation of certified association executive.

CONTEXT MATTERS: BUILDING STRATEGIC HR FROM THE OUTSIDE IN

Charles G. Tharp

Human resource professionals are responsible for the key tasks of growing talent, building capabilities, and shaping the culture of their organizations. While it is widely recognized that deep mastery of the body of knowledge in HR and an in-depth understanding of an organization's strategy and operations are important to success, there has been less emphasis on mastery of the context within which HR professionals function. By context I am referring to the various external influences that shape the effective practice of HR. These important contextual influences include but are not limited to the following:

- Legislative and regulatory mandates in the various geographic locations in which an organization operates
- Cultural differences across geographies
- Industry trends and competitive practices
- Demographic shifts and corresponding attitudes and expectations of employees
- Technological changes, especially those innovations that enable flexibility in the location and manner in which work is conducted

- Increased communication and networking of employees with one another and access to a variety of information sources
- Impact of special interests groups, activists, and other social trends (e.g., social responsibility, environment, increased income inequality)

Increasingly it will be important for HR professionals to develop skills in anticipating and monitoring the external influences that impact and shape the pool of available talent and the organization's culture. Interpreting the potential impact of these external influences—and creating appropriate forward-looking programs and processes to enable the organization to effectively deal with contextual issues—is a key skill for success. Among the key external influencers are customers, regulators, investors, and partners at various stages of the supply and distribution chain. However, given the virtually unlimited influences that may impact an organization, there is a need for HR professionals to develop not only skills in managing the context but also the ability to discern which external influences are important to their organization and to develop effective policy, practice, and program responses to address the issues of highest importance.

PRIORITIZING CONTEXTUAL FACTORS

There are countless external factors that may have an impact on an organization's strategy, talent, and culture. However, any organization's time and resources are limited, thereby requiring that HR professionals develop filters through which to prioritize those external factors that may have the most significant impact. The key filters that HR professionals can use to prioritize the importance of external influences are (1) the business strategy of the organization and (2) the corresponding talent strategy required to deliver a requisite workforce to enable accomplishment of the business strategy. Looking at external factors through these two lenses will provide a touchstone for the HR profession when seeking to prioritize the significance and potential impact of various influences on an organization's talent and culture.

By way of example, assume that an organization has a strategy of creating competitive advantage by being a low-cost producer and that one of the external influences is the increased attention globally to the issue of income inequality. Efforts by external influencers such as government agencies or unions to address income inequity may take the form of raising the minimum wage, limiting tax benefits to organizations with high levels of pay disparity, or blacklisting government contractors that have excess levels of pay inequity. In this example, it would be important that the HR professional monitor minimum wage legislation, union organizing activity, and legislative and tax initiatives addressing pay equity given the significant impact each of these factors could have on the organization's employment costs and business strategy.

By contrast, a company that competes on the basis of technological innovation may be concerned about congressional action to limit the number of H-1B visas, which would affect the supply of scientific researchers and other highly skilled workers. While the H-1B visa issue is important to many companies that compete on the basis of innovation, it is unlikely that it would be a significant contextual issue for firms that compete on the basis of cost. Viewing the external context through the lenses of business strategy and the corresponding talent strategy allows the HR profession to allocate time and resources devoted to monitoring and addressing contextual factors in a more effective and efficient manner.

IDENTIFYING SOURCES OF INFORMATION

Once the key external factors that may significantly impact an organization are identified, the next challenge is to identify the information sources that would allow the HR profession to monitor emerging trends and developments important to the organization's talent strategy. A first step may be to determine which periodicals the organization's business leaders read and the sources of information that inform the business strategy. Such sources of information are most likely to be industry or trade journals, the information provided by the organization's governmental affairs offices in key markets, and key themes surfaced during internal operational and strategic reviews. Reading the poplar global business press may also be a rich source of information on influences that may impact the organization.

In addition to industry and general business periodicals, there are also more focused sources of information to help HR professionals assess and identify important trends and influences impacting the workforce. Professional organizations such as SHRM, HR Policy Association, the Chartered Institute of Personnel and Development, and various university and academic research and policy centers (e.g., the Center for Effective Organizations at USC, the HR Policy Institute at Boston University, and Cornell's Center for Advanced Human Resource Strategy) are among the organizations that can provide information and access to leading thinkers on issues impacting talent and organizations. Other sources of information are professional

HR journals, conferences, and social networks focused on the HR community. The challenge for the HR professional is to interpret the importance and applicability of such information within the context of the organization's business and talent strategy.

POINTS OF LEVERAGE

While monitoring external influences and trends and developing appropriate responses within the talent strategy and practices is important, it is equally important for HR professionals not to be passive observers of external influences. A challenge for the HR profession is to help shape the external context. The manner in which the HR professional attempts to shape a contextual issue will vary based on the specific issue and the position of the organization. For example, if the organization takes a visible pubic position or is outspoken on a potentially polarizing issue such as access to health care coverage, minimum wage, or executive compensation, the organization may open itself to negative reactions from its customers, politicians, or regulators—or become a target for campaigns by parties advocating for a particular issue. Similarly, a relatively small organization may not have the market or political clout to have a meaningful influence on a particular issue important to its business or talent strategy. In these situations, it may be beneficial to identify external alliances to help influence a particular issue of concern.

Professional associations are often effective channels through which to have impact on important contextual issues. Identification of the specific professional association that may be a helpful ally is often contingent upon the issue of concern. For example, issues of employee benefits, workplace safety, compensation, or discrimination may best be addressed through professional groups having these issues as their primary focus. However, there are often situations where greater impact can be achieved through industry groups (e.g., the Pharmaceutical Manufacturers Association or the National Association of Manufacturers) or through general business associations (e.g., the Business Roundtable or the Chamber of Commerce), given the size and scope of their membership and the financial resources they can dedicate to a particular issue. A further advantage of working through a professional association or business group is the anonymity it provides for the individual organization that may not want to be singled out on a potentially contentious topic.

DEVELOPING A SYSTEMATIC APPROACH

In view of the increasing importance of external influencers on business and talent strategies, it is important that HR professionals be keenly aware of the important contextual issues impacting their organizations today and anticipate emerging trends. As with any important management process, adopting a systematic approach to monitoring and anticipating significant contextual issues is essential. Outlined below is a simple model that may be helpful in developing the HR function's approach to managing contextual issues that are important to their organization.

- *Identify.* In view of the organization's business strategy and corresponding talent strategy, what are the contextual issues and external influencers that would have the most significant impact on organizational success today and in the future?
- *Monitor and anticipate.* What are the sources of information on current and emerging external influences that can significantly impact the organization?
- *Prioritize.* Working with the management team, prioritize the issues that are of highest importance to the organization and allocate the HR function's time and resources accordingly.
- *Respond.* Develop programs, practices, and policies to anticipate and respond to key external influences. Monitor the effectiveness of the responses and adjust accordingly.
- *Shape.* Work with professional, industry, and business associations to help shape the key contextual issues that are important to the organization and its workforce.

It is increasingly important that HR professionals develop competency in monitoring, anticipating, and shaping the contextual issues that have an impact on their organizations. Building a greater focus on managing the business and talent context will be a critical enabler of the HR professional's ability to be an active participant in shaping the organization's strategy and ensuring success.

About Charles G. Tharp

Charles G. Tharp is the chief executive officer of the Center on Executive Compensation, where he is responsible for setting the organization's overall policy positions and research initiatives. He is also executive vice president of the HR Policy Association, a visiting lecturer in the School of Industrial and Labor Relations at Cornell University, and a Fellow and research scholar at Boston University's Human Policy

Institute. Tharp has more than 25 years of corporate experience, having held key human resource positions with General Electric, PepsiCo, Pillsbury, CIGNA, Bristol-Myers Squibb, and Saks Inc. Earlier in his career, he served as an executive compensation consultant for the global consulting firm Towers Perrin. He has held teaching appointments at Cornell, Northeastern University, and Rutgers University, and has taught graduate courses in executive compensation and HR leadership. In 1998, Tharp was elected a Fellow of the National Academy of Human Resources, and in 2010 was elected a Distinguished Fellow, the highest honor in the HR profession. He holds a PhD in labor and industrial relations from Michigan State University, a JD from the Quinnipiac School of Law, an MA in economics from Wayne State University, and a BA from Hope College, where he was Phi Beta Kappa and a Baker Scholar.

HR AS ORCHESTRA CONDUCTOR

Ian Ziskin

Peter Drucker said, "The best way to predict the future is to create it." HR leaders have an unprecedented opportunity to create the future of HR by understanding where we have been as a profession, identifying strengths and gaps, and taking high-priority actions to close the gaps. HR people must also develop a shared understanding about the evolving business context and environment in which HR and other business leaders operate—as well as the resulting required changes in work, the workforce, and the workplace.

SIX FACTORS CHANGING THE HR LANDSCAPE

There is a seemingly endless array of shifts taking place in where, how, and when work gets done, and by whom. For purposes of this essay, let's briefly address six such factors to set the context.

1. ***Jobs*** are scarce as a result of the economic downturn that has gripped the global economy since 2008. Economists at the time predicted it would take five years for the economy to fully recover, but things have improved more slowly. This recovery has, in fact, been the slowest in history. But we are finally reaching the point where the economy is growing, jobs are being created at a steady pace, and unemployment is below 6 percent and dropping. Despite these improvements,

we continue to face the dilemma that many of the jobs being created do not match the skill sets of available talent, and these people may therefore remain structurally and permanently unemployed or under-employed.

2. While **globalization** has been on the radar screen for a long time, only in recent years has it become obvious that the majority of jobs, growth, and the math and science skills required to do them are increasingly located outside the United States. This shift is putting significant pressure on US companies that need to find and keep talent.

3. From a **technology** standpoint, the internet is often credited with creating 2.6 jobs for every job it has destroyed. That's the good news. The bad news is that there is a complete disconnect between the technology-based jobs being created and the skills possessed by many of those looking for work. This skills mismatch is a fundamental source of tension in job markets around the world.

4. A scarce supply of talent inevitably leads to questions about workforce **engagement** and the ability to attract and keep key people. Several engagement studies suggest that 25 percent or more of high-potential employees are at significant risk of leaving their current companies within the next year. This challenge is becoming even more pronounced as the economy slowly but steadily improves, thereby creating more opportunities and less anxiety related to the risks of changing jobs and companies.

5. Likewise, the very **nature of work** and the definition of "employee" are also rapidly evolving. Increasingly, people are looking for short-term, project-based gigs rather than traditional long-term, full-time employment relationships. They want to work where they want, when they want, on what they want, with whom they want—and then move on to the next thing when they are ready, not when the company is ready. Think about the challenges associated with employee engagement when we are trying to engage people who are not employees by traditional definitions.

6. In large measure, when it comes to the workforce **demographics** challenge, demographics are destiny because the numbers are what they are. For example, in the United States, 10,000 Baby Boomers will turn 65 every day for the next 19 years. That's an aging population, and an aging workforce. Critical skills will be leaving the workforce in droves, even if people are increasingly delaying their retirement due to personal financial pressures.

The above external environmental factors provide a contextual backdrop for other trends shaping the future of HR, including:

- Agile co-creativity and open innovation
- Analytics and big data
- Collective leadership
- Gamification
- Generational diversity
- Globalization
- Mass customization
- Personal technology
- Social media
- Sustainability

To learn more about these and other key trends, visit: http://www.sciencedirect.com/science/article/pii/S0090261611000568.

MASS CUSTOMIZATION: A DEEPER DIVE EXAMPLE

For purposes of illustration, let's consider the implications of just one of these trends—mass customization. Mass customization at its core is a marketing concept that focuses on combining the mass production and delivery of products or services with specific customization to individual consumers or consumer groups. At its most extreme, it means creating and building each product or service to a specific customer's set of requirements while maintaining large-scale production and delivery.

Examples of mass customization include NikeiD, which allows consumers to design their own sneakers with patterns and colors to fit their style; Chocomize, which allows consumers to create their own gourmet chocolate bars by adding fruits, nuts, and even sugared rose petals; and Pandora, which streams music to personalized "radio stations" by learning listener preferences.

Mass customization in HR will include shifts from employment value proposition to personal value proposition and from sameness to segmentation. Both concepts employ the use of marketing-related principles to solve people-related organizational challenges.

The theory behind the employment value proposition is that if we can convince people how great a place our organizations are to work, employees will be less inclined to leave and more inclined to stay or join. This line of thinking is very valid, but it is not sufficiently precise. In addition to making our companies compelling places to work, we are also going to need to be more laser-like in focusing on the needs and interests of select pivotal talent segments and individuals with critical skills. This new emphasis implies a shift from the generic employment value proposition to a more customized personal value proposition.

As consumers, people have learned to expect and value some choices within a reasonable range of alternatives. For example, when purchasing a new car, consumers have a choice of colors, interiors, electronics, and the ability to buy or lease.

The shift from sameness to segmentation is a related trend that continues to build on the notion of using accepted marketing principles to address people issues. It is probably the shift that makes HR leaders uncomfortable more than any other, because it challenges our definition of fairness.

Fairness taken to extremes has evolved into sameness. We have equated fairness with treating everyone the same because it is easy to explain and defend, both practically and legally. In an environment of scarce resources, however, organizations can no longer afford to peanut-butter-spread solutions and programs across all employees in an effort to keep everyone happy.

As HR leaders, we must begin to shift our perspective from a focus on sameness to an emphasis on segmentation. Rather than practices that ensure we treat everyone the same, HR leaders will instead be called upon to segment talent, identify pivotal roles and individuals, understand their unique needs, and fashion compelling ways to attract, retain, develop, reward, and engage these key people.

The question we might ask ourselves as HR leaders is, "Can we reasonably expect employees and potential employees to be satisfied with the same one-size-fits-all HR practices and other elements of the employment value proposition, when they are increasingly becoming beneficiaries of segmentation and mass customization as consumers?"

IMPLICATIONS FOR REACHING OUT BEYOND HR

A survey that John W. Boudreau and I conducted a few years ago with more than 300 HR people from 11 different companies revealed four very enlightening things:

1. Some of the trends listed above have already arrived for most HR leaders. Trends such as globalization, generational diversity, sustainability, and social media are in evidence in daily work challenges and routines.
2. Other trends have not quite arrived but are increasingly being felt and talked about, including personal technology, mass customization, open innovation, big data, and gamification.
3. There is a significant gap between the role HR people are playing today regarding these trends and the role they think they should be playing in the future.
4. HR people want to be equally involved in all the above future trends—as well as many others—whether they have already arrived or are still emerging. We want to be great at, and directly involved in, virtually everything.

These findings beg some questions. Is it possible or even desirable for HR leaders to be equally knowledgeable about and personally prepared to contribute to each of these trends on behalf of their organizations? Furthermore, can HR leaders expect to master these trends fast enough to keep pace with their organization's need to address them?

I believe the answer is "no," on all counts. It would not be possible for HR people to become equally knowledgeable or prepared, nor could they address these things simultaneously. It would not even be desirable for them to try. And, they could not move fast enough to be personally relevant and savvy in all these areas.

We might eventually learn how to address many of the present or emerging trends facing HR leaders. But we don't need to. That is not our role or the best way to approach the challenge. Our role is to lead, follow, or get out of the way—to reach out beyond the boundaries and traditional disciplines of HR to bring together expertise and capabilities from multiple functions. We don't necessarily need to solve big hairy problem by ourselves, but we do need to ensure they are solved.

To learn more about how HR needs to lead, follow, or get out of the way, visit: http://www.talentmgt.com/authors/966-john-boudreau-and-ian-ziskin.

HR AS ORCHESTRA CONDUCTOR

Most challenges that organizations face today and will confront in the future are large, complex, multidisciplinary, and cross-functional in nature—including the issues mentioned in this essay. And, like the mass customization trend described above, they imply the need for solutions that extend well beyond the traditional boundaries of HR.

HR executives will therefore be challenged to reach out to other disciplines to deliver an integrated set of solutions to complex organizational challenges. Think of HR as an orchestra conductor, bringing together a highly diverse set of people and capabilities to harmonize answers to these complex organizational issues.

The symphony orchestra conductor is not an expert at playing the violin, clarinet, flute, trumpet, and timpani. Rather, he or she is adept at finding the very best musicians who are expert at their respective instruments and bringing them together to produce beautiful music. The differentiating leadership role is orchestration, not universal expertise.

The orchestra conductor metaphor suggests a new role for emerging HR executives. Bring together and partner with experts from a variety of disciplines such as anthropology, communications, finance, law, marketing, project management, statistics, and supply chain management. Reach out beyond the traditional boundaries and comfort zones of HR. Orchestrate integrated solutions to multidisciplinary problems.

It is probably impractical for us to start hiring a bunch of PhD anthropologists or experts in customer intimacy into our HR organizations. And, we might be thinking to ourselves, "Why would these non-HR people want to work in HR anyway?"

They may or may not want to work in HR, but they may be very interested in solving complex organizational challenges. We need to engage these experts on a part-time or full-time basis. Let's bring them into HR, second them to HR for a specified period, or simply partner with them across boundaries. The willingness and ability to orchestrate business solutions to complex issues may indeed by the single most important factor that will differentiate the next generation of highly successful HR leaders from all the rest.

CEOs and other operating leaders don't care where these integrated solutions come from, or who leads them. They don't care whether they fit neatly into the traditional HR competency or operating models. All they care about are solutions and results. So, why don't we HR leaders take the lead in orchestrating these solutions? That's what organizational capability is all about. And, who better to deliver it than us?

About Ian Ziskin

Ian Ziskin is president of EXec EXcel Group LLC, a human capital coaching and consulting firm he founded in 2010 following a highly successful 28-year career as a corporate business executive. Ziskin delivers services to clients as a board advisor, coach, consultant, teacher, speaker, and author. His global leadership experience includes serving as CHRO and in other senior leadership roles with three Fortune 100 corporations—Northrop Grumman, Qwest Communications, and TRW—where he had a track record of designing and implementing innovative business and human capital solutions for complex businesses with combined revenues of $68 billion and 300,000 employees in more than 25 countries. A contributor to numerous books and periodicals, he is the author of "WillBe: 13 Reasons WillBe's Are Luckier Than WannaBe's" (2011) and a contributing author to "The Chief HR Officer: Defining the New Role of Human Resource Leaders" (2011). Ziskin serves on the board of directors of Axion Health and on the advisory boards of Humantelligence and RiseSmart; he is also an executive in residence with the Center for Effective Organizations at USC's Marshall School of Business and an executive advisor to Executive Networks Inc. He holds a bachelor's degree in management (magna cum laude) from Binghamton University and a master's degree in industrial and labor relations from Cornell University. In 2007, he was elected a fellow of the National Academy of Human Resources, considered to be the highest honor in the HR profession.

2 ORGANIZATION

ORGANIZATION

Introduction

For years (some say decades) HR professionals have pleaded to be more involved in business discussions, captured by the metaphor of being "at the table." As indicated in the essays throughout this anthology, HR has been increasingly invited to participate in business discussions. The more relevant question today is: What does HR bring to the table? Kristi McFarland, chief people officer at New Seasons Market, calls for HR professionals to step up to leadership opportunities rather than ask to be invited to business discussions. As leaders, HR professionals help set strategy, drive value creation, develop and inspire people, and model the way forward.

As McFarland implies, HR is at a crossroads—not in having access but in leading on the right issues. Traditionally, HR brought information about administrative efficiencies (e.g., cost per hire per employee) and policy administration (e.g., compliance with regulation). More recently HR has been focused aggressively on talent, serving up HR solutions that bring talent into the organization, enhance talent throughout the organization, and move talent out of (or keep it within) the organization. The flow of talent in, through, and out of the organization has been a primary HR contribution to business success in recent years.

The essays in this section propose that talent is not all that HR contributes to business success. HR can also contribute to business success through conceiving, crafting, and institutionalizing the right organization. To help HR professionals do this, it is useful to ground their understanding of the "right organization." **Table 1** offers a brief historical review of organizational thinking.

TABLE 1. APPROACHES TO CREATING THE RIGHT ORGANIZATION

THEME OF THE ORGANIZATIONAL MOVEMENT	FOUNDING OR EXEMPLARY AUTHORS	HOW TO CHARACTERIZE AN ORGANIZATION	FOCUS OF ORGANIZATIONAL IMPROVEMENT	CURRENT APPLICATIONS
Efficient	Frederick Taylor	Machine with parts	Standard operating procedures	Reengineering to drive efficiency
Bureaucracy	Max Weber Alfred Sloan	Morphology and shape by looking at clear roles and specialization	Clear accountability with roles and responsibilities	Multi-divisional firm; strategic business units; matrix; delayering
Systems thinking	Bob Katz and Daniel Kahn; Jay Galbraith; Dave Nadler and Mike Tushman; Dave Hanna	Organization aligned to environment; integrated systems within the organization aligned	Connecting systems to one another (e.g., socio-tech); organizational diagnosis of systems	Customer-centric organizations; horizontal organizations; organizational audits
Capability	CK Prahalad; George Stalk; Bob Kaplan and Dave Norton; Dave Ulrich and Norm Smallwood	Capabilities within the organization	Diagnosing and investing in key capabilities	Cultural audits; process improvements

Following the logic in this table, HR professionals help create the right organization by making it more efficient by reengineering work, clarifying roles and responsibilities through organizational design choices, aligning and integrating systems through organizational audits, or defining and delivering the right capabilities through cultural audits.

In this section of essays, there is a elaboration on what "capabilities" an organization needs to be successful. Dave Ulrich's essay lays out a way to think about capability, culture, and management action that attempts to clarify the often confusing thinking about how to define an organization. He offers HR professionals specific ideas and tools for doing capability assessment and culture change.

Other essays in this section suggest emerging capabilities that organizations should adopt through thoughtful HR work.

A company's culture, as a capability, is often easier to sense or feel by employees or customers than it is to diagnose and shape. Hugo Bague, Group Executive, Organisational Resources at Rio Tinto, suggests that HR professionals consider culture as the glue to building a system that connects vision/values, mission/strategy, organizational philosophy, and an operating model to deliver performance metrics. He proposes that business performance is more influenced by systems and processes that reflect the organization's culture.

Strategy execution has been an important pivot for the last few years in strategic thinking. It is often easier to propose a future state than to realize one. Organizations with the capability of executing strategy are more likely to succeed than those that merely articulate them. In their essay, Kenneth J. Carrig, CHRO at a number of companies, and Aki Onozuka-Evans, HR advisor, focus on three organizational requirements that will enhance an organization's ability to execute strategy: alignment (unity or shared direction), ability (human capital or talent pools), and architecture (organizational blueprint or governance).

Increasingly, complex business requires more collaboration than independent action. Organizations that master the capability of collaboration do a better job of managing teams, accomplishing mergers and acquisitions, and adapting for the future. Lynda Gratton, a London Business School professor and esteemed thought leader, suggests that because of globalization and technology, HR should be crafting more collaborative organizational cultures. She believes that collaborative organizations not only perform better in the short term, but will help an organization's lifespan match increasing human life expectancy.

With unprecedented access and availability of information, organizations have to learn how to use, share, and manage information in a more transparent world. Transparency, as an organizational capability, enables organizations to increase commitment from customers and employees, share a common direction from the top to the bottom of a company, and meet promises to investors and customers. Susan Meisinger, HR advisor and former CEO of SHRM, makes a strong case for HR professionals to become much more transparent and to recognize transparency for all organizational actions. Information ubiquity will lead to more transparent organizations, leaders, and policies.

No one can dispute the increasing pace of change. When organizations adapt their internal governance to match the external pace of change, they are more likely to succeed. Building agility as an organizational capability becomes central to most organizations today. Arthur Yeung has been CHRO and advisor for multiple Asian companies and is generally considered the leading thought leader for Chinese HR practices. He highlights the dramatic societal and business change associated with mobile internet and suggests that organizations have to build the capability of agility (speed, responsiveness, change) through more adaptive HR practices.

Defining the right capabilities for an organization does not start just with what the organization is good at, but with what customers and consumers outside the organization need the organization to be good at. Creating customer-centric capabilities shifts HR from an internal employee to an external marketing focus. Libby Sartain has been CHRO in many companies and a long-time thought leader in HR (and co-editor of this volume). Her view is that HR professionals must acquire marketing savvy so that they can connect external customer brand promises to internal employee actions. When HR adapts marketing principles, organizations will increase consumer and customer centricity.

Creating organizations with a focus on capabilities means shifting organizational thinking from hierarchical organizations with clear roles, rules, and responsibilities to organizational platforms. The pillars or the systems sustaining a platform become the capabilities an organization requires to succeed. Regis Mulot, executive vice president at Staples, makes the case for building organizational platforms where there will be increased global collaboration, shared (matrix) decision-making, agility and speed of response, and inclusive leadership. He believes that organizations with platforms of these capabilities will win in the global marketplace and that HR will play a key role in making this happen.

As suggested, the authors in this section offer provocative insights about what the capabilities will be for the successful organization:

- Leadership throughout the organization as modeled by HR leaders
- Culture, or glue, that holds organizational systems together
- Strategy execution through alignment, ability, and architecture
- Collaboration both inside and outside the organization
- Transparency of information and action
- Agility or the ability to adapt to change quickly
- Customer centricity so that there is a line of sight between customer and employee brand
- Organizations built on platforms that adjust rather than hierarchies that are stable

While it may not be clear which of these capabilities (or others) matter most to any specific organization, it does matter than HR professionals come to business discussions with the ability to offer insights on the organization, not just its talent. By doing so, HR professionals show up "at the table" of business not by accident, as guests, or as stewards, but as fully engaged members of the management team.

THE IMPORTANCE OF CULTURE TO ACHIEVING SUPERIOR BUSINESS PERFORMANCE: A LEADERSHIP OPPORTUNITY FOR HR

Hugo Bague

Fundamental to an organization's ability to deliver on its strategic goals is an embedded culture aligned to those goals. Cultural misalignment is often cited as the reason why mergers or acquisitions prove unsuccessful—yet is not often given the same focus as an organization's strategic goals. Given its impact on business performance, an organization's culture must not be left to chance. Rather, it must be proactively developed, led, managed, and reviewed.

Culture is expressed in the way people think, feel, and act. It often sums up the personality of an organization—"the way we do things around here"—and is a "group" experience. It exists whether an organization aims for a desired culture or simply allows one to evolve. Ultimately, culture drives behaviors and therefore how decisions are made—irrespective of the systems, processes, and tools that are put in place. Thus the importance of making sure the right culture exists.

How does an organization's culture impact the effectiveness of the HR function? Amid ever-increasing demands on our HR professionals' time, it is vitally important that our HR investment is focused on the levers that can have the most dramatic impact in areas such as employee engagement, health and safety, and capability building—all of which are proven key drivers of productivity and therefore competitiveness.

Too often, HR professionals are consumed by low-value reactive work at an individual level. When change is desired, the focus shifts to large initiatives and programs designed to fix processes and tools blamed for perceived organizational failings. While undoubtedly undertaken with good intent, such initiatives—which by their nature are often far-reaching, lengthy, and complex, especially in global organizations—are almost doomed from the start if the root causes of issues are not addressed.

As the HR function continues to grow and evolve, the demands on HR professionals to manage business processes such as talent management, performance and reward processes, recruitment, and employee relations will also continue to increase. However, unless this is balanced with a significant level of effort to embed the desired culture across the organization, the outcomes of such processes and the associated investments made in them will at best remain limited and the overall contribution of the HR function diminished.

Consequently, if the HR function and its professionals were to invest a greater proportion of their time ensuring the organization has not only the right structural elements in place but also the right culture, rather than focusing on individual matters related to each business process in isolation, their impact will be far more profound.

SO WHAT IS REQUIRED?

Within the overall organization, strong and clear alignment of key structural elements, complemented by an appropriate culture, must be in place to achieve continued improvement in business performance. The key elements can be best described as the chosen organizational design and structure, accompanied by performance measures used to gauge the success of delivering the organization's strategic goals.

These elements must be brought together with enough structure to provide a clear line of sight and linkages between them without "hard-coding" them into a single "system." There is a natural order to these elements; a good mental image to use is a pyramid, in which the elements would appear in the following order, from the top:

- *Vision and values* – The vision should act as a guiding light, laying out where the organization wishes to head. The values describe what is important within the organization and help guide behavior and the way that work is conducted. To be successfully translated, they must be embodied in everything the organization does.
- *Mission and strategy* – The mission outlines "why the organization exists" and what will be done, while the strategy describes how it will be achieved—the "competitive game plan."
- *Organizational philosophy* – This tells the story of how value will be delivered. It features key themes that help keep the organization focused and are often used in decision-making processes to help guide leaders and managers at all levels.
- *An operating model* – The operating model defines how the organization is structured and provides a high-level set of principles for how the many parts of an organization will work together. The operating model must align with the organization's vision, values, mission, and strategy, as these form the context in which leaders will apply it. The model views the business as a system and answers the question, "How are we going to make money to survive and grow?" For example, it could be a high-level representation of the business that shows the grouping of activities or capabilities into operating units; how these units will interact with one another and with external groups (customers, suppliers, other business functions); and key design decisions (where relevant) around decision rights, sourcing, location of work, and technology.
- At the foot of the pyramid is a set of *business performance metrics* that show how success is measured within the organization. These metrics are understood by all and used to measure progress and performance.

Misalignment between any of these elements increases the risk of having duplicate authorities and activities, difficulty identifying who is accountable for what outcomes, and, on an individual level, increased stress and poor performance. Conversely, strong alignment will create an environment in which continued development, growth, and achievement of superior performance are more likely. For example, it is important to explicitly provide guidance and expectations as to how the operating model should be used to drive business value, including how the operating model translates to workforce design.

Critical to making these elements work in practice is *culture*. Indeed, culture is the glue that holds them together. A defined culture must underpin the organization's strategy and its chosen values, as the culture of an organization shapes the experience of the people who work with and within it. Culture is commonly considered to be shared basic assumptions about the way that an organization operates; the symbols, values, beliefs, and behaviors that are considered appropriate; and how individuals are recognized and rewarded.

WHAT ROLE MUST HR PLAY?

Senior HR professionals must play a lead role in the design process for each of the described structural elements. Once defined, the broader HR function has a critical role to play in ensuring:

- Leaders understand the overall organizational construct, including how the operating model and organizational design support their business objectives
- Employees understand the operating model and how each part works together
- The operating model is translated into workforce design so that employees understand their role within the organization and are clear about their accountabilities and authorities
- Common cultural attributes exist that the organization believes are fundamental to align its systems, processes, and practices to the design of its organization

The organization's culture and the "way it does things" must be congruent with its strategic direction. Once a level of understanding has been built throughout the organization of the overall organizational construct, and the desired culture emerges through visible examples of behaviors and values in action, the complementary process and task-level activities will truly begin to deliver results. Ensuring that key processes that drive behaviors and influence decision-making are deeply understood and implemented in accordance with their intent and original design is of great importance for HR professionals. Examples of this in action include:

- *Industrial relations*, where consistency is incredibly important in the relationships with all stakeholders involved. While content and personnel will change, having defined values and a defined culture will help the organization to navigate these relationships over time.
- *The reward and recognition system*, if used as a critical lever, should underpin the overarching organizational philosophy by aligning it to decision-making

processes and key focus areas. Doing so can energize the organization rather than being perceived as an administrative burden by leaders.

- By embedding the organizational and cultural elements in **training and development** programs, discrete knowledge will be transformed into practical business insights and skills into strengths.

In conclusion, it is critical that HR professionals acknowledge that business performance is influenced by far more than systems and processes within an organization. Rather, the organization must have the requisite constructs and elements in place—from its vision down to common business performance management metrics. Exponential value can only be unlocked if these elements are underpinned by behaviors and values that build a culture aligned with the organization's operating model, operating philosophy, and strategy. Unless the HR function ensures that its resources focus on these aspects at an organizational level as well as at the individual process level, further examples of organizations failing to deliver on their promises through a lack of cultural alignment will continue to persist.

Given that leaders often underestimate the role they play in building a culture through their own behaviors and actions, this area represents an opportunity for the HR function to lead the organization as much as partnering with it. Arguably no function is better placed to influence this critical business opportunity, and as an HR function we must grasp it with both hands.

About Hugo Bague

Hugo Bague is group executive for organizational resources at Rio Tinto, a British-Australian multinational metals and mining corporation with headquarters in London. His responsibilities include group-wide accountability for a range of functions, including media and communications; shared services covering information systems and technology, procurement, finance services, group property, and people services; and human resources. Bague joined Rio Tinto in 2007, serving as global head of human resources until assuming his current role in 2013. Previously, he worked at Hewlett-Packard as the global vice president of human resources for the company's technology solutions group. Bague has been a non-executive director and member of the compensation committee and the nominating and governance committee of Jones Lang LaSalle Incorporated, a global real estate services firm, since 2011.

THE FUTURE OF HR IS BEYOND "HR"

Kenneth J. Carrig and Aki Onozuka-Evans

It's time to rethink the future of HR transformation. In the past 10 years, we have transformed ourselves from a reactive, task-focused department into a results-oriented department that is more strategic, streamlined, and cost-effective. HR has also expanded to focus more on organizational design and talent development while managing constantly growing back-end operations. But this is not enough. HR has to change itself into an entity that exploits opportunities to directly and tangibly contribute to company financials.

One way to reshape HR's impact is to facilitate strategy-execution capabilities throughout the organization rather than focusing solely on human capital. In this capacity, HR leaders may be cast as structural engineers of a sort to build an infrastructure where people are aligned, talent capacity grows, structure is reimagined, and processes are reengineered. Beyond a focus only on human assets, HR can play an active role in improving a comprehensive set of components that really matter for strategy execution.

At SunTrust Banks, we recently conducted an in-depth study to identify what really enables companies to succeed. We realized that focusing on execution is as critical as having the "right" strategies. "Organizationally healthy"[1] companies are successful in execution as well as in defining directions of their businesses. But there seems to be no common answer for what creates a truly healthy organization. We decided to develop a quick diagnostic tool that describes most of the organization, instead of finding ways to evaluate every component. We selected only foundational elements that are critical to the core functionality. This approach proved to be concise and realistic enough to make timely, yet meaningful, interventions.

EXECUTION CAPABILITY MODEL: ALIGNMENT, ABILITY, AND ARCHITECTURE

We identified three core factors that make strategy execution possible: alignment, ability, and architecture. These three are integrally related, interdependent, and mutually causal. Although our forthcoming empirical study will refine our model, we believe these three factors are the most robust and practical tools to diagnose organizational health.

Alignment is the foundational factor of organization health because it represents the common framing, purpose, or strategic intent of the organization. In our experience, without alignment, nothing else matters. And there is consensus among the executives with whom we have worked that achieving alignment is the first priority in the pursuit of organizational health (or execution capability). When the organization is united around a set of clear goals, performance expectations, culture, and accountabilities, employees are more focused and able to prioritize activities that drive performance.

Alignment also acts as a bond to keep the organization together, especially when facing changes, by orchestrating individual activities that are purposefully combined to create synergies. The power of alignment is underestimated; it should be reevaluated for its valuable capacity to challenge employees to go beyond what their current skill set can offer.

Ability refers to an organization's greatest intangible assets: human capital. Now being recognized as a source of competitive advantage, talent management is one of the major contributors to bottom-line results. Leaders are committed to cultivating the company-wide capability, seeking ways to translate intellectual capacity into cash flow. This goes beyond mastering all the facets of talent management, such as recruiting, training, and performance evaluation. It means that leaders have to continually commit to creating a talent pool of high performers so that critical businesses can operate at full capacity. The same goes for building a leadership pipeline to insure themselves against potential shake-ups and leadership shortages. Ability, therefore, is more than building a collection of superb individual capacity; it is a company's ability to optimize talent potential and overall human capital ROI and create an organization-wide climate where people are encouraged and empowered.

Architecture is a blueprint of an organization. It is a framework in which individual and collective efforts are organized and maximized to yield the best outcome through focused, coherent, and stable processes. A simplified structure, built with clear lines of authority and decision rights, is a key ingredient for proper architecture. Streamlined processes are also critical because they eliminate needless complexity, reduce waste, and simplify workflow. Both simplified structure and streamlined processes are underpinned to a well-designed information system to endorse well-informed decisions. Such a system can transfer information seamlessly to the right people at the right place while keeping transparency. Organizations that have reliable, scalable, and durable performance can differentiate their competitive positions through architecture in these ways and become more resilient to outside forces.

MAKING THE LEAP FORWARD: COMPETENCIES AND TOOLS

Implementing the execution capability model will require a fundamental change in HR structure. HR would need to shift from focusing on centralized expertise and process efficiency to engaging in practice application and integrated process. On top of the structural transformation, HR professionals will have to master some critical competencies to make this leap. Without these additional competencies, HR will lose opportunities to apply human capital knowledge to strengthen business, which can hinder company's growth.

COMPETENCY 1: KNOW YOUR BUSINESS INSIDE OUT (BUSINESS ACUMEN)

Having strong business acumen will be the first step in breaking away from the traditional mindset of HR as an administrative function. HR professionals must be able to use profound business logic to institute human capital application and also be ready to take responsibilities and be held accountable. To do that, HR professionals need to showcase both business and HR technical skills and be recognized as ambidextrous.

Having a solid business foundation in topics such as performance metrics and profit-making mechanisms would be a mere prerequisite. Successful HR professionals would have to understand the projected direction of business so that they can judge opportunities that represent the most potential for HR strategy application. Setting precedents and building a portfolio of successful contributions will ground HR as a part of the strategy group and foster a relationship with businesses.

COMPETENCY 2: ACT AS A SEARCHLIGHT (STRATEGIC ADVISOR)

It is not uncommon for companies to underestimate the amount of internal work required to properly execute strategies. Particularly when a company is facing an imminent threat, executives are forced to jump right into battle. Because of this "quick decision and fast execution" mentality, problems emerge due to operational deficiency or overcapacity and unclear decision rights.

HR professionals can articulate what's necessary to properly execute a given strategy, specifying when and where bottlenecks could occur in terms of competency gaps, resource capacity, process flow, and decision rights. HR professionals can also prioritize structural issues by impact level and develop remediation plans. As a strategic advisor, HR will not only give voice to future implications but will also translate them into actions to remove roadblocks.

COMPETENCY 3: SEEING IS BELIEVING (CULTURAL STEWARD/CREDIBLE ACTIVIST)

These two roles—cultural steward and credible activist—are frequently discussed separately, but their interdependencies cannot be ignored; HR professionals should have qualities of both because they are complementary. Credible activists commit to a realistic and practical approach and make a direct impact on business performance. This is how HR professionals build trusting relationship with businesses. Speaking the same language, offering practical observations, and sharing goals are some of the ways to become a credible activist, but it boils down to an ability to make impactful changes that promote corporate culture.

Being a cultural steward is built on the reputation of being a credible activist. Too often, culture is intangible and abstract. However, by being a cultural steward, HR professionals can turn it into a more tangible strategic issue, using their position to validate their argument. Cultural awareness penetrates deeper when linked to specific behavior and business outcomes. This integrated view will help HR to be more successful in reshaping and reinforcing the culture throughout the organization to better organize activities and eliminate unproductive activities.

COMPETENCY 4: BE AN EXPLORER (DATA ANALYST)

The rise of digital technology and big data opened a whole new array of possibilities for HR to provide insights through data analytics. Multiple databases (including ones devoted to people management, business performance, and compensation) are being consolidated onto a single platform, which will allow HR to identify previously hidden patterns and trends by linking business performance data with human capital data (such as competencies, career background, training courses, historical compensation, and turnover).

A robust analytical capability will lead HR to palpable actions backed with evidence, informing businesses where to invest and divest in terms of human asset ROI. Moreover, as HR becomes an expert in organizational metrics, it could generate a predictive analysis, revealing embedded trends that may arise in the future and allowing a business to mitigate problems in advance.

COMPETENCY 5: BUILD A NETWORK (TALENT DEVELOPMENT FACILITATOR)

HR professionals have to become diligent and ingenious communicators to facilitate organization-wide talent development efforts to identify, invest, and develop human assets to optimize their overall contributions. HR's ability to construct effective communication networks will help build a holistic system where talent responsibilities are woven throughout the organization and promote collaborative efforts. In order to strategically enhance the exchange and collection of feedback, HR professionals will need to employ a mix of strategic communication channels, techniques, and technology to boost collaboration within the organization. Such a strategic communication capability will help HR consolidate widespread commitment across diverse constituents.

COMPETENCY 6: SEARCH FOR INNOVATION (DIVERGENT THINKER)

HR is known as the least innovative function in the organization, bound to laws, regulations, and processes that haven't changed much over the years. However, there will be a growing demand for HR to be more creative in finding ways to approach pre-existing goals and functions. One way to be more innovative is through a total rewards system, which balances human capital expenses and compensation/ benefit competitiveness. Out-of-the-box thinkers could come up with entirely new approaches to maximize total return on human capital investment. To foster this, HR as a function has to cultivate an innovative culture where new ideas are generated and tested. This is not a natural transition, but it will be impactful if HR establishes a position as a forward and innovative thinker, taking a salient position to promote such a culture to the rest of the organization.

CONCLUSION

HR began its evolution long ago. But the change we are facing now is unprecedented. What we are aiming for is a broad spectrum of change, from fundamentally reconstructing HR competencies to widening a scope of work to execution capabilities. This will take some time, but we should not hold back.

Our first step is to recognize the importance of three core functionalities: alignment, ability, and architecture. This is our foundation. Designing and strengthening these key components will create unprecedented opportunities for organizations. Our second step is to zero in on reconstructing HR's competencies so that the HR role will not be limited to improving talent, but will include building an infrastructure where human assets are explored and optimized. The final step is to reorganize HR based on alignment, ability, and architecture so that each function will get a dedicated team to reinforce and measure organizational capabilities for continuous improvement. This may be idealistic at this stage, but it is a pragmatic approach if we are going to be in the center of this new frontier.

Let's not forget that there is still much more to be done in human capital optimization. "Human" is one of our foundational words, but to really harness the power of human capital to improve HR and business performance, HR will need to go beyond "human" and adopt the mindset of organizational engineer, so that every process and decision led by HR will address execution capabilities. This is a fundamental transformation of the function in terms of its practices and processes as well as its competencies and capabilities. A new developmental phase for HR is going to be nothing short of revolutionary, setting off a substantial culture change both within and outside of HR.

About Kenneth J. Carrig

Kenneth J. Carrig is corporate executive vice president and chief human resources officer for SunTrust Banks Inc. In this role, he oversees human resources strategy, talent management, employee benefits, compensation, staffing, human resources systems, operations and payroll, compliance, employee relations, human resources policies, and training and development. Prior to joining SunTrust in 2011, he was executive vice president of human resources for Comcast. He previously held similar roles with Sysco Corporation and Continental Airlines during his 30-year human resources career. Carrig is a member of the advisory boards of the Cornell Center for Advanced Human Resource Studies and PearlHPS, a predictive execution analytics software company. He also serves on the boards of Operation HOPE and the Atlanta Botanical Garden. Carrig became a National Academy of Human Resources Fellow in 2004 and was named an Academy of Management Distinguished Human Resources Executive in 2010. He is co-author of the 2006 book "Building Profit Through Building People," the proceeds of which benefit Share Our Strength, an organization dedicated to fighting childhood hunger. Carrig earned his undergraduate degree in labor economics from Cornell University and has participated in leadership development education and training at Columbia University and Yale University.

About Aki Onozuka-Evans

Aki Onozuka-Evans is principal at AOSIS Consulting LLC and a management consultant with more than 15 years of experience in national and international strategic planning and human capital projects. Her expertise includes identifying growth opportunities at both the corporate and business unit levels; facilitating the development and implementation of strategic plans to drive results; and analyzing industry structure and competitive landscapes to identify emerging trends and potential future challenges. During her career at Monitor Group and BearingPoint, she managed various multidimensional project initiatives by promoting a holistic approach and participated in a broad range of industry engagements—including finance and banking, retail and distribution, and IT. Her past clients include SunTrust, Oracle, H.E.B., Merck, Goldman Sachs, LG, Hitachi, and NTT

Data. Her key projects include corporate growth strategy, human capital, market/share growth, organizational capability analysis, business process reengineering (BRM), strategic marketing and brand strategy, data visualization, and financial modeling. Onozuka-Evans holds a BA in international relations and economics from American University and an MBA from the McDonough School of Business at Georgetown University.

---

[1] The term "organizational health" was introduced by McKinsey Solutions. "Organizational Health Index" is one of its solution offerings.

HR AS GUARDIAN OF THE FUTURE

Lynda Gratton

The forces shaping our world are having a profound impact on organizations and on the HR professionals within them. That is why over a decade ago my colleagues and I founded the Future of Work Research Consortium (FoW). Our aspiration was to engage with HR people from around the world to consider the forces that they believe will shape their function and the roles and responsibilities within it. More than 80 corporations, NGOs, and government think tanks have been involved in this joint exploration of the real changes that are taking place and how corporations can best adapt to them.

It is clear that the forces of technology and globalization have shaped business models and will continue to do so. Take, for example, one of our FoW members, Tata Consultancy Services. A decade ago, their business strategy of high-impact, medium-cost IT support and consulting would not have been possible. Yet today they have the technology and the culture to link more than 300,000 employees in hundreds of fast-paced learning communities, enabling them to meet their clients' needs with speed and scale. What is clear is that this scale of mobilization is only possible now.

It is not just the forces of technology and globalization that are shaping our world. Workforces are impacted by intense demographic trends as working lives elongate and family size decreases. They also operate under the shadow of resource constraints and climate change that will have to be addressed in the coming decades. We can expect that the very forces that are shaping business models will have a profound impact on the HR strategies, practices, and processes that support them. So what does this mean for the future of HR?

BUILD COLLABORATION INSIGHT

The primary design principle emerging from the forces of technology and globalization is collaboration. We now have access to the technological might to connect many millions of people—and the potential is there for them to engage in highly effective communities, sharing information and solving problems. But, as many companies have found, while the technology can be an enabler to speed and innovation, it is often the culture of the company that acts as a barrier to collaboration.

Culture—the norms of behavior and general expectations of performance—is fiendishly hard to shape or control. Yet what we have seen in many companies is that the HR practices and processes often inadvertently create a barrier to collaboration and innovation. Misaligned remuneration systems, poor executive role modeling, unclear job design, and poorly managed teams are all barriers to the extraordinary potential of collaborative technology. They are also practices and processes within HR's sphere of influence. Making changes to these practices is hard—but crucial.

This is why I believe that it is imperative for the HR profession to have deep strategic insight into the role that practices and processes can play to support a culture of collaboration. The strategic understanding of the alignment between business goals and HR practices and processes was the centerpiece of "Living Strategy," one of the first books I wrote for the HR community. A decade later, this is as important as ever. It requires understanding the organization as a system, working through the levers that have the greatest influence on culture, and then having the courage and commitment to change those that are a barrier and strengthen those that are potential enablers.

Understanding how cultures of collaboration are built is a crucial capability for HR professionals. Moreover, measuring the current state of collaboration can bring real understanding. It seems to me that the research and insight from network theorists can be of significant use to us. Their research has highlighted the importance of weak ties, helped us understand the role of boundary spanners, and taught us a way of thinking of companies not as organizational charts of power but as networks of influence. That is why, in my executive human resource strategy program at London Business School, I now partner with my colleague Professor Raina Brands to support each participant in understanding more fully their personal networks of influence.

Take, for example, a senior HR member of a rather traditional bank. Her hope was to influence the senior team to act more collaboratively. But when she looked at her personal influence network, she found that most of her strong relationship ties were with other members of the HR function. In working so much to support her HR peers, she had failed to reach out to her business colleagues and to really invest in building those relationships. As a result, she had little traction when it came to influencing them.

What the participants discovered was that understanding more about how networks operate can be a significant tool for them, and one they can take back to use within their companies.

Yet while technology and globalization are reshaping corporations and work, there is another force that is beginning to be felt. Across the world, through a combination of healthier lifestyles and medical advances, many people are expected to live a great deal longer than their parents or grandparents.

PREPARE FOR LONGEVITY

My colleague, the economist Andrew Scott, and I are fascinated with this and have spent the last couple of years studying what happens when many people live to be 100. What we have found is that the impact is felt across the trajectory of a lifetime—from young people who want more time to explore, to those in their 30s wanting to make a significant transformation, to those in their 50s wanting to build a new portfolio of work. Our economic modeling and development of various scenarios shows that for most people, an important result will be long working lives, with people remaining in the workforce into their 80s.

Those working for so long will want engaging, meaningful work; the capacity to take breaks to recuperate and learn; and the support to build valuable skills to prepare for portfolio stages in their career. Many will want balanced family partnerships to help shoulder the financial burden of longer lives. That means both men and women will want more flexible ways of working. The scenarios we modeled for future careers often contained many more stages and a great deal of variety as people forge their unique pathways.

Yet our initial research into current corporate practice showed that few HR teams are fully aware of the implications of longevity and are still basing their people practices on the traditional three-stage path of education, work, and retirement. It seems to me that a crucial HR capability going forward will be understanding the implications of longevity and how best to create an environment in which people can work a great deal longer, rather than retire at the age of 60. That means doing away with many of the stereotypes about the "over 60s," and disconnecting pay and service so that older people are more economically attractive. It means establishing strong mentoring roles and creating opportunities for work to be part of a broader portfolio of activities.

CONSIDER CLIMATE CHANGE

One of the consequences of globalization has been a depletion of natural resources and unpredictable weather patterns. For many companies, particularly those with extended supply chains, these new realities are increasingly hard to ignore and indeed are often a risk to them.

In thinking about these consequences, Unilever CEO Paul Polman set the goal of reducing the company's carbon footprint by 50 percent. He tasked the HR teams with understanding how this goal could be met. Their first project was to analyze carbon use across the company. What they quickly discovered was that much of the carbon created within the company and in the supply chain came as a result of traditional work practices: moving employees around on multiple flights, putting employees to work in centrally located offices, and encouraging them to commute every day into a city. Changing these work practices proved to be a tough but rewarding process. It also brought a higher level of flexibility and encouraged managers to think more creatively about how they supported virtual working and performance management.

More and more CEOs are as engaged as Polman in the debate about climate change. Some are also determined to make a difference. What is clear is that the HR function has a key role to play, both in understanding where carbon is created and in reshaping work practices to ensure that it is significantly reduced.

What Polman and his colleagues have realized is that making change at the level of the globe requires an understanding of how to make multi-stakeholder alliances work. In a sense, this is the most complex extension of the collaboration challenge I referred to earlier. There are many stakeholders with an interest in climate change—governments, NGOs, citizens groups, employees. Bringing these disparate interests together is tough, but as I argued in my latest book, "The Key," it is corporations that can make this happen. Of course, this takes me back to my opening comments about collaboration. It is only through collaboration that corporations can become a force for good—and the HR function plays a key role in building a context in which collaboration can flourish.

So what does this all mean for the way we structure the HR function? There are many others much better placed than I to comment on this. But I would make these simple suggestions. First, let the HR function be a guiding light on how the corporation as a whole should function. Model collaboration, work with ease across boundaries, and use network tools to understand and build communities of practice. Next, appreciate that multi-stakeholder decision-making will be increasingly important, and that the way that the function approaches sharing ideas and engaging others in change should follow this. Finally, realize that of all the functions in a company, it is HR that is the guardian of the future—and it is HR that must continuously imagine what the future could bring.

About Lynda Gratton

Lynda Gratton is a professor of management practice at London Business School, where she directs the "Human Resource Strategy in Transforming Companies" program—considered the world's leading program on human resources. Gratton is founder of the Hot Spots Movement and for more than six years has led the Future of Work Research Consortium, which brings executives from more than 80 companies together both virtually and on a bespoke collaborative platform. Over the last 20 years Gratton has written extensively about the interface between people and organizations, and her eight books have been translated into more than 15 languages. Her latest book, "The Key" (2014), looks at the impact of the changing world on corporate practices and processes and on leadership. Gratton has won the

Tata HR Leadership Award in India and in the US has been named a Fellow of NAHR and one of the top 15 business thinkers in the world by The Times/Harvard Business Review. A Fellow of the World Economic Forum, she has chaired the WEF Council on Leadership; serves as a judge on the FT Business Book of the Year panel; chairs the Drucker prize panel; and is on the governing body of London Business School. Most recently she received the 2014 WFPMA "George Petitpas" award for her outstanding contributions to the advancement of the HR profession.

STOP ADVISING, START LEADING

Kristi McFarland

In many organizations, the role of human resources leaders has been to advise and counsel other business leaders. Relationships of deep trust and open communication are built over years of working together, where the HR person and the business person both benefit: The business leader benefits from having a safe place in which to wrestle with leadership challenges and decisions, and the HR person benefits from being a valued confidante, mentor, and coach. It's often mutually fulfilling. The relationship deepens, and both parties may grow significantly in the process. Some of my most treasured professional and personal relationships have been born of this dynamic, and for that I am incredibly grateful.

It can also be a very limiting model for the business and for HR professionals. Being in service is comfortable, and gratifying. You feel good at the end of the day for having helped your partner work through a difficult situation or decision. Yet the decision is ultimately someone else's. The HR leader is absolved of accountability. In what other leadership role is this the norm or acceptable?

For many HR leaders, achieving a seat at the table is the primary goal. From this seat, we can be heard, or offer an opinion. Too often, however, that opinion is on what other leaders should do, rather than a point of view on what's right for the business—one that we can own and where we can be accountable for the outcome. We must shift our thinking from having earned the right to be at the table to having earned the right, and the responsibility, to lead.

In order to step into this leadership role, we must first examine the some limiting beliefs that are common in our profession, and bust a few myths.

1. *Leaders are business people in revenue-generating roles, with big titles.* Hogwash. Leaders are people who set a strategic course for the company; create value for customers and stakeholders; develop, inspire, and enable others to achieve results; and serve as role models for the company's vision and values. These traits can be embodied by anyone, at any level, in any functional area. They are not the purview of sales, product, and operations folks. There is leadership talent in every corner of our organizations, and we miss out on innovative solutions by selectively listening only to those in sanctioned leadership roles.

2. *Our customer is the employee, and our client is the line organization.* Nope. The customer is the customer. When employees are highly satisfied and engaged, they are much more likely to deliver an outstanding customer experience. And that's a great place to start. But where can we add value directly to the customer experience versus indirectly through employees? For example, one of HR's core capabilities is training and education. That capability could be used to improve the customer experience. Similarly, rather than treating line business partners as clients, where can we get our hands dirty and directly improve business operations? Our analytical skills could be put to good use here. We can add value. We'll only know by becoming intimately familiar with the needs of our customers (the real ones who pay for our products and services). For me, taking leadership roles outside of the HR career path has been immensely helpful in this process. Look for opportunities to lead a product launch, open a new market, or tear apart and rebuild a core business process. You'll learn more than you expect and begin to see your customers in new ways.

3. *Focusing on compliance helps keep our organization safe.* Sure. But safe doesn't grow. Many HR folks have been taught that it's their job to be keepers of the rules, and to ensure that the company stays out of hot water. Just like the advisor role, this is a distanced role, an "I told you so" position. It's our job to help define the boundaries for strategies and practices in alignment with the company's core purpose and vision. Boundaries imply freedom within a

framework, adaptability, and fluidity. Rules set limits on action. They are very different. In a business climate that is increasingly more complex, with a high degree of change, to be a "rule keeper" is to inherently freeze your organization in one particular context and block change. A boundary keeper, on the other hand, makes space for messiness and risk, creativity and innovation. A boundary keeper makes it safe for the organization to explore the edges of its strategic options, helping to guide the right choices at the right time and reducing the need to let the rules make choices for us.

So if we free ourselves from these myths, what does our role become? What does a leader do?

LEADERS SET STRATEGY

It starts with a deep understanding of the competitive landscape and how your organization differentiates itself. Shop the competition. Get feedback from people outside your industry and outside your functional expertise as input to the strategy-setting soup. Pull a diverse team together to stimulate the best thinking. Strategy development is a highly collaborative process that undulates between exploring a wide range of possibilities and making surgical decisions. It requires us to look at the business as a whole system within the context of competitive, regulatory, technological, and social trends. Staying in your functional lane prevents the best thinking from emerging.

At the same time, as an HR leader you have a unique role to play in developing your organization's strategic focus. The culture and vision of your organization serve as the decision-making, go/no go criteria that act as guardrails on your growth strategy. Be willing to challenge your peers when strategic choices bump up against those guardrails. Be willing to test assumptions. Be willing to highlight the impact on people and culture that your strategic choices will have.

LEADERS DRIVE VALUE CREATION

Your company's people practices are core business processes, just as essential as product development, go-to-market pathways, operations, or distribution channels. Who you hire defines your capabilities. How quickly you develop them meters the pace of your growth. How you do business defines who will do business with you. All of these choices and processes are building blocks to your business model and determine whether your organization's people will be a core differentiator or a constraint.

Having a clear assessment of your people and practices gives you a platform from which to innovate. Where can you take low-value work out of the system and focus people on what matters most to customers? How can cost savings be turned into growth-generating investments? One of my favorite tools for this is the Business Model Canvas developed by Alexander Osterwalder and Yves Pigneur and shared in their book "Business Model Generation."

The Business Model Canvas enables you to work with the variables that create customer value, play up your differentiators, and reframe the competitive context. With a clear and engaging strategy, and a business model that aligns the organization to deliver, your next step is to develop and enable people to act.

LEADERS DEVELOP AND INSPIRE PEOPLE

This should be our sweet spot. We know how to hire, onboard, train, manage performance, and develop careers. Others come to us for those services. Unfortunately, the flipside of our service orientation is that we often put the HR team at the back of the line and focus on other parts of the organization first. Is the HR team getting the best of what we have to offer? Are we hiring innovators or administrators? Are we developing the next generation of versatile business leaders? Where does an HR career go?

Make your department a magnet for talent from other parts of the business, a fun place to work, and great team to be a part of. Be the best boss your folks have ever worked with. That means being present and patient. Teach, coach, mentor. When you focus your attention on the executive team, the board, or other business units, your team feels it. One simple step is to pilot career development programs with your own team first so that they know you are investing in their growth, and so that they can be advocates for the process in other parts of the company. Go first, and set the pace.

LEADERS MODEL THE WAY

If you don't wholeheartedly believe in the vision, mission, and values of your organization, work somewhere else. As HR leaders, people in our companies watch our actions and decisions closely and expect that we will embody what the company stands for. Yes, that's a high bar. It's a role with symbolic weight. And it's fun to show people that it can be real. It's fun to watch the skepticism dissolve when people see that the company really does make decisions based on its values.

While the CEO is often the one to make the inspiring speech or kick off the big company event, your personal leadership style says volumes about what the company rewards and tolerates. There are certain messages that can only come from you. There are times when the organization needs to hear your voice, when they need to see your face, when your leadership presence (or absence) sends a clear signal about what the company really holds dear. Step out from the behind-closed-doors advisor role, and lead.

WHERE DO I START?

Shifting your thinking is a major step forward. Shifting the focus of our time, resources, and energy—now that's the harder part. Here are a few ways you might reflect on your leadership role.

Where do you spend your time, and to whom do you give your attention? Make a pie chart that shows how much time you are spending with each of the following groups:

- Executive team and board
- Other business partners or "client groups"
- Your HR team
- Total company or general employee population
- Customers and community

What do you notice when you assess where your time is spent? How much of your time is spent advising? How much of your time is spent leading a core business process that adds value to your customers and stakeholders? What would happen if you allocated 10 percent more of your energy to the most important pie piece in your chart?

Today's business environment is fast-moving, ever-changing, and increasingly complex. The HR function has evolved from being primarily transactional (administering practices and policies) to more consultative (advising leaders on talent strategy, building adaptive organizations, and enhancing culture). A positive step forward indeed, but we cannot stop there. The consultative role leaves us distanced from the heartbeat of the company. Do you want to be known for having done something to move the company forward, or for having told an executive what to do? The next phase is for HR leaders to shape strategy, build businesses, and truly lead alongside our peers in other parts of the business.

Yes, there is a stack of work on your desk. Yes, the day-to-day fires will pop up and require your attention. And yes, it is certainly easier to administer and advise than to take risks and be bold. But there is deep wisdom in our community. There is insight, there is innovation, and there is rock-star talent.

Stop advising, start leading.

About Kristi McFarland

Kristi McFarland joined New Seasons Market in March 2014 as chief people officer, responsible for all aspects of the company's human resources practices in support of more than 3,000 staff and for continuing to strengthen New Seasons Market's position as a progressive employer. She has also led the new store opening team and plays an integral role in shaping the company's growth strategy. With 20 years of experience in retail and consumer products, McFarland understands that great customer experiences are created by great employee experiences and deeply rooted in the company's vision, mission, and values. Previously, she served as vice president of people and culture at Peet's Coffee and Tea, where she led the human resources function; led global leadership development for Gap Inc.; and held HR and organizational development roles for Banana Republic and Williams-Sonoma. McFarland believes in creating a culture where people can grow and foster their full potential in support of the company's mission. She has spoken at conferences about her passion for employee engagement, company culture, and innovation. She's committed to building the capabilities that a company needs to grow while enabling the unique culture and customer experience to flourish.

---

[1] Alexander Osterwalder and Yves Pigneur, "Business Model Generation" (Hoboken, NJ: Wiley and Sons, Inc., 2010), pages 18–19.

HR AND TRANSPARENCY

Susan Meisinger

When Dave Ulrich invited me to submit an essay for a book that would be shared with HRCI certificants, I was honored. Dave has been one of the most thoughtful and prolific contributors to helping the HR profession add value to organizations, and I was happy to join his latest effort. Of course, whenever I'm asked to join a conversation about the profession, I'm in.

But I almost declined the invitation when he told me that my essay should answer the question, "What do HR professionals need to know or do to be effective in today's and tomorrow's business world?"

There's so much that an HR professional needs to know and do to be effective in today's environment. How could an essay do the subject justice? I found it hard to focus on just one thing for HR professionals to do or know. I kept thinking about the screensaver Mike Losey, a former CEO of SHRM, always had running across his computer: "HR is not a profession for wimps!" There's just so much to know, and so much to do, to be really effective and successful in the function. But it's because there's so much to know that it's such a great career. There's real opportunity to impact people's lives in a positive way.

As an HR professional:

- You must understand the business and the context within which the business is operating, and be able to leverage your HR expertise to help drive business performance.
- You must understand the business's strategy and be able to link it to the talent acquisition and retention strategy—not just for the short term but for the longer term, whatever longer term means in your industry.
- You have to be able to develop the talent that you've acquired and know how to manage performance to keep your workforce engaged and committed to whatever it is that your business is trying to achieve.
- You must be able to design a compensation strategy that fits the business strategy and that rewards the outcomes and behaviors that the business demands.
- You need to keep up with emerging and new technologies. This is true not just for those that allow you to automate HR functions but for your business in general. Emerging technologies have implications beyond staffing levels or productivity improvements. They have the potential to offer insights that might change the very nature of your business.
- You must be a risk manager, remaining current and ensuring compliance with ever-changing government mandates, which are continuing to add levels of complexity and costs to operating a business.
- And you have to be skilled as a coach and counselor for managers and executives who may need your help desperately—even if they don't know it or want it.

All of these responsibilities are important, and research-based competency models developed for the HR profession offer useful road maps for those interested in learning more about how to add value to their organizations.

OUR TRANSPARENT WORLD

While these responsibilities or deliverables of the HR function have grown over time and have seen changes in emphasis, I think the world in which we now operate requires something even more. I think HR professionals will need to spend more time thinking about and developing strategies for operating in what has become a transparent world.

What do I mean by operating in a transparent world?

For me, it means operating in a world where immediate access to information over the internet has raised everyone's expectations of what information should be freely available. With so much information readily available, employees, customers, and the public now expect to be able to get just-in-time information: the information they need, when they need it.

Just as importantly, the public expects access to information that wasn't easily available in the past. What most thought of as private in the past—political contributions, criminal records, real estate/tax payments, a person's age and address—are all now a few key strokes away. Information on competitors—from their pricing to products to personnel—are all easily discoverable by spending some time on their website or through simple searches across social media tools.

In a transparent world, customers and employees expect to get immediate answers to their questions with a simple query and assume that the information provided by the company will be accurate and useful. If a web search doesn't provide answers, a query over social media channels is likely to provide an answer.

This includes information about the inner workings of organizations. Not only is the entire employment cycle accessible to candidates and employees, it's visible to customers and the general public as well. Wondering what it's like to work at a company? Just Google it. Curious about what questions might be asked in an interview? Send out a query on social media to see if anyone has recently been interviewed by the company. Wondering how to get better customer service from a company? Tweet out a complaint.

Interested in what a company pays? Just check Glassdoor.com to see what employees have reported. Where compensation information was once treated as confidential and not to be shared with anyone but an employee's family, more and more salary information—some accurate, some not—is now freely available.

Operating in a transparent world also means operating in a world where privacy may be promised but cannot be guaranteed. Workers and customers who once felt that their personal information, and private communications, were protected from public view or unauthorized access now know from widely publicized security breaches that this may be false confidence. Internal communications that are at odds with external messaging from a business or corporate executive are vulnerable to discovery and wide distribution, putting at risk the trust that's been built with employees or customers.

In a transparent world, corporations can be victimized by hackers from anywhere in the world for the purposes of theft, extortion, or just to embarrass the enterprise or make a political statement.

So, what do I think this means for HR executives?

First, it places great responsibility on HR executives to manage the risk of private information becoming public by ensuring that confidential employee information is only accessible to authorized personnel. And while HR professionals don't need to be IT security experts, they need to have a solid working relationship with those security experts in their organization to ensure that adequate protections are in place.

Similarly, it means that HR executives need to be constantly vigilant and remind other executives and employees that anything they communicate, no matter how they communicate it, is subject to discovery and disclosure. While discovery and disclosure have, in the past, usually been as a result of litigation, in a transparent world they may be the result of hackers or disgruntled employees.

But while I believe that HR needs to be vigilant in helping organizations protect confidential information and communications, I also believe that HR executives need to be communication ninjas, working to ensure that their entire organization has a bias toward sharing information where it can. In a transparent world, where there is a constant tension between the expectation of easy access to information and the fear that confidential information will become public, HR needs to play a leadership role in helping the organization make more information available while also managing the risk of sharing too much.

For internal processes that are likely to become known to the public, this means planning and designing them with information sharing in mind. Consider, for example, recruitment. Where once this process was basically know to the hiring official, HR, and the candidate, this isn't true any longer. Information on the process and how someone was treated is now easy to discover through various websites or social media. HR executives have to help their organizations understand that in a transparent world, it will quickly become known to the public when a company fails to treat a candidate with respect. Indeed, in a study of 4,500 workers in the US, 78 percent said they would talk about a bad experience they had with a potential employer with friends and family, 17 percent said they would post something about their negative experience on social media, and 6 percent said they would blog about it.[1]

It means employment policies—however stringent or loose they may be within your organization—need to be available and communicated to workers in a manner that is accessible and understandable. Technology now makes it easy to make this information widely available to employees, but it falls on HR to actually make it happen.

It means that HR executives need to ensure that managers and supervisors are trained to clearly communicate performance expectations and to provide employees with the information and guidance they need to do their jobs well. This includes ensuring that training resources are available—whether through managers or from a desktop—and that they contain information and answers to any questions an employee might have about how to do a job or improve their performance.

It means transparency and open communication about promotional opportunities and development opportunities within your organization, so that employees feel that they have the information they need to have a fair opportunity for advancement.

It means providing more transparency and communication to employees about how compensation and benefits decision are made, and how jobs are valued. Keeping salary information secret, or forbidding employees from discussing compensation information, may have worked in the past. But in a world where this information is likely to be discoverable anyway, sharing it may make more sense, especially when combined with information that educates the workforce on how compensation is determined.

It means helping the organization communicate to employees about how the business is doing, and how employees' individual contributions add value to the enterprise. It means communicating to employees that they should expect to be treated with respect, and that they, in turn, are expected to treat others with respect. And it means helping the other leaders in your organization understand that their actions, decisions, and communications are all at risk of disclosure in a transparent world, requiring greater vigilance in how all are handled.

These aren't new requirements of HR, to be sure. But I believe that now, more than ever before, HR professionals have to approach their role by constantly reminding their organization to consider the question: What would happen if an employee or customer saw this, or if this appeared on the front page of the newspaper?

Because in a transparent world, it's very likely to happen.

About Susan Meisinger

Susan Meisinger, SPHR, JD, is a widely read columnist on HR leadership for Human Resources Executive Online. She speaks and consults on human resource management issues, and is the former president and CEO of the Society for Human Resource Management (SHRM). Prior to joining SHRM, Meisinger was appointed by President Ronald Reagan as deputy under secretary in the US Department of Labor, where she was responsible for more than 4,000 employees and the enforcement of more than 90 US employment laws. Meisinger is a former board member for the World Federation of Personnel Management Associations, SHRM, the HR Certification Institute, and the Certified Financial Planners Board of Standards. She also has corporate board experience and is a Fellow of the National Academy of Human Resources and the Human Resource Policy Institute. She currently sits on the Kronos Workforce Institute's advisory board and the National Academy of Human Resources' board of directors. Meisinger also co-authored and edited "The Future of Human Resource Management," which was published in 2005 by John Wiley & Sons.

---

[1] "Your Company's Open Position as a Consumer Product: How and Why Candidates Consider You and Buy," a nationwide CareerBuilder and Inavero study, March 2011. (http://img.icbdr.com/images/jp/reports/Your-Position-As-A-Consumer-Product.pdf?sc_cmp2=JP_Report_ConsumerProd)

HR FROM AROUND THE WORLD … LET'S UNITE!
From Corporate HR to Global Human Capital Platform

Regis Mulot

Each management generation faces two or three major and unique business transformations (and sometimes one revolution) during their career. Here are the ones that corporations have recently been addressing:

Globalization. Companies have been operating (or trying to) across the world for the past 400 years. The modern challenge is figuring out how to harmonize across cultures in a multicultural world where customers' needs are different—in other words, how to be global and act local. Global is about distance, diversity, cultural differences, long-term goals and vision, culture sensitivity, domination, and more. Today, being "global" is less than a two-second click away, from anywhere in the world.

Managing virtual teams located across multiple locations. We have learned to operate in a world where there are no physical boundaries, wall constraints, or building limitations. Some organizations encourage associates to be located anywhere around the world. Every place is now the right place to work: home, coffee shop, office, cafeteria, rental space, hotel, car, plane—the list goes on. What had been a challenge even 10 years ago and required a lot of air miles has become easier to manage at a distance through Skype, webcasts, telepresence, instant messaging, FaceTime, and more. Not only is distance "virtually" disappearing, but the need to train teams across the organization is different. We now have intuitive learning programs where trainers and operating guidelines are no longer needed.

Working in a matrix environment. This is still a challenge, but again not a new one. Complex organizations require intensive collaboration, information exchange, and knowledge sharing. Even if "matrix" is not a "natural" way to organize a group, leaders with the right mindset can make it happen and use organizational development tools (RAPID, RACI) to clarify the most efficient way of working. Today, it is not about controlling my resources or building my team independent from another. Rather, it is about destroying silos, removing barriers, and leveraging resources from other teams.

THE PLATFORM REVOLUTION

What new business challenge are leaders facing today? And how can human resources professionals help to address them? The greatest emerging challenge we now face is much bigger than any of the above and may even qualify as a revolution— as important as when, 125 years ago, corporations started to rise and become the foundation of modern western capitalism. In their book, "How Google Works," Jonathan Rosenberg and former Google CEO Eric Schmidt share the observation that our economic model is moving from corporation to platform. That's the revolution— and that's the revolution HR professionals need to address and to leverage.

Fortune 1000 corporations won't disappear overnight, but we need to watch for this change. In a "platform" world, value is not created by bringing together and efficiently organizing workforce and capital, but by partnering and cooperating using common technology with multiple corporations, partners, nonprofit organizations, educational institutions, and so on. Diverse groups of individuals or organizations can temporarily partner together without sharing the same long-term objectives. Universities and other research centers that share and partner with corporations are the closest to this model already.

This new economic model will require new ways of working, where actors take risks and push boundaries, where failure is part of being innovative, where knowledge management tools are critical, where hierarchy is replaced by collaboration, where bureaucracy and complexity are replaced by agility, where continuous learning is more important that personal status, and where inclusive leadership and dialogue are the norm. Our rules, practices, organizational design principles, regulations, business confidentiality principles, non-compete agreements, and company cultures will be irrelevant if we fail not only to adapt to the new model but to reinvent our framework.

A NEW HUMAN CAPITAL FRAMEWORK

This new economic model will be characterized by inclusive leadership, collaboration, agility, collective knowledge sharing, continuous learning, fulfilling work, and innovative mindsets.

- Successful ventures will be the result of strong inclusive leadership—not traditional hierarchical decision-making and managing paradoxes.
- We'll have a culture of innovation where perfectionism is no longer a goal. Instead, our cultures will be highly adaptive, we will learn through shared knowledge, and failure will be encouraged and rewarded.
- Silos and secretive mindsets will be replaced by collaboration within and outside an organization.
- Business models will encourage go-to-market agility and speed, focusing on meeting customer demand before creating shareholders and corporation value (and not the reverse!).
- Collaborators will be able to fulfill their work through continuous learning and credible activism. They will be players, not spectators, to borrow the words of Tony Blair.

How can HR professionals help make the shift to operating in a platform ecosystem? How do we communicate this vision to our workforce? How do we ensure that the individual assessments previously developed are applied to all individuals working together on the same platform? How do we develop individuals and share knowledge while at the same time protecting confidential information? How do we retain the best contributors and encourage them to work together on the same platform?

Answering these questions will be critical in the coming years. Already, more and more companies are leveraging this "open business space" to innovate (Procter & Gamble has been using its Connect + Develop open innovation process to help deliver leading innovations); to increase their market share (Google encourages other companies to use Android open source); to partner with experts who will not work long term with them (H&M partnering with fashion designers); to build new concepts without a dedicated corporate team (Wikipedia Foundation's crowdsourcing model); and to get access to the contingency workforce.

How do we get these individuals, groups, and entities (business or not) working together and sharing the same passion, vision, and purpose? By going back to the fundamental of trade and business that we may have lost during the past decade: customer centricity—customers first!

That's what will be common on this platform: developing solutions and products that answer customer needs. The absence of organizational structure will not be a competitive barrier but a real advantage when it comes to creating customer centricity.

EXISTING HUMAN CAPITAL PROCESSES WILL NEED TO BE ADAPTED

- It is already challenging to assess the human capital value of a corporation. So how will we be able to assess it in a "platform" model? What role will government play? Will it regulate the relationships between individuals and organizations, or develop a human capital environment where individuals and groups will partner? Singapore is an interesting example of a country investing in human capital to attract individuals and organizations to create wealth in and for the country.
- What does a platform world mean for human resources practitioners? We could argue that it doesn't change our objectives and ways of operating; we still need to provide human resources services. But how will HR experts support leaders and colleagues (associates, consultants, third-party organizations) to achieve their new business objectives?
- How do we align performance and corporation objectives across a diverse group of individuals and organizations that are partnering together, and how do we do this when we are not connected anymore to the same corporation?
- We have step-by-step transformed the science and art of recruiting, mastering assessment techniques and even using mining data to forecast a person's contribution and performance. How are we going to apply that same rigor when we select our platform partners?
- Human capital is a competitive asset. So how do we maintain this asset, and is it okay to share it and develop it for other platforms too?
- How do we celebrate individual or collective success or create alignment when we

no longer have a common vision for our organization or our team but rather one for our customer? What will be our common commitment?

- Do we develop our business plans differently? Do we need to forget everything we've learned during the past 50 years related to business strategy and strategic planning to adapt to the new platform model?
- How do we comply with federal and state regulations that haven't adopted the platform model? What will labor, tax, immigration, and other regulatory constraints—which are based on an employment relationship framework between an individual and a corporation—mean for collaboration? Will it be okay to work together and share the same tools and objectives without having a formal employment relationship?
- What role will employee groups like unions, which have been built to protect individuals "against" corporations, have in a platform world?
- How will we communicate? How will we share knowledge and at the same time protect confidentiality and not breach confidential data disclosure?
- Will turnover reports be something from the past, because we will no longer measure employee loyalty, instead measuring an individual's partnership strengths?

A NEW HR COMPETENCY MODEL AND MINDSET WILL BE REQUIRED

Human resources objective will have to be different, focusing on a customer-centric culture instead of a high-performance company-centric one. There may be an opportunity to build and manage for the first time a global human capital platform in cooperation with other HR practitioners, instead of focusing on our individual corporate human resources structure.

We may migrate by 2025 to a universal HR service, where governments (or why not the United Nations!) regulate this global platform by aligning human capital practices through standardization instead of regulation. And we may see an HR ecosystem where HR practitioners are leveraging the same tools, frameworks, and processes to embed business integration, collaboration, and human capital portability with:

- A *common leadership competency model* across the US (and maybe the globe) boosted by a technology platform offering seamless integration solutions.
- A *homogenous performance management model* and assessment tools that are portable and universally structured and captured in databases owned by individuals, not corporations.

- *Non-cash recognition tools* that are common to multiple organizations (like frequent flyer programs where miles can be claimed or used with other airlines).
- Back to "welfare," with governments offering *common health/medical benefits* and retirements tools accessible to all. Companies will no longer be involved in benefits plan design or administration, and collaborators will have their own health care and retirement plans that will move with them from one platform to another.
- A *structured talent database* owned by individuals and accessible to all and no longer the property of an organization. LinkedIn has already done this, with hundreds of millions of individuals sharing professional information through its site.
- Worldwide, a *structured and professionalized HR community* (much more like the finance, legal, and accounting communities) created through a consolidated and powerful HR trade organization—in other words, a new environment through which HR professionals from all over the world will unite!

About Regis Mulot

Regis Mulot is executive vice president of human resources for Staples, responsible for the company's global HR strategies and programs that support 80,000 associates located in 25 countries. Previously, Mulot served as vice president of HR for Staples International, based in Amsterdam, the Netherlands, where he built an integrated HR team across Europe, Asia, Australia, and Latin America. Mulot is also executive vice president of the Staples Foundation. Prior to joining Staples, he served as vice president of HR, Community and Corporate Citizenship, for Levi Strauss, based in Brussels, Belgium, where he supported employees in 24 countries across Europe, the Middle East, and Northern Africa. Earlier in his career, located in Paris, Brussels, or London, Mulot held senior HR leadership roles at Broadnet Europe (a telecom startup), GTECH EMEA (a world-leading lottery system supplier), and Chronopost (a French Post Office company). He sits on the board of NextStep (Cambridge), an organization helping young adults with life-threatening diseases, and is chairman of the Business Advisory Council of Simmons School of Management (Boston). A French national, Mulot earned his BA in public law at Paris II-Assas University and his MA in public administration at Paris IX-Dauphine and Paris XI-Sceaux Universities.

THINK LIKE A MARKETER!

Libby Sartain

My answer to the question, "What do HR professionals need to know or do to be effective?" might surprise you. I believe that HR needs to know more about marketing—to think and act more like marketers.

THE IMPORTANT CONNECTION BETWEEN PEOPLE AND BRAND

At Southwest Airlines, we realized early on that our key differentiator was customer service. So we marketed our service, and thus our people strategy became critical. Recruiting and retaining the right employees, a culture that reinforced desired behaviors, and strongly aligned leadership were essential to delivering our brand promise. Our simple philosophy took hold: Employees are our most important customers. Our CEO, Herb Kelleher, famously coined a controversial phrase— "employees first, customers second"—that defined our desired leadership behavior and culture.

As our company grew, a big brand emerged. And as our marketing evolved, so did our thinking around employees as customers. Our people were our brand. Eventually it dawned on us that creation of an employer brand was as important as our corporate brand—and thus that HR and marketing should be attached at the hip.

CREATING SOUTHWEST'S EMPLOYER BRAND

At Southwest, we were charged with instilling our brand—"A Symbol of Freedom"—in the hearts and minds of our employees. At first marketing and HR worked separately, trying various campaigns and programs that didn't resonate with employees. Eventually, marketing and HR partnered together, abandoning our silos. Our new blended project team asked, "What if the experience of working at Southwest was a product? How would we sell it? What differentiates us from our competitors? What do we offer that is unique?"

An employer brand (EB) soon emerged that articulated the experience the company committed to creating for employees so that they in turn would commit to delivering the brand promises we made to our customers. We identified eight basic "Freedoms" the company provided to employees: the freedom to pursue good health, create financial security, learn and grow, make a positive difference, travel, work hard and have fun, innovate, and stay connected. Our employer brand message was, "At Southwest, Freedom begins with me."

From there our work began. Instead of delivering HR programs, we began to brand the employee experience just as marketing would brand the customer experience. Each stage of the experience would have its own look, feel, and personality aligned with the messaging used to market the company brand. The candidate experience was uniquely Southwest, as was every learning and development offering, recognition and reward, and ultimately every departure and retirement. This formed a functional connection around the work experience and EB, as it defined the "what" and "how" of the employee value proposition (EVP).

To make an emotional connection to our employees, each "Freedom" would be tied to outcomes and messaging. We worked with our advertising agency, benefits consultants, and staffing partners to create products and services for employees tied together under the Freedom brand with creative on-brand messaging and packaging. We also applied marketing techniques to engage employees around the brand, creating an army of brand ambassadors.

Marketing recognized that if we didn't have the right employees and if staffing priorities were not met, our organization would not live up to our brand. So they became our partner in recruiting. A small portion of marketing spend was diverted to our talent branding efforts. Messaging and advertising for candidates and employees had the same "look and feel" as outreach to customers. Working with marketing resulted in a more creative approach to our employment advertising and messaging.

An EB is the way to bring a culture to life in the hearts and minds of employees and to communicate a unique EVP to workers and prospective workers. It is the way a business builds and packages its identity, origins, and values, and what it promises to deliver to emotionally connect employees so that they, in turn, deliver what the business promises to customers.[1]

MARKETING TOOLS AND TECHNIQUES

Marketing tools can also add value to strategic workforce planning and talent management. Just as customer analytics related to consumer behavior can inform business decisions around products, services, marketing messages, and CRM, employee analytics can provide insights that strengthen the EVP and the promotion of the EVP inside and outside the organization. Employee segmentation can be as powerful as customer segmentation in determining offerings to the employee audience.

At Yahoo!, we divided our offerings by customer segment so that we could deliver the appropriate products and services to each segment. Working with marketing, we also developed a segmented approach to talent acquisition in the talent marketplace. To use our employer brand to its full potential, we needed a customized approach for certain groups of workers and potential workers. We asked our market research partners to provide insights from segments of potential employees to inform our efforts. We learned that tech talent required smart and edgy messaging and a targeted candidate experience, while for creatives it was more about design. Ultimately, we established two entry points on our career site, one tailored for techies and the other for creatives.

BEGIN WITH THE CUSTOMER

When HR thinks and acts more like marketing, we begin with the end customer in mind. For example, when thinking about strategic workforce planning, the conversation starts with "How the customers will be served?" versus "How many heads will we need by segment?" Insights can also be analyzed to tie employee behavior to the customer experience; measuring employee engagement against customer loyalty will reveal a correlation between the variables.

Doing this dramatically changed our thinking around diversity at Southwest. Rather than focus on outreach to employees, we charged our diversity affinity groups to help us better market to diverse customers. They worked with marketing on brand messaging and HR on our talent brand. And, we tied the service of these customers to having the right employees in customer-facing jobs. Now these groups were strategic and important to brand strategy versus just a support or networking group, and the result was better inclusion for all.

At Southwest, our "employee as customer No. 1" philosophy was the underpinning of our customer service program. We made a commitment to provide employees with the same respect and caring attitude that they are expected to show externally to every Southwest customer.

SOCIAL MEDIA CHANGES EVERYTHING

Organizations can no longer spin internal PR or brand campaigns to create an employer brand. With the prevalence of social media, organizations will have an employer brand whether or not it is deliberate. The employer is no longer totally in control of its own reputation. Much like a reality show, the camera is following what happens inside and outside our organizations 24/7, and commentators—lots of them—are putting their own spin on what is happening.

So many messages out there from official and unofficial sources create new challenges as organizations work to make sure the right messages get through. In this age of transparency, employees are the media and HR is essential to marketing, as they deliver on the brand promise day in and day out. What employees do, how they interact, and what they say to others and in social media either reinforce or undermine the brand.

The "holy grail" for most organizations is to be Facebook or LinkedIn worthy, giving your employees bragging rights and acting as a magnet for the right candidates. To do that, the employee experience must authentically live up to, or perhaps exceed, expectations. Having an authentic culture that helps workers understand the identity, origins, and values of the organization is the best place to start connecting leadership with employees. Without the classic line of sight between workers and leaders, it is more imperative than ever that business leaders deliver what the organization promises.

Social media can also be used for "employee listening." Online consumer discussion boards, as well as product rankings, ratings, and reviews posted online, have revolutionized the world of market research, offering businesses a massive source of data on what customers think about them and their products. Tools are being developed to enable marketers to listen to the "voice of the customer." Web-scraping tools or apps can be used to find out what employees and candidates are saying online as well. Sites like Glassdoor, LinkedIn, and Vault provide such insights.

THE NEW CONSUMER OF WORK

Today's workers are consumers—consumers of work. They approach the search for a job with highly developed consumer sensibilities. They use the web and resources similar to Consumer Reports, TripAdvisor, or Yelp to find out about an employer. And the search doesn't end with the attainment of a job. These days, everyone has his or her profile online. Many are open to new opportunities at any given time. This is a huge challenge for HR. We can't just think about filling job requisitions. We have to think about continually re-recruiting our own people, keeping them engaged, and providing a culture that nurtures their professional and personal growth.

MEASURING BRAND VALUE AND EFFECTIVENESS

Marketers have tools and rankings to measure the value of their consumer brands. The Net Promoter Score (NPS) is used to measure a customer's experience and quality of the brand. NPS asks customers if they would recommend a brand or product to a friend. To date, no universal tool has been developed to measure the value delivered and progress made on the employer brand. To track progress, a dashboard can be developed use the following elements:

- NPS for the employer brand: "Would you recommend a friend work at this company?"
- Number and quality of candidates
- Recruiting costs
- Retention rates
- Engagement measures
- Values and cultural assessment measures
- Media coverage as employer of choice
- "Best company" reports
- Insights from social media and employee listening
- Customer loyalty measures

WHAT YOU STAND FOR

Brands do more than sell a product or service. Brands connect the public with a big idea or concept. A brand can connect a customer to what a business is all about—its character, personality, and values. A brand can give a face to a business and can create a sense of comfort, a degree of security, a spirit of hope. It can symbolize the larger meaning of what a business stands for—the idea, experience, or relationship. An employer brand, done well, can have the same effect.

Perhaps the strongest measure of the success of your employer brand is whether or not any employee or candidate can tell you what the company stands for. Do workers understand the business strategy and how their work contributes to company performance?

Few organizations can make that claim. Yet more people look for businesses they can believe in and proudly tell others they work for. People respond to values and traditions. When people know their impact on the company strategy, they are more engaged and productive. It is no surprise that, inside many businesses, stories about legends of the business pass from person to person as if to preserve the humanity of the legend and what the brand stands for.

When HR professionals think and act like marketers, our work and programming related to recruiting, rewarding, and developing talent resonate throughout the organization. Everyone who works for the organization understands their role as brand deliverers and will join in that work. The people agenda aligns with the organization's strategy around customers, and the work is simplified. The employer brand becomes essential to the strategy of the business, just like the corporate/consumer brand.

About Libby Sartain

After a distinguished 30+ year career in human resources, Libby Sartain is now an active business advisor, board member, and volunteer. As head of HR at Yahoo! Inc. and Southwest Airlines, Sartain led significant business transformation initiatives and guided global human resources efforts focusing on attracting, retaining, and developing employees. Both Yahoo! and Southwest were listed in Fortune's "100 Best Companies to Work For in America" and in the Fortune 500 during her tenure. Sartain serves on the board of directors of ManpowerGroup and AARP. She was on the board of Peet's Coffee & Tea Inc. from 2007 to 2012. She is on the board of the SHRM Foundation and is a trustee for the National Academy of Human Resources Foundation. She advises several startups and Fortune 500 organizations on HR, employer branding, and talent management. Sartain served as chairman of the board of the Society for Human Resource Management in 2001 and was named Fellow of the National Academy of Human Resources in 1998. The co-author of several books, she was named one of the 25 most powerful women in HR by Human Resources Executive in 2005. She holds an MBA from the University of North Texas and a BBA from Southern Methodist University.

---

[1] "Your Company's Open Position as a Consumer Product: How and Why Candidates Consider You and Buy," a nationwide CareerBuilder and Inavero study, March 2011. (http://img.icbdr.com/images/jp/reports/Your-Position-As-A-Consumer-Product.pdf?sc_cmp2=JP_Report_ConsumerProd)

CHROS NEED TO MOVE FROM INFLUENCING TO BEING ACTIVELY ENGAGED IN THE BUSINESS

Padma Thiruvengadam

For a CHRO to be successful in today's world, having the ability to influence will not cut it. Given the highly matrixed operational models most companies work in, the ability to influence is a "must have" skill at all levels and no longer exclusive to the top HR roles.

Major changes in the marketplace are pushing companies to operate much differently than they have before:

- Data and information are flowing at a greater speed than in the past.
- Not all critical decisions need to be directed to the CEO; the hierarchical decision-making model is obsolete.
- Price and margin wars are no longer subtle.
- The world is more geopolitically and economically volatile.
- The move from "learning organizations" to "knowledge organizations" is more of a challenge, as employees treat employment as contracts; tenure is becoming less important.

In the past, a good CHRO was considered a sounding board for the CEO—a trusted advisor who also had good relationships with the rest of the executives and could manage sticky issues. While those qualities still hold true today, they are not sufficient. I believe that when Ram Charan challenged HR to be split into two, he did not question the role of the CHRO but the value proposition a CHRO offers in the complex environment in which we now conduct business.

Change has always been around us, but the pace and complexity of change is nothing we have seen before. Yet it is something all CHROs must contend with. In order to add value, a CHRO is expected to be "actively engaged" in the business. But what does this mean? It means that CHROs need to know a tremendous amount about the business and the context surrounding it, just like the CEO. CHROs must understand:

- Economic trends and what they mean for their industry and the markets they serve
- The immediate and long-term impact of geopolitical issues
- The competitive landscape for their company, not just focused on talent
- The performance and potential of their company's inline and pipeline of products
- The products and product mix that will differentiate them from their competition
- Key business processes, including how the company conducts business, whether changes should be made to these processes, and why this provides/may provide a competitive edge
- The company's financial performance and analyst reports
- What changes in the landscape mean for their talent needs

Being steeped in the strategy and operations of the company helps a CHRO actively participate in strategic discussions, deliver on immediate and long-term goals, and add shareholder value.

A CHRO needs to begin with understanding the strategy of the company. In order to deliver on the multiyear strategic plan, a company needs to determine how it wants to operate efficiently—its key business processes. This operational framework determines the company's capability and capacity requirements and forms the basis for the development of organizational structure, workforce planning, and skill requirements. This model needs to be regularly revisited and adjusted. This avoids having to make major shifts that can place the company at greater risk. We have to ask ourselves: How can a CHRO develop an organizational structure that is meaningful or will yield business results if he or she doesn't actively participate early in the process?

BUSINESS CYCLE

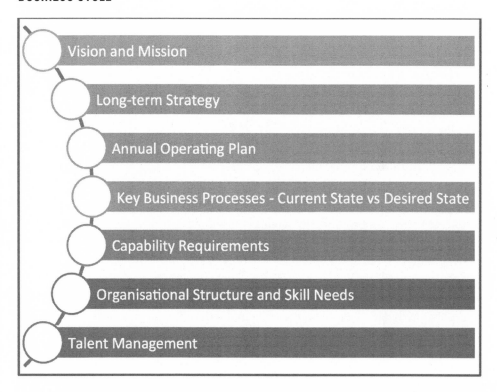

Every company revisits its strategic plan annually. Current-year performance and any adjustments to the strategic plan shape the operating plan for the next year. Of course, market conditions and other aspects mentioned above will play a key role. With changes coming at us with speed and intensity, every company is asked to test how they conduct business. Changes to any of the elements above will require reevaluating the organizational platform—capability requirements, organizational structure, and talent needs.

The role of the CHRO is rapidly changing. For CHROs to succeed, they need to be comfortable speaking the language of the business. They need to be actively engaged in every aspect of the business and not limit themselves to "supporting" the company. With talent being one of the top three priorities of most CEOs, CHROs need to embed themselves and participate in the business.

Below are some areas that a CHRO should intimately understand in order to align strategy and execution and deliver on the company's short- and long-term objectives:

• The company's multiyear strategic plan and annual operating plan
• Its financials and how various factors impact financial performance
• Its portfolio strategy and multi-generation portfolio planning; pipeline management for both inline products and funnel; margins for various products; and how the product mix creates advantage in the market
• The company's position in various markets and its plans to maintain or grow share (e.g., through price increases, geographic expansion into new markets vs. new clients in existing markets, and penetrating existing accounts)
• For manufacturing and other capital intensive industries, capital and inventory management, supply and demand planning, and how well they align with revenue forecasting
• Who your competitors are and how are they performing

There is a direct link between managing a company's talent game plan and each of the factors listed above. For example, understanding a company's growth plan will determine the type of salespeople the company will need in each area in the short term and long term. This will help drive talent acquisition, development, and management strategy.

Of course, each company will have it is own set of unique and critical areas that a CHRO will need to deeply understanding. Knowing the HR playbook is the baseline—but knowing the business, knowing the markets the company serves, and knowing its customers and products are also essential. Customizing the company HR playbook in the context of these factors to realize the long-term strategy creates a world-class people platform that is essential to every company. And it's what every CEO looks for from his or her CHRO.

About Padma Thiruvengadam

Since 2011, Padma Thiruvengadam has served as CHRO for the medical device company Integra Lifesciences, where she is responsible for providing leadership in developing and executing human resources strategy in support of the organization's overall strategic direction. She also leads the company's strategic initiatives, operational excellence, and information systems functions, with a focus on delivering on the company's long-term strategy by leveraging its technology platform for effective data and customer management. Prior to joining Integra, she was with Pfizer as Vice President, Asia Pacific and Canada Operations for the Oncology Business Unit, where she was primarily responsible for P&Ls, sales force and product performance, as well as Research and Development. Previously she was the Vice President, Business Integration, leading integration activities globally for Pfizer Oncology for the Wyeth merger. Padma first joined Pfizer as Vice President, Human Resources, where she provided overall HR strategic counsel to Pfizer Oncology and worked closely with the President and General Manager of Pfizer Oncology in creating and operationalizing the new "Business Unit." Earlier in her career, she held HR leadership roles at Bank of America, Loral Space & Communication, and Bowne & Co. An experienced senior HR executive, Thiruvengadam has a proven track record in developing and implementing leading-edge business and people strategy solutions by integrating market dynamics, product and process technologies, innovative business solutions, and operational excellence. She holds a master's degree from Madras University and received her bachelor's degree from Osmania University.

FROM WAR FOR TALENT TO VICTORY THROUGH ORGANIZATION

Dave Ulrich

I like quantitative data that provides empirical answers. But I also like qualitative data that enables me to investigate questions without clear answers. Recently, I was interviewing a new CHRO who came into HR with a systems and manufacturing background. As he reflected on his first 90 days as CHRO, he noted that HR folks seemed consumed with improving talent processes. He observed that they had developed many good disciplines for bringing people into the organization and helping them be productive. He said that he felt that they were 65 percent to 75 percent up the "S curve" of managing talent.

He also realized that the challenge in his organization was not about talent alone, but about building a culture. He shared that his organization was changing its business focus and merely getting good people into the organization was not enough; the organization needed to create a more adaptive culture. He believed the tagline "Culture eats strategy for lunch," and he felt that HR should be the steward of culture as well as talent.

This conversation has been reinforced by my experience and the insights of others. Wayne Brockbank points out in a marvelous essay:

*The vulnerability of the talent paradigm is that it focuses on optimizing individual contributions. The term talent inherently focuses on ensuring that companies have the individual talent necessary to achieve their purposes. Certainly this is a critically important agenda for any organization. However, by focusing primarily on individual contributions, the talent movement, by definition, succeeds in making the organizational whole **equal** to the sum of the parts. This overlooks the central contribution of organization to make the organization whole **greater** than the sum of the parts. It is this integrating and leveraging function of organization that creates sustained competitive advantage.[1]*

In the last 15 to 20 years, the HR profession has been shaped by remarkable work captured in the "war for talent."[2] Many have built systems for bringing people into the organization (sourcing, having a value proposition), moving them through the organization (development, performance management, engagement), and removing them from the organization (outsourcing).[3] The war for talent was a great battle, but we now need to turn to victory through organization.

Talent is not enough. HR professionals need to establish organizations that leverage individual talent through collective actions. The whole organization should be greater than its separate parts. United states are stronger than individual states. Teams outperform individuals. Individuals are champions, but teams win championships.

I believe that in any business dialogue (being at the table), an HR professional can proffer three unique contributions:

1. **Talent** – To what extent do we have the right people with competence (right people, right skills, right job), commitment (engagement), and contribution (meaning) to win in the marketplace?
2. **Leadership** – To what extent do we have branded leaders who deliver results in the right way?
3. **Organization** – To what extent do we have the right organization to deliver sustained business goals?

In today's rapidly changing business world, the challenge of building the right organization complements and supercedes the talent challenge. It is interesting to note that the Chartered Institute of Auditors has prepared recent documentation to help auditors monitor culture.[4] One of the challenges for HR professionals to facilitate building the right organization is that there are related concepts, terms, and prescriptions that require clarity. Are organizations to be thought of as resources,[5] core competencies,[6] health,[7] climate,[8] processes,[9] values,[10] shared mindsets,[11] organization types,[12] or systems?[13]

With these confusing concepts, no wonder HR professionals have difficulty creating competitive organizations. The concept clearly matters, but it seems impossible to articulate or define with any precision. Let me propose a three-step process (summarized in **Table 1**) for HR professionals to bring discipline to creating victory through organization.[14]

TABLE 1. THREE DIMENSIONS OF COMPETITIVE ORGANIZATION: CAPABILITY, CULTURE, MANAGEMENT ACTION

SUMMARY LOGIC	KEY QUESTION AND FOCUS	PREVIOUS RESEARCH	AUDITS THAT CAN BE DONE	ANALOGUE WITH INDIVIDUAL
Capability	What is the organization good at doing and what should it be known for? Competitive differentiators.	Resources Strategic capabilities Core competencies	Capability audit: What do we have to be known for and good at to win? This should be tightly linked to strategy. Measure the extent to which priorities are shared about capabilities required to win.	What is my personality? We each have a personality that can be dissected into five core personality traits based on what comes naturally to us.
Culture	How do we shape the right patterns that will enable us to win? How the organization works: event, pattern, identity.	Competing values Organizational types Organizational health	Cultural audit: Do we have the right patterns for thinking and behaving? Measure the clarity and accuracy of the culture.	What habits inform my lifestyle and identity? We each have habits or routines that determine who we are.

Management Action 1: Intellectual agenda	Create a clear message about the desired culture to share inside and outside.	Shared mindset Values	Unity audit: Do we have a shared culture? Do we recognize implicit assumptions? Measure unity of culture and clarity of assumptions.	What are my thought patterns? (schema)
Management Action 2: Behavioral agenda	Turn cultural identity into employee actions.	Climate	Behavioral audit: Do employee behaviors link to the culture? Measure behavioral alignment and change.	What are my daily actions? (calendar test)
Management Action 3: Process agenda	Create, shape, and reinforce culture through management practices.	Systems – 7s – STAR – High-performing work system Organizational processes	Process or system audit: Do we have processes that reinforce and embed the culture? Measure process alignment and change.	How do my emotions shape my experience and sustain my desired routines?

First, organizational capabilities represent what the organization is known for, what it is good at doing, and how it allocates resources to win in its market. Organizations should be defined less by their structure and more by their ability to establish the capabilities required to win—that is, to serve customers in ways that competitors cannot readily copy. Organizational capabilities might include the ability to respond to or serve customers, drive efficiency, manage change, collaborate both inside and outside, innovate on products and the business model, access information, and establish the right culture. HR professionals can facilitate capability audits to determine if the organization has prioritized the right capabilities to win (see **Table 2** for the steps to a capability audit).[15]

TABLE 2. ORGANIZATIONAL CAPABILITY AUDIT

STEP	QUESTION	OUTCOME
1 Select organizational unit for audit.	What organizational unit should be the target of the capability audit?	Define organizational unit where the capability audit will occur (corporation, business unit, region, plant).
2 Create content of the audit.	What are the key capabilities that an organization might consider?	Prepare a list of possible capabilities that an organization might possess; tailor the generic capabilities to the organization.
3 Collect data through surveys or interviews.	How do different groups (leadership team, employees, customers, suppliers, partners) prioritize these capabilities?	Involve multiple stakeholders to determine which capabilities should be priorities.
4 Synthesize data to see priorities.	What are the top two to four capabilities for this organization?	Look for patterns in data to identify the top two to four priorities most likely to help the organization succeed.
5 Create a capability action plan.	How can the organization implement the chosen capabilities throughout the organization?	Prepare an action plan for each capability with definitions, decisions to implement, and actions to move forward.
6 Follow up and monitor progress.	How can the chosen capabilities be institutionalized?	Track the progress of capability implementation and improve as required.

Second (in **Table 1**), culture represents the pattern of how people think and act in the organization. While organizations can have many capabilities, culture is likely to be the key to future success. The right culture takes what the organization should be known for by target customers and uses this external identity to shape internal thought and action. HR professionals can audit the extent to which an organization has the right culture.

Third (in **Table 1**), management actions can be identified and implemented to create and sustain the desired culture. My colleagues and I have classified these actions into intellectual, behavioral, and process agendas. Intellectual agendas ensure that managers create a shared culture inside and outside the organization;

behavioral agendas show the extent to which all employees behave consistently with the desired culture; and process agendas institutionalize the culture through management practices.

The three dimensions in this organizational logic parallel psychologists' understanding of individuals. Individuals have personalities (parallel to organizational capabilities) that have been categorized into the "Big 5": openness, conscientiousness, extraversion, agreeableness, and neuroticism. These five personality traits capture domains that can be observed and measured. Individuals then have habits (organizational culture or patterns) that determine how they approach life. Psychologists say that 50 percent to 80 percent of what people do comes from habits or routines. These habits show up in how people think (cultural intellectual agenda), act (cultural behavioral agenda), and manage emotions or sentiment that signal and sustain behaviors (cultural process agenda). Psychologists who diagnose individuals look at each of the three levels (personality, habit, action). Likewise, HR professionals who assess organization can look at three levels (capability, culture, and management action).

The implication for HR professionals: While talent may be 65 percent to 75 percent of the way up the "S curve," creating competitive organizations is likely only 15 percent to 25 percent up the "S curve." As HR professionals bring similar rigor to organization as they have to talent and leadership, they will add even more value to their organizations. Through ensuring talent, HR enters the business game; through building organization, HR wins the business game. The wars for talent will be changed into victories through organization.

About Dave Ulrich

Dave Ulrich is the Rensis Likert Professor of Business at the Ross School, University of Michigan, and a partner at the RBL Group, a consulting firm focused on helping organizations and leaders deliver value. He studies how organizations build capabilities of leadership, speed, learning, accountability, and talent through leveraging human resources. He has also helped generate award-winning databases that assess alignment between strategies, organizational capabilities, HR practices, HR competencies, and customer and investor results. Ulrich has published more than 200 articles and book chapters and more than 25 books. He edited Human Resource Management from 1990 to 1999, served on the editorial boards of four journals, on the board of directors for Herman Miller, on the board of trustees at Southern Virginia University, and is a Fellow in the National Academy of Human Resources (NAHR). Ulrich has consulted and done research with over half of the Fortune 200 and received numerous honors for his research and thought leadership. In 2014, he was ranked the No. 1 speaker in management and business by Speaking. com. In 2011, he was ranked the No. 1 most influential thought leader in HR by HR Magazine. The following year, the magazine honored him with a Lifetime Achievement Award for being "the father of modern human resources."

1 Wayne Brockbank, "Balancing the HR Agendas: Talent and Organization," Harvard Business Review blog, 2014.

2 Ed Michaels, Helen Handfield-Jones, and Beth Axelrod, "The War for Talent" (Cambridge, MA: Harvard Business School Press, 2001).

3 Justin Allen and Dave Ulrich, "Talent Accelerator: Secrets for Driving Business Growth in Asia" (Singapore: RBL Group and Ministry of Manpower, 2013).

4 "Culture and the Role of Internal Audit: Looking Below the Surface," Chartered Institute of Internal Auditors, 2014. (http://www.iia.org.uk/policy/culture-and-the-role-of-internal-audit/)

5 The resource-based view of organizations has a more academic tradition in work by: J.B. Barney, "Firm Resources and Sustained Competitive Advantage," Journal of Management, 17(1), 1991, pages 99–120; R. Makadok, "Toward a Synthesis of the Resource-Based View and Dynamic-Capability Views of Rent Creation," Strategic Management Journal, 22(5), 2001, pages 387–401; J.B. Barney, "Is the Resource-Based Theory a Useful Perspective for Strategic Management Research? Yes," Academy of Management Review, 26(1), 2001, pages 41–56.

6 Approaching organizations as core competencies has been captured in work by C.K. Prahalad and Gary Hamel. See C.K. Prahalad and Gary Hamel, "The Core Competence of the Corporation," Harvard Business Review, May–June 1990, pages 79–91.

7 Scott Keller and Colin Price, "Beyond Performance: How Great Organizations Build Ultimate Competitive Advantage" (Hoboken, NJ: John Wiley & Sons, 2011). See also Scott Keller and Colin Price, "Organizational Health: The Ultimate Competitive Advantage," McKinsey Quarterly, June 2011; and Aaron de Smet, Bill Schaninger, and Matthew Smith, "The Hidden Value of Organizational Health—And How to Capture It," McKinsey Quarterly, April 2014.

8 D.M. Rousseau, "The Construction of Climate in Organizational Research," in International Review of Industrial and Organizational Psychology, edited by C.L. Cooper and I. Robertson (London: Wiley & Sons, 1988).

9 The process approach to organization may be seen in the balanced scorecard work of Dave Norton and Robert Kaplan. See their works: "The Balanced Scorecard: Measures That Drive Performance," Harvard Business Review, January–February 1992; "The Strategy-Focused Organization: How Balanced Scorecard Companies Thrive in the New Business Environment" (Cambridge, MA: Harvard Business School Press, 2000); "Strategy Maps: Converting Intangible Assets Into Tangible Outcomes"

(Cambridge, MA: Harvard Business School Press, 2014).

[10] Edgar Schein, "Organizational Culture and Leadership: A Dynamic View" (San Francisco, CA: Jossey-Bass, 1992); T.E. Deal and A.A. Kennedy. Corporate Cultures: The Rites and Rituals of Corporate Life (Reading, MA: Addison-Wesley, 1982).

[11] The concept of mindset comes from cognitive psychology and is called automatic thoughts, schema, or mental models. See P. DiMaggio, "Culture and Cognition," Annual Review of Sociology, 1997. In organizations, we have talked about a shared mindset, or culture, being the shared cognitions in an organization. See Dave Ulrich and Dale Lake, Organization Capability: Competing From the Inside Out (New York: Wiley, 1990).

[12] Daniel Denison, "Corporate Culture and Organizational Effectiveness" (New York: Wiley, 1990).

[13] Russell Ackoff, "Re-Creating the Corporation: A Design of Organizations for the 21st Century" (New York: Oxford University Press, 1999).

[14] Dave Ulrich, "Leadership Capital Index" (forthcoming, 2015); Dave Ulrich and Norm Smallwood, "Capitalizing on Capabilities," Harvard Business Review, 2004, pages 119–128; Dave Ulrich, "What Is Organization?" Leader to Leader, 1997(5), pages 40–46.

WINNING IN THE MOBILE INTERNET ERA: WHAT SHOULD HR KNOW AND DO TO BE EFFECTIVE?

Arthur Yeung

Mobile internet has changed how we communicate, shop, entertain, and learn—but more important, it has transformed how companies are organized and how they compete with one another. With the prevalence of iPads, smartphones, and other smart devices, people can now connect to other people, information, content, services, companies, and things much more quickly, easily, and cheaply. Although the term "connectivity" was coined in the late 1990s, the true realization of connecting people, information, and organizations anywhere at any time is a recent phenomenon, occurring with the arrival of mobile internet in the last few years.

Enabled by the accessibility of mobile phones, the capability of location-based services, and the convenience of secured mobile payment, companies such as Uber and Didi Taxi have enhanced our transportation experience, which would not have been possible without mobile internet. Similarly, Twitter, Facebook, Amazon, WhatsApp, WeChat, and others would not have been so valuable and powerful without the prevalence of smartphones and supporting services.

This wave of mobile internet is strong and only gaining momentum. It is going to challenge and redefine established business models in almost all industries, including communications, media, retail, entertainment, banking, education, publishing, and health care. It will continue to create innovative business opportunities for companies that embrace it (including Apple, Facebook, Uber, Alibaba, and Tencent) and cause the downfall of others that fail to respond fast enough (such as Nokia, Motorola, BlackBerry, Dell, or Borders).

IMPLICATIONS FOR THE ENVIRONMENT, ORGANIZATIONS, AND PEOPLE

Surviving and thriving in the mobile internet era is no easy task for many companies. The new era presents a drastically different business environment than what many firms grew accustomed to in the twentieth century. This new business environment has three salient characteristics:

1. The ***magnitude of change will become more radical*** as newcomers take advantage of the new enabling connectivity to challenge the existing business models of established players across many industries. For example, e-retailers including Amazon have disintermediated traditional retailers, putting companies such as Borders out of business.
2. The ***rate of change will increase*** as the rise and decline of new product and service applications occur in exponentially shorter amounts of time. For example, while it took about 12 years for Tencent's first-generation instant-messaging product, QQ, to reach 100 million users, it took only 433 days for its second-generation product, WeChat, to reach the same size user base. Similar trends can be seen in the accelerated popularization of products such as Facebook, Twitter, and WhatsApp (and, simultaneously, in the replacement of their substitutes).
3. ***Competition will be fiercer*** as traditional barriers to entry such as capital requirements, operating infrastructure, and sales and service channels drop substantially. Today, only a small team of people is required to make a big impact in the mobile internet era. Small startups such as WhatsApp and Instagram are telling examples. If a company has great talent and product ideas, financial capital is never the primary constraint, as vehicles such as venture capital funds or crowdsourced funding models are constantly searching for investment opportunities and enticing them with resources. Operating, infrastructure, and sales channels are also less of a concern given the prevalence and accessibility

of cloud services and internet platforms such as Amazon Marketplace, Alibaba's Taobao, and Google Play. More than ever before, talent is the ultimate scarce resource. Great minds, such as those of Steve Jobs, Jeff Bezos, Larry Page, Mark Zuckerberg, Jack Ma, Pony Ma, or Lei Jun, surrounded by core talent teams and driven by customer-centric organizational cultures, are the ultimate source of competitiveness.

Given this fast-changing and hypercompetitive business environment, what kind of organization will succeed? Clearly, it will not be those with a traditional hierarchical organizational model. Frederick Taylor and Max Weber, key advocates of the scientific management approach, suggested that the organizational form of hierarchy—with many organizational layers, fine division of departments, clearly defined roles, and numerous standard operating procedures—is the most efficient organizational model to ensure the reliability and consistency of business operations. Yet this is a poor fit in the fast-changing, uncertain, and hypercompetitive business environment of today. Moreover, this organizational model works well only when products are tangible and the final output can be clearly defined.

To ensure the quality and efficiency of production, standardized processes were the key to success when people played a relatively less important role. However, in the mobile internet era, most of the tasks are creation-based, the products and services (e.g., games, internet platform, and social media) are not tangible, and their final outputs cannot be perfectly specified at the design stage. Creativity is needed to envision a great product or service offering and then implement quick iterations of improvement to continuously enhance user experience. Instead of a hierarchical organization, more agile, autonomous, and collaborative organizational forms (e.g., elite troops or sports teams) are likely to thrive in the mobile internet era. My recent research with a group of prominent internet firms—including Google, Facebook, Amazon, Netflix, Riot Games, Uber, Alibaba, and Xiaomi—indicates that these companies share the following similarities in organizing and managing their people for business competitiveness:

- *Winning capabilities* – These firms organize their people in ways that focus their competencies, commitment, and contribution around the capabilities of customer centricity, innovation, and agility. These capabilities are critical to success in the internet mobile era.

- *Hiring the best* – These firms adopt strict hiring standards (for characteristics including learning agility, passion, cultural fit, and professional skills) and rigorous screening processes (such as Amazon's "bar raiser" program or Google's hiring committees) to ensure that only the best will join the company.
- *Firing fast* – These companies do not hesitate to replace underperformers and employees who negatively impact the overall performance of the team. Companies including Zappos even pay employees to leave as a way to quickly filter those who are not committed. The opportunity cost of missed business opportunities is too great in a fast-changing and highly competitive environment.
- *Aggressively rewarding and retaining talent* – Retention is a big challenge for many internet firms. As on sports teams, people are remunerated based on their external market value, not internal equity. At Netflix, line managers can increase an employee's salary anytime (with no need to stick to a merit increase schedule) once they know that a competitor offers a more competitive package. They will also consider how much it costs to hire a new candidate with a similar profile and adjust employee compensation packages accordingly. All these companies are also generous with stocks and stock options, based on differentiated performance.
- *Instilling strong mission and values* – In a fluid environment with uncertain tasks, standardized rules and procedures are not well suited. Instead, shared mission and values can guide employee decisions and behaviors in developing world-changing products and quickly improving user experience based on instant customer feedback.
- *Organizing in flexible and multiskilled teams* – These companies often arrange teams of five to 10 people with different skills (such as coding engineers, user-interface designers, and data analysts). The self-contained teams are designed to minimize the time-consuming and energy-draining coordination across teams or functions that is typical in many traditional companies. Moreover, teams are fluid and are formed or dissolved based on the mission and assignment rather than rigid administrative structure.
- *Communicating frequently and transparently* – Within the company, top management strives to be transparent about the company's strategy and recent developments or bottlenecks, so that loosely coupled autonomous teams can align their tasks with the company's overall direction. Google's weekly TGIF meetings or Facebook's all-hands meetings are great examples.
- *Empowering small teams for agility* – While major product innovations may come from the top down, fast-paced improvements are often carried out from

the bottom up. Teams are empowered to release new product versions based on user feedback and market data.

IMPLICATIONS FOR THE HR FUNCTION AND HR PROFESSIONALS

As the established hierarchical organizational form becomes outdated in the mobile internet era, the established principles and practices of HR embedded in this model are likewise fading in relevance. Most current HR practices favor standardization, consistency, and equity—outgrowths of the organizational setting where standardized processes, not individual talent, matter most. As we embark on the mobile internet era, where talent working in a customer-centric organizational culture is of paramount importance, we may need to reflect, unlearn, and then relearn what the HR function and HR professionals should do and not do to be effective. Based on my observations of evolving HR practices at some pioneering internet firms, here are a few starting points:

- *Process-driven vs. talent-centric* – Over the decades, HR has developed an array of standardized tools and processes that may be overengineered or perceived as bureaucratic among internet firms. For instance, HR traditionally spends a lot of time chasing line managers to create performance plans, provide feedback, and fill out evaluation forms that link to year-end merit increases and bonuses. However, I found that companies including Netflix, Riot Games, and Xiaomi are not as obsessed with performance planning and reviews, as managers can easily assess employee and team performance based on real-time market data rather than following a quarterly, biannual, or annual cycle.

The emphasis has switched to feedback and coaching rather than performance evaluation. Instead of depending on rigorous annual talent reviews (similar to GE's Session C), these companies rely on line managers to categorize the performance and potential of their team members on a quarterly basis. This also creates a faster cycle of promotion or share granting. Instead of sticking to many conventional HR practices, companies including Netflix have even scrapped basic HR policies such as annual leave and give employees unlimited leave time. All these practices sound "unprofessional" based on established HR standards. However, given the shift in these companies' business environment and organizational models during the mobile internet era, it has become clear that their HR practices also need to be more agile, customer-centric (or talent-centric for HR), and innovative.

- *Equity vs. contribution* – Equity is regarded as one of the key principles in designing a compensation system. Yet the principle of internal equity based on job grading and external equity based on annual market surveys may not be as relevant in organizational settings, where the contribution of one talented product engineer or a team can create tremendous market value. Individual market value based on contribution and performance (think basketball stars or football stars) seems to be more relevant in the new era, especially for key talent. Job grading and salary banding may still be useful for deciding base salary for lower-level employees.

  However, when it comes to equity incentives or year-end bonuses, contribution and performance rather than internal equity are the overriding principles. Some companies have even explicitly tied an individual's bonus or share award to a percentage of the profit or market value that their team creates. This fosters a strong sense of ownership among team members, as their wealth is tightly tied to the ultimate competitiveness of their products and services rather than the performance of the overall company or business unit.

- *HR vs. line managers* – As talent becomes more idiosyncratic in needs, styles, professional skills, and contributions, line managers who work closely with top talent should be given more autonomy and discretion in decisions around hiring, promotion, termination, and rewards. Instead of designing and enforcing a standardized set of HR policies and processes, the HR function and professionals may need to reexamine their value-add in the organization by (1) architecting more fluid and agile teams; (2) instilling strong company mission and values; (3) attracting the best talent; (4) coaching line managers to do their jobs; (5) using data to assess the effectiveness of current HR and management practices; and (6) providing resources and tool kits for line managers and talent to help themselves.

  Such trends are best reflected in Netflix's HR function, where all traditional HR processes and routines are now organized under the finance function and HR serves only as the talent scout and coach. While many HR functions will not follow Netflix's example to this degree, it serves as a telling example for HR to reexamine and redefine what HR should and should not do in the mobile internet era, when talent, not process, matters most.

About Arthur Yeung

Arthur Yeung is the Philips Chair Professor of Human Resource Management at China Europe International Business School (CEIBS). Before his recent return to academia, Yeung was chief learning officer and subsequently chief HR officer at Acer Group. He also founded the Center of Organizational and People Excellence (COPE) and the Organizational Capability Learning Association, where CEOs of more than 100 Chinese firms meet regularly to learn how to grow and succeed in China and beyond. The author of 10 books and dozens of articles, Yeung also serves as global editor (Asia-Pacific) for Talent and Strategy Journal and is an editorial board member for the Human Resource Management Journal (US), Harvard Business Review (China), Human Relations Journal (US), and Thunderbird International Business Review (US). In addition to research and teaching, Yeung has also been involved in training and consulting projects for numerous major corporations in Asia and North America, including Alibaba, Bank of China, China Mobile, Ford Motors, Lenovo Group, Philips, Tencent, and United Microelectronic Group. He also serves as board director for five corporations and one nonprofit organization, and advises CEOs of several leading Chinese firms. At CEIBS, his outstanding teaching has been recognized through numerous awards. He also teaches regularly in executive programs in association with Harvard, INSEAD, and Michigan.

3 TALENT SUPPLY

TALENT SUPPLY

Introduction

No discussion of the role of HR now or in the future can be complete without exploring the complex issue of talent, talent supply, and the marketplace in which we compete for talent. While hiring and retaining top talent is often one of the top goals for a CEO and for HR, some ask whether or not HR has the right mindset and competencies for the challenge. No business can reach its strategic objectives—no matter what business it is in, its marketplace, global economic conditions, or the regulatory environment—without first attracting and retaining the right talent in the right roles at the right time.

As we look at what is happening in talent, a topic brought to the forefront almost 20 years ago by McKinsey in "The War for Talent" as a critical driver of business performance, we realize that challenges predicted 20 years ago with regard to the talent supply chain are now affecting our businesses. As Lance J. Richard's essay points out, there is not necessarily a shortage of people in the world who are available to work—but there is a shortage of people with the skills we need in the workplace today across the world. In his essay, Carl Rhodes outlines many other obstacles in the talent marketplace and how HR is adapting to this new world of talent. This talent mismatch is part of a complex equation, as organizations are looking for workers whose talents and skills match the job and whose work styles and values match their culture.

China Gorman's essay examines how great corporate cultures can lead to enhanced and sustainable performance. She shares examples of organizations where CEO and HR goals are aligned, and thus have a competitive advantage over those without such alignment. In the current marketplace for talent, the workers we want and need are in the driver's seat, with higher expectations about what the company will deliver. Workers of all generations want more from their work. They want an experience that provides meaning and fulfillment beyond the traditional job description.

As Gorman explains, culture is created by everyday relationships and what workers experience day in and day out with their leaders, co-workers, and the work itself. Trust is the foundation of these relationships, as is pride in the work product, and co-workers with shared values. Indeed, a strong culture can be the glue that holds the right talent in place.

With more agile organizations, the workforce is increasingly becoming more diverse and globally dispersed. The work itself is no longer just a full-time job but more project based, able to be accomplished by part-time, contingent, or virtual workers. Amy Schabacker Dufrane and Iona Harding look at the topic of driving high-potential talent in this environment. They advocate that potential trumps all other qualities in this new age. Mara Swan points out that the employee/employer model has evolved from a net present value model to a cost model and now to talent as a total value asset.

Talent is defined by several of the authors in this section. For Dufrane and Harding, talent is defined by potential. Richards sees talent as the ability to convert data into actionable knowledge. He sees the need for HR to become involved earlier in the pipeline, through our educational systems, so that we can ensure that the talent we need will be generated. Swan calls the environment in which we are operating "The Human Age," a time when HR must develop expertise in supply and demand of talent and HR must be able to customize offerings to employees to engage and motivate.

HR must work with their teams at the top to take charge of securing and optimizing the talent supply by segment through various supply chains and pipelines to meet the talent needs of their organization. Rhodes encourages HR teams in global organizations to embrace a robust strategic workforce planning (SWP) as part of an effective talent strategy. Research conducted by Human Capital Institute (HCI) and Workday showed that while most organizations consider workforce planning to be a high priority, few organizations are prepared for their talent needs of the future.

To date, HR has not embraced a standard model for SWP that can be adopted across all companies, and very few organizations are using vendor-provided solutions. Rhodes shares HCI's model that can be tailored to the needs of each organization, and emphasizes the importance of fully integrating SWP with existing strategic business planning processes in the organization.

In her essay, Swan writes that a collision of macroeconomic forces have brought about "The Human Age," where demand is unpredictable and companies need to be agile and flexible in order to drive value and compete in new markets. Of course, this cannot be done unless HR and their organizations can access, mobilize, and engage the right talent. Swan argues that rather than one workforce strategy for one work model, organizations must shift to a workforce strategy that supports multiple work models as needed to tackle a transient competitive advantage. The infrastructures deeply ingrained in HR have become not only an obstacle but also a liability when faced with a need for agility.

The focus on talent as a differentiator requires new ways to deliver for HR and brings about a multitude of new cultural and social implications. Swan believes that now is the time for HR to be experience driven, which will require mindset shifts focused on driving more time to value. It means that we must understand where value is created and what experiences customers are willing to pay for. We must create value from our efforts. Competitive advantage is transient, so agility will be a key contributor to our success.

We should not overlook the HR talent supply. Dufrane and Harding present some compelling research on the correlation between certification and potential and advocate that certified HR professionals display higher levels of potential and performance than non-certified, and are better able to handle the challenges of the changing workplace and a rapidly evolving workforce.

In this section, all of our authors offer strong advice for what HR needs to know and do to ensure a supply of the right talent. The following are a few highlights:

- Articulate the business strategy link to strategic workforce planning to support and sync talent with organizational objectives and expected results.
- Encourage your leadership to make the important connection between talent, performance, and culture.
- Immerse yourself in the educational infrastructure from kindergarten through university to make sure the talent available in the future has the potential needed by organizations.
- The HR mindset must change. We need to abandon prior focus on control and programming and move toward roles that enable HR to drive more time to value.
- HR must continually improve its own capabilities and competencies. A rigorous certification process is a proven way to demonstrate that to employers.

HRCI CERTIFICATION AS A LEADING INDICATOR OF HIGH-POTENTIAL HR TALENT

Amy Schabacker Dufrane and Iona Harding

Nearly anyone who studies the human resources profession today is bound to encounter a reference to "potential" in their research on employees and the companies that hire them.

Executive search firms clamor to find high-potential candidates to help their clients with succession planning. Talent managers inside firms exert special effort to ensure that especially promising workers get the support they need to succeed. Meanwhile, high-achieving employees actively seek opportunities to hone their skills, increase their wages, and stretch their capabilities, frequently opting to abandon their current positions if companies don't harness their skills and talent.

What is the context fueling these new methods of selecting, retaining, and developing employees? Clearly, the workplace and the workforce are evolving at a rapid rate. Organizational structures are flatter, more agile, and often more amorphous than ever before. The workforce is increasingly diverse and more globally dispersed. Assignments transcend traditional full-time employment to include contingent, project-based, part-time, and virtual workers. And there is a global scarcity of critical skills.

THE RISING IMPORTANCE OF "POTENTIAL"

In 2014, with these changes in the air, executive search consultant Claudio Fernández-Aráoz penned a much-discussed essay in Harvard Business Review titled "21st-Century Talent Spotting: Why Potential Now Trumps Brains, Experience, and 'Competencies.'" In the article, Fernández-Aráoz argues that an employee's capacity to adapt to increasingly complex circumstances—described as their "potential"—is a better predictor of success at work than mere assessments of their leadership skills, or competencies.

Because of this, Fernández-Aráoz suggests that hiring and talent managers need to look beyond competencies alone and evaluate both current and prospective employees on a number of factors that indicate their deeper potential—including motivation, curiosity, insight, engagement, and determination. Taking the idea a step further, he also suggests that managers can help star performers improve their already high performance—and further tap into their potential—through challenging assignments and clever retention practices.

Not only do these insights figure into the counsel that HR professionals provide to employers about approaches for finding and keeping good workers, but they are also highly relevant to our own job prospects as well. The HR field is predicted to be one of the top areas for job growth in the next decade. HR management positions in the United States are forecasted to grow by more than 13 percent, compared to 7 percent for management positions overall.

So with demand and competition for people in the HR sector expected to increase in the years ahead, how can leaders identify, attract, and retain top HR talent—the high potentials, if you will? And how can HR professionals demonstrate to current and would-be employers that we have the kind of potential Fernández-Aráoz says they should look for?

WHY CERTIFICATION MATTERS

There are perhaps multiple answers to these questions, but new research conducted by the Alexandria, VA-based Human Resources Research Organization (HumRRO) suggests that certification from the HR Certification Institute (HRCI) is widely considered a strong indicator of professional potential in our field. In a 2015 report titled "An Evaluation of the Value of HR Certification for Individuals and Organizations," HumRRO assessed the significance of HRCI certification and found that HRCI-certified professionals stand out among their peers when it comes to job performance, future potential, and expertise.

HumRRO's study of the value of HR certification is one of the biggest and most comprehensive to date. HumRRO surveyed enormous samples of HR professionals for its study, including nearly 12,000 individuals with certification (either SPHR or PHR) from HRCI, about 5,600 without HRCI certification, and about 2,400 supervisors who make hiring and promotion decisions about HR teams within for-profit, nonprofit, and public-sector organizations. The study was commissioned by HRCI.

Ultimately, HumRRO found that within the HR profession, HRCI certification is closely associated with important outcomes that include stronger job performance, stronger capability to handle strategic activities, better potential for higher-level positions, and more advanced technical expertise. Importantly, these judgments were made by the direct supervisors of HR professionals and are not based on the potentially biased viewpoints of certificants themselves.

While HumRRO's study cannot prove that HRCI certification causes all of the positive outcomes listed above, it did show that this certification is related to these outcomes *above and beyond* any effects due to level of HR experience, level or type of education, current job level, and industry.

For example, today's organizations need HR professionals with the proven ability to think and perform strategically in order to meet the needs of the evolving workplace and workforce. So HumRRO's researchers asked the 2,400 supervisors who participated in the study whether HRCI-certified HR professionals perform better on strategic tasks than non-certified professionals. The vast majority of supervisors said that those holding the SPHR certification from HRCI consistently performed at a higher level on strategic tasks—such as providing counsel on likely barriers to and enablers of organizational performance—than their uncertified counterparts. The same pattern held for those holding a PHR certification from HRCI, although the difference was not as pronounced.

In order to evolve, today's organizations need HR professionals who can anticipate barriers and opportunities and lead the way through them. When asked to rate the ability of HR professionals to anticipate future organizational priorities and develop processes to meet them, the surveyed supervisors gave stronger evaluations, on average, to HRCI certificants than to non-certificants. The supervisors also said that HRCI certificants were more likely to provide timely and accurate consultation on potential barriers to organizational performance than non-certificants.

The HumRRO study also assessed whether HRCI-certified professionals possess more expertise in core bodies of human resources knowledge than their non-certified counterparts. Across all areas, certified professionals were rated as having more expertise, especially those holding the SPHR certification. The areas of expertise included in the survey—business management and strategy, risk management, employment law, workforce planning and employment, human resource development, and employee and labor relations—are critical for helping organizations position themselves for the future. They are also critical for ensuring HR professionals' own future success in the field.

Finally, supervisors noted that HRCI certificants appeared better equipped to handle the many challenges of the changing workplace, including high degrees of ambiguity, uncertainty, complexity, and volatility.

LEVERAGING HR CERTIFICATION: THE ORGANIZATION'S PERSPECTIVE

The HumRRO study strongly suggests that HRCI certification is both a reflection and a marker of an HR professional's potential in the field. It further suggests that organizational leaders should consider HRCI certification as a factor when hiring or promoting HR professionals—and also that organizations would benefit from supporting their current HR professionals in becoming certified.

The HRCI certification process is designed to help talent professionals build their potential. For example, the initial certification process requires demonstrated HR experience, knowledge, and skills in several critical areas. Once certified, talent professionals must renew their certification every three years by taking a certification examination and/or participating in approved professional development activities. HRCI strongly supports the dual purpose of these professional enrichment activities, as they provide a means for certified professionals to ensure they are continuing to develop, stay relevant, and keep pace with changes occurring both in the organizations they serve and in the marketplace.

Indeed, the survey results show that many supervisors already view HRCI certification as an indicator of potential. Two-thirds of supervisors said their organization prefers to hire HRCI-certified professionals for at least some positions—and 20 percent said their organization *requires* certification by HRCI for some or all positions.

LEVERAGING HR CERTIFICATION: THE INDIVIDUAL'S PERSPECTIVE

Becoming certified by HRCI is a good way for HR professionals to demonstrate their skills and potential to current or would-be employers. At the most direct level, certification enhances an HR professional's level of expertise, and the HumRRO study strongly suggests that supervisors recognize this fact. Indeed, having a higher level of expertise may well impact organizational leaders' perceptions of an HR professional's value to the organization and his or her potential to capably perform strategic activities and handle challenging problems.

The HumRRO study also found that HRCI certification is associated with several other outcomes that matter to individuals. For example, certified professionals were less likely to report being unemployed or underemployed than their non-certified peers. This suggests that when employment is tight, having an HRCI credential may make a difference in obtaining or maintaining a job.

Also, HRCI certified professionals reported much higher compensation than those without this certification. Self-reported current annual income was $4,547 higher, on average, for PHR certificants than for non-certificants, and $19,712 higher, on average, for SPHR certificants. SPHR certificants in private-sector (or for-profit) companies reported earning significantly more than those in nonprofit and public-sector organizations. This cross-sector disparity did not appear between PHR certificants and non-certificants.

Moreover, income growth over time was higher for HRCI certificants than for non-certificants, even after factoring for differences in experience, education, job level, and industry. For PHR certificants, income growth was $292 per year higher, on average, than for non-certificants; for SPHR certificants, it averaged $938 per year higher. HRCI certificants also reported much higher career satisfaction than non-certificants.

SUMMARY

The HumRRO study presents a compelling argument that HRCI certification is a good indicator of the type of potential that matters to both individuals and organizations. Supervisors who make critical hiring and promotion decisions report that HRCI certificants bring an array of workplace-enhancing qualities to organizations compared to professionals who have not yet sought or achieved such credentials. They rate certificants' job performance much higher than that of non-certificants; indicate that certified HR professionals have more potential to perform well in higher-level positions and in challenging situations; and say that certified HR professionals have better technical expertise. While the study cannot prove that HRCI certification is the direct or sole cause of these positive outcomes, it did rule out several potential competing explanations (such as differences in HR experience or education level).

HumRRO's investigation reaffirms what past studies and abundant anecdotal evidence have told us for years: that HRCI certification reflects the motivation to build potential and credibility as a talent professional, and to maintain those qualities through recertification activities. Surely it is not a coincidence that supervisors understand, value, and rely on HRCI certification as a marker for potential when making hiring and promotion decisions. And it is yet another reminders that, now as ever, our profession must continue to keep the certification process rigorous and relevant to the work of human resource management.

About Amy Schabacker Dufrane

Amy Dufrane is CEO of the HR Certification Institute, where she focuses on developing collaborative long-term partnerships with individuals and organizations looking to create and deliver change around human resources. Before joining HRCI, she spent more than 25 years in leading human resources functions with organizations including the Municipal Securities Rulemaking Board, The Optical Society, Marymount University, and Bloomingdale's. Dufrane has been an adjunct faculty member at the Marymount University School of Business Administration in Arlington, VA, since 1998. She also serves on the advisory board of Columbia Lighthouse for the Blind and is a commissioner for the National Commission for Certifying Agencies (NCCA). She is a recipient of the Leadership Non-Profit Award from HR Leadership Awards of Greater Washington. Dufrane holds the HR Certification Institute designation of Senior Professional in Human Resources (SPHR) and the Certified Association Executive (CAE) credential from the Center for Association Leadership. She also holds a doctorate in education from George Washington University; an MBA and MA in human resources from Marymount University; and a BA in management from Hood College.

About Iona Harding

Iona Harding is a human resource leader and educator with a passion for helping organizations and the human resources profession grow. The focus of her firm, Harding Resources LLC, is to improve business and human capital performance by increasing leadership and workforce capability. She is also an adjunct professor in the MBA program at St. Peter's University in Jersey City, NJ, and in the MBA and EMBA programs at Sasin Institute for Business in Bangkok, Thailand. Prior to starting her own consulting firm, Harding worked in the telecommunications industry for more than 20 years. She was the global HR vice president for Lucent Technologies' $10 billion global mobility business, where she supported and coached leaders and organizations throughout North America, Europe, the Middle East, and Asia. She also served as the interim human resources vice president for Lucent China. Prior to moving into HR, she held management positions in finance and marketing. Harding is a certified HR professional holding both the SPHR and GPHR certifications from the HR Certification Institute (HRCI). Currently she sits on HRCI's board of directors and is a frequent speaker on topics including the value of certification, measuring the effectiveness of human resources, and organizational culture. She holds master's and bachelor's degrees in business education from The College of New Jersey.

CEOS WANT BETTER PERFORMANCE. GREAT CULTURE CAN MAKE IT HAPPEN.

China Gorman

Planning ahead is essential to success. As radio icon and comedian Eddie Cantor astutely observed, "It takes 20 years to make an overnight success." Of course, making future plans in a modern work environment that is continually in flux can be tricky. But the good news is you already have a strategic advantage. As an HR leader, you have a deeper understanding of people, how they work, and the impact they can have on your company. After all, it's your job. And while people do evolve (despite occasional acts of Neanderthal behavior), there are some things about them that never change. In fact, as I will demonstrate later, there are some things about people that you and your company can bank on, quite literally.

One of the most predictable aspects of people in the workplace is that they have needs that are directly related to the goals they want to achieve. As an HR professional, you need to attract, hire, develop, and deploy the best people you can find to ensure you meet the goal of helping your company continue on an upward trajectory. However, you report to an executive leadership team, and their needs, at first, seem quite different from yours. C-level executives need to improve company performance, foster innovation, and increase profitability. Shareholder happiness and their jobs depend on it. So what do their needs and goals have to do with yours? Everything.

I believe the companies that have the most promising future and the best chance of outperforming their competitors are those in which HR and CEO goals have come together. Recently, the Korn Ferry Institute released a report that looks at the leadership traits of top executives, and the important relationship between CEOs and CHROs. The report "CEOs and CHROs: Crucial Allies and Potential Successors," confirms that for C-suite roles, the executives in the top 10 percent of pay for their function tend to have leadership styles that motivate employees, develop future leaders, and create appropriate cultures. The workplace is beginning to evaluate leaders on how they treat people, foster the right work environment, and encourage future leaders—and these are all areas where HR can become a CEO's greatest ally. As Korn Ferry's report asserts, "Well-managed talent, leadership, and culture are what enable sustainable customer, operational, and financial results."

CULTURE AS A CATALYST

When HR and leadership are united through a common goal, great things happen, as the Korn Ferry report and other research has proved, time and again. The best part is that the solution is simple, so simple in fact that it boils down to just one word: culture. Culture is the catalyst that connects executive leadership goals to HR goals and creates a perpetual winning environment. In short, creating a culture of success is the primary path you need to pursue in order to meet the needs of both executive leadership and HR.

Regardless of your size, industry, current environment, or any other variable that may attempt to present itself as an obstacle, you can set the course for your company to develop a great culture. Yes, it will require hard work, patience, and diligence—but the future results are worth it. It is important to note that your culture will not look and feel exactly like another's. However, just as every person has needs, studies have shown that all great cultures have three things in common. Namely, they are cultures in which employees:

- Trust in the people they work for
- Have pride in the work they do
- Enjoy the people they work with

In other words, great cultures are not formed by a checklist of programs and benefits. They are created through the everyday relationships that employees have with leaders, with their work, and with one another.

The most critical variable is trust. Building trust and fostering pride and happiness in the workplace are not impossible goals, and yet they elude most companies. While most HR professionals are acutely aware of the positive impact culture has on their ability to attract and retain the best people, a disconnect often happens at the executive level. Many C-level leaders have failed to see culture as a strategic part of making their company a contender in the marketplace. It's simply not a priority for them because they are focused on their immediate needs—performance, innovation, and profitability. They are big-picture thinkers, but so are you, and your vision as an HR leader can help them understand how making culture a priority will yield big returns in their areas of need.

One of the easiest ways to get leadership to partner with you to create a great workplace culture is to speak their language—numbers. A simple Google search of workplace culture and business success will yield countless studies that have all discovered the same thing: There is a direct correlation between a great workplace culture and strong financial performance.

Perhaps one of the most compelling long-term studies on culture and performance was conducted by Harvard Business School professor James Heskett, who later wrote a book entitled "Corporate Culture and Performance." In his book, which chronicled his study of more than 200 corporate cultures and how they impact performance over an 11-year period, Heskett discovered some shocking differences, reflected in the table below.[1]

	AVERAGE INCREASE FOR 12 FIRMS WITH PERFORMANCE-ENHANCING CULTURES	AVERAGE INCREASE FOR 20 FIRMS WITHOUT PERFORMANCE-ENHANCING CULTURES
Revenue Growth	682%	166%
Employment Growth	282%	36%

Stock Price Growth	901%	74%
Net Income Growth	756%	1%

Like Heskett, Russell Investments, an independent firm, has been tracking the performance of Fortune Magazine's "100 Best Companies to Work For" for nearly 20 years. These companies are selected each year by the Great Place to Work® Institute, and the primary criteria is employees that report high levels of trust, pride, and camaraderie as measured by the Trust Index Survey. Each year, Russell Investments compares the stocks of these 100 companies with the S&P 500 and the Russell 3000 indices, and each year these companies outperform all others, delivering nearly twice the return on investment as their competitors.[2]

If your company competes in the global marketplace, the numbers in this arena are even greater. A recent paper published by the European Corporate Governance Institute[3] studied data from 14 countries and concluded that the stocks of companies that made a "best workplaces" list consistently outperformed other companies in the stock market. For example, in India, companies on these lists outperform overall India stock market indices by more than four times. In Denmark, companies rated "best workplaces" deliver three times the revenue growth of other Danish companies.[4]

THE MERIDIAN EXAMPLE

If you really want to get your executive leadership's attention focused on culture, simply share with them the story of Meridian Health, a nonprofit health care system based in New Jersey. The organization came about as the result of a merger between three distinct hospitals. CEO John K. Lloyd knew he wanted Meridian to be known for providing the best health care experience in New Jersey, but he also knew he would need to create unity across its disjointed expanse of 2,100 doctors, 12,000 team members, and four unions. He determined that the best way to accomplish his goal was to make it everyone's goal. The journey to define the "Meridian Way" (their culture) had begun, and in 2006, an official program was launched called the Meridian Chain of Excellence.

To foster a sense of unity among Meridian's people, Lloyd looked to his HR department to help develop a training program that would equip all employees to embrace and work the Meridian Way. On their first day of work, every new team member, leader, and physician takes a "Traditions" course. The class teaches the Meridian Way with regards to heritage, traditions, culture, vision, mission, service standards, diversity, and inclusion.

"But you can't just hear about it once and then be done," says Patrice Ventura, Meridian's director of HR operations and organizational effectiveness. "We reinforce this learning as often as we can. 'Traditions' is followed by 'Beginnings,' where team members receive site-specific information as well as mandatory orientation information. The shared values, traits, and behaviors that define Meridian are integrated into everything we do. It starts from the top, with the belief that success is not just about business results, but also about the behaviors that get you there."

According to Sherrie String, Meridian's senior vice president of HR, it is their deliberately designed and tirelessly maintained "Culture of Excellence" that has made them one of the top-rated health care systems in New Jersey. However, String is also the first to admit that it has been a journey to get there and that culture is something that must be continuously nurtured. "Never take a breath and say 'we made it,'" says String. "This is when you go backwards."

The impact of Meridian's commitment to use culture as a catalyst for change has produced dramatic results in every area of its performance. Over a seven-year period, operating revenues increased 50 percent, going from $862.5 million to over $1.3 billion. Voluntary turnover dropped drastically from a national average of over 16 percent to just 5 percent. And last year, Meridian received 60,000 applications for just 1,200 openings. Meridian has also been named to Fortune's "100 Best Companies to Work For" list every year since 2009.

THE KEY INGREDIENTS OF A STRONG CULTURE

When you partner with leadership to create a culture of success, the most important thing you will work on developing together is trust. In the workplace, trust comprises credibility, respect, and fairness. While trust may be an intangible quality, it can be cultivated through very tangible steps. Leaders who desire to build credibility with their people must be willing to invest time and be both patient and consistent. Some of the steps leaders can take to demonstrate credibility and trustworthiness to employees include:

- Being approachable and promoting two-way communication
- Being transparent, sharing information, and communicating a clear vision
- Demonstrating competency by matching actions to words

The second aspect critical to developing a trust-based culture is respect. Your employees need to feel they are respected as people and as professionals. A few of the practical ways you can demonstrate respect for employees include:

- Investing in training and development
- Providing special benefits such as paid volunteer time, gym memberships, and flexible scheduling options
- Giving employees a voice in matters that pertain to them

The third and final aspect of trust essential to a successful culture shift is fairness. Your people need to feel that they are on a level playing field and have equal opportunities for recognition and advancement. Practical steps for promoting fairness include:

- Working with leaders to design and implement training and development opportunities
- Posting jobs internally and striving to promote from within
- Sharing profits equitably
- Ensuring people are paid fairly for their work

Like trust, pride is another intangible quality inherent to the most successful corporate cultures. To foster pride in the work employees do, it's imperative to show them how their jobs impact your company's success. A few simple ways you can help your company foster pride include:

- Work with departments to recognize employees who have demonstrated "pride" in their work. This can be done publicly at company meetings or on-the-spot with a simple, "Great job!"
- Share thank-you letters from customers that laud employee performance with all employees via the company newsletter and/or company and department meetings.
- Develop a weekly/monthly awards program that recognizes outstanding employee

contributions with useful awards such as $25 gift cards to a local coffee shop or restaurant.

- Enlist the accounting department's help in creating quarterly diagrams that show how each department's contribution impacts financial performance.

As noted earlier, the third ingredient in a great culture is enjoyment of the people one works with. As you might suspect, this is one of the most fun and easy cultural elements to develop. A few of the ways you can help foster enjoyment include:

- Hosting regular department lunches so employees get a chance to share a meal and spend quality time with one another
- Making a point of celebrating birthdays, work anniversaries, and holidays with on- and off-site parties
- Engaging employees' help in selecting a charity to volunteer time with and then sponsoring a volunteer day where employees work together to benefit that charity
- Encouraging employees to have fun while working by having team-based competitions to achieve various goals

As all of these steps demonstrate, creating a culture of success doesn't have to be expensive or time-consuming, but it does require planning and intention. One of the most important things to bear in mind with regard to culture is that it is not a destination, but a journey. Culture requires daily care and preparation in order to continually flourish. To that end, it is imperative that once you have worked with leadership to define the goals of your culture, and you have cultivated an atmosphere where employees and leaders are equipped to meet these goals, then you must be vigilant about protecting what you have created.

The best way to protect your culture's integrity is to be meticulous in only hiring people who fit within it. Yes, it will be tempting to hire people who have amazing skills but may not fit your culture. Don't do it. Don't even think about it! Just as one bad apple can spoil the bunch, so can one bad hire throw a wrench in all the hard work you and your company have invested in creating a unique and wonderful culture. Always remember that skills can be taught, but culture fit is like style— people either have it or they don't. Great culture is about never settling. It's about doing the right thing, even when it's hard. So wait for the right person. You'll be glad you did, and so will everyone in your great workplace culture.

FOCUS ON PEOPLE FIRST

Kip Tindell, CEO of The Container Store, the nation's leading retailer of storage and organizational products and perpetually ranked on the "100 Best Companies to Work For" list, is the perfect example of a leader who empowers his teams to hire only the best and the brightest. Tindell's hiring philosophy is "one great person is equal to three good people," which means one great person can deliver the productivity of three "good" people. To ensure great people are hired, hiring managers are given the freedom to conduct as many as seven or eight interviews of potential candidates. Fellow store employees are also regularly included in these interviews since they will be working directly with this potential hire.

Here, it's easy to see how great culture is perpetuated, not just in hiring the right people but in building trust with current employees by including them in the process and valuing their input on potential new employees. Tindell credits the double-digit, year-over-year growth rates the company has enjoyed since 1978 in part to the company's focus on people and the preservation of its culture through this hiring approach.

The Container Store's "employee-first" mentality enables it to bring great people on board, pay them well above the industry average, provide them with outstanding training and development opportunities, and empower them to unleash their creative genius. This has resulted in an environment where employees, customers, vendors, and, ultimately, shareholders win. In a speech Tindell gave to executive leaders who wanted to replicate his success, he told them, "If you take care of the employees better than anyone else, they will take care of the customer better than anyone else. If the employees and the customers are ecstatic, the shareholders will be ecstatic, too."

I believe that the workplace of tomorrow is one that HR leaders must actively champion, cultivate, and protect. In order for you, as an HR leader, to be effective in tomorrow's business world, you must help your leadership make the connection between people, performance, and culture. To recap, I recommend that you:

1. Recognize that culture is a catalyst.
2. Partner with leadership to create a great culture.
3. Work with leaders to foster trust.
4. Be culture-centric and hire only those who fit your culture.

As you invest the time, budgets, and energy to make culture a priority, you will soon discover that there is no downside to becoming a great workplace. Companies with great cultures don't just survive, they thrive. They draw the best and the brightest. Tenure goes up. Turnover goes down. Customers report better experiences. Shareholders are happier because stocks outperform the market. As for you, you will relish the satisfaction of knowing you have achieved true greatness, for your leaders, for your company and most importantly, for your people.

About China Gorman

China Gorman is CEO of Great Place to Work®, a global human resources consulting, research, and training firm specializing in organizational trust. With 30 years' experience in successfully leading professional services firms within the human capital management sector, Gorman has firmly established herself as a thought leader, writer, and sought-after speaker. Previously, she served as COO and interim CEO of the Society for Human Resource Management (SHRM); president of Lee Hecht Harrison, the global consulting division of Adecco, which became the performance leader in its industry under her leadership; president of DBM North America; and CEO of the CMG Group. In support of her lifelong commitment to leading and supporting organizations that make a difference in the world and in the lives of individuals, Gorman is the past board chair of the Chicago-based Council for Adult and Experiential Learning and currently serves on the board and executive committee of Jobs for America's Graduates. She also serves on the strategic advisory boards of RiseSmart and CVCertify. A native Midwesterner, she holds a bachelor's degree from Principia College and has completed significant post-graduate work in organizational development. When she is not at work, you'll find her spending time with her husband of 30 years, a former NFL coach.

---

[1] http://www.forbes.com/sites/johnkotter/2011/02/10/does-corporate-culture-drive-financial-performance/

[2] http://www.greatplacetowork.net/our-approach/what-are-the-benefits-great-workplaces

[3] Alex Edmans, Lucius Li, and Chendi Zhang, "Employee Satisfaction, Labor Market Flexibility, and Stock Returns Around The World," European Corporate Governance Institute (ECGI), Finance Working Paper No. 433/2014, July 2014. (http://papers.ssrn.com/sol3/ papers.cfm?abstract_id=2461003)

[4] Great Place to Work® Institute, "Dawn of the Great Workplace Era," October 2014. (http://www.greatplacetowork.net/best-companies/worlds-best-multinationals/2014-report)

STRATEGIC WORKFORCE PLANNING: PREPARING FOR TODAY AND TOMORROW

Carl Rhodes

The future is full of uncertainty, and that is especially true for HR professionals. As technology continues to evolve, needed job skills continue to shift, and the demands placed on HR continue to rise, gaining the knowledge and expertise to overcome these challenges has become a priority across companies of all sizes and industries. Not only is mastering these challenges necessary for the relevance of the HR profession, but it is also essential to the sustainability of the entire organization. Without a solid understanding of the issues facing HR practitioners today—and those that will emerge in the future—it will be difficult to chart the appropriate course and ensure continued success.

The HR landscape today is characterized by a multitude of obstacles, from increased competition for talent and growing disengagement among employees to rising demand for flexible work arrangements. Because these challenges continue to increase almost daily, the ability to address them in real time with the latest best practices and proven strategies is essential. Workforce planning has emerged as a crucial factor in ensuring an effective talent strategy that meets the needs of organizations, both today and far into the future.

For the last 10 years, the Human Capital Institute (HCI) has been working with global organizations and federal agencies to train HR teams on the process of strategic workforce planning (SWP) to define and deploy the mission-critical talent needed to align their organizations strategically with their future goals and objectives.

CHALLENGES OF STRATEGIC WORKFORCE PLANNING

Despite the growing focus on workforce planning, the function continues to be an area in which many organizations struggle. From getting executive buy-in for the program and securing necessary budgets to fostering a culture where all parties play their role in building alignment between talent and business priorities, implementing an effective SWP program is no easy task. The companies that get it right understand that it must be a collaborative process, requiring full alignment between people, data, and technology. When these are in place, we begin to see real results.

We recently completed research on the topic of strategic workforce planning with our partners at Workday. I have to admit, I wasn't surprised to see that there continues to be a disconnect between expectations and results. Although 69 percent of our survey respondents reported that workforce planning is an essential or high priority at their organizations, almost half (45 percent) reported that their organization is unprepared for the talent needs of the future. Factors such as a lack of resources and commitment to the process, an unclear definition of workforce planning, and poor technology continue to be the biggest barriers to success with the initiative.

Although the challenges in implementing a successful SWP strategy are numerous, such a program is necessary to protect the company's future. Our research shows that organizations with a robust program are better prepared to address business challenges—and more likely to take effective action with their talent information, evaluate their talent proactively, and prepare their organizations for the talent needs of the future.

Another issue is that there is no standard model or one-size-fits-all approach that can be used across all companies. Instead, SWP is a unique journey for each organization, being driven by its current status, goals, and culture. It is also important to recognize that workforce planning must be integrated with other planning processes, including strategic business planning and budgeting, as the workplace and workforce continue to change.

THE RIGHT PATH FORWARD

Given these struggles, what can companies today do to drive a robust and effective workforce planning strategy? At the end of the day, the organizations that understand how analytics, technology, and collaboration intersect are best positioned for success in workforce planning. For our HCI strategic workforce planning certification course, we have developed a model that organizations can use to streamline their SWP processes—and we recommend this model be tailored to the unique needs of each individual organization:

- Articulate the business strategy to link workforce planning processes that support and sync talent with organizational objectives and expected results.
- Segment roles to determine how each position contributes value and which roles are a priority or in the periphery.
- Conduct an environmental scan to continuously identify and monitor trends that affect the workforce and the organization.
- Analyze the current state to evaluate, benchmark, and inventory today's workforce.
- Construct a detailed future of how the organization, environment, technologies, and operational norms will look in the coming years.
- Identify gaps between the current and the desired future workforce and organizational state.
- Create an action plan to address, design, or restructure pieces (or all) of the organization's structure and talent initiatives, ensuring the company has the right talent in place to address current and future skills gaps.
- Monitor and report with quantitative and qualitative benchmarks and milestones that are identified in the action plan. Report findings to stakeholders and management.

Though implementing SWP may be daunting for many organizations and HR professionals, the bright side is that many are already doing some of these steps well. According to survey respondents, role segmentation, environmental scanning, and current state analysis are areas where organizations feel confident in their capabilities. However, other areas, such as future scenarios and action plans, continue to challenge most HR teams and their ability to conduct successful workforce planning.

The real issue here is that HR should not be the sole owner of the workforce planning process. Instead, it should truly be an organization-wide initiative. Overall, 56 percent of our survey respondents said that HR owns SWP in their workplace, while a mere 5 percent of managers own the SWP process. Even more striking, fewer than half of respondents (44 percent) said that their company provides SWP training to the individual responsible for the process, and 52 percent admitted that their organization is not adequately staffed to conduct SWP.

COLLABORATION, DATA, AND TECHNOLOGY

In order for this to change, we recommend establishing cross-functional teams to ensure proper alignment—and there are several characteristics shown to be indicative of effective cross-functional groups. These include strong team leadership to serve as active liaisons between management and team leaders, support from top management, and formal and informal communication across departments.

In addition to cross-function collaboration, SWP also requires that accurate and timely data be used to inform proper decision-making and planning. Only 19 percent of respondents agreed that they are proficient at predictive analytics, highlighting a significant gap between data and results. Without a clear understanding of the data, and a method for accessing and integrating a variety of quantifiable talent metrics, it will be difficult to achieve the full promise of SWP.

So, what is preventing organizations from leveraging data effectively? Our survey suggests that the main barriers are inadequate analytic skills and minimal data integration. Also problematic is the fact that practitioners must often collect data from a wide variety of disparate sources. Though most is derived from the HR function (92 percent) or the HRIS system (84 percent), the data needed for effective strategic workforce planning can span numerous departments, including finance, IT, learning and development, marketing, and even external vendors.

Given the sheer volume of data systems in use across workforce planning and the numerous sources of data, it is essential to integrate human capital management systems and provide executives and leaders with a real-time view of their workforce. Integrated technology solutions can deliver the much-needed link between that talent data and SWP. The benefit of such a solution is clear; a large majority (79 percent) of companies that do not use a technology solution from a vendor report that their SWP technology is either very far or far from the ideal, compared to those that do use a vendor-supplied technology solution. In addition, they are more likely to struggle to access timely, internal data.

Most survey respondents indicated that the tools and technologies they use for SWP do not work together effectively. Moreover, it is not uncommon for companies to have one tool for goal setting and performance management, another system for applicant tracking, and separate spreadsheets for succession planning, talent management, and development. Put more simply, many organizations are missing the crucial piece that can tie these systems together.

AN EFFECTIVE APPROACH TO SWP

To be successful in today's dynamic human capital landscape, and to continue to thrive in the future, business leaders must understand the link between their talent needs and overall goals. They must also acknowledge that workforce planning is no longer just under the jurisdiction of HR—it is an essential function requiring full integration with the existing strategic business planning processes that occur across the organization. When assisted by the right tools and processes, companies can hone an effective approach to strategic workforce planning, enabling them to improve their preparations for business growth, enhance operational efficiencies, and address growing skills gaps.

Of course, there are some people, such as noted workforce management expert Peter Cappelli, who would suggest that such extensive planning efforts are a waste of time. As uncertainty grows and the economy remains dynamic, they argue that once workforce planning is complete, the landscape has changed so much that those planning efforts are futile. This is certainly a valid point; it is impossible to account for every contingency and scenario. However, the fact remains that companies with a robust SWP strategy will be better prepared to address that uncertainty and ensure that the right talent is in place no matter what the future holds.

Overall, SWP can help companies overcome the talent challenges they face today—and those in the years to come. But key to success is understanding how the intersection of collaboration, analytics, and technology can bring together the people and the data that enable effective workforce planning.

About Carl Rhodes

Carl Rhodes is chief executive officer of the Human Capital Institute (HCI). Prior to joining the organization in 2009 as its chief operating officer, Rhodes was co-founder and general manager of Kairos Networks and a senior leader with the Corporate Executive Board, where he specialized in developing and scaling new products and services for networks of senior executives in general management, strategy, IT, and HR. His work has been cited in Harvard Business Review, The Economist, and The Washington Post, among other media outlets. Rhodes started his career as a professor of methodology and American politics at the University of Cincinnati. There, his work appeared in leading academic journals, in a volume compiled and edited by a Nobel Laureate, and was competitively funded by the National Science Foundation. He holds a PhD from Rice University and a BA from Colorado College.

WAKE UP, HR! YOUR TALENT SUPPLY CHAIN HAS A PROBLEM.

Lance J. Richards

I'm going out on a limb to argue that McKinsey might have erred a bit. (Very tough to argue against McKinsey research, right?)

Contrary to McKinsey's 1997 assertion, the "war for talent" isn't destined to continue through 2050.

It's over. Done.

Battle lost.

Talent won.

We, as employers and engagers of talent, lost. We, as HR professionals, are now having to adapt to this brave new world—whether we like it or not.

But this is actually no surprise. We've seen the demographics, we know the tightening in supply and demand. We know that the supply and demand equation for skilled talent is upside-down for the first time since...when? The Great Plague?

And we are faced with an inexorable problem.

We have people in the world. Lot's of people. Six billion people and growing.

But people, quite simply, do not always equal talent. Our core challenge today is converting all these people into skilled talent.

So first, how do we define talent? Well, it's clearly "something above the ordinary." There are a lot of definitions floating out there, but first I'll give you mine. Talent, I believe, exists along a Bloomesque hierarchy. At the bottom of that hierarchy is simple data, simple counting of items or reading of information.

A simple understanding of data, though, is insufficient to qualify as talent. I'm seeking people a couple of steps further along this continuum. I view talent as the ability to take data and turn it into information. Then, talent (as I define it) can use this information to process and understand further data, to synthesize multiple information streams, and to apply that synthesis to create projections and situation resolutions. Simply: Talent can convert data into actionable knowledge.

All of this requires an educational infrastructure. That is, we need a K–12 and college/university construct (let's call it K–16) that effectively generates talent that can fulfill the myriad needs—and the various needs of the myriad components—of an existing, effective economy. (These needs are even more prominent in developing economies.)

It requires an educational infrastructure that converts people into the talent that our markets are demanding today, as well as tomorrow. If we can do that, then the talent shortage problem goes away. If we can't? Oops—the shortage continues.

The challenge is that emerging markets, where population growth has the highest velocity, frequently lack the educational infrastructure to effectively convert people into talent. This is a problem when education is a core driver of talent, and therefore business.

In mature markets, where we do have strong educational infrastructure, our population growth is declining. We can convert people into talent, but we don't have enough people to convert.

Then, to make things worse, we have a very real disconnect between what employers depend on and expect from new entrants into the workplace and what our K-16 educational infrastructure is delivering. This is exacerbated by the lack of communication and coordination between the business community and the educational community.

In fact, I'd argue that, to a very real extent, we have lost sight of the purpose—the end use—of education.

But there is light on the horizon. *HR has a unique opportunity to lead the development of the world's talent through a focus on engagement, involvement, and leadership in the current educational infrastructure.*

WHAT HAPPENS IF HR *DOESN'T* TAKE THE LEAD

To be clear, I believe that the end consumer of education is not solely the young girl in middle school; it's not solely the young man entering college. They are, at least temporarily, the primary end consumers of the education process and industry. Their parents are proxies, of course, but more importantly, they may simply be billpayers. (The disengagement of parents in education is a subject for a very different essay.)

Once the K–16 educational infrastructure has completed its work, and a newly minted graduate—strike that, newly minted *talent*—enters the workforce, the end consumer of that education is now the employer.

In 2022, my daughter Brianna will head off to college. In 2026 or 2028, she will exit college and enter the workforce. Will she—along with all her peers—bring to our workplaces the things we need?

I'm not terribly concerned about core skills; I think that's probably under good control. Work ethic? Employability? Workplace behaviors? There, I'm concerned.

My issues revolve around the application of skillsets, competencies, and behaviors—the abilities required to take data and convert it into information, and then synthesize that information into projections, understandings, analysis, and more.

And what about global consistency? Does freshly minted talent bring consistent behaviors and employability to the workplace? I have firsthand knowledge of one single school system in Michigan. But what's going on in Haderslev, Hangzhou, Houston, and Harare? From a global perspective, are they "pulling their weight"?

Can this fresh talent do all that? Who taught them? Were they even taught?

So, fast forward.

It's now 2026. We welcome my daughter and her peers into our workplaces. Then, stunningly, we realize that they enter with very different expectations, behaviors, knowledge, reasoning skills, and more. Our incoming workforce doesn't have what we need! They lack key elements of employability; they lack important thinking capabilities; they lack micro-cultural understanding of the workplace. Their skill sets? Well, the '90s called and asked if we could drop off some of their "taught" skillsets at the Smithsonian.

What happened?

Like any good HR professionals, we launch into a flurry of activity. Knowledge management mechanisms are supremely advanced by now. We have embraced the difference between know-who and know-how. We understand the clear difference between "accessing" talent and "owning" talent. Further, we've leveraged all the available technology to reduce the impact of this disconnect and to mitigate the challenges to our business.

But what have we really done? Where do we go from here? There's still that disconnect. So we start the gap analysis, and the root cause analysis.

Of course, there are things we *could* have been doing back in 2015 that would have made this far easier—things that may even have prevented us from getting to a place where the talent we hire lack the skills and capabilities our organizations need to succeed in the marketpace of 2026 and beyond.

ENGAGING WITH STUDENTS AND EDUCATORS—EARLY AND OFTEN

We, as HR professionals, must immerse ourselves in the educational infrastructure—

at both the K–12 and college/university levels.

Here's what we should be doing.

K–12
What is your engagement with the K–12 schooling system? In Germany, Siemens has been investing in science and engineering kits and distributing them in grade schools to encourage early identification of engineering and mathematical potential and interest. Initiatives like this aren't cheap, but they're certainy cheaper (in the long term) than doing nothing.

If a school in your general area is having a "career day" (yes, they still do that!), you should be ready to send over not just one professional from your company but several. Identify people in finance, IT, operations, HR, and marketing. And make sure they're ready not only to give realistic job previews but to talk about the skills and behaviors needed to succeed in work.

They will need to be able to discuss how work is done, what an office is, how we leverage technology in the workplace, etc. And they must be able to articulate this to students (remember, they process differently) and, frankly, to their teachers as well.

Every time you talk about a work situation and a high-school teacher says, "I didn't know that!" then you've delivered on your goal.

Does your K–12 system have a business group, like an FBLA?

You should be all over them.

Here's why: Our government (and whether or not this is right is a very different discussion) has imposed a Common Core curriculum. School administrators and teachers have a very thin layer of discretion as to what to teach, and early "test runs" in various states have shown markedly lower scores than under "No Child Left Behind." Although the goal is to unwind "teach to the test," I'm still not sure we're on the right track toward "college and career ready."

What is not included in that remit is anything resembling "How do you interact with people in the workplace?" or "How do you develop and deliver thinking skills?" K–12 is obligated by law to deliver passing grades against a nationally standardized curriculum.

They are *not* focused on how these students are going to work out in the workplace.

ACTION ITEMS FOR HR:

- Find the three or four local middle schools and high schools in the area around your business.
- Invite yourself over and chat with guidance counselors.
- When they have a career day, offer to bring managers from your company from several disciplines.
- Offer up classroom discussions during the year in different areas. Use these opportunites to help students and teachers understand what the workplace is seeking.
- Explain the difference between skills and behaviors.
- Explain why competency matters—and what it is!
- Talk about social media and how they need to approach it now (in school) and when they get to your place. Explain its importance to their future. Talk about background checks!
- Talk about how technology is (and isn't) used in the workplace.

Are you telling them that, in the future, you'll need them more than they need you? Yep, pretty much. But you're also helping them understand that you only need them under X, Y, and Z circumstances. If they are talent, you need them.

Colleges and Universities

What is your engagement with colleges and universities? Are you popping in once a year for a quick presentation and a few interviews with MBAs with 4.0s? Or are you contributing? What are you doing during the school year? How many times a year does someone from your company visit a college career planning office to give presentations? How are you working with professors in your industry space to deliver guest lectures? (Hint: A guest lecture from a corporate executive means it's one less class the professor has to teach!)

When you deliver these talks, what do you talk about? Are you explaining the key competencies and behaviors that your company (and everyone else) needs? Or are you saying something else?

ACTION ITEMS FOR HR:
- Become involved.
- How many professors at your nearby colleges are you having regular discussions with?
- What are you talking with them about? Are you discussing the content of their curriculum? Are you discussing the "soft skills" your business needs from college graduates?
- Are you helping them understand the skills, behaviors, and competencies that your business (whatever that might be) needs?
- Are you discussing social media?
- Are you offering to guest lecture, so that you can directly tell students what sorts of behaviors and skills might be needed in the workplace—whether it's your workplace or not?

A FINAL WORD ON ENGAGEMENT
So, is this just a rant about education? Not at all.

I'm flagging this as an area that HR needs to focus on in order to impact a very real future. As an organization inside of a business that is ostensibly tasked with the attraction, development, and retention of talent, we've got to start looking much further back, much earlier, in the talent supply chain if we want to really make an impact.

I am advocating that HR become more engaged in shaping and managing the front end of the development of talent. I believe that to do so, we must become directly involved in our K–16 education system.

(And yes, I think the K–16 education system needs to become more involved in business. But that's a different paper for a different book!)

About Lance J. Richards

Lance J. Richards is a thought leader and workforce futurist, with a long career in human resources. He has more than 30 years of HR experience, with the last 20 years focused on global HR. Most recently he served as vice president of innovation for Kelly Services. He also headed the company's global HR consulting practice, based in Singapore. He joined Kelly in 2003 as head of international HR, accountable for HR across 26 countries and for more than 4,000 employees. Richards is also a visiting professor at the Sasin Graduate School in Bangkok, where he developed and teaches their MBA coursework in global human capital management. He previously held senior HR roles at Bell Canada, Verizon, and British Telecom, and has lived and worked in China, Singapore, and Thailand. A globally sought-after speaker, Richards has presented at dozens of conferences and seminars around the world. He currently serves as an Advisor to HR Unconferences and HR Tech Tank. Richards holds four globally recognized certifications in HR: the GPHR, SPHR, HRMP, and SHRM-SCP. He is co-author of "The Leadership Deficit" and "Don't Manage Me, Understand Me," as well as the 2013 Amazon release, "Gen Now."

DRIVING TIME TO VALUE IN THE HUMAN AGE

Mara Swan

Time to value—that's the one thing that human resources executives need to focus on to be successful in the "Human Age." Why is time to value so crucial to success? The Human Age has been brought on by a collision of macroeconomic forces—economic, demographic, technological, and social—that have created an environment of unpredictable demand and increased transparency. Many companies now face economic uncertainty and value/margin compression and no longer have the benefit of sustainable competitive advantage and the stability that this brought.

Companies need agility and flexibility in order to create new markets through innovation and to seize transient competitive advantage to drive time to value. None of this will be achieved without accessing, mobilizing, and engaging the right talent. Human resource executives will need to ensure that their companies can make the shift away from a stable business model environment where they have one workforce strategy characterized by one work model, one set of people practices, and one major talent source. They need to move their companies into the Human Age, where their companies will be operating with different business models supported by a workforce strategy with several work models, people practices, and talent sources (see **Figure 1**).

FIGURE 1. BUSINESS STRATEGY REQUIRES AGILITY

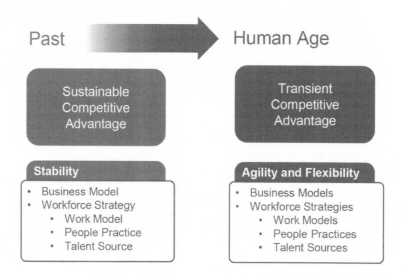

In the developed world, we have spent the last several decades creating more and more sophistication in HR. This sophistication was necessary to professionalize the management of people as we experienced accelerated growth in our industrial economy and as work moved from an owner model to a corporation model. But our deeply ingrained systems and structures have now become a liability—because in order to compete in an uncertain environment, businesses require speed. This is one of the major reasons we have heard so much recent discussion on whether HR delivers value, and why so many CEOs are now talking about the need for simplicity.

CEOs will see their HR teams as an asset if we adjust to this new environment— but they will see us as a liability if we stay steeped in what we have delivered in the past. ManpowerGroup CEO Jonas Prising summarized it well: "I need an HR team who can drive value for the company by focusing on the outcomes that drive value for our business—speed, quality, and service. I need simple people systems and processes that deliver the outcomes our clients expect and that create the environment where high-performing people want to work and contribute. I don't need more perfected processes."

TALENT AS THE KEY DIFFERENTIATOR IN THE HUMAN AGE

The CHRO is the person best suited to set the direction and engage the organization in achieving this outcome. Because in-demand talent has more access to the labor market and is less dependent on the corporation as an intermediary, one of the first things we need to do is rethink the employee model in the Human Age. In-demand talent must be viewed as a total value asset. What are they bringing to the company, and what is the company bringing to them?

In the past, we employed a net present value model for talent. Under this model, we would hire raw talent—high-school graduates, trade-school graduates, and university graduates—and invest in them over time so that they could contribute more to the enterprise. When they finished contributing or could no longer contribute what the company needed, we would pension or outsource them. This "job for life" model engendered long service and loyalty because employees were dependent on the corporation for their livelihoods, their careers, and their training and skills.

As growth slowed, companies started to move the employee relationship into a cost model. Over the past two decades we have seen a series of reductions in staff, benefits, promotions, and security as companies came to view employees as a cost. This "job for now" model has resulted in reduced loyalty to match the reduction in job security and has shifted the employee/employer relationship away from dependence to "I will get what I can while I can."

This model will not work for in-demand talent who have more choice and more freedom to access the market directly. Companies must give in-demand talent a reason to bring their skills to bear for the business—in other words, the model must shift to a "career for me" (see **Figure 2**). These employees will bring with them their reputations, social profiles, intellectual property, and ability to collaborate to drive innovation and productivity. They will therefore have more power in the employee/employer relationship and expect more from the company. At the very least, you will need to give them a compelling reason why they should bring their talents to your company. Employees care less about belonging to the employer's brand and being tied to what the company will give them and more about how a particular job will enhance their own careers.

This environment demands a whole new level of thinking from HR executives who were brought up on "one size must fit all." It also creates new and different cultural and social complications for corporations. Differentiating talent with in-demand skills (who will likely need highly customized approaches to attraction and retention) from talent with ubiquitous skills (who will most likely still be managed in the cost model) will require political and innovative finesse that was previously not demanded from HR executives. This bifurcation of the workforce into those with in-demand talents and those in high supply will require new ways of thinking about work models, people practices, and talent sources. It will also create new corporate social responsibility issues that will develop around how we can create opportunity for those with high-supply skills, and how to properly allocate our finite resources.

FIGURE 2: EMPLOYEE/EMPLOYER DYNAMICS ARE SHIFTING

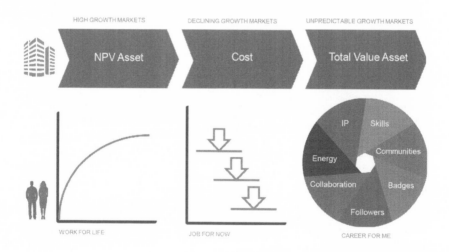

A NEW MINDSET FOR HR

In this new competitive environment, companies need to be more agile and flexible. We need to innovate more quickly in order to capture transient competitive advantage and we need to woo in-demand talent. This means that HR needs to shift from being internally focused and program-driven to focusing on time to value, which requires us to be more outside-in and data-driven. We must understand where value is created and what experiences customers are willing to pay for (see **Figure 3**).

Customers want a great service experience. But what will drive that? We need to move away from the business partner model where we create processes driven by internal client needs and ensuring that our *internal* clients are happy. We must move to identifying our external customer needs, focusing on how we can drive the shortest time to value by designing the simplified processes that drive these outcomes. Unfortunately, many HR teams have not yet successfully moved away from administratively driven mindsets and processes, so they have a long way to go before their function is no longer seen as a liability, let alone one that can be experience-driven.

FIGURE 3: SHIFTING THE HR MODEL TO DRIVE VALUE

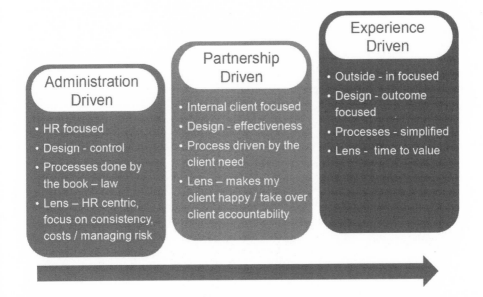

An experience-driven HR function will require a new mindset—and this must be addressed before any model change is undertaken. I believe there are five major shifts that must occur for a model change to be successful. These shifts can be seen in **Figure 4**.

FIGURE 4: MAJOR MINDSET SHIFTS

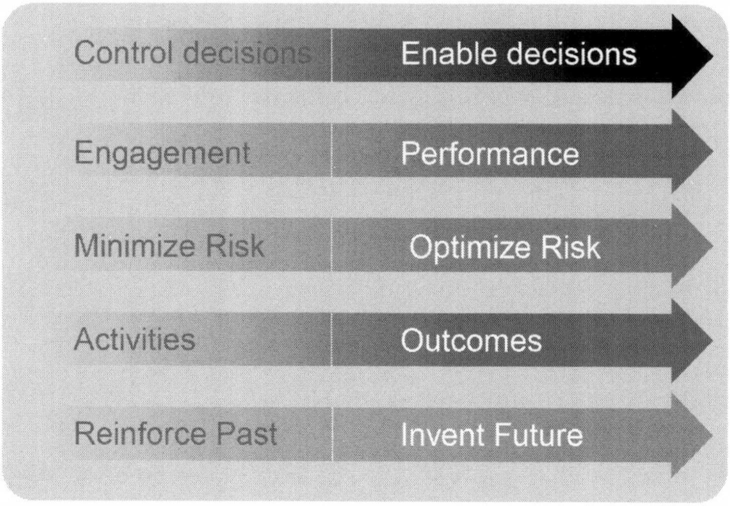

Control decisions	Enable decisions
Engagement	Performance
Minimize Risk	Optimize Risk
Activities	Outcomes
Reinforce Past	Invent Future

These shifts will help move HR to a more value-driven function and to rise to the challenge the Human Age presents. In addition, HR will need to take on some new roles that enable us to drive more time to value:

- **HR as supply and demand experts** – HR as the de facto expert and advisor to drive the alignment between the business strategy and talent strategy
- **HR as marketers** – HR utilizing consumer marketing principles and expertise to deepen the understanding of talent needs and wants and connecting them to customized offerings that motivate and inspire talent to "buy again"
- **HR as designers** – HR needs to redesign work models, reimagine people practices, and optimize talent sources

Because talent plays a predominant role in the success of businesses, the Human Age creates an opportunity for HR to play a larger role in our companies. The intermediary value of business has declined as transparency has increased. This has resulted in less stability in business models, so those companies with talent that can be agile and flexible will be the ones to innovate and capture transient competitive advantage in the marketplace. Those who do not will see their futures dwindle.

CHROs always seem to be looking for ways to make the business world take our function more seriously or ways that our roles can have a greater impact. Now is the time to stop looking and seize the opportunity that the Human Age presents. Talent matters. Let's make it matter by leading our organizations during this era of unprecedented change. We will lead our companies forward by changing the employee/employer model, by creating an HR model that is focused on outcomes that drive time to value for our customers, and by changing our mindsets to adjust to our new reality. Most of all, we will change our contribution by changing ourselves.

About Mara Swan

Mara Swan was appointed ManpowerGroup's executive vice president of global strategy and talent in 2009. In 2014, she assumed global brand leadership for the "Right Management" business. Swan joined the company as senior vice president of global human resources in 2005 and has had a significant impact on talent development and shaping the business strategy. A recognized expert in human resources, Swan is regularly featured as a speaker at high-profile events, including the annual meeting of the World Economic Forum in Davos, where she has provided council on women in leadership. In addition, she co-chairs the World Economic Forum Global Agenda Council on Gender Parity. In recognition of her success, she was named "HR Executive of the Year" in 2012 by Human Resource Executive magazine. Swan was also named one of Diversity Journal's "Women Worth Watching" in 2010 and a "Women of Influence" by the Milwaukee Business Journal in 2008. A veteran of the human resources profession, Swan joined ManpowerGroup from the Molson Coors Brewing Company, where she served as chief people officer for its global operations. Swan was elected to the National Academy of Human Resources (NAHR) National Class of 2012 and is on the executive committees of the Personnel Roundtable and the HR Policy Association. She holds a bachelor's degree in business administration from the University of Buffalo and a master's degree in industrial relations from the University of Minnesota.

4 TALENT OPTIMIZATION

TALENT OPTIMIZATION

Introduction

This section of the book contains an eclectic collection of refreshing thoughts, challenges, and ideas from notable academics, practitioners, and thought leaders related to optimizing talent in organizations. Human resources—people, and the talent they bring—are increasingly a higher percentage of total costs and a bigger predictor of success for most organizations. This certainly is true in an expanding service economy in which most of the intellectual capital comes and goes with the people who pervade the organization. Even manufacturing organizations are requiring more specialized and expensive employees to run the technology of the factories of tomorrow.

So the question one needs to ask is: "Are we leveraging the investment in talent—the collective knowledge, skills, experiences, and behaviors of our people—in the most effective way possible?" The authors in this section come at this from a variety of avenues, with a common theme of the role of HR in helping the organization optimize this critical resource.

One recurrent theme throughout the entire anthology is the need for HR leaders to understand the business in which they are working, and this logic clearly applies to optimizing talent. As Andy Brantley states, "I made it my business to know the business in which HR was functioning." He goes on to challenge HR leaders with a key question: "Are you and your HR colleagues viewed as critical to the development and execution of your organization's mission and key work?"

David Shadovitz, editor and co-publisher of Human Resource Executive magazine, discusses the importance of and challenges related to employee engagement. In a piece citing HR Executive's "What Keeps HR Leaders Up at Night" survey, he reports that "ensuring workers are engaged and productive consistently occupies the top spot." In fact, in the magazine's 2014 survey, 36 percent of 400 HR executives identify engagement as their greatest challenge. This is a far cry from a decade ago, when many HR leaders were either trying to get their arms around engagement or struggling to sell its importance to the C-suite.

Gallup, Metrus Group, Aon-Hewitt, and others have argued that there are far too many disengaged or partially engaged workers, with huge economic consequences to organizations.[1] Shadowitz offers some practical approaches to address the gap, beginning with better efforts to tailor organizational programs to a segmented workforce. One-size-fits-all approaches are becoming relics in organizations that want to succeed. Another key step is not only conducting regular workforce surveys but ensuring the findings can be analyzed by relevant segments of the workforce. With today's technology, it is relatively easy to compare pivotal to non-pivotal roles, high to low performers, or high to low potentials. Increasing transparency, more effective onboarding, and smarter career development round out additional strategies that organizations should be examining if they wish to grow engagement.

Sandy J. Wayne challenges the traditional idea of equal treatment of all employees, arguing that equal is not fair, and fair is what attracts, grows, and keeps talent. She notes that HR has long been locked into one-size-fits-all programs and policies, often to the detriment of overall performance. She also discusses *servant leadership*, a concept introduce by Robert Greenleaf in the 1970s that flips the traditional organizational hierarchy on its head. Leaders who embrace this approach[2] look to maximize the individual's contribution to the organization by providing the leader support needed for individuals and teams to thrive.

Linda A. Hill discusses the growing urgency for innovation in a world of constant change in a piece with an intriguing title—"Leave No Slice of Genius Behind."

Given this world of ubiquitous turbulence, she asks, "How will we develop the leadership talent we need to build and sustain innovative organizations?" She discusses a Harvard research effort that arrived at conclusions challenging traditional assumptions about leadership. Interestingly, her study challenges the widely accepted notion of the leader as visionary. She goes on to say, "Instead of creating a vision and inspiring others to execute that vision," excellent leaders from her study "considered it their role to create a community around shared purpose, values, and norms, and to build organizational capabilities required for innovation."

In other words, these leaders believed that everyone has a slice of genius, and that "seemingly ordinary people have the potential to make extraordinary contributions to innovation." Hill goes on to discuss how leaders can unleash people's talents and passions to create important solutions in the throes of a continuously changing environment.

Paula Caligiuri makes a case for stronger efforts in corporate social responsibility (CSR), arguing that the "benefits of employee volunteerism programs include increased employee engagement and retention, enhanced employer reputation and attractiveness, and developed leadership competencies." She goes on to discuss volunteerism and the impact that it has had in a number of organizations on talent attraction, retention, engagement, and talent development. She also provides a number of management practice recommendations in this space.

William (Bill) G. Ingham provides a rather unique perspective among a sea of thought leaders arguing for an "outside-in" approach, arguing that we need to find our own resilient center before we can truly support others. The notion is akin to airline messaging that asks us to put on our own oxygen mask before helping others. Ingham proposes that "success is based on two characteristics: long-term resilience and the ability to be centered, or 'in the zone,' more frequently." When those two traits are combined, he believes it leads individuals to a "resilient center"—a place where individuals are at their finest. He describes five dimensions that are important to finding this center, noting that it is a personal journey of discovery that subsequently will allow you to enable others. "We should find our resilient center emotionally, physically, spiritually, financially, and in relationships; establish where we are in relation to our center; then learn how to guide ourselves toward it."

Lastly, diversity is a major theme in this section, espoused and elaborated in essays by Andy Brantley, Tacy M. Byham and Debbie McGrath, and Carole Watkins. Women in particular are the focus of both Byham and McGrath's and Watkin's essays, providing a rich discussion of the reality and challenges regarding opportunities for women, ranging from cultural biases to programs to overcome those biases. Byham and McGrath challenge women to change their own thinking, which often limits them according to their research and experiences. They advocate for the idea of seeking out "micro-mentors" over different stages of one's career.

Watkins challenges men to become more involved in advancing and mentoring women, arguing that too many assumptions are made about women that may not be real. She argues for "sponsorship" rather than simply coaching or mentoring, saying "coaches talk 'to' you, mentors talk 'with' you, but a sponsor talks 'about' you." Sponsors advocate and help build recognition by others of your skills, abilities, and aspirations. A sponsor is also the one to close the door and give "real" feedback. Protégés expect sponsors to be their "truth tellers."

All in all, this section provides some great thinking on alternative ways to optimize talent in organizations and offers some challenges to traditional thinking. Many of the writers in this section provide practical organizational examples of what has worked—ranging from the proven to the exploratory—that readers can use as jumping-off points for discussion in their own organizations. Key themes include the importance of engagement, the leverage of women in the workplace, the value of knowing yourself, the impact of creating a community of shared purpose, and the criticality of looking at each individual uniquely rather than applying one-size-fits-all programs to broad classes of the workforce.

---

[1] Aon Hewitt, "Engagement 2.0," 2011; "State of the American Workplace: Employee Engagement Insights for US Business Leaders," Gallup Inc., 2013; W.A. Schiemann and J.H. Seibert, "Optimizing Human Capital: Moving Beyond Engagement," People & Strategy Journal, Vol 36(1), 2013.

[2] Note: In the XX section of this book, Stan Sewitch and Garry Ridge also mention this as part of their working philosophy at WD-40 Company.

HR AS ORGANIZATIONAL LEADER AND CHAMPION OF DIVERSITY AND INCLUSION

Andy Brantley

There are many opinions on the type of work that HR must view as essential in order to remain relevant. This topic is often difficult to contemplate as we rush about our day dealing with legislative or regulatory compliance challenges, recruiting and retaining talented individuals, or balancing benefits budgets. However, the bottom line is that our future relevance depends less on the support roles we perform and more on the leadership roles that are integral to organizational success.

There are differing opinions regarding exactly what this means for HR, but I believe that our future relevance is contingent upon our ability to be an organizational leader versus "just" an HR leader. Our future also depends on our ability and willingness to commit to diversity and inclusion as a core expectation of ourselves, HR, and the entire organization.

LEADER OF THE ORGANIZATION VERSUS LEADER OF HR

I am one of those rare HR professionals with undergraduate and graduate degrees focused in human resources. I left college with a great foundation in the core areas of human resources and ready to tackle the most challenging employment, compensation, or benefits challenges for the organization that hired me. Little did I know that my academic work had been significantly enhanced by my employment experiences, which included positions as a resident assistant, graduate resident, summer conference manager, and leader of a prominent campus student organization.

I began my career at the Chrysler Corporation. On my first day, I accompanied the negotiating team to a meeting with union representatives. The smoke-filled room (it was the late '80s) and the words used during negotiations (ones that I had never imagined hearing in the workplace) provided a glimpse into an unexpected side of human resources. As a labor relations representative, it was imperative for me to know the functions of all the core areas of HR, but I quickly realized that my success or failure was not based just on my knowledge and understanding of HR.

When I was 27 years old, the University of North Carolina at Asheville took a risk by selecting me as their director of human resources. I was young, but eager to learn and contribute. As part of a small organization with a five-person HR staff, I had the chance to be involved in every area of HR. I worked with my staff to ensure that we all had the core technical HR knowledge necessary to meet and exceed the expectations of the campus community. I also had almost daily interaction with the chancellor and vice chancellors and served on several campus-wide committees. (Higher education loves committees!) My knowledge and understanding of HR were important, but my interactions with campus leaders required me to think broadly and contribute much more than just my HR knowledge.

My appointment at UNC at Asheville was followed by an appointment as chief HR officer at Davidson College. The Davidson experience was transformative for me. I was given the opportunity to design new benefits plans and classification/compensation systems, redesign recruitment and selection processes, and incorporate meaningful performance planning and review into the culture for the first time. I also led the implementation of the college's first true HR information system. I will never forget meeting with the vice president for business affairs on my first day and being told that the college had purchased "this technology thing" that needed to run payroll in six months! The new human resource information system did run payroll six months later, but my success at Davidson was driven not just by new HR projects. It was primarily driven by the opportunity to be truly involved in the leadership and the life of the campus. The core HR competence that I developed for myself and instilled in my HR colleagues was the baseline that opened the door for broader, more meaningful leadership of the entire campus. My position as chief HR officer at the University of Georgia provided similar opportunities on a much larger scale.

The common theme through all of these experiences is that I made it my business to know the business in which HR was functioning. At Chrysler, I quickly realized that my work with the union representatives was less about the organization's benefits and compensation structure than it was about how employees were treated and valued by their supervisors. Making it my responsibility to know and understand more about the "Quality Is Job One" motto and supervisors' production challenges (which frequently created conflict with some employees) helped me better represent HR as part of the solution to these challenges.

In my experiences as the head of HR at UNC at Asheville, Davidson College, and the University of Georgia, I did not wait to be "anointed or appointed" to committees or task forces. I asked questions, expressed interest, and worked really hard when given the opportunity to participate and lead. The HR organizations that my colleagues and I created were not "HR in a box," but rather integral parts of the life and leadership of the campuses. Are you and your HR colleagues viewed as critical to the development and execution of your organization's mission and key work? How can the core work of HR be used to emphasize that those in HR are willing, responsible, well-informed, effective, creative leaders?

The understanding of the core areas of HR that I gained during undergraduate and graduate school created the baseline competence I needed to be relevant as an HR practitioner. The experiences that I gained though my positions in residence life and leading a major student organization helped prepare me to be an HR practitioner and a leader. I am far from perfect, so I will always continue my efforts to learn and grow so that I can improve as an HR professional and as a leader.

DIVERSITY AND INCLUSION: SO MUCH MORE THAN AFFIRMATIVE ACTION AND EQUAL EMPLOYMENT OPPORTUNITY

I grew up in a rural part of middle Georgia. Of the 110 students in my graduating class, approximately half were white and half were African-American. Most families lived below or slightly above the poverty level. Everyone was Protestant. No one was openly gay. We viewed ourselves as inclusive, but the racial divide was pretty clear. Our senior year of high school was disrupted when members of the Ku Klux Klan and civil rights advocates descended on our small town for rallies that required the Georgia State Patrol to line the middle of the streets to separate the two groups. Those incidents shook all of us, but the groups disappeared as quickly as they appeared, and life returned to "normal" for the small town.

Leaving for college provided opportunities for me to interact with and become lifelong friends with people from very different backgrounds. I didn't really understand at the time that I was becoming more aware of my biases, both intentional and unintentional, but I was—and this quest to be aware of my biases continues to this day. I also did not realize just how much this awareness would impact my future career.

Fast forward many years later: I have always viewed myself as open and inclusive (in spite of my intentional and unintentional biases), but I had never really related these qualities to my role and responsibilities as an HR professional. Sure, I helped lead the effort to create a position focused on diversity and inclusion at the University of Georgia, but I didn't see it as "part of HR." That changed in 2010, during a meeting of the board of directors of the College and University Professional Association for Human Resources (CUPA-HR). A member of our board challenged us to consider our personal and professional commitment to diversity and inclusion. That interaction—and the work that I have been involved in since—has transformed my personal commitment to diversity and inclusion and my view of HR's responsibility (not role) to lead this important work for our organizations.

Why is this HR's responsibility? Our workforce is changing and becoming increasingly diverse in many ways, including gender, sex, sexual orientation, language, age, ability status, national origin, religion, race/ethnicity, and heritage. Those who manage and develop the workforce need to be prepared to address the environmental factors that influence performance and impact employees' overall well-being. Yet many who are positioned to influence performance are stuck in a mid-twentieth-century mindset that says some talent can be dismissed while other talent should be valued. This mindset serves no one well, nor does it help build the interpersonal and performance competencies that *all* individual employees need or the capacities for agility that organizations need to thrive in an increasingly complex world.

This work is familiar to some HR professionals, but not all. We have always provided employees with talent development opportunities in compliance with affirmation action and equal employment opportunities. However, a clear and unabashed focus on diversity and inclusion to advance organizational excellence and success may be unfamiliar to some. HR must help instill a new mindset—one that goes beyond merely complying with non-exclusionary laws, but truly commits to core values and believes that, with guidance, every employee has the capacity to perform at high levels.

Why now? Because the work is needed now, and because we can. Because *every* employee interacts with HR, we are in a position to take a leadership role. The expertise and assistance that HR professionals are best suited to provide differs throughout our organizations, so we must equip ourselves *now* to provide the best guidance and resources possible to all employees to make certain that our organizations achieve their excellence goals and remain vital well into the future.

I encourage you to develop your own personal commitment to diversity and inclusion, as well as an organizational commitment in the form of a plan that ensures an open, inclusive environment that values every individual, and works with and through these colleagues to achieve organizational excellence and success.

As HR professionals we face many challenges, but our biggest challenge is to change our mindset from HR leader to organizational leader. What are we doing every single day to emphasize our leadership of the entire organization? We must also be fully committed on a personal and professional level to creating and supporting a diverse, inclusive workplace. What are we, as HR professionals and organizational leaders, doing every single day to emphasize our commitment to creating and sustaining a workplace that values and encourages diversity and inclusion?

I recommend the following specific actions:

- Demonstrate expertise in the core areas of HR. (This is the baseline expectation instead of the only expectation.)
- Find meaningful ways to engage with other organizational leaders. Don't wait to be anointed or appointed—create opportunities to lead.
- Find meaningful ways to engage with employees at all levels in the organization. Be a real person instead of "just" HR.
- Learn the business of the organization so that you can truly be an organizational leader instead of an organizational supporter. Ask questions and understand all facets of the business.
- Understand your intentional and unintentional biases. Ongoing learning and development of HR professionals must include a commitment to understand our own personal biases and how these impact our ability to lead and support our colleagues.
- Acknowledge that most supervisors have had little to no guidance regarding the importance of creating a diverse and inclusive environment for employees. Our organizational leaders need guidance and support from HR as the workforce becomes more and more diverse.

About Andy Brantley

Andy Brantley has served as president and chief executive officer of the College and University Professional Association for Human Resources (CUPA-HR) since July 2005. During his tenure, CUPA-HR has grown from 1,500 to 2,000 member institutions and from 6,600 institutional representatives to more than 18,000, and the organization's annual revenue has doubled. Prior to his appointment as CUPA-HR's president and CEO, Brantley served the association for a number of years as a volunteer leader at both the regional and national levels. He is also a recipient of the association's highest honor, the Donald E. Dickason Award, which recognizes distinguished and continuing service to CUPA-HR and excellence in the field of higher education human resources. Previously, Brantley worked for 17 years in higher education, serving as associate vice president and chief human resources officer at the University of Georgia, director of human resources at Davidson

College, and director of human resources at the University of North Carolina at Asheville. A frequent keynote and workshop presenter at meetings across the country, he has written extensively on the challenges faced by higher education human resources professionals and the higher education workforce, and serves on a number of higher education and workforce management-related boards. He completed his MBA in 1986 and began his professional career as a labor relations representative for the Chrysler Corporation.

THE HR AND CSR PARTNERSHIP: TALENT-RELATED BENEFITS FOR EMPLOYEE VOLUNTEERISM

Paula Caligiuri

Human resources has successfully partnered with various functional areas for many years. Finance and HR partner to manage costs and optimize the value of compensation packages and other employee rewards. Operations and HR partner on devising solutions for work design, scheduling, and staffing. Marketing and HR partner to convert the firm's brand into organizational culture and an employer brand.

In the recent past we have seen HR partnered with another functional area—corporate social responsibility (CSR)—given that CSR initiatives, specifically employee volunteerism programs, have talent-related benefits. The Committee Encouraging Corporate Philanthropy (CECP) identified the following categories of employee volunteerism programs:

- "Dollars for Doers" (a per-hour employee incentive for every hour of volunteerism up to a certain cap)
- Paid release time for volunteerism
- Company-wide day of service

- Employee recognition awards for extraordinary volunteerism
- Flexible scheduling for volunteerism activities
- Family volunteerism opportunities
- Team grants for volunteer projects
- Programs to encourage retiree volunteerism
- Pro bono advisor programs (or international corporate-sponsored volunteerism programs)

The benefits of employee volunteerism programs include increased employee engagement and retention, enhanced employer reputation and attractiveness, and developed leadership competencies. When employee volunteerism programs are designed in such a way to optimize both CSR and HR goals simultaneously, these talent-based benefits also positively affect the company's image for social responsibility, increase its social license to operate, and make a positive difference in communities being served. This HR-CSR partnership is a "win-win-win" for the firm, employers, and the beneficiaries of employee service.

INTERNATIONAL CORPORATE-SPONSORED VOLUNTEERISM PROGRAMS

In the recent past we have seen a particularly effective HR-CSR partnership emerging around international corporate-sponsored volunteer (ICV) or global pro bono advisor programs. ICV programs provide opportunities for a firm's skilled employees to go "on loan" as pro bono advisors to nongovernmental organizations (NGO) in developing countries. The participating employees provide short-term, project-based technical expertise for projects identified by the NGO, the deliverables of which are aimed at NGO capacity-building.

In the past 10 years, we have seen a fourfold increase in ICV programs such as the Dow Sustainability Corps, IBM's Corporate Service Corps, GlaxoSmithKline's PULSE Volunteerism Partnership, and Pepsico's PepsiCorps. The accelerated increase in the initiation of these programs began during the recessionary years. While cash donations declined between 2005 and 2010, there was a rapid increase in the number of firms adopting corporate-sponsored volunteerism programs during that same period. In today's post-recessionary period, the trend toward employee volunteerism programs has continued on a rapid upward trajectory, growing faster than any other category of corporate philanthropy.

Firms structure ICV programs in two ways:

1. *ICV programs for high-potentials* – These ICV programs are designed for a targeted group of high-potential employees or are structured within a global leadership development rotational program. When designed for rotational programs, the in-country service is scheduled between rotations when employees' absence is less disruptive for business.
2. *Open-application ICV programs* – These ICV programs are open to the employee population, with a selection process in place to match applicant skills with NGO requests.

Whether targeted or open-application, ICV programs vary in terms of team size, duration, location, and virtual interactions:

- *Team size* – Some ICV programs' projects are team-based, with associates from different countries and functions. The added developmental benefit is the multicultural team operating in a host country familiar to none of the team members. In other cases, the projects are individual assignments, situations in which the development of cultural agility can occur quickly without the cultural buffer of the firm's associates.
- *Duration* – ICV programs also vary in duration, from weeks to months spent in the host country. Some programs serve continuously in-country for a period of time, some serve intermittently in-country (with multiple short-term visits), and some are staggered with team members going in-country a few members at a time.
- *Location* – Locations can be selected to gain awareness of a specific country or to foster positive relationships in a given community.
- *Virtual Interactions* – All ICV programs rely on some virtual meetings with the NGO staff and/or fellow team members before departing to the host country to make the best use of time in-country. Some programs have virtual consultation after the in-country portion is completed.

An example of an ICV program is the Dow Sustainability Corps, a skills-based pro bono advisor program that engages employees to help solve pressing problems around the areas of clean water, agriculture, housing, education, health, sanitation, and energy. According to the website Dow Sustainability Corps website (http://www.dow.com/company/citizenship/corps.htm):

"Dow Sustainability Corps (DSC) is part of Dow's approach to meet the world's most basic needs by matching interested and capable employee(s) with nongovernmental organizations (NGOs), social entrepreneurs, and local government agencies that need support for sustainable development projects, especially in emerging geographies and areas of growth for Dow."

TALENT-RELATED BENEFITS OF ICV PROGRAMS

One reason for the accelerating popularity of ICV programs such as the Dow Sustainability Corps is the additional benefits above and beyond philanthropy and CSR—especially the talent-related benefits. The 2014 CECP report noted that employee volunteerism programs are "crucial to helping leading companies engage staff, boost morale, and improve overall job satisfaction."

The talent-related benefits of corporate volunteerism—employee attraction, employee engagement and retention, and talent development—collectively make a compelling argument for ICV programs specifically and the CSR-HR partnership generally.

- *Employee attraction* – A PricewaterhouseCoopers (PwC) study of Millennials at work found that the majority of new college graduates (almost 90 percent) actively seek employers that share their values for social responsibility. Volunteerism programs "get the word out" about an organization's positive reputation for social responsibility. Reports have found a greater number of good news stories are generated about employee volunteers compared to other forms of philanthropy. This reputation-enhancing media coverage, in turn, increases employer attractiveness.

- *Employee engagement and retention* – Research that Ahsiya Mencin, Kaifeng Jiang, and I conducted found that employee engagement can be increased through corporate volunteerism programs, especially when the experiential opportunities are structured well.[1] When compared to employees who do not (or rarely) volunteer, the Deloitte Volunteer Impact Survey found that employees who frequently volunteer through company-sponsored volunteerism opportunities are almost 30 percent more likely to rate their employers' corporate culture positively, 19 percent more likely to say they are proud to work for their employer, and about 20 percent more likely to express a higher level of loyalty toward their employers. Retention rates are also higher among employees who participate in volunteer activities compared to employees who do not. IBM, for example, reports that 80 percent of its Corporate Service Corps participants agreed that the international volunteerism experience significantly increased their likelihood staying at IBM for the duration of their careers.

- **Talent development** – A survey of global CEOs found that a dearth of global business leaders is one of the greatest risks to a firm's future growth—and developing global business leaders is critical to their competitiveness. Our research found that well-designed employee international volunteerism programs build participants' global leadership competencies and their understanding of key issues in key emerging markets. In another recent research study, I found a change over time in critical competencies necessary for cultural agility, including tolerance of ambiguity, perspective-taking, and humility.

CRAFTING ICV PROGRAMS TO MAXIMIZE TALENT-RELATED BENEFITS

It is important for HR and CSR to work together to craft ICV programs that will be developmental and increase engagement while fulfilling the CSR mission. Professors Nicola Pless, Thomas Maak, and Guenter Stahl, in an evaluation of PwC's "Project Ulysses" service-learning program, found that developmental volunteer assignments provided participants with "exposure to adverse situations, forcing participants out of their comfort zones, confronting them with cultural and ethical paradoxes, and motivating them to change their perspectives on life and business." Stretching an ICV participant's skills in this novel context was considered highly developmental.

The employees participating in ICV programs should be assigned to *meaningful* projects. The volunteerism assignments should enable them to provide significant value to the NGO and use their relevant professional expertise, such as supply chain, operations, marketing, finance, strategy, and HR. As pro bono advisors, ICV participants will want to know that they are making a positive difference in the lives of those they are serving by increasing the NGO's capacity. Routine or back-office administrative work—without any attachment to the NGO being served—is not sufficient for volunteers to experience the affect-enhancing "buzz" that comes from volunteering. It is this affecting-enhancing experience that is so important to increasing employee engagement and, in turn, retention.

From the perspective of enhancing talent development specifically, we want volunteerism experiences to be significant enough that ICV participants experience the limits of their functional knowledge in the local context. Regardless of how skilled participants are in finance, supply chain, etc., success should require local knowledge they do not possess. Projects requiring symbiotic partnership with NGO leaders foster ICV participants' humility, encouraging openness and a willingness to learn from the host national and NGO environment. Fostering humility is one of the many sub-benefits of ICV programs.

Finally, ICV participants should be placed in assignments where NGO managers and staff are supportive of the participants in their volunteer activities and want to be mutual partners in this symbiotic relationship. Volunteers should feel comfortable interacting openly and demonstrating acceptance and respect for NGO leaders and staff—and feeling the same in return.

In an article Christian Thoroughgood and I have written on "Developing Responsible Global Leaders Through Corporate-Sponsored International Volunteerism Programs,"[2] we encourage the following five talent management practices to maximize the talent-related benefits of ICVs.

1. *Select ICV program participants carefully.* Employee participants should be selected for their open-mindedness, interpersonal orientation, and emotional strength. Being motivated to help others is another important selection criterion.
2. *Prepare ICV participants for success.* Participants should be trained on cross-cultural nuances of the host country and technical skills needed for success (e.g., consulting skills). Using platforms such as the Cultural Agility E-Learning Program, it is also important to build participants' self-awareness of their cross-cultural competencies and give advice on their development.
3. *Craft the international volunteer assignment for development.* As noted in the previous section, ICV projects should enable participants to engage with their surroundings, practice newly learned behaviors, receive feedback on cultural effectiveness, and feel emotionally safe to try new approaches.
4. *Foster communication during the international volunteer assignment.* Volunteers should share their task-specific experiences, appreciation for the opportunity, and lessons learned with their colleagues back home.
5. *Reintegrate skills gained after the volunteerism experience.* The firm should recognize and leverage any knowledge volunteers acquire during their experience.

In conclusion, CSR-based initiatives—specifically ICV programs—have talent-related benefits with tangible "win-win-wins" for companies, employees, and communities in need. The research is compelling, with stakeholder results pointing to an accelerated future for ICV programs. Speaking on the fifth anniversary of the IBM Corporate Service Corps, Stan Litow, IBM's vice president of corporate citizenship and corporate affairs and president of IBM's foundation, offered a call to action for the Fortune 500. He said:

"Just imagine, if every Fortune 500 company sent only 100 of their top employees a year on a program similar to IBM's, well, instead of thousands, we could be impacting millions of communities and people around the globe. If we want to continue affecting real change, then this is certainly an important and effective way to do it."

I could not agree more—and look forward to working with the HR professionals who partner in answering this call.[3]

About Paula Caligiuri

Paula Caligiuri is a D'Amore-McKim School of Business Distinguished Professor of International Business and Strategy at Northeastern University, where she researches and teaches in the area of cultural agility and global leadership development. Caligiuri works extensively with leading organizations across a wide range of industries, including private sector, military, and nonprofit organizations. She is also the HR area editor for the Journal of International Business Studies and the director of Northeastern University's Cultural Agility Leadership Lab, a corporate-sponsored international volunteerism program in partnership with the National Peace Corps Association. A frequent expert guest on CNN and CNN International covering career and management-related topics, she is the author of several articles and books, including "Cultural Agility: Building a Pipeline of Successful Global Professionals" (2012). She holds a PhD in industrial and organizational psychology from Penn State University.

[1] Paula Caligiuri, Ahsiya Mencin, and Kaifeng Jiang, "Win-Win-Win: The Influence of Company-Sponsored Volunteerism Programs on Employees, NGOs, and Business Units," Personnel Psychology, 2013, pages 825–860.

[2] Paula Caligiuri and Christian Thoroughgood, "Developing Responsible Global Leaders through Corporate-Sponsored International Volunteerism Programs," Organizational Dynamics, in press.

[3] Northeastern University and the National Peace Corps Association run a joint program called the Cultural Agility Leadership Lab (CALL). The CALL program is a turnkey solution for companies initiating ICV programs.

LEAVE NO SLICE OF GENIUS BEHIND: SELECTING AND DEVELOPING TOMORROW'S LEADERS OF INNOVATION

Linda A. Hill

There's no question that tomorrow's organizations will need to innovate not just once, but time and again, if they are to address the challenges we face as a global community. In an age of increasingly scarce resources and economic uncertainty, innovations in the private and public sectors—whether incremental or breakthrough, singular or systemic—are critical to remaining competitive or tackling such intractable problems as poverty, global health, or fiscal crises. This elicits a question that concerns me as a business professor: How will we develop the leadership talent we need to build and sustain innovative organizations?

In 2003, I teamed up with three collaborators to conduct a decade-long study of innovative organizations around the globe, and in 2014 we published our findings.[1] Many before us had written about how innovation works—through a collaborative process of problem-solving, discovery-driven learning, and integrative decision-making—but there was a relative dearth of literature about the role that leaders play in enabling and facilitating this process.

We studied 16 master innovation leaders from around the world, including men and women in 12 industries and seven countries, in order to understand their mindset, behaviors, and personal qualities. Interestingly, the leaders in our study all rejected the widely accepted notion of the leader as visionary. Instead of creating a vision and inspiring others to execute that vision, our leaders considered it their role to create a community around shared purpose, values, and norms, and to build organizational capabilities required for innovation. Our leaders also embraced a fundamental belief that we saw reflected in their talent practices: Everybody has a slice of genius.

Innovation leaders deeply believe that seemingly ordinary people have the potential to make extraordinary contributions to innovation. The leader's job, they believe, is to unleash people's talents and passions, and to harness those slices of genius into a collective solution to a problem. An unsettling fact is that leaders who possess this mindset and the skills required are, frankly, difficult to find. Because we are only just beginning to understand how exceptional innovation leaders think and behave, many HR professionals do not know how to attract, select, and develop the kind of leadership talent their organizations need to innovate now and into the future. The time has come to challenge our conventional wisdom about great leadership.

In a 2010 IBM study based on conversations with 1,500 global chief executive officers, the CEOs identified "creativity," "integrity," and "global thinking" as the three most important leadership qualities their organizations would need over the next five years. Leaders, the report stated, must be comfortable with ambiguity and committed to ongoing experimentation.[2] As the study suggests, the ability to creatively solve problems has replaced having a vision and setting direction— qualities we typically associate with good leadership—as the most highly valued traits in the C-suite. Yet the executives I meet today frequently tell me their firms continue to be plagued by a lack of innovation. Because leadership is critical to creating an environment for innovation, two possible conclusions are that our current talent practices are either failing to identify individuals with the potential to lead innovation, or failing to adequately develop and prepare those individuals to lead innovation. The correct answer may be both.

IDENTIFYING "THE RIGHT STUFF"
Vision, decisiveness, smarts—these are all traits we have come to expect of leaders. But what if our narrow criteria for identifying leadership potential are leaving

important talent sources untapped? Our study comprised leaders of different ages, genders, cultures, and backgrounds, and yet, after spending hundreds of hours with them, we identified several personal qualities they all had in common. Leaders of innovation are:

- *Idealists, yet pragmatists.* They are attracted to incredibly complex, difficult problems and are willing to put their arms around very big challenges. They push the boundaries of what is possible, yet remain aware of the practical steps necessary to overcome challenges along the way. They are at once boldly ambitious and levelheaded.
- *Holistic thinkers, yet action-oriented.* They think about problems in all their complexity and nuance, but understand that solutions emerge from action through trial and error. They understand organizational context, but avoid becoming so caught up in the big picture that they cannot see the way forward.
- *Generous, yet demanding.* They are comfortable sharing power and letting others take the spotlight, despite being geniuses in their own right. They have a deep sense of ownership for a problem, but are willing to share credit for its solution. They are often reluctant to be singled out for an accomplishment. At the same time, they have high expectations and hold people accountable for results.
- *Human, yet highly resilient.* They are far from perfect and not afraid to let their vulnerability show. Like all of us, they make mistakes, but they see intelligent failures as opportunities for learning. They accept and acknowledge their anxieties and fears, and cope well with uncertainty. In this way, they exude calm where there is chaos or ambiguity. They are open to seeking help because they recognize the slices of genius in others.

Having seen our leaders in action, my collaborators and I were not surprised to find that they appeared to possess nontraditional—or even paradoxical—leadership traits. This is not to say they lacked vision and intelligence or that they lived constantly on the fence of decisions. To the contrary, each of our leaders was a visionary in his or her own right. Quite often, they did have the answers. When a situation was urgent, they exercised their decision-making authority. But because they understood what the hard work of innovation requires of people, they embraced those qualities most conducive to unlocking the best in others for the collective good of the organization.

Consider the traits most organizations seek when identifying candidates with leadership potential. "Idealistic," "generous," and "accepting of ambiguity and uncertainty" are unlikely to top the list. Yet these are the kinds of qualities we see in leaders who are skilled at creating innovative environments. Truly effective innovation leaders are sensitive enough to a situation's demands to display their more conventional leadership qualities selectively. However, this presents a challenge to HR professionals and managers, whose pool of high potentials may be limited by a leadership model based primarily on an ideal of take-charge, direction-setting behavior that is not well suited to innovation.

People with potential to lead innovation are often difficult to identify. In fact, they sometimes fade into the background—not because they are less capable, but because they are more concerned with creating solutions than claiming the spotlight. They see their role as being more of a stage-setter than a performer. Talented people in the ranks who have precisely "the right stuff" to build innovation capacity may risk becoming what we call "stylistic invisibles." Too often they fail to be spotted and, consequently, are passed over for leadership opportunities and positions of influence because of their more inclusive, collaborative style.

SELECTING TODAY'S HIGH POTENTIALS

If we hope to avoid overlooking key talent, it is time we rethink our criteria for selecting high potentials and embrace an alternative model of leadership. IBM's Steve Kloeblen, one of the leaders in our study, did just this—and found he unleashed a well of untapped innovation talent within the company.

Then the vice president of business development, Kloeblen was responsible for acquiring new businesses—and thereby bringing new talent into the firm. However, Kloeblen could not help feeling that people within IBM's ranks had innovative business ideas that were being overlooked. After attending a lecture about business opportunities at the "bottom of the pyramid" (BoP), Kloeblen decided to test his assumptions. He sent an email to several mentees, suggesting they get together and brainstorm how IBM technologies could address issues affecting the BoP. "I don't mean philanthropy," he wrote. "I'm talking about business development, our business." Almost immediately, several people had committed to work on the project in addition to their day jobs.

The group soon assigned itself a name, the World Development Initiative (WDI), and within six months grew to include more than 100 volunteers from across the company. Kloeblen let the group define the project's mission. He didn't inspire them with stirring speeches. He was pretty unassuming, actually, keeping a low profile at meetings and often qualifying his comments with "We could do this" or "We could do that." He led mostly from behind, not from the front, persistently nudging the team along and helping them gain access to key resources. Within three years, membership in the group had quadrupled.

WDI set the ambitious target to create $1 billion in revenue for IBM while helping to improve the lives of 1 billion people. Holding virtual weekly meetings, they formed ad hoc teams to explore business opportunities related to their personal interests. Some teams coalesced around issues such as health care or microfinance, and others around regions of interest including India and China, but all were aimed at the BoP. They researched opportunities and prepared business plans to present to senior management. Many, although not all, of their ideas gained financing, and WDI members then had the challenge of implementing their plans. Their innovative projects ranged from helping to create Spoken Web, a platform for illiterate clients in India to access employment and social services, to the Africa ThinkPlace Challenge, an open online forum designed to foster global collaboration and innovation to promote economic development in Africa.

Many projects became growth opportunities for the company in the developing economies they aimed to serve. Without diminishing the value of the innovative ideas the WDI helped develop, we suspect that its greatest "product" was a new generation of leaders of innovation now applying their talents across IBM. In sub-Saharan Africa, for instance, members of the WDI are playing important leadership roles in the growth of IBM's presence in more than 20 countries.

If Kloeblen had chosen a different route—hand-selected a team instead of sending out that email—would WDI have produced the same results? True, Kloeblen might have selected some of the same mentees who first stepped forward to volunteer. However, he might have overlooked other individuals—equally talented, maybe stylistically different—who were both willing and able to innovate with him. Instead, those who volunteered were all united by a common purpose: to improve the lives of 1 billion people at the bottom of the pyramid. Arguably, it was their passion, dedication, and persistence—as well as their talents—that ignited the imaginations of 400 others and allowed the community to flourish.

Of course, "stylistic invisibles" are not the only people who risk being passed over for leadership opportunities. We must also be cautious to avoid overlooking "demographic invisibles," groups of people frequently neglected due to preconceived notions about their race, ethnicity, nationality, class, age, or gender. They often remain invisible due to explicit limitations—such as lack of political rights or hierarchical cultural attitudes in some regions—or implicit biases that limit equal access to the networks and tools that could help them grow into leadership roles. Some of the leaders we studied sought out these populations (for example, women in Korea and the United Arab Emirates), provided them with opportunity and development, and watched their businesses grow as a result.

DEVELOPING TOMORROW'S INNOVATION LEADERS

If we truly want to build organizations that can innovate time and again, it is clearly not enough to rethink our criteria for selecting high potentials. We must also ask ourselves: What are the stretch assignments or the growth opportunities that will help people develop the mindset and skills required to lead innovation? Formal leadership development programs—or, at least, our current conception of them—may not be the way.

In Kloeblen's case, the voluntary makeup of the WDI, coupled with the ambiguous nature of the work, necessitated that team members learn to do bold thinking and self-manage. In actuality, many struggled initially; this was very different than working on a team in a consulting or financial services firm where there was an assigned leader and clearly defined objectives. To be effective, they had to learn how to build a sense of community around shared purpose, values, and rules of engagement with diverse teams of people who were scattered across the globe and over which they had no formal authority. They had to learn to be design-thinkers, acting their way as opposed to planning their way to new business models. (When you are looking for breakthroughs, by definition you don't have the answer or know what direction to go in.) They had to devise integrative solutions, because their passionate colleagues wouldn't compromise or be dominated.

Not surprisingly, those who succeeded were idealistic, generous, and accepting of uncertainty. They persisted when faced with challenges, investing significant time and energy despite knowing their projects might never be funded. "It wasn't my initial intention," Kloeblen said of WDI, "but I soon realized that I was also creating an excellent leadership development crucible." More than a dozen WDI members were later promoted to key executive leadership roles within IBM.

For HR professionals and hiring managers, there are many lessons to be gleaned from stories like Kloeblen's. The first is awareness that our current systems for identifying leadership potential are no longer adequate and that we must broaden our definition of good leadership. Secondly, relying on formal development mechanisms alone may be hindering organizations everywhere from building their innovation capacity. Are the high potentials in your organization encouraged to identify and take on self-managed entrepreneurial projects with groups of diverse people? Our leadership development efforts will need to be critically reimagined, and more inclusive, if we hope to develop a new generation of innovation leaders.

Until this sea change comes, the best way to develop innovation leaders may be to provide people with opportunities to self-nominate—and the space and support to pursue a particular passion—and collaborate with others with diverse points of view and talents in order to discover along the way, through trial and error, what it takes to lead an innovative effort.

About Linda A. Hill

Linda A. Hill, PhD, is the Wallace Brett Donham Professor of Business Administration at the Harvard Business School. She is faculty chair of the Leadership Initiative; has chaired numerous HBS executive education programs; and was course-head during the development of the new Leadership and Organizational Behavior MBA required course. Her books include "Being the Boss: The 3 Imperatives of Becoming a Great Leader"; "Breakthrough Leadership," named one of the "Five Business Books to Read for Your Career in 2011" by The Wall Street Journal; "Becoming a Manager: How New Managers Master the Challenges of Leadership";

and "Collective Genius: The Art and Practice of Leading Innovation," named by Business Insider as one of "The 20 Best Business Books" in summer 2014. She is author of numerous course modules and award-winning multimedia management development programs; author or co-author of numerous HBR articles; and has also been named by Thinkers50 as one of the top 10 management thinkers in the world. Hill has consulted on leadership development, talent management, and other issues for numerous organizations—including General Electric, Reed Elsevier, Pfizer, IBM, Mitsubishi, Morgan Stanley, the National Bank of Kuwait, and The Economist—and sits on numerous boards. She holds a PhD in behavioral sciences from the University of Chicago, an MA in educational psychology from the University of Chicago, and a BA, summa cum laude, in psychology from Bryn Mawr College.

---

[1] Linda A. Hill, Greg Brandeau, Emily Truelove, and Kent Lineback, "Collective Genius: The Art and Practice of Leading Innovation" (Boston, MA: Harvard Business School Publishing, 2014).

[2] IBM, "Global Chief Executive Officer Study: Capitalizing on Complexity," IBM Global Business Services, 2010, page 25.

FINDING OUR RESILIENT CENTER

William (Bill) G. Ingham

It is the nature of good business and driven leaders to look for ways to reach goals and be more effective. Traditionally, the HR community has done this in a number of ways. We look toward a "north star" or a vision statement. We study competitors and business trends around the world. We search best practices for topics such as talent development and attend programs that teach us to be analytical and innovative.

While looking elsewhere, we have failed to take care of ourselves first—a fundamental and easily overlooked step. Because when we are healthy, with the self-awareness to know when we are at our best, we bring new courage and authenticity to our clients to help them be at their best, too.

OUR "RESILIENT CENTER"

Erwin McManus, the principal visionary and primary communicator of Mosaic in Los Angeles, has said that the most successful people are not always the most talented, smart, hardworking, well educated, unique, creative, or best networked. However, they all share one thing in common—they are resilient. I propose success in any field is based on two characteristics: (1) long-term resilience and (2) the ability to be centered, or "in the zone," more frequently.

Combining these two traits creates a "resilient center"—a place where we are at our finest without conscious effort. This is an aspirational state that comes and goes; it is not a constant, nor an annual goal that is replaced every year with a new one. Just as a pendulum swings, we are challenged to stay at our resilient center as positive and negative things occur in our personal and professional lives.

The aim is to be aware enough to understand when we are at our resilient center and to realize when we're not there and why. With that understanding, we can bring our best selves to leaders, employees, friends, and family.

When we reach this center, we also develop a natural authenticity rather than one created through a contrived declaration. Just as a work of art does not try to be authentic, authenticity is not something we should strive for. Instead, it is at its best when it comes naturally through our unique experiences and self-awareness: our resilient center.

THE RESILIENT CENTER'S FIVE DIMENSIONS

This resilience center spans five aspects of our lives: our emotions, our physical selves, our spirits, our finances, and our relationships.

1. *Emotionally*, we must identify our place of calm and steadiness while giving ourselves permission to be "off center" at times, with boundaries. While we want to be aware of our place on the spectrum, it's actually more important to understand why we are where we are. From that understanding, we can work to return to our center.
2. *Physically*, maintaining a resilient center requires consistent exercise, proper diet, and plenty of rest. We know the realities of daily life can get in the way and temporarily throw us off our center. The key is finding balance over the long-term and understanding why we are off target.
3. *Spiritually*, it's important to find the resilient actions that center us—whether it's regular attendance at a place of worship or simply taking a few minutes of silence to appreciate life—and to realize what puts us off balance.
4. *Financially*, we've reached our resilient center when we're earning enough to focus on other parts of our lives or work—in other words, when we are comfortable and money is not the top concern. Our financial resilient center can also emerge when we realize the importance of living within our means and the gift to *ourselves* of being generous with others.

5. The fifth and final aspect involves ***relationships***. If our emotional pendulum swings positively through the birth of a child, or negatively through a divorce, we can lose sight of our resilient center and act without authenticity. This is perfectly acceptable for a while, but over time, we need to refocus. At work, we often think of building relationships in terms of networking opportunities—something to gain, long term or short term. In this context, we are at our resilient center when we build and maintain relationships naturally, without a conscious purpose. That's not to imply there won't be gains from these relationships, but rather that our center doesn't think in those terms.

Intertwined with these five fundamentals is how we prioritize them as we move through the different stages of our lives. For example, finances will seem much different when we're just starting out compared to when we're about to retire. The importance is being able to identify where we are in life, and giving ourselves permission to change priorities.

Also, it's important to consider our "whole" life collectively rather than looking individually at the roles we play as spouses, parents, children, business leaders, and community volunteers. We would gain different insights by considering each of the five areas solely in terms of our business role, for example, which would not be a complete picture.

HOW TO IDENTIFY YOUR "CENTER"

Defining the center in each of these areas is not easy, and to be realistic should be completed over time. Just as each person's center will be different, individuals also may use different paths to discover it.

One way to begin is to commit to the following exercise, which takes about six months. Every 30 days, write down what you believe to be your resilient center in each of the five areas, without reading the previous months' lists. Ask yourself key questions, reflecting on when you were at your most satisfied or productive. If you find it difficult to identify those times once a month, try keeping a running diary to identify when you were feeling great, and why. At the end of six months, review all the lists and look for recurring themes.

Once you've identified the activities or moments that bring you to your center, you can take the additional step of creating a motivational phrase to repeat to yourself when you're feeling off. This can be an ongoing tool to help you return to a more productive frame of mind as you go through changes in your life.

These steps can be helpful at several points in our lives, such as when we feel "off center," reach significant milestone birthdays, or during work anniversaries.

A faster and perhaps more simple way to return to our center is to focus on ourselves first across the five dimensions we've discussed. This should not be considered selfish, but rather a starting point for helping others. A colleague compared it to a plane's safety instructions—put on your own mask first. In his book "How to Be an Adult in Relationships," David Richo encourages us to learn and give ourselves affection, appreciation, attention, acceptance, and most of all "allowing"—meaning allowing ourselves to be our true, authentic selves.

No matter how we learn about our resilient center, identifying it shows us how close or far away from it we may be. Once again, this brings up the challenge of understanding why you've strayed. Sometimes it's obvious, such as a significant life event, a health issue in the family, a new job or responsibilities, or marriage. Other times, we may need to ask close family, friends, business colleagues, or a professional counselor to help us figure out why we are off balance.

Once we define our center and learn how to get closer to it, we become more effective leaders, coaches, and partners.

TAKING YOUR JOURNEY TO WORK

Significantly, this self-awareness gives us exponentially more courage, capability, vulnerability, and authenticity to lead other leaders and organizations. It builds a foundation from which we can provide authentic coaching of the same ideas.

I have discovered these capabilities as an unexpected spinoff of my own journey following a divorce, a job change, and a geographic move. These life events are not unusual for HR professionals or our clients, so we should be more willing to explore them together openly for personal and professional reflection and self-improvement.

Bringing our own HR teams through these exercises build the self-awareness of "looking inward" to help the group, and by extension, our clients. These ideas also can be used for executive coaching, with expansive conversations about personal and business lives. We can share our experiences, and ask the right questions to help leaders gain perspective about their own journeys. Then we can help executives gain deeper insight into their lives and their leadership.

This framework, with some flexibility, also can be used to build effective teams. Financially, the team's resilient center could be effective, proactive cost discipline while meeting business or division financial goals, including stock price. Spirituality is likely to be more about team culture and operating principles, and be closely tied to relationships. The framework is flexible enough to be appropriate in different situations.

We often coach others to be authentic, and providing a broader understanding of the "whole self" is a unique approach to doing just that. Ultimately, as we know, an authentic leader with strong team dynamics will generate business results. Being an HR strategist who sparks this transition will add significant value to a business.

CONCLUSION

Many companies are learning new ways to support employees and culture, seeing the value of offering something more experiential than regular pay and a pension. As HR professionals, it's our responsibility to lead this work in genuine ways.

Before asking others to be authentic and consider their "whole self," we should start with ourselves. We should find our resilient center emotionally, physically, spiritually, financially, and in relationships; establish where we are in relation to our center; and learn how to guide ourselves toward it. Then we will have new courage, capability, vulnerability, and authenticity to teach others to be authentic, too.

About William (Bill) G. Ingham

William (Bill) G. Ingham is vice president of global HR for Visa Inc., where he partners with business leadership teams to drive the global business and talent agendas. His career spans multiple industries—including high tech, retail, and consumer products—and his expertise includes all areas of human resource management, with special emphasis in talent management. His passion will always be driven by his love for talent acquisition, branding, cultural transformation, and being a catalyst for leadership team effectiveness. Prior to Visa, Ingham led international HR for the Banana Republic Brand at Gap Inc. in San Francisco, CA, and spent eight years with the Clorox Company in Oakland, CA, where he led HR for a $2 billion business unit. Earlier in his career he was with PeopleSoft, where he built the strategy for PeopleSoft's human resources business process outsourcing division in addition to leading global staffing. He started his career at Oracle as the first compensation analyst for the company. He had the pleasure of building out the first compensation programs at Oracle and dabbled in executive and sales compensation as well as in college recruiting. Ingham attended the University of Western Ontario and Evangel University in Springfield, MO. He holds degrees in communications and psychology.

THE WISDOM OF WOMEN (AND MADONNA)

Tacy M. Byham and Debbie McGrath

"Women need to shift from thinking "I'm not ready to do that" to thinking "I want to do that—and I'll learn by doing it." – Sheryl Sandberg, "Lean In: Women, Work, and the Will to Lead"

Although women are making real and steady gains in higher education and working entry-level jobs in fields previously dominated by men, they have made few inroads into upper-leadership positions in most organizations. A quick look at the numbers shows that the glass ceiling is alive and well: Women comprise 53 percent of entry-level workers, 40 percent of managers, 35 percent of directors, 27 percent of vice presidents, 24 percent of senior vice presidents, and 19 percent of C-suite execs.[1] Female Fortune 500 CEOs? About 5 percent.[2] The rise of women to senior leadership positions—whether as executives, board members, venture-backed entrepreneurs, or in government—simply has not happened.

At the same time, the business case for gender diversity has never been stronger. Development Dimensions International (DDI) and the Conference Board's Global Leadership Forecast (GLF) found that organizations with more women consistently perform better financially. As shown in **Figure 1**, companies in the bottom 20 percent of financial performance have only 19 percent women in all leadership positions; companies in the top 20 percent have 37 percent—almost twice as many.[3]

FIGURE 1. MORE WOMEN LEADERS = BETTER COMPANY PERFORMANCE

Organizations with Better Financial Performance Have More Women in Leadership Roles

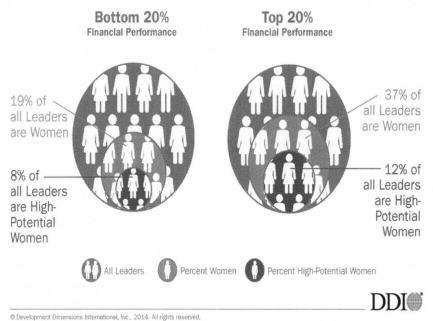

Bottom 20%
Financial Performance

Top 20%
Financial Performance

19% of all Leaders are Women

8% of all Leaders are High-Potential Women

37% of all Leaders are Women

12% of all Leaders are High-Potential Women

All Leaders   Percent Women   Percent High-Potential Women

DDI

So why are women falling off the management ladder? Here's one possible answer: Female talent opts out after their first experience at the frontline level. Business culture also remains an issue. With a diminishing number of available female leaders seeking to advance, there are fewer women to observe as role models. This means fewer opportunities to influence an organization to embrace the benefits of true diversity.

In 2008 Hewlett Packard conducted an internal study to learn why more women weren't applying for senior leadership jobs. It seems to be a pretty cut-and-dried case of male versus female personalities at work. Men apply for a job when they meet only 60 percent of the stated job qualifications. Women apply only if they can show they meet 100 percent.

Research clearly shows that there is no real difference between genders in terms of leadership ability. And women know this. According to the Global Leadership Forecast 2014–2015, female leaders rated themselves as effective as males on an entire array of competencies—the important skills that make leaders truly effective.[4] Multiple other studies show that female leaders are every bit as competent as their male counterparts. In fact, DDI's own testing and assessment processes—which measure real behavior, not survey data—show little difference in leadership ability when it comes to gender.

So, what's holding women back? Women polled in the GLF study cited a lack of opportunities to lead teams and gain global leadership experience. These experiences, rich with potential, are important proving grounds for career advancement. Additionally, they provide a strong boost to leaders' capabilities and confidence. And this is where we women can do ourselves—and the women leaders we supervise—some real good. We need to proactively identify key leadership development assignments and ensure that our best-laid plans become realities.

IS IT A MATTER OF CONFIDENCE?

According to "The Confidence Code" by Claire Shipman and Kitty Kay—both prominent broadcasters—confidence is a key differentiator.[5] A quote from their book sums up the situation: "Men think they can and women think they can't." DDI's GLF research on gender differences (see **Figure 2** below) echoes this theme, with women tending to self-evaluate themselves as less-effective leaders than their male peers. In other words, we have a paradox—based on this survey data, women perceive themselves to be *less effective as leaders* than men but at the same time *slightly more effective in leadership skills*. So, is it a matter of confidence?

FIGURE 2. WHERE ARE THE GENDER DIFFERENCES?

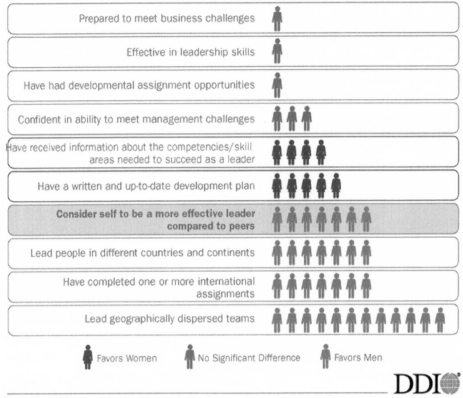

Another possible interpretation comes from author Tara Sopher Mohr in a post for Harvard Business Review.[6] After surveying more than 1,000 men and women, she discovered that the primary reason both genders cited for not applying for a job for which they lacked some of the qualifications was, "I didn't think they would hire me, and I didn't want to waste my time." While lack of confidence can hold women back in the workplace, so too might a failure to understand just how the workplace systems actually operate. That is, applying for jobs with just *some* of the stated credentials is actually "how it's done." For the inside track on how your company operates, particularly for women leaders, you'll have to tap into your own network. And that, of course, takes a good bit of confidence.

The September 2014 Real Simple/Time Magazine Success Poll surveyed 1,000 women on how they define success, how much importance they attach to it, and the risks they've taken to achieve it.[7] The poll found that only 8 percent of women consider themselves a success all the time. And, 36 percent of women often feel people at work think they're more qualified than they actually think they are.

So, what we women need is an attitude change. Or a different voice in our head guiding the way. A great voice is Sheryl Sandberg, who said, "Women need to shift from thinking 'I'm not ready to do that' to thinking 'I want to do that—and I'll learn by doing it.'"[8] Admittedly, learning on the job takes courage, but the risks are worth it.

THE WISDOM OF WOMEN (AND MADONNA)

For Tacy's upcoming book with co-author Rich Wellins, "Your First Leadership Job," she wanted to gather a collection of women's voices.[9] So, she started up a conversation—four dozen conversations to be precise—with top women leaders around the globe who are ahead of their game. The following list represents advice and personal wisdom from these women, who are climbing the ladder themselves.

Don't settle for a ho-hum work life. The women we spoke to consistently demonstrated passion for their roles. It was passion that helped them face obstacles head-on, and passion that allowed them to address the complex challenges that came their way. One woman leader said, "When I'm happy at work, it makes everything else in life hum." They also spoke of the importance of "having a connection to an underlying purpose," "needing value alignment," and, ultimately, choosing a job and career that you actually want to devote your energies to. According to one, "I'm a true believer that if you enjoy what you do, your performance will be higher and you will be more successful." When you find your passion, you can inspire yourself and your team to greater levels of performance.

Fail often, fail well. Know and understand what is important to you, and be very clear about the goals you want to achieve. However, don't be afraid to fail along the way. "Success is about working out what you want to do, not necessarily driving for the name or title, but more about the richness of what you're doing," one of our female senior leaders said. In other words, failure is not about failure; it's about failing forward and learning from the experience.

And that's not all. Failure provides opportunity to recalibrate our internal report card, listing areas of personal strength and understanding our weaknesses. Failure is often described as key to innovation and real breakthroughs as leaders. The senior women we interviewed would coach others to not miss opportunities for reflection, self-insight, and learning. According to one, "You need to understand yourself and what is right for you, not what the organization thinks is right for you."

Rethink mentorship. Finding a good mentor is like winning the lottery for any new professional. And DDI research shows that if you find a good candidate and ask for their sponsorship, they will likely say yes.[10] But finding the right person is no easy task. And many young women resist asking. It feels needy, like you're asking someone to "like" you. And your career may languish in the meantime.

Our best advice? Look for *micromentors*—people who can give you feedback about your career as it evolves, particularly if you're facing a stretch assignment, like delivering an important presentation or bringing a new business unit online. It's less about your overall career and more about finding an expert who can help you *now*. And don't ask just women! Because there are fewer women in leadership ranks as you go up, why limit yourself? Female mentors can provide advice based on the wisdom gleaned from their career paths. Male mentors can advise you on how you're coming across to others in the workplace. Both can help you enhance your political savvy.

The following exercise gives you a good excuse to expand your network without feeling like you're asking someone to go steady with you forever.

DDI Pro Tip: Create your own three-person affinity group. Take it upon yourself to find one promising woman one step below you in your organization and one who is one step above you. Create a small networking and support group that helps each of you grow as professionals yet also navigate the specifics of your company.

This advice was echoed by our panel of senior women, who would encourage you to find people who believe in you even more than you believe in yourself. Mentors and sponsors will be able to provide you with insight, guidance, and advice, even with challenges you haven't yet encountered. "Make yourself meet these people, and continue to meet them within the organization," one senior woman said. Because if you choose the right ones, they'll back you when you need it most.

In addition to organizational resources, these highly successful female senior leaders also had support systems beyond work. Many told us about the importance of personal relationships with friends and family—"an unspoken support that is without much acknowledgment," but one that is of great value in buffering both stress and pressure at work. For many of them, success is defined by balancing work-life priorities, as this allows you to "give yourself some purpose in life other than work."

Tacy now recognizes that this is a secret to her personal success, as she has a core group of powerful female friends who serve as her executive advisory board. "We're always on call to cheer each other on or hash through the big life issues when they arise. So, I encourage you to find your 'girl posse' and lean on them."

Declare yourself early and often. While everyone needs to declare their readiness for the next step up, women often miss cues such as when and how often to remind people what they *can do* now and what they *want* to do in the future. And as conscientious rule followers, women might miss the point that merely following instructions is not enough to win the day.

Be sure to demonstrate results and make them visible. Because remember that doing a good job is not defined by long hours, but rather by the outcomes you deliver. "Earning respect and doing a good job of what you do gets you a long way."

For women, the declarative conversation carries real weight. This call to action applies to all women—single, married, working moms, blended-family moms. Any woman who is balancing it all needs to step away from the fray and daily struggles of being their best, keeping their head above water, and getting things done to focus on the future—*their* future as a leader—and declare themselves.

Be "Madonna-like" and vogue. Take a moment to notice what your body language is when you join a meeting. Are you shrinking into a corner, or are you striding into a meeting looking ready to take charge? I challenge you to channel your inner rockstar—in this case, Madonna. One of the things that Madonna (and performers of all types) master is to seize the stage with an air of confidence. Were they born this way, or did they develop this skill?

It's likely that the confidence they project to the audience was developed over time. As a young singer, Madonna most likely was scared silly on the inside, but didn't let those emotions show on the outside. Even now, after performing for more than 30 years, Madonna admits that she still gets nervous before a show. But, she marches forth anyway, taking on new challenges (like a Super Bowl halftime show).[11]

But this advice is not just for rockstars. Wearing a mantle of fearlessness, backing yourself, and having the tenacity to get back on the horse when you fall off were all cited by our women leaders as critical characteristics in their move up the ladder. In fact, one savvy leader offered the following advice when women do hold themselves back from that next opportunity: "When you feel envy, question why you haven't gone for it yourself."

How do we become "Madonna-like"? Well, this is a bit of a cheat, but it works: If you strike a power pose before an important meeting or conversation, you will feel more powerful. Get pumped! Every meeting is an opportunity. Join the 8 percent of women leaders who know their power.[12]

#LeadLikeAGirl. In 2014, a new video redefined the phrase "like a girl" as something strong and powerful. It was part of the larger #LikeAGirl campaign by Always, the feminine hygiene brand owned by Procter & Gamble. In the video, a cast of men and women of all ages were asked to describe what they think the phrase "like a girl" means. The result was troubling. Waving hands and flipping hair, the participants pretended to run "like a girl" and throw "like a girl." Everyone—except, notably, the young girls—demonstrated that "just like a girl" is often perceived as an insult. Yet the young girls demonstrated purposeful, athletic motions.

So, in closing, we've confirmed that organizations with more women consistently perform better financially. In other words, it's good to #LeadLikeAGirl. And, perhaps you didn't need your own personal wake-up call, but I hope we, and the senior leaders who lent their insights, have inspired you to take a chance, seek a mentor, and strike a pose, like Madonna in her "Vogue" video. Others will see you as poised, credible, and confident. And, in turn you'll build your own inner confidence to stretch, grow, sometimes fail, and learn.

"A woman is like a tea bag. You never know how strong she is until she gets in hot water."
— Eleanor Roosevelt

About Tacy M. Byham

Tacy M. Byham, PhD, is senior vice president of DDI and will soon be taking over as CEO. An expert in unique solutions to address talent management challenges, she brings her experiences in assessment centers, 360s, development planning, and customized leadership solutions to maximize growth for individuals across the leadership pipeline. Her clients include Sam's Club, ADP, BNY Mellon, Lockheed-Martin, and Texas Children's Hospital. Byham is an energetic and thought-provoking presenter at industry conferences and events—including the ASTD International Conferences in 2012 and 2014, Conference Board events, and Society for Industrial and Organizational Psychology events—on topics such as the "talent driver seat" and innovation. She co-authored chapters in the ASTD Leadership Handbook in 2012 and 2014 titled "Managing from the Middle" and "Leadership Development Strategy." Her new book, "Your First Leadership Job," with co-author Rich Wellins, will be published in May 2015. Byham also received the national ASTD Dissertation Award in 2006 and was selected as one of Pittsburgh Magazine's "40 Under 40" award winners in honor of her professional and volunteer accomplishments in the Pittsburgh region. She holds an BA from Mount Holyoke College and an MS and PhD in industrial/organizational psychology from the University of Akron.

About Debbie McGrath

Debbie McGrath founded HR.com in 1999. HR.com is in business to help build great companies by connecting them with the knowledge and resources they need to effectively manage the people side of business. As the global authority, HR.com delivers HR best practices to help organizations build great companies through community, collaboration, research, shared best practices, events, and measurements. McGrath has an extensive background in HR, publishing, and the internet. Before starting HR.com, she owned The CEO Group, a Canadian and European entity that created job board software, talent management software, HTC Career Magazines, and High Tech Career Fairs, which was sold to The Washington Post in 1998 and is now part of IBM/Kenexa. She earned her degrees in computer science and business administration from the University of Guelph.

[1] Joanna Barsh and Lareina Yee, "Unlocking the Full Potential of Women at Work" (New York: McKinsey & Company, 2011), page 3.

[2] "Catalyst Census: Fortune 500 Appendix 1—Methodology," Catalyst Census (New York: Catalyst, 2013).

[3] DDI and The Conference Board, "Ready-Now Leaders: Meeting Tomorrow's Business Challenges, "Global Leadership Forecast (Pittsburgh: Development Dimensions International, 2014), page 40.

[4] Ibid., page 41.

[5] Katty Kay and Claire Shipman, "The Confidence Code: The Science and Art of Self-Assurance—What Women Should Know" (New York: HarperBusiness, 2014).

[6] Tara Mohr, "Why Women Don't Apply for Jobs Unless They're 100% Qualified," Harvard Business Review, last modified 2014, accessed December 17, 2014. (https://hbr.org/2014/08/why-women-dont-apply-for-jobs-unless-theyre-100-qualified)

[7] "Work & Money," Real Simple, September 1, 2014.

[8] Sheryl Sandberg, "Lean in: Women, Work, and the Will to Lead" (New York: Knopf, 2013).

[9] Tacy M. Byham and Rich Wellins, "Women and Leadership," Chapter 23 in Your First Leadership Book (Hoboken, NJ: Wiley, 2015).

[10] Stephanie Neal et al., "Women as Mentors: Does She or Doesn't She? A Global Study of Businesswomen and Mentoring" (Pittsburgh: Development Dimensions International, 2013), page 7.

[11] People.com, "Madonna Is 'So Nervous' About Super Bowl Performance," last modified 2014, accessed December 17, 2014. (http://www.people.com/people/article/0,,20565802,00.html)

[12] "Work & Money," Real Simple, September 2014, page 196.

HR IMPERATIVE: RAISING THE BAR ON ENGAGEMENT

David Shadovitz

In April 2014, Amazon announced the launch of its "Pay to Quit" program, patterned after a program previously introduced at the company's Zappos unit. Under the initiative, the online retailer offers to pay its associates to quit, beginning at $2,000 the first year the offer is made and climbing $1,000 a year before capping at $5,000.

According to CEO Jeff Bezos, the goal of the program is to encourage employees to think about what they really want. "We want them to stay," Bezos told shareholders. But, over time, "an employee staying somewhere [he or she doesn't] want to be isn't healthy for the employee [or] the company."

True enough. I doubt many companies will follow in Amazon's footsteps and offer employees such an out anytime soon; they may not want to risk losing talent they would be smart to keep. But there's no denying it's a bold way for the Seattle-headquartered company to get the attention of workers and let them know it only wants people who are engaged in what Amazon is doing and who *really* want to be there.

To be sure, HR professionals have many issues on their plates these days, ranging from leadership development and talent retention to more closely aligning HR to the business and controlling health care costs. But each year, when Human Resource

Executive sends out its "What Keeps HR Leaders Up at Night" survey, asking readers to name their most pressing concerns, "ensuring workers are engaged and productive" consistently occupies the top spot. In HRE's latest study, featured in the magazine's August 2014 edition, roughly 36 percent of the more than 400 HR executives surveyed identified this as their greatest challenge. (By comparison, 28 percent cited developing leaders, 24 percent said retaining key talent as the economy improves, and 21 percent said aligning people strategies to business objectives.)

Why is this the case? Because highly skilled employees in today's knowledge-based, technology-driven economy need the right resources at their fingertips. And they expect, like never before, employers to be sensitive not only to their work needs and career development but to life demands that can distract them from the crucial work that needs to be done. Unlike decades ago, when bored or distracted workers could slip up on an assembly line, disengagement or dissatisfaction today could lead to supply chain disruptions and huge delays in product development and innovation—not to mention the loss of a precious leg up on competitors in fast-moving, knowledge-driven industries such as pharmaceuticals, aerospace, and telecommunications.

Not that all of this should come as a huge surprise to HR professionals, especially when the costs of a disengaged workforce are considered. In its 2013 "State of the American Workplace" report, Gallup found that 30 percent of Americans with full-time jobs are engaged and inspired at work, while 20 percent could be considered actively disengaged. The other 50 percent, Gallup reported, are simply *not* engaged. Put another way, these workers may be present on the job, but they aren't contributing to their organizations in any meaningful way.

As the Gallup report points out, engaged workers can have a huge impact on a business and its financial success. Researchers at the firm found that "organizations with an average of 9.3 engaged employees for every actively disengaged employee in 2010 and 2011 experienced 147 percent higher earnings per share [than] their competitors in 2011–2012." In contrast, organizations with an average of 2.6 engaged employees for every actively disengaged employee experienced 2 percent lower earnings per share over that same period compared to their competitors. Gallup estimates that active disengagement costs US businesses between $450 billion and $550 billion per year.

Given these figures, it's no wonder HR professionals view engagement as their top worry and are increasingly making it a top priority. Likewise, study after study suggest many CEOs are acknowledging this as a principal concern. They're looking to HR to provide essential leadership and find new and innovative ways to ensure employees aren't just showing up but are fully engaged in the business and its goals. While progress is certainly being made in this regard, indications are that much still needs to be done to keep workers—especially the highest-performing ones— firing on all cylinders.

SEGMENTING THE WORKFORCE

Certainly, everyone has an important part to play as far as engagement is concerned. But I believe no one is better positioned to move the needle here than the HR leader. Like most challenges facing HR leaders today, there's no single magic bullet for addressing the issue of engagement. Nevertheless, there's little question that HR professionals who are able to implement strategies and practices that can result in a more fully engaged workforce will give their businesses a clear advantage over their competitors.

What those efforts will look like obviously differs from organization to organization. Yet there are some proven strategies that all HR practitioners should keep in mind as they formulate their engagement game plans.

They should start by customizing their efforts to a segmented workforce. As most of us know firsthand, what motivates one demographic group won't necessarily motivate another. Similarly, what drives someone in one department might not matter to someone in another department. To make engagement happen, organizations must craft strategies specific to each generation, job type, job level, and employee personal interest.

Take Millennials, who are expected to represent 75 percent of the nation's workforce by 2025. As most HR leaders already know firsthand, Millennials have a very different approach to work than their Gen-X and Baby Boomer counterparts. They care more about corporate social responsibility, community service, and better work/life balance, for example, than previous generations. Given this, employers have to deploy a very different set of strategies and practices in order to motivate and engage them.

This point isn't lost on corporations such as Merck, the Whitehouse Station, NJ-headquartered pharmaceutical company. In HRE's September cover story, "Doing the Right Thing," writer Will Bunch details a few of Merck's programs and tools, including the launch of a website called "Merck Gives Back" that enables workers to learn about charitable opportunities, swap insights and inspirational stories, and unite with like-minded volunteers across the company's diverse units.

Another Merck initiative featured in the story is a three-month intensive fellowship that connects key talent at the company with nongovernmental organizations dedicated to tackling difficult medical problems in underdeveloped nations. Beyond giving up-and-coming leaders a once-in-a-lifetime experience, the initiative provides Merck with valuable insights that can sometimes lead to new global strategies or products.

Though these two programs obviously have broad appeal, they can be especially attractive to Millennials, who are much more likely to seek out and *remain* at organizations that are attempting to "make a difference."

Other approaches to customizing work by demographics include flexible scheduling, innovative project and team assignments, and mobility (both within and outside the organization).

MOVING BEYOND SURVEYS

Nowadays, it's rare to find an HR leader whose organization isn't conducting annual employee engagement surveys—or more frequent "pulse" surveys—to generate valuable insights about the mindset of their workforce and use those insights to inform their decision-making. Indeed, thanks to new technologies that have emerged in recent years, organizations are now able to analyze the data they generate by workforce segment and apply these insights in much more meaningful ways.

At the same time, more and more HR professionals are beginning to leverage technology to speed up the collection and analysis of survey data and apply those insights to action plans in a much more timely fashion. However, the most effective HR leaders understand that these tools are no substitute for time spent on the front lines and in face-to-face interactions with employees. Hence, we're seeing more and more organizations leveraging small-group discussions and town hall meetings with C-suite leaders to ensure that their leaders understand what's happening inside the organization and use those insights to help shape strategies.

Senior HR professionals at leading organizations also seem to understand that greater transparency is key to building a culture of engagement. Reflecting on the stories we've published in recent years, more and more of them realize that such openness needs to be part of an organization's DNA in order for engagement to take hold.

At AT&T, for example, Bill Blase, senior executive vice president of HR, has been instrumental in spearheading a program called "Leading with Distinction," an initiative aimed at ensuring that everyone, from the top down, knows where AT&T is going and why. Launched in 2007, the effort occurs on an annual basis over a five-month period and involves either in-person meetings or live webcasts. In 2014, for the first time, the initiative was expanded to include employees who are part of a bargaining unit.

ENGAGING TALENT EARLY

Increasingly, organizations are also addressing talent engagement as part of their onboarding processes—sometimes even before an offer is made. For example, while not onboarding in the traditional sense, some organizations, as a part of their recruiting process, are videotaping managers and potential co-workers—and posting those clips to their website—so that passive candidates have a greater frame of reference and potential sense of belonging before even applying for a job.

In a recent report produced by Seattle-based i4cp titled "Six Talent Practices That Boost Engagement and Market Performance," researchers suggest that engaging talent needs to start from day one. In a report summary, the company references a process at Microsoft that "jumpstarts employee engagement early on through a collection of onboarding experiences that fulfills the needs of new hires around the world on multiple levels." In addition to its new hire orientation program, Microsoft provides new hires with a state-of-the-art online program called "The Welcome Experience," which the summary describes as a virtual campus from which participants can view executive messages and access learning content personalized to their role.

Other suggested approaches featured in the i4cp report include assigning mentors to new employees at the time of hire and involving family members in the familiarization process.

Yet while rethinking the onboarding process is certainly a natural place to start, any effort to address engagement will inevitably miss the mark if it fails to address the issue of career development, which consistently emerges in studies as the most important driver of talent engagement. Naturally, more and more HR leaders are making this a top priority. Some companies are starting this process on day one of every employee's job. Career development might take the form of stretch assignments, rotational posts, or leveraging new technologies that give talent greater access to career and development opportunities. Whatever form it takes, there's no denying that HR professionals are increasingly realizing they can no longer afford to relegate career development to the back burner if they ever hope to engage their talent.

As I stated earlier, there are some very good reasons why HRE's readers, when polled, consistently cite keeping employees engaged and productive as their top challenge. I would be surprised if this issue weren't at the top of the list of concerns when the magazine polls its readers again in 2015. Talent engagement isn't simply a challenge but an extraordinary opportunity for HR leaders to demonstrate their leadership and impact their organizations in unprecedented ways.

About David Shadovitz

David Shadovitz is editor and co-publisher of Human Resource Executive, a leading magazine for executives in the human resource profession, and has more than 25 years of experience in publishing. He also serves as vice president of editorial for the LRP Magazine Group, publishers of Human Resource Executive and Risk & Insurance magazines. Shadovitz joined the LRP Magazine Group in 1987 and worked on the start-up of both publications. Previously, he was editor-in-chief of Gordon Publication's Computer Dealer magazine. In addition, he has held senior editorial positions for several industrial magazines. Shadovitz is a recipient of a number of editorial awards, including three Jesse H. Neal Editorial Achievement Awards. In 1996, he was inducted into the National Academy of Human Resources, one of the HR profession's most prestigious honors.

ENGAGING WHITE MEN TO DRIVE DIVERSITY AND INCLUSION

Carole Watkins

The time has come for men to "lean in" and become full partners for increasing diversity in leadership in our corporations. This requires moving beyond creating initiatives that become window dressing to proactive leadership actions that drive real culture change. And that is just what the men at Cardinal Health are doing.

CURRENT REALITY IN DIVERSITY AND INCLUSION

While we would probably all agree we've made progress relative to diversity and inclusion in the workplace, the facts stand as a reminder that we still have a long way to go. Today women earn more college degrees than men, and within the next decade Caucasians will become a minority in the United States. White men are promoted at significantly higher rates than women and ethnically diverse talent. Articles, papers, and studies continuously espouse the benefits of diversity in our workforce. And, over and over again, the results show that companies that have more women and cultural diversity in their leadership perform and serve their customers better, attract top talent, have higher employee engagement, and are more innovative. Yet, while women represent more than 46 percent of the US labor force and 87 percent of consumer buying decisions, they represent only 4 percent of CEOs, 16 percent of board seats in Fortune 500 companies, and only 17 percent of US House and Senate seats.[1] And ethnic representation is even lower.

For years the corporate world, various professional organizations, universities, and agencies have offered leadership classes and seminars for women, African Americans, Asian and Pacific Islanders, and other minorities focused on "improving the leadership" skills of these constituents. Mentoring programs, networking groups, and many initiatives focused on women and ethnically diverse talent are available inside and outside of our organizations. Yet, why has the number of women and ethnically diverse leaders barely increased? To make real and lasting change, inclusion must be treated and led with the same attention and importance as any other business imperative. And that means men must actively engage to drive results.

THE CARDINAL HEALTH EXPERIENCE

After grappling with our own diversity and inclusion imperatives, more recently we accelerated our progress and momentum by actively engaging white men and raising the visibility of this business imperative. The impact it is having on our culture, and on them as individuals, is remarkable.

Cardinal Health is a global Fortune 22 health care products and services company. We are the business behind health care. We are working to make health care more cost effective so providers can focus on their patients. We, like many others, have had diversity and inclusion programs and initiatives for many years. Recently we took a small but bold step. We not only named our chairman and CEO George Barrett (a white man) to lead our Diversity and Inclusion Council, we named the CEO of our largest segment, Mike Kaufmann (another white man), as executive sponsor of our Women's Initiative Network. Our belief was, and still is, that if we FULLY engage our male leaders in our efforts, more progress will be made than when efforts were driven exclusively by women or ethically diverse talent—or, as we say, than when just women talked to other women and ethnically diverse talent talked to one another. Let me be clear: This is NOT about women or ethnically diverse talent needing help from men to be successful. This is about getting men involved in a cultural shift and building awareness of how unconscious biases and beliefs influences behavior and ultimately organizational culture.

We started somewhat cautiously and began by providing "Unconscious Bias" training across the organization; implementing a women's leadership program that focused on women driving business projects that demonstrate measurable, significant business results; and setting "bold goals." Those goals included requiring diverse slates on all open positions and providing new and targeted assignments for high-potential females and ethnic minorities. We engaged an external expert to be our advisor and to push us to be even bolder.

Our progress was steady but, under our own critical eye, not good enough. The next year, we set goals to promote women at a rate closer to white men. The following year, we launched our broad "Engaging Men for Gender Partnership" initiative—a multipronged effort designed to create a more diverse and gender-balanced culture with a common commitment to maximize all talent. This is truly when we began to see our culture change accelerate.

PARTNERS LEADING CHANGE

One of our most effective moves was to launch our Partners Leading Change (PLC) program. Facilitated by our outside advisor, Rayona Sharpnack, CEO of the Institute for Women's Leadership, this three-day seminar is designed to move beyond unconscious bias awareness to personal insights regarding behaviors and actions that are "gendered" and create unintended consequences. Over the course of the three days, participating men learn and reflect on their styles; build understanding of how men and women see the world through different contexts; and build skills to leverage the full contribution of both men and women.

Each participant commits to working on a project or initiative that will contribute to transforming the enterprise culture, leading to more women in leadership positions. A few of these projects include: a gender compensation study; a sponsorship program for women and ethnically diverse talent; a program to build support at home for partners of women who work at Cardinal Health; and creating a job rotation program for high-performing women in order to prepare them for general manager positions.

The results and impact have exceeded our expectations. More than 100 male leaders have participated in this program. The vast majority of participants reported that, while the experience was "uncomfortable" and while they thought they understood issues women face because they have a wife and daughters, they came to realize that they "didn't know what they didn't know." For example, they learned about some of the basic differences in the aspirations of men versus women:

- *Men often see themselves and their skills differently from women.* If there are five requirements for a position and a man has two of them, he will ask for the position. But a woman who may have four of the five qualifications will *not* likely put her hand up because she doesn't have the fifth. Men who participated in the program now recognize this difference and are reaching out to those women to encourage them to apply for positions rather than waiting to apply.

- *Assumptions are often made about women's personal and professional desires.* In the past, men were making assumptions without consulting the potential women candidates—for example, assuming a woman who is qualified for a promotion wouldn't want it because she has small children and the job requires extensive travel. Assumptions might seem appropriate and even protective but they are actually self-censoring and limiting. Participants are now allowing potential female candidates to make that call.

- *Decisions made without applying a gender lens often have unintended consequences.* Initiating conversations with women on their team about gender differences awakened male participants to how decisions they make may have unintended consequences. For example, a leader in our nuclear pharmacy business was finding it difficult to hire women, who today are the majority of pharmacy graduates, to move to some of our newer locations. When he probed more, he discovered that since the nature of the nuclear pharmacy business requires pharmacists to work during the dark early morning hours or late night hours, women were not comfortable with the current locations. He needed to consider location (in safe neighborhoods), good parking, and proper outdoor lighting before he could attract top female pharmacists.

- *Day-to-day conversations.* Today's business meetings are full of sports and military analogies. After talking to many women, male participants realized many of these were lost on the women in the room. The decision was made to begin a "fine" system. If a sports or military analogy is used, the person has to contribute to a fund donated to a local nonprofit focused on women's issues.

PLC participants also reported having different, more meaningful conversations with spouses, partners, daughters, and sons about the impact of unconscious bias, asking them questions about its impact on them and sometimes leading to life- and relationship-changing conversations. Meanwhile, at Cardinal Health, female promotions as a percent of total promotions jumped from 33 percent to 55 percent in one year. We believe this program played an important role in the improvement.

SPONSORSHIP

Our sponsorship program has also proved to be one of the contributing factors to our early success. Sponsorship is different from coaching or mentoring. Coaches talk "to" you, mentors talk "with" you, but a sponsor talks "about" you. Sponsors advocate and help build recognition by others of your skills, abilities, and aspirations. A sponsor is also the one to close the door and give "real" feedback. Protégés expect sponsors to be their "truth tellers." Sponsor relationships are not to be entered into lightly. The sponsor has to know the protégé well and be able to see them perform. The protégé needs to trust that the sponsor has their best interests firmly at heart.

We began our program by asking every senior vice president in our organization to select two individuals, one of whom needed to be a female and/or ethnically diverse, to sponsor. This way the SVPs were selecting individuals they could advocate for, give direct feedback to, and promote throughout the organization. HR provided simple and targeted training and toolkits to help these relationships form in a new and productive way. Again, the results have been positive. Sponsors are intervening to ensure the company is retaining, promoting, and recognizing the contributions of their protégés. Protégés are getting assignments, promotions, and lateral moves at a significantly higher rate than others. And the sponsors are learning more from their protégés than imagined—an unexpected bonus.

The program has been so successful that a few of our PLC participants developed a project to expand the program to lower levels in the organization. Seventy more leaders, at the VP level, have been trained as sponsors and each selected two protégés, again with at least one being female or ethnically diverse.

WIDEN THE CIRCLE

Our focus is not solely inside the walls of Cardinal Health. Our chairman and CEO, George Barrett, championed the launch of Widen the Circle—an initiative to make Central Ohio, where we are headquartered, the best place in the country for women to grow their careers. To engage more companies in this work, Cardinal Health partnered with The Columbus Partnership, an organization made up of CEOs of major Central Ohio corporations.

To launch the Widen the Circle initiative, we hosted actor Geena Davis, whose foundation works to change how women are portrayed in the media, as the keynote speaker at a community-wide event attended by hundreds of leaders. Davis praised the initiative, saying that she believes Central Ohio "will become a model for the whole country." Work to date includes creating a benchmark of data on the current state of women in leadership in Central Ohio; creating a council of HR leaders in the community who are sharing best practices; conducting cross-company unconscious bias training; and launching "Lean In" circles across gender and companies. Columbus Partnership CEOs have also agreed to sponsor women leaders to serve on public company boards.

RESULTS

While we are far from claiming victory, we are convinced that actively engaging men in our diversity and inclusion initiative is effectively driving the right conversations, awareness, and accountability for this critical business imperative. It has also provided other tangible results:

In 2010, Cardinal Health had no female presidents. By early 2014, four of nine presidents were women.

1. We hold dedicated "diverse talent reviews" focused solely on discussing diverse employees, their talents and capabilities, and the next steps for their careers. This allows sponsors to advocate for and recognize their protégés so others are aware of their talents.
2. The inclusion index, which is part of our annual "Voice of the Employee" survey, has increased 10 percentage points.
3. In 2014, turnover for females at the manager level and above is 5.2 percent—which is lower than it is for their male counterparts (6.3 percent).

The business case for inclusion has been proved. But continuing to deliver on the benefits in our ever-more diverse business environment and engaging ALL our leaders in the process—especially white male leaders—will be critical. Moving beyond the comfort of just "helping" women or ethnically diverse leaders to driving culture change that allows everyone to thrive and do their best work everyday is the key. Culture change takes time. At Cardinal Health, we believe we are accelerating the necessary change—and hope that many other companies will join us in this important work.

About Carole Watkins

Carole Watkins is chief human resources officer of Cardinal Health, a $103 billion health care services company headquartered in Dublin, Ohio. She became CHRO in 2005, after serving in numerous roles of increasing responsibility in the HR function since joining the company in 1996. She also serves on the company's executive committee and on the Strategy and Innovation Council led by the CEO. In her role as CHRO, she leads all of HR, security, aviation, corporate communications, real estate, and facilities. She is also the management advisor to the HR and Compensation Committee of the board of directors and serves on the Cardinal Health Foundation's board. Prior to joining Cardinal Health, Watkins gained more than 20 years of HR experience with companies including The Limited, O.M. Scott & Sons, and Huntington Banks. She serves or has served on the boards of numerous organizations and volunteers with the American Heart Association, serving on the executive leadership team for the Central Ohio "Go Red for Women" luncheon. In 2013, Watkins was named a Columbus YWCA Woman of Achievement and was inducted into the National Academy of Human Resources. She also co-chairs the CHRO Board Academy and is a member of the Human Resource Policy Association, the Personnel Roundtable, and the Healthcare Business Women's Association. She earned her bachelor's degree in business from Franklin University.

---

[1] Sources: Bureau of Labor Statistics, Catalyst, Center for American Women & Politics, The White House Project.

ATTRACTING AND RETAINING TALENT THROUGH DIFFERENTIAL TREATMENT

Sandy J. Wayne

Many HR professionals focus on developing or implementing policies and procedures that ensure that employees are treated in the same way or behave similarly in performing aspects of their job. Standardization was a hallmark of early HR departments, as the prevailing view of many HR professionals was that formal HR policies were key to managing a growing workforce. This view proliferated in the 1960s and 1970s with the passage of equal opportunity employment (EEO) legislation.

While contemporary HR practices have evolved, HR professionals continue to be responsible for creating an employee handbook containing policies and procedures that enhance efficiency and serve as a control mechanism for employee behavior. HR policies and procedures that achieve these purposes of efficiency, guiding employee behavior, and achieving EEO are critical and should *not* be abandoned.

Although HR policies and procedures are beneficial, they should not prevent differential treatment of employees. In this essay, I caution HR professionals from developing policies and procedures that restrict managers from treating their employees differently. Further, I argue that HR professionals should be dissuaded from overlooking the potential benefits of individualized treatment and, in fact, encourage such practices.

This view is contrary to the intent of many HR policies and practices, which is to create consistency in the treatment of employees by managers within a firm. The underlying premise of such guidelines and policies is that workplace fairness is achieved when managers treat their employees in the same way. Yet this assumes that employees behave in the same way and perform at the same level, which is improbable in most organizations.

WHAT IS DIFFERENTIAL TREATMENT—AND WHY IS IT IMPORTANT?

Differential treatment in the workplace focuses on customizing employees' jobs or conditions of employment based on their performance or unmet needs. The result is a work environment with aspects that are uniquely suited for individual employees. This is in contrast to standard employment arrangements, which comprise policies that impact a group of workers in the same way, perhaps based on level in the firm (employee versus manager) or job type.

Examples of standard employment arrangements include employees in the same firm sharing the same insurance benefits or a firm where employees who have similar tenure receive the same vacation benefits. In many of today's workplaces, individuals negotiate customized features of their employment that supplement these standardized work arrangements. An example is a new hire who negotiates an earlier start and end time for his or her work schedule in order to manage work-family challenges, resulting in a schedule that is unique compared to that of other employees.

There are certainly a number of important arguments that cannot be ignored for why HR professionals may be hesitant to encourage customized work arrangements within their firms. Yet there are a number of labor market trends that support customized work arrangements. These include:

- *A reduction in collective bargaining.* In the past, collective bargaining restricted employers from individualizing employment conditions. According to the Bureau of Labor Statistics, the percentage of the workforce covered by collective bargaining went from 20.1 percent in 1983 to 11.3 percent in 2013. The implication is that fewer firms are required to treat employees in the same way based on a collective bargaining agreement.

- **The preferences of Millennials.** A 2011 PricewaterhouseCoopers survey of more than 4,000 Millennials suggests that this segment of the workforce desires a work environment free from rigid hierarchies and outdated management styles (i.e., they desire flexible approaches). Customized work arrangements are well suited for a generation that expects employers to meet their individual needs.
- **Increased competition for top talent.** This has resulted in more employees proactively negotiating preferred work arrangements. Not fulfilling these requests due to a desire to treat all employees the same means the highest performers are most likely to leave, as they also tend to have the greatest number of job opportunities.

These are some of the most pressing reasons why HR professionals need to abandon a "one size fits all" approach and consider effective ways to individualize the workplace.

IDIOSYNCRATIC DEALS AND THEIR BENEFITS

Recent scholars have referred to customized work arrangements as "idiosyncratic deals," or i-deals, defining them as personalized work arrangements of a nonstandard nature that employees and their employers negotiate for mutual benefit. I-deals vary in terms of their timing and content, and they may be negotiated by employees during the recruitment process or after joining the firm. Interestingly, empirical studies have found that employees negotiate i-deals more frequently after they join a firm than during the hiring process. One explanation is that new hires need to "prove their worth" and distinguish themselves from others to their manager, typically through their performance, in order to be successful in negotiating special arrangements.

I-deals come in many forms. Four of the most common are:

1. **Schedule flexibility i-deals** – Modifying an employee's schedule to accommodate his or her needs
2. **Location flexibility i-deals** – Allowing an employee to work from a location outside the office
3. **Task i-deals** – Allowing individuals to negotiate to create or alter the content or responsibilities of their job

4. *Developmental i-deals* – Special opportunities an individual negotiates in order to use or expand his or her knowledge and skills

Numerous empirical studies have explored the consequences of i-deals for their recipients. While the magnitude of the consequences vary by i-deal type, there is evidence that those who successfully negotiate i-deals have higher job satisfaction, stronger commitment to their employer, lower intentions to leave their firm, and higher work engagement. Importantly, recipients of i-deals were rated as higher performing by their managers than those who had not received customized work arrangements.

THE SERVANT LEADERSHIP APPROACH

Another form of individualized treatment that is receiving attention is servant leadership. While i-deals are typically initiated by employees, servant leadership is an approach to managing whereby the leader strives to meet the needs of each employee. In contrast to i-deals, which are provided to select employees, servant leadership strives to prioritize the needs of each employee.

This approach to management was first explored in a series of essays by Robert Greenleaf in the 1970s. According to Greenleaf, one of the primary distinguishing characteristics of servant leadership is a focus on developing employees to their fullest potential. In order to accomplish this, leaders must rely on one-to-one communication to understand the abilities, needs, desires, goals, and potential of each individual.

My colleagues at the University of Illinois at Chicago and I developed a measure of servant leadership that could be used in academic research but also in organizations to assess the degree to which managers engage in this form of leadership. Our research identified seven dimensions of servant leadership: emotional healing, creating value for the community, conceptual skills, empowering, behaving ethically, helping subordinates grow and succeed, and putting subordinates first.

These last two dimensions imply that servant leaders must understand the needs of each employee and create a work environment whereby they can develop their competencies and fulfill their goals. A servant leader's behavior is not based on what the leader desires for the employee but rather what the employee desires for him or herself. A servant leader understands what each employee strives to achieve in the workplace and makes it a priority to assist them in succeeding.

THE RISKS OF CREATING A CUSTOMIZED WORKPLACE

The most obvious risk is that treating employees differently will create questions that managers must be prepared to address. If one employee is given a preferred work schedule, will coworkers resent the employee? Will employees always view customized work arrangements provided to some individuals and not others as unfair? Are others' concerns silenced if the justification for differential treatment is based on an employee's high performance? To what extent is performance evaluated accurately? Is servant leadership the best approach to differential treatment? How likely is it for servant leaders to meet the needs of all followers?

These questions imply that customizing work arrangements comes with challenges. When employees are treated the same, managing is easier and there are fewer questions such as those listed above. But doing so risks having your highest performers leave the firm. HR professionals have long advocated linking pay and performance such that the highest performers receive the highest pay. Why, then, shouldn't customized work arrangements be provided to high performers?

There are certainly some situations that are more suitable for differential treatment than others. Differential treatment should be the norm in situations where there are clear differences among employee performance and it is clear who is a "star performer" based on their results or output. A recent study by O'Boyle and Aguinis involving 198 samples and more than 600,000 individuals found that a significant amount of an organization's output or performance is driven by a small group of elite or star performers. As these authors pointed out, star performers "make or break" an organization. Losing these individuals would have significant negative consequences for the firm.

In conclusion, I am *not* advocating for the elimination of HR policies and procedures that improve efficiency, guide employee and manager behavior, and create an equal employment opportunity workplace. Even with such policies and procedures, there should be room for customization of the workplace and treating employees as individuals. The challenge for HR professionals is to achieve this balance. By doing so, HR can play a key role in retaining and motivating top talent.

About Sandy J. Wayne

Sandy J. Wayne, PhD, is professor of management in the College of Business Administration (CBA) at the University of Illinois at Chicago (UIC), where she has been a faculty member for 25 years. She is also director of the CBA's Institute for Leadership Excellence and Development (iLEAD). Wayne's research focuses on relationships in the workplace, including employee-leader relationships and employee-organization relationships and the antecedents and consequences of these relationships for organizations and their members. She has published more than 50 articles in leading management journals on these topics and has received numerous awards for her research, including the S. Rains Wallace Dissertation Award and the Ulrich & Lake Award for Excellence in Human Resource Management Scholarship. She was elected as a Fellow of the Society of Industrial and Organizational Psychologists; serves on the editorial boards for six journals; is past chair of the human resources division of the Academy of Management; and recently completed a three-year term on the Academy of Management board of governors. Through her applied research projects, Wayne has provided consulting services on human resource management issues for Allstate Insurance, BMC Software, Bristol Myers Squibb, Busbank, Caterpillar, ConAgra, FMC, Jason's Deli, Merisant, Motorola, Mercy Hospital, Osram Sylvania, Sara Lee, Texas Instruments, Trilogy Software, UPS, USG, W. W. Grainger, and Western Building Products. Wayne received her PhD in management in 1987 from Texas A&M University.

5 INFORMATION & ANALYTICS

INFORMATION & ANALYTICS

Introduction

As Richard Beatty acutely points out in his essay in this section, for many HR professionals, measures are a foreign language. This is akin to the worn and ineffective strategy of hoping that expatriates will be successful without understanding the culture or language of the country they are working in.

Beatty goes on to state that "HR analytics and metrics present a significant opportunity to impact the HR profession. In fact, effective use of analytics and metrics may be the biggest contributor to the building of great, sustainable organizations." Wayne Brockbank goes even further as he reports on a tracking study that his organization conducts regularly on the role of HR competencies, saying, "The scarce but vital competency...is the ability of HR professionals to help architect the flow of business information—not just HR information but business information."

If we think about a hierarchy of measurement as depicted in **Figure 1**, it is probably not surprising that much of what HR and organizations track is at the transactional level. As pointed out by several of the authors, the use of analytics and measurement should be driven by strategy, not by what's available or easy to collect. What is the theory of the business? What are the talent and organizational implications and requirements? Given the talent and organizational needs, what are the important metrics that HR or the organization should be tracking? Beatty says metrics should be answers to the right questions—before discussing "how" to measure, "we need to explore what might be worth measuring."

FIGURE 1. HIERARCHY OF MEASUREMENT

Looking at the top of the pyramid, Mark Huselid goes on to argue that HR professionals need to focus more on differentiation. Who are the high performers, what are the critical roles, and what are the most strategic requirements of the business? Only then should hypotheses be developed that analytics can help answer. If a business's value proposition is to be the most customer-intimate organization in its sector, then the measures that are used in its business, talent, and HR scorecards will be different from those of competitors who are differentiating themselves in other ways. And, the analytics that are employed should focus on the connection of talent, customer-facing processes, and technology to customer and market goals.

This leads to observations by several authors regarding the dangers of benchmarking when you are comparing your measures to those who may well have different business and talent strategies. If you look again to **Figure 1**, the easiest level to benchmark is the transactional level; things like training hours per head, turnover rates, time to hire, cost per hire per employee, and so forth. However, this level is the least useful to organizations strategically. These measures may capture efficiency but not effectiveness. A manager leading recruiting may have a time to hire average that is better than some benchmark, but if the organization is losing those hires quickly, is it really effective?

Furthermore, at the strategic impact level, if that same organization has great recruiting speed and high retention, but those hires are driving customers away because they are not service oriented, then the aforementioned strategy of being customer intimate is thwarted. Zappos, which is renowned for its high customer service, would have no way of knowing if it was achieving differentiated service if the metrics could not detect both their levels of service and how they compare to the competition.

Most of the authors in this section argue for "outside-in" thinking. For too long, HR (and, for that matter, organizations in general) generated metrics from the "inside out." Once you are looking through the eyes of the customers of the organization or the stakeholders of HR, the game changes. They, and only they, can provide insights into how they see value being created (or not).

William A. Schiemann and his colleagues at the Metrus Institute have been tracking such value for HR and many other organizational functions since the early 1990s. They have found that while overall ratings of functions on the value they are producing has increased greatly over the past 20 years (e.g., HR scores have gone from near 20 percent favorable on value delivered to 40 percent during that time), HR is behind other functions due to a variety of factors: strategic thinking, business acumen, and proactive versus reactive actions, among others.[1] Furthermore, in studies that have included raters from more than 4,000 organizations, they report large variance in reported ratings across HR organizations.[2] Why are some HR organizations getting strong value ratings from their stakeholders (ranging from funders to users), while others are receiving "no confidence" votes, often leading to their becoming outsourced?

For example, Mark James, named CHRO of the year by HR Executive magazine in 2013, leads a global HR organization at Honeywell that receives high scores from its stakeholders. In his essay, he shares several factors that have led to these outstanding ratings and have contributed to their success. These include truly knowing the business—how widgets are produced—and taking the proactive step to know what your stakeholders need and whether you are fulfilling what they need to execute the business strategy. This is not about making stakeholders happy, but about driving business results.

William A. Schiemann calls for a more strategic set of workforce metrics (the top level of **Figure 1**) by discussing the work that he and the Metrus Group have done to identify truly strategic workforce factors that drive business results, such as quality, customer loyalty, and financial performance. He discusses the ACE dimensions—Alignment, Capabilities, and Engagement—that comprise a concept called People Equity, and why they are a good surrogate for understanding and assessing how well talent is being optimized in the organization.

Many of the authors in this section and elsewhere in this book have reiterated the huge cost and critical role that human capital plays in organizations. Schiemann argues that organizations must optimize that investment, and goes on to discuss how each of the three ACE factors can be customized to the business strategy and how the analytics applied to surveys and other tools must provide insights about the unique drivers of high People Equity.

Finally, Denise M. Rousseau makes a compelling argument for evidence-based management. The time for folklore and anecdotal stories is over. Organizations that manage by fact will leave their competitors in the dust. But facts must also not become obsession. Facts must lead to decisions at lightning speed in order to adapt to the incredibly rapid changes in the environment described by Wayne Brockbank in his essay.

In sum, these authors call for a more strategic approach to measurement and analytics. Start with the market and the strategy, and work back to talent requirements, and only then to HR metrics. And, develop measures that are answers to important strategic questions. In today's data-rich environments, the risk is creating organizations that are choked by hundreds if not thousands of transactional or tactical metrics, and in doing so, missing the important signals that should be conveyed by "critical few" scorecard metrics. Metrics should help provide evidence that authenticates or invalidates great hypotheses about what drives value in the organization. And think about metrics and analyses that help the organization understand how well talent is being leveraged, or not, and where the most fruitful opportunities for improvement are. After all, talent is viewed by most CEOs as their most important asset. Perhaps it is time to measure it more effectively.

It is an exciting time for those who can embrace measures and analytics without getting caught up in esoteric findings or undue complexity. Instead, use smart measures and the right analytics to focus the organization, optimize talent investments, evaluate progress, and help the organization adapt its strategy in the rapidly changing marketplace.

---

[1] J.H. Seibert and J.H. Lingle, "Internal Customer Service: Has It Improved?" Quality Progress, March 2007, pages 35–40.

[2] Seibert and Lingle, 2007; J.H. Seibert and W.A. Schiemann, "Power to the People," Quality Progress, April 2010, pages 24–30; J.H. Seibert and W.A. Schiemann, "Inside Job," Quality Progress, November 2013, pages 31–37.

HR ANALYTICS AND METRICS: SCORING ON THE BUSINESS SCORECARD

Richard W. Beatty

Numbers are often the language of an organization. But for many, numbers are a foreign language, as well as a reason that many college students choose to major in the soft sciences and avoid more rigorous math-based subjects (or major in HR so they can "work with people"). However, HR analytics and metrics present a significant opportunity to impact the HR profession. In fact, the effective use of analytics and metrics (through math and statistics) may be the biggest contributor to the building of great, sustainable organizations in the future, as well as a significant HR career opportunity.

To build an effective metrics system, HR needs to first consider the organization's context. Too many HR functions seek "available" metrics instead of strategic metrics that fit their organization. Choosing strategic metrics involves discerning the firm's strategy, its competitive environment, and the workforce's role in realizing its strategic success. We should also realize that, in an ever-changing business environment, organizations only change when people change their decisions and behavior. Well-designed metrics can also change behavior.

Workforce metrics are strategically important for firms because the workforce is most firms' single largest expenditure—and the least scrutinized in assessing its impact on value creation. More slack likely occurs in the management of the workforce than in any other organizational asset. Most other resources have relatively well-tested metrics that are designed to impact the firm's success: Financial resources are held accountable through budgets, material resources with supply chain metrics, time by schedules, etc. But what is the metric system for allocating and holding accountable the firm's most expensive resource? The challenge is to identify the metrics that enable workforce decision-making, which impacts the firm's strategic success and sustainability.

Commonly available HR metrics seldom impact the firm's scorecard. Even if a firm is "world class" in its implementation of traditional ways to measure the workforce (e.g., turnover, job satisfaction, time to fill, cost per hire, etc.) the firm is unlikely to become world class. Commonly used metrics constitute "metrics jeopardy," providing answers to questions the firm should not necessarily be asking. Metrics should be answers to questions! If you don't ask the right questions, you will never get answers that allow you to successfully intervene and produce the desirable result. The real purpose of metrics is to intervene and assure that the firm's strategic targets are realized. Seldom do traditional HR metrics provide this possibility.

ASSUMPTIONS ABOUT IMPROVING ANALYTICS

Before beginning a discussion of how to measure, we need to explore what might be worth measuring. This is the analytics component of building a robust set of HR function and workforce measures. A few assumptions are necessary:

1. *Use interventional metrics.* Effective metrics should be interventional so that they can dictate actions to significantly improve the outcome of a desired organizational target.
2. *Score on the business scorecard.* The selected metrics should enable HR to impact the business scorecard—by improving business process success (e.g., productivity, efficiency), customer success (e.g., market share, net promoter scores) or investor success (e.g., financial returns, profitability, earnings per share, market value). The workforce should also be a component of the firm's business model (see **Figure 1**), with the appropriate metrics designed to influence the behaviors that impact the components of the business scorecard.

FIGURE 1. THE CONTEXT OF WORKFORCE METRICS: SCORING ON THE BUSINESS SCORECARD

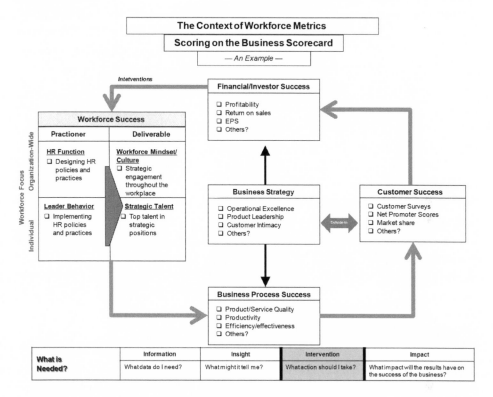

3. *Focus on the impact HR should deliver.* HR should focus not on what it does, but on what it delivers that impacts the scorecard of the business: firm success and sustainability. HR's major deliverable should be the workforce/workplace and the strategic engagement of the workforce, to impact the creation of customer and economic value.

4. *Remember that leaders also have HR responsibilities.* HR must also remind itself that leaders influence the workforce more than HR does, no matter how well HR functions. Leaders should own HR work, including performance management, selection, employee development, rewards, work design, and communication. How well leaders discharge these responsibilities obviously influences the culture of the organization and the attraction, growth, performance, and retention of direct reports. HR should architect

the blueprint for the organization to build a successful workforce. Thus we need to include metrics that measure how well leaders execute their HR/ workforce responsibilities.

Following these four suggestions can help HR analyze a firm's unique situation, determine appropriate metrics investments, and design powerful measures that will enhance performance in other organizational functions. HR's efforts impact the outcomes of other functions (such as marketing, manufacturing, and finance), thus cross-functional metrics enable the organization to become an interdependent system. Organizations should be a whole and not a heap!

DEVELOPING STRATEGIC METRICS

The development of HR metrics should begin by asking what HR should deliver. Obviously, HR should operate its back office efficiently and effectively, but HR cannot "save" the organization to prosperity and must focus on delivering outcomes that enable top-line growth through the firm's strategic mindset and by leveraging the performance of individual roles that impact value creation and top-line growth.

Meaningful mindset metrics would include whether your workforce has the knowledge to enable it to become "strategically engaged." What do you want your workforce to understand about your organization that will influence behaviors that make it inordinately successful? The answers might include your firm's business strategy, brand, values, and governance system.

Ideally you would like to attract a workforce that knows what your firm does, believes in what it does, and wants to contribute to those achievements. Employees with those characteristics are much more likely to become strategically engaged. The last person you want to hire is someone who wants a job but has learned very little about your organization before applying.

The metrics used to assess workforce culture and mindset can be captured through informational surveys that use multiple-choice and true/false questions to assess whether your workforce understands the strategic interests of the enterprise. Such surveys not only collect data about your workforce's strategic engagement, but also communicate what is expected of an employee.

You may also wish to know how your workforce feels about your organization (the most common purpose of workforce surveys today) through questions that assess an employee's "strength of sentiment" about organization-wide policies, leadership, coworkers, or their job duties. These approaches can be combined in the same survey and tied to each work unit and manager to provide insight into the culture and mindset under each manager's jurisdiction.

Beyond what you would like your entire workforce to understand, there are roles that have a profound impact on the firm's ability to create customer and economic value. Therefore, the question to ask is: What are the positions that are intended to impact the creation of value for our firm? Usually it is a surprisingly small number, but these positions have a dramatic impact on the firm's customer and economic success. Knowing what these positions are—and the effectiveness of the talent in these positions—is a critical workforce metric. Talent in these positions should be assessed in categories such as "Top Talent," "Emerging Talent," "Career Level," and "Does Not Meet Position Requirements." This enables a firm to build a current strategic talent inventory and provides insight to the talent supply chain required to meet future talent challenges, as shown in **Figure 2**.

FIGURE 2. STRATEGIC TALENT INVENTORY

BUSINESS LEADER RECAP AND POSITION SCORECARD

Line of Business: Retail Appliance Division
Business Strategy: Low cost producer and major provider to "Big Box" retailers for highly price sensitive retail customers

STRATEGIC CAPABILITIES	STATUS				
	Abysmal (1)	Less Competitive (2)	Competitive (3)	Very Competitive (4)	World Class (5)
Executive Leadership			3 ⟶		
Manufacturing Excellence				4 ⟶	
Sales/Marketing				4	
R&D/New Product Development		2 ⟶			

INFORMATION & ANALYTICS

STRATEGIC POSITIONS	Number	Top Talent	Emerging Talent	Career Level	Move	Action Plans
Executive Leadership						
VP Marketing	1		1			Develop more talent from sales and marketing
VP Mfg.	1			1		Consider early replacement of VP Mfg.
CFO	1	1				
Manufacturing						
Plant Managers	16	4	3	7	2	Exit moves and "careerists." Hire developing talent. Hire and move "top talent" into the 38 career level/move positions
Area Supervisors	48	7	3	33	5	
Sales/Marketing						
Marketing Directors	6	2	1	1	2	Exit moves and initiate campus recruiting and career development plans to strengthen marketing talent at all levels
Brand Managers	5	1	1	3	0	
Consumer Insight Specialists	7	2	4	0	1	
Merchandising Managers	6	1	0	5	0	
R&D/New Product Development						
Design Engineers	11	3	0	8	0	Initiate external hiring program for "top talent" at all levels. Begin to exit careerists – we have 14 of 20 in this category.
Cooling Specialists	4	1	1	2	0	
Laundry Specialists	5	1	0	4	0	
	111	$\sum = 37$		64		

Mentors Needed

We have discussed two major metrics targets for organizations: culture/mindset and strategic talent. How this data is interpreted determines what strategic metrics can be used to intervene and impact the firm's strategy. Proper interpretation of the data is essential. For example, understanding the overall level of mindset—the firm-wide average—is not as important as knowing the source of the data (whether it's coming from a certain business unit, manager, or individual performer). In fact, the use of averages may cause you to select the wrong intervention. For example, deciding that your firm's job satisfaction scores are low and you need to intervene to make your employees "happier" might cause you to provide excessive benefits or higher compensation, which might have a negative impact on the firm's performance. The source of this data provides more strategic information. The changes might be satisfying only your lowest-performing employees, many of whom you wish were no longer with your firm. A simple solution is to ask "What is your latest performance rating?" on every workforce survey. This enables you to cut the data and answer a very important strategic question: Who is more satisfied with our organization, our top performers or our worst performers? Once you have this information, you will know what to do!

In many respects, averages are deceptive metrics for HR ("the mean is a mean HR thing"). Looking at ranges and variances, as well as knowing the source of the data, can provide significant opportunities for strategic workforce interventions that impact the firm's success.

For talent metrics, knowing what roles significantly impact value creation for the firm, to what extent the top talent is in strategic positions, and targets for top talent in these positions is critical. Certainly, if the firm is underperforming, this is a priority relative to the workforce's overall job satisfaction. A simple rule of thumb is that if there is a single incumbent in a strategic position, they should be a top talent. But when many employees are in a single job title, a firm should aspire to have a disproportionate share of top talent relative to the labor market in those roles that have a profound impact on the firm's success, especially related to the competition.

Other common measures using such a strategic perspective would include:

- **Turnover** – Who is turning is more important than a percentage or average turnover. Are you losing A players in A positions (regrettable losses) or C players in A positions (nonregrettable losses)? It makes a huge difference! In fact, if you have very low turnover, the labor market may not want your employees. Low turnover is not necessarily a positive outcome.

* ***Time to fill*** – Are you looking at average time to fill all positions or time to fill strategic positions?

STRATEGIC INTERVENTIONS AND CONCLUSIONS

Metrics are answers to questions. If you don't ask the right question, it is difficult to get a useful answer, especially one that can lead to actions for a more desirable outcome (see **Figure 3**).

HR metrics should help deliver business results. Be certain to understand what information might enable you to make better workforce decisions. Once you have data, ask, "What is this data telling me?" All data tells a story—what is the story that gives insight and points toward appropriate action?

We should also remind ourselves that not all data is quantitative. Qualitative data often enables us to identify organizational mysteries to solve, anomalies to resolve, or questions to ask. However, making progress in resolving those issues may require quantification. Then plan your intervention: What will you differently? If you want different, you must do different. Once you have intervened, ask, "What difference has my intervention made?" Here is where metrics earns its keep, by enabling a firm to assess if it is on target or in the ditch, by suggesting what corrective action might be taken, and by measuring the effectiveness of the corrective action. One final caveat: As the context of your organization changes (e.g., changes in strategy, competitive challenges, new entrants, or technology advances), your workforce metrics will also need to change.

FIGURE 3. TRANSITIONING HR PRACTICES: WHAT QUESTION ARE YOU ANSWERING? / SHOULD BE ANSWERING?

	OLD FOCUS			NEW FOCUS		
	Question Asked	**Data Needed**	**Decisions Made**	**Question Asked**	**Data Needed**	**Decisions Made**
Communication	Is our workforce satisfied / happy?	Traditional job satisfaction survey	Give the workforce more "satisfiers"	Is our top talent in strategy position thrilled with our firm?	Strategic engagement survey	Provide top talent what is needed to retain and motivate them
Work Design	How do we do our work?	Job descriptions	Did we accurately capture how work was done?	Are we focusing on value creation in every job?	Performance Appraisal data/ information	What work is strategic? Support? Surplus?
Selection	Are we "fair" in our selection process?	Adverse impact analysis	Remove all selection tools that have an adverse impact	How well does our top talent in strategic roles compare to the labor supply?	External market assessment of our talent	Keep and reward top talent that benchmarks well against the external labor supply
Training/ Development	How did our participants feel about our training?	Conduct post training "smile" surveys	Remove unpopular instructions	How can we accelerate the skills of our emerging talent in strategic roles?	Identification of developmental needs of emerging talent	Develop rotational, mentors / coaches and training programs for emerging talent in strategic positions
Performance Management	Are performance appraisals completed and on time?	Submission on due date and complete	Withhold increases until performance appraisal forms are completed	Is our performance management system a tool to execute business strategy?	Analysis of alignment of performance management systems	Use zero-based strategic work planning/ budgeting
Rewards	Is our program fair?	Analysis of distribution of increases	Everyone gets a raise	Are we adequately rewarding our value creators for their success?	Assess relationship between strategic performance and extraordinary rewards vs. lower performers	Assure that we never abuse our best performers with inadequate rewards (or over reward our poor performers)

About Richard W. Beatty

Richard W. Beatty's interests focus on strategic workforce planning, HR metrics, rewards, and performance leadership. Beatty has published more than 100 articles on workforce issues in business and management journals as well as 19 books, including "The Workforce Scorecard: Managing Human Capital to Execute Strategy" (Harvard Business School Press, 2005), named a top 10 must-read by Human Resource Executive. His experience in executive education is also extensive. He serves as a core faculty member at the University of Michigan's executive education program and has presented executive education programs at Cornell, Wharton, Dartmouth, Pittsburgh, Utah State, and the Indian School of Business (Hyderabad). Beatty has worked with more than half of the Fortune 100 firms, addressing issues in strategic workforce planning, workforce metrics, and organizational change, and has had long-term working relationships with General Electric, General Motors, Lockheed Martin, ITT, Precision Castparts (PCC), Nissan, NovoNordisk, and Pfizer, among others. A former associate editor of Human Resource Management Journal and the Academy of Management Review, in 2013 he was named one of the 20 most influential "International Thinkers on the Global Workforce" by HR Magazine (UK). He received his BA from Hanover College, his MBA from Emory University, and his PhD from Washington University.

HR'S ROLE IN A WORLD OF PERVASIVE INFORMATION

Wayne Brockbank

Every five years since 1987, the University of Michigan, the RBL Group, and major HR institutions from around the globe have conducted the Human Resource Competency Study,[1] the longest ongoing study of global trends in the human resource field. The study identifies HR competencies and agendas throughout the world that are not done well but, in the pockets where they are done well, have the greatest impact on business performance. This intersection of high impact and low effectiveness is the sweet spot of potential opportunity, future value creation, and emerging competitive advantage.

In our research over the past 25 years, two interesting dynamics have occurred. First, every five years, our findings are initially met with skepticism and doubt. Why? Because these findings show that most competencies and agendas in HR are generally not done well, except in a few select high-performing companies. Thus, the initial and frequent response is, "This is not what HR does in our company." Second, within the subsequent five years or so, skepticism and doubt are generally replaced with commonplace acceptance and the belief that, "Of course, this is what HR does!" In the meantime, the early responders have moved ahead in creating competitive advantage, while others are left in the dust.

- In our first Human Resource Competency Study in 1987, we identified for the first time that HR professionals around the world did not have high levels of business knowledge. However, companies whose HR professionals did have high levels of business knowledge outperformed those that did not. Over the next five years, the assertion that HR professionals should have business knowledge became commonplace. But in 1987, when we made our first assertion, the response was frequently disbelief or outright rejection.

- In our second study in 1992, we identified that HR professionals did not generally have strong change management skills. However, we also found that HR professionals in high-performing companies did have the skills of change management. Again, our data was frequently met with strong skepticism: "OD folks are responsible for change management, not HR professionals." However, within a few years, it became generally accepted that HR departments play a central role in change management initiatives.

- The data from our third study in 1997 identified that HR professionals did not function well as business partners except in the highest-performing firms. Following a few years of skeptical doubt, HR as a business partner was strongly accepted as an HR mantra.

- We conducted our fourth study in 2002. Our research found that linking culture management to external customers was not generally done well, but it was done well in small pockets of high-performing firms. The frequent response was, "Your findings are wrong. We create cultures that focus on employees. Corporate cultures should be internally not externally focused." Today, with the exception of a few monopolistic or oligopolistic firms, it is generally accepted that corporate cultures need to focus on the logic and behavioral patterns that are required by the realities of the competitive marketplace and its external customers.

- By our fifth study in 2007, the data revealed that HR professionals did not generally contribute to the formulation of business strategies, but such was the case in high-performing firms. Today we are seeing a substantial increase of senior HR professionals in the C-suite, and more HR professionals are coming from the business side into HR.

Thus, over the years, the Human Resource Competency Study has been a reasonable predictor of agendas and competencies that have become commonplace, but they were anything but commonplace at the time they were initially identified.

In the 2012 version of our research, more than 20,000 individuals from around the world responded to our survey. The 2012 findings were among the most dramatic of the past 25 years. As in past versions, we sought to identify the HR competencies and agendas that are the weakest among HR professionals but have the greatest business impact. The scarce but vital competency and agenda that emerged in 2012 is the ability of HR professionals to help architect the flow of business information—not just HR information, but business information.

Before diving into the details of the implications of these finding for HR professionals and departments, I will first review the several reasons why this trend has so quickly entered the HR arena. Today, in an average 48-hour period, more information is generated than in the preceding 30,000 years of human history. By the year 2020, this number will shrink dramatically to one hour.[2] Much of this change is being driven by processing capacity and the speed of microprocessors. One of the founders of Intel, Gordon Moore, projected in 1964 that the speed of information processing would double every 18 months. Thus, in the last 50 years, the speed of information processing has increased roughly 850 billion percent.

At the same time, a unit of information that cost $1 to process in 1964 has dropped to millionths of a cent. Furthermore, it is projected that in the next 10 years computer speed will increase approximately 6,500 percent. Not only is information faster, but its exponential proliferation continues to increase at mind-numbing rates. Intel estimates that by 2015, there will be approximately 1,200 quintillion transistors on Earth, or about 1.7 billion for each person.[3] Meanwhile, the cost of international communications has shrunk to almost zero; 200 million photos are uploaded on Facebook every day;[4] and the global YouTube audience logs 6 billion hours every month.[5] And so it continues.

Within this context, there is little wonder that information is transforming virtually every industry and redefining the strategy and functioning of almost all companies. Creating information asymmetries that increase customer awareness, drive top-line growth, and substantially reduce costs is emerging as the source of competitive advantage in this generation. As the definer and creator of organizational capability and differentiating talent, HR cannot help but move into the most fundamental and dramatic trend in global business.

The Human Resource Competency Study has picked up the early warning signals of the implications of information for HR professionals and departments. While there were several important findings in the 2012 study, the most dramatic addressed HR's role relative to different aspects of information. In 2012, we found three information-related subfactors as part of the "technology proponent":

1. HR's role in leveraging social networking is not done well throughout the world and has the lowest impact on business performance.
2. HR's ability to apply information technology to itself (so-called HR analytics) is also not done well and has medium to low impact on overall business performance.
3. Most importantly, HR's role in architecting the flow of information is likewise not done well. But in pockets where it is done well, it has the greatest impact on business performance of any activity in which HR professionals might be involved.

It is on this last finding that the remainder of this article focuses. Specifically, we found that there are four issues that statistically form the subfactor of "designing information flow." They are as follows:

In high-performing firms, HR professionals identify external information and import it into the firm. They spend the time and effort necessary to understand industry structure, competitive trends, customer buying habits, and social, political, and economic dynamics on a global scale. As a result, they are able to identify the most important information on which their firms should focus. With such targeted information identified, they can then ensure that mechanisms are in place to bring such information into the firm.

Examples include the Timken Corporation, in which HR has helped arrange for satisfied and less satisfied customers to speak at annual officer meetings. Through such meetings, senior executives have been given the opportunity to hear and discuss customer reality in a real-time manner. The Disney Corporation frequently uses its front-line employees to conduct market research. This process is facilitated by training, job expectations, communication, and empowerment practices that are provided by HR. GE has developed internal individual and departmental big data analytical capability by recruiting the right talent, providing the appropriate performance metrics, and applying organizational design capabilities that occur through forward-thinking HR practices.

In high-performing firms, HR professionals design practices that encourage and facilitate the electronic and social sharing of information. The BlackRock Investment Institute, for example, provides communication forums in which individuals meet to share important global economic and investment trends with other individuals with whom they would not normally have much contact. In these and multiple related forums, carefully selected and trained individuals glean insights from their discussed and shared information, which enables BlackRock to continue as one of the world's highest-performing investment institutions.

High-performing firms have worked to ensure the optimal sharing of information by overcoming the generally pervasive "Kerr Paradox," which is: "Other than the fact that those who have information do not want to give it and those who need it do not want to receive it, the sharing information is not a problem." Dow Chemical works to overcome this organizational pathology by including collaborative information-sharing in 360s and cultural audits at the department and organization levels. CalSTRS hires and promotes people on the basis of their collaboration capabilities. At CalSTRS, non-collaboration is grounds for dismissal.

In high-performing firms, HR professionals ensure that their collective HR practices are aligned with external customer requirements by taking an "outside in" perspective. And they do so with discipline and focus. Whereas many HR departments maintain a limited line-of-sight to internal operation, the highest-performing firms maintain a disciplined line-of-sight to the outside—to customers, competitors, shareholders, etc. For example, as a central aspect of its management trainee program, Hindustan Unilever Limited in India has new trainees spend up to a month or more living in remote villages among the poor, who comprise "the wealth at the bottom of the pyramid." In those locations, these high-potential university graduates internalize the lifestyle of the company's present and future customers. GE invites key customers to its senior-level leadership courses. The customers receive a world-class training experience while GE's employees get in-depth exposure to their most important customers.

Finally, in high-performing firms, HR professionals recognize that organizations have limited cognitive space. If they are to increase the organization's processing of important external information, they must concurrently reduce processing of less important internal information. To increase the organization's ability to amplify weak (but important) signals, they must reduce the pervasiveness of strong (but less important) signals. This is the intended outcome of GE's well-documented WorkOut. Designed and facilitated by HR professionals, GE's WorkOut enables teams to reduce the low value-adding internal information that exists in the form of meetings, reports, approvals, paperwork, and processes.

As a result of this research, I have spent the last two years visiting with 29 of the leading technology and investment organizations around the world. One of the questions that I have asked is, "Who is the chief information architect?" Frequently, the response was: "The chief information officer." Then I would respond: "I don't mean the chief information officers who overlook the IT systems. I mean who is responsible for architecting the total flow of information into, around, and through the company? Who is it that thinks through big data analytics or morphs unstructured data into quantifiable spread sheets? Who thinks through rigorously designed and executed social algorithms that trump the competition?"

In two of the 29 companies, the CEO was identified as playing that role. In one case, that role was occupied by individuals with strong OD and HR backgrounds. In the remainder, this role was ambiguously fulfilled or nonexistent, and I received a resultant blank stare. Given the centrality of information for competitive advantage, these results are a bit troublesome. Thus, the opportunity to add value through this centrally important agenda is open to HR professionals who can grasp the importance of information and are willing to lead.

In summary, HR's activities relative to architecting the flow of business information are not currently done well in most companies around the world—but where they are done well, they create substantial value. Thus these activities represent potential competitive advantage. As given above, this paper has provided several insights about HR that might influence this centrally important organizational agenda. In the next five to seven years, HR's role in leveraging business information as competitive advantage will be more commonplace. In the meantime, architecting the flow of information is a profound area of opportunity for HR. Rather than respond to the future that others create, HR departments and professionals can create the future for others.

About Wayne Brockbank

Wayne Brockbank is a clinical professor of business at the University of Michigan's Ross School of Business and a co-faculty director and core instructor of its Advanced Human Resource Executive Program. Over the past 20 years, the school's HR executive programs have been consistently rated as the best in the United States and Europe by The Wall Street Journal, BusinessWeek, and Leadership Excellence. Brockbank is also a distinguished visiting professor at IAE Management and Business School, Universidad Austral (Buenos Aires, Argentina), and has been on the visiting faculty at universities in numerous other countries. In 2013, he was acknowledged as one of the top 20 global HR thinkers by HR Magazine. His research and consulting focus on linkages between business strategy and human resource practices; creating high-performance corporate cultures; and key levers that drive business performance. He has published seven books (with colleagues) and numerous articles and book chapters on these topics. Outside of his university teaching and research responsibilities, Brockbank serves as an advisor to the management committee of the Abu Dhabi Investment Authority on issues of strategy, organization, and HR. He has consulted in these areas with major corporations on every continent. He has also served on the board of directors for the Society of Human Resource Management and the Human Resource Planning Society. Brockbank completed his PhD at UCLA, where he specialized in organization theory, business strategy, and international business. He received his BA and MA in organizational behavior from Brigham Young University.

---

[1] Dave Ulrich, Jon Younger, Wayne Brockbank, and Mike Ulrich, HR from the Outside In (New York, NY: McGraw-Hill, 2012).

[2] Eric Schmidt and Jared Cohen, The New Digital Age (London: John Murray, 2012).

[3] Dave James, "Intel Predicts 1,200 Quintillion Transistors in the World by 2015," TechRadar, 13 September 2011. (http://www.techradar.com/news/computing-components/processors/intel-predicts-1-200-quintillion-transistors-in-the-world-by-2015-1025851)

[4] http://expandedramblings.com/index.php/by-the-numbers-17-amazing-facebook-stats/

[5] https://www.youtube.com/yt/press/statistics.html

HR DISRUPTED: THE NEXT AGENDA FOR DELIVERING VALUE

Diane J. Gherson

It isn't often that a group of professionals can say with confidence that they stand at an important moment in history. This is one such moment for HR.

If that sounds like overreach, step back and consider the moment in which we find ourselves today. Over the past decade, we have seen the convergence of three historic shifts that are reshaping business and technology.

- **Data** – The volume, velocity, and variety of data and analytics provide more granular and customized information about not just past patterns and trends but inferences from the "big data" created by the internet revolution and predictions about the future. Analytics change how we do work and make decisions. Predictive analytics have led to prescriptive analytics and reshaped entire industries, as Netflix has done in home entertainment.
- **Cloud** – This is not just a source of greater productivity but the basis for fundamentally new business models. Information (data, movies, high-school term papers, etc.) can now be managed and stored "as a service," without the need for on-premise servers and licensed applications. This allows for much more flexibility, mobility, and agility in managing information.

- *Social engagement on mobile platforms* – Individuals are now interacting in new ways with institutions, reframing their relationships. Physical locations matter less than social connections. Facebook-type technologies inside the enterprise have allowed people to share and build on one another's ideas, data, and work products, creating a richer dialogue and workspace than ever before (and certainly a step change from email).

Any one of these forces would have been enough to usher in a new era of technology. Together, they are redefining the agenda of global business.

And these technology trends are reshaping HR. For example, we can now buy HR software and HRIS as a service on the cloud, instead of investing in costly and inflexible on-premise systems. We now make people-related decisions and compensation or training investments through advanced analytics rather than standardized processes or benchmarking. We now serve up more and more of our programs—from learning to health care enrollment—on mobile devices. We use social chat features to enhance management development or respond to issues. And we find ourselves managing a litany of new business controls to ensure protection of personal and confidential data.

At the same time, these trends are radically reshaping expectations of what HR can and should deliver—both in terms of HR services and in terms of strategic impact.

What will HR services look like when we focus on user experience in the era of cloud, analytics, mobile, social, and security technologies? Certainly the recruitment function is leading the way, with a shift to passive recruiting using Google+, Instagram, Xing (Europe), WeChat (China), Weibo (China), RenRen (China), and YouTube—as well as through online contests, video interviews, and integrating the candidate experience on smartphones.

But while advancements in recruiting offer a glimpse into the future, by and large the rest of HR services still feel less like Zappos and more like the IRS. So how can we modernize our approach? I believe there are two main areas that will have a disproportionate influence on the future of our profession—analytics and engagement.

IMPORTANCE OF HR ANALYTICS

There was a time when HR advice relied heavily on benchmarking. We would ask, "What do most/other successful companies do?" Today, with analytics, we can mine huge amounts of data and offer more granular, customized solutions, including more flexible responses. Using outcome data like revenues, productivity, hiring yield, individual performance, or employee engagement, we can help our leaders understand the probability of success of certain decisions. For years, we have struggled with sales incentives and tried to create norms and rules for how incentives would change people's behaviors. With modern analytics, we can define more accurately which incentives work with each employee and for which assignment. We can also define the extent to which goals should be "stretch" versus doable, and we can change goals depending on the situation.

At IBM, analytics now enable us to predict an employee's propensity to leave. In fact, several of our HR employees have obtained a US patent for our proactive retention algorithms. Each year, we run proactive retention programs where we increase the salaries of employees with a high propensity to leave. This program has resulted in net savings of $131 million, with savings measured as the avoided cost of hiring a replacement, net of the investment to retain the employees. Using control groups, we have validated the "propensity to leave" calculation within less than one point of attrition.

With the availability of social engagement and analytics, HR programs have moved from annual events to ongoing works in progress. For example, at IBM, we recently rolled out a recognition program where 57 percent of receivers were very satisfied or satisfied. Our vendor informed us this compared favorably to the industry average of 40 percent in the first year of implementation—but is this really acceptable? We were able to quickly ask those not satisfied how we might modify the recognition program to better meet their needs. We now have a granular understanding of what kind of recognition has the highest impact on different populations.

Social analytics also give us advance warnings of what might be happening among our employees. We monitor blog posts about the company by employees and others. While respecting privacy, we can gauge positive, neutral, or negative trends from social media. We have been able to anticipate employee engagement scores by tracking social media trends. In some emerging markets, we have been able to anticipate labor unrest and respond before the unrest led to disruptive actions.

Another strategic use of analytics is workforce management, where headcount management has given way to skills management. Skills—including depth of skill—have become an important currency in flatter, more fluid organizations, and there is an increasing need for real-time assessment of skills gaps and redundancies. Analytics can be used to infer employee expertise from the vast data sources inside companies—blogs, publications, resumes, projects, and so on.

Because skills are changing so rapidly in technology, skills inventories are hard and complex to keep up to date. At IBM, we developed an app to find employees with specific expertise, anywhere in the world. The search returns each expert's areas of expertise, organizational chart, common connections, and smartphone contact information. This is now being used at an enterprise level for workforce planning, such as to identify gaps in "hot" skills for recruitment and training investments.

HR professionals need to develop analytics capabilities. Hard as it is to imagine, there was a time only 30 years ago when professionals believed that typing proficiency was not a necessary skill. I believe we are now in the same situation with analytics. HR professionals have rich data at our fingertips, and tools to undertake predictive and prescriptive analytics. It won't be long before analytics departments go the way of typing pools.

SHIFTING FROM HR PROCESS TO EMPLOYEE EXPERIENCES

And all this is happening at a time when our employees are experiencing a revolution in their consumer experience outside of work. With the move to mobile access and social technology, employees experience organizations differently than in the past, and their bar is much higher. Their experience on retail platforms has taught them to expect a high level of personalization, feedback, transparency, and adaptation in real time. They want all systems to know them; they want to participate in the design and improvement of programs that affect them; and they want to be able to give feedback or ask questions in the moment and get a response within 30 minutes.

How do our HR systems and programs do against these expectations? For the past two decades, HR has been all about process efficiency—standardization, outsourcing, globalization, and manager self-service—all so HR professionals could focus on more strategic issues. The unhappy byproduct of this era is the employee experience. While each of our processes— compensation, recognition, global mobility, benefits, internal transfers, and so on—became more streamlined and more efficient, we outsourced the coordination across these silos to the manager and the employee. While we may be more efficient than ever before, the experience we deliver comes up short compared to what our employees experience every day on retail platforms.

For example, a new employee needs to get a laptop from IT, a badge from security, office space from administrative services, benefits and payroll paperwork from compensation, onboarding from learning, and a welcome from her manager. We need to offer employees a customized and integrated onboarding experience, including a chance to socialize with other new hires and share questions and answers.The same can be said of employee separations, which often generate a painfully complex array of disparate tasks for the manager.

And this brings us to the real potential of combining analytics and employee experience. We will be able to anticipate what employees may need. Using agile methods, HR professionals will operate less as subject matter experts and more as custodians of the employee and manager experience.

No matter how you come at this, the answer isn't extending existing HR practices. It's completely reimagining how our work is done, how processes run, and how we integrate the core of the enterprise with the capabilities of individual professionals. When we do these things in HR, we can create a workplace that is more effective for our people, and one where they feel like they matter—and have a say in the things that matter to them.

I am an optimist about the future of our profession. For years (or even decades), HR has sought to make an impact. Technological advances are once again enabling HR to shift to higher ground, just as we shifted from personnel to human resources years ago. Today, it's about how we capture the incredible wealth of data and insight about talent that will shape a company's future. Talent is the center of everything we do. To compete in new industries, we have to create an environment that builds talent—with people who can learn, adapt, lead, and innovate in a workplace that is interactive and transparent. HR, with a focus on analytics and employee engagement, becomes the transformative force to shape the future of the enterprise.

About Diane J. Gherson

Diane J. Gherson is senior vice president of human resources at IBM, responsible for the 400,000 employee company's quality of leadership and talent, workforce strategies, and HR operations worldwide. Prior to this role she served as IBM's vice president of talent, leading the company's leadership development and succession planning, learning, career development, workforce management, global mobility programs, and recruitment functions worldwide. During her tenure in this role, IBM was named No.1 in Fortune's "Global Top Company for Leaders" study—the first company to earn this recognition two consecutive times. She also was awarded a US patent in the field of predictive analytics. Previously, Gherson led human resources for IBM Global Business Services and served as IBM's vice president of compensation and benefits, transforming the company's $30 billion portfolio to drive greater value for the enterprise. Before joining IBM in 2002, she spent eight years as a partner in the consulting firm Towers Watson, leading the firm's worldwide employee and performance management compensation practice. Gherson holds a BA with honors from Trinity College, University of Toronto, and an MA in industrial and labor relations from Cornell University. She also completed her course work toward a PhD in management at MIT's Sloan School of Management.

WORKFORCE ANALYTICS FOR STRATEGY EXECUTION

Mark Huselid

Business leaders face substantial challenges and opportunities in the current global economic environment. Customer expectations for faster, better, and cheaper goods and services are increasing at an accelerating pace, in no small part due to the creation of global markets and distribution systems. And, more and better data and information have enabled precise segmentation and targeting of customers, suppliers, and even the workforce.

The rapid development of these trends has created what might be called a global "arbitrage" of talent, where employees are much more likely than ever to (1) work for multiple employers and (2) live in different cities or countries than their employers (including this author!). The upside of these trends is that leaders now have unfettered access to a global market for talent. The downside is that their competitors have these same opportunities. In a highly competitive market, one of the last sources of competitive advantages is talent, and by extension the way in which talent is managed.

What are the implications of these trends for workforce management? It's an old saying in the field of organizational design that human resource management practices should be "as common as possible—but as different as necessary." But a segmented, differentiated, and highly competitive customer space means that a conventional, hierarchical approach to workforce management may no longer be effective. Indeed, many firms routinely spend 50 percent to 70 percent of their revenues on direct and indirect workforce costs, but often these investments are not well measured or managed.

Addressing these issues means that leaders (both HR and line) should be prepared to develop a comprehensive understanding of *how* the workforce contributes to their strategic success. This means that firms needs to manage their workforce strategically, including (1) identifying the *strategic work* that is truly necessary to execute firm strategy; (2) investing in *differentiated management systems* that support that work; and (3) designing and implementing *targeted measurement systems* (HR function and workforce scorecards) designed to help to hold line managers accountable for the firm's most expensive resource, the workforce. HR managers and HR activities in the future should be grounded in these three activities.

IDENTIFYING STRATEGIC WORK

In "The Differentiated Workforce,"[1] my co-authors and I made several key points about the importance of effectively managing a global workforce:

- There are many, many roles that can destroy wealth in organizations—but only a very few roles that can actually create great wealth. Identifying and managing these roles is a key component of strategic workforce leadership.
- In contrast to the conventional wisdom, you probably don't need—and truly can't afford—world-class talent in all positions.
- All (or at least most) jobs are *important*, but only a few jobs are truly *strategic*.
- "A" or *strategic positions* are those that impact strategy and exhibit high variability in employee performance. Simply put, these are the positions that provide the greatest potential upside for improved organizational performance. Improving the talent in these roles can have a significant impact on your strategic success.
- Strategic positions can appear at any level in the firm. In fact, because employees in lower-level positions have shorter job tenures and have generally experienced fewer developmental opportunities, they often represent the greatest ROI investment opportunities.

DIFFERENTIATING WORKFORCE MANAGEMENT SYSTEMS

Because some work—and some jobs—have relatively greater impact on strategy execution than others, it should follow that a strategic approach to workforce management should identify and help to improve the performance in these roles. In "The Differentiated Workforce" we also argued that:

- Great firms manage their workforce like a portfolio and leverage its return—investing disproportionately in the highest-return *strategic work* and *strategic positions*.
- But…most organizations continue to invest in talent by hierarchical level, not by strategic impact.
- As a result, over time firms tend to *under*invest in strategic work and *over*-invest in nonstrategic work.

What this means is that leaders need to identify the work that they need to execute their strategy, and then to make sure that top talent holds the jobs that contain this work. Implementing these concepts in practice will require us to make strategic (and often tough) choices about how and where we are going to invest in the workforce.

DEVELOPING AND IMPLEMENTING WORKFORCE ANALYTICS

So where does this leave us? We believe that there is an "information failure" concerning talent in most firms, in that the most expensive asset with the greatest upside potential (talent) is the least well measured and managed. Solving this problem will require measures that are as differentiated as the talent and the HR practices they are intended to monitor and help to implement. Simply put, a differentiated approach to workforce management means that the analytics we employ need to be differentiated as well. But this approach is often at odds with conventional approaches to HR and workforce measurement.

FROM SCORECARDS TO ANALYTICS

Interest in the measurement of the workforce and the HR function has a long history in the social sciences—well over 100 years. For much of this time the focus has been on identifying and measuring benchmark data associated with the activities housed in the HR *function*. What is new and potentially important is the availability of significantly enhanced data and informatics, and a simultaneous shift in emphasis from the activities of the HR function to the productive outcomes of the workforce.

The critical element is to move from a focus on *levels* associated with a particular workforce attribute (e.g., What is our cost per hire?) to understanding the *impact* of the workforce on business-level outcomes (e.g., How might an increase in the quality of our project managers affect new product cycle time?). In short, the emphasis of the current focus on workforce analytics is no longer about justifying the existence of the HR function but about executing the firm's strategy through the workforce.

MEASURES ARE ANSWERS TO QUESTIONS!
The process of executing strategy through the workforce begins with the identification and quantification of the strategic capabilities—bundles of information, technology, and people— that drive strategic success. The next step in the process is to quantify the gaps in the requisite strategic capabilities and the work that is required to close those gaps. This work can then become the focus of managers' efforts at performance improvement, which begin with a series of questions that ask, in essence, "Where do we start?" For example, managers could begin by asking:

- What strategic capabilities are needed to win, and how do we measure the activities (strategic work) that help to create those capabilities?
- How well is our strategic work currently being performed? What work needs to be added or deleted?
- What are the key strategic positions in our firm and how should they be managed?
- What is our inventory of talent in our strategic positions?
- What do we need to do to close the gap between the talent that we have and the talent that we need?

The next step in the process of driving managerial accountability for the workforce is to clearly operationalize the "destination metrics" associated with workforce success. While necessary, metrics are not sufficient to drive a strategic approach to workforce management. Also required is a very clear understanding of "what causes what" in your workforce.

How do we develop such an understanding? The process begins with the development of a theory or model (based on the previous academic research as well as your unique understanding of your business) that shows *what causes what* in your organization. The next phase in the process is data collection and analysis.

But first determine *what to measure—then* collect reliable and valid data. Don't let data availability drive the questions that you ask. Instead of asking "How can we used the data we have to help the business?" ask instead "What questions must the business be able to answer, and where will we find the data?" Put differently, don't start by asking "What data do we have?" Start by asking "What data do we need?"

Finally, use analytical tools to estimate the impact of talent on the organizational outcomes you care about. Conventional approaches employ correlation and regression analyses. More recent advances and innovations (many facilitated by the availability of "big data") include network analyses, neural networks, and a variety of new machine learning techniques. Finally, data processing platforms such as Hadoop and a wide variety of data visualization tools have been developed that can help turn data into usable information for executives. Completing this work may mean that the HR team will need to develop or acquire new competencies in workforce analytics.

STRATEGIC HR PERFORMANCE MANAGEMENT: A NEW COMPETENCY

Many authors have written extensively about the importance of talent in executing strategy, and the competencies and behaviors needed from the HR managers charged with helping the organization making this happen. For example, Dave Ulrich and his colleagues have identified HR manager competencies associated with positioning the workforce (and workplace) for competitive advantage, becoming an activist for the workforce, building workforce capabilities, becoming a champion for change, and innovating HR practices and information technology.[2]

Going forward, how can we ensure that both HR and line managers effectively adopt workforce analytics? We believe that both groups of managers will need to develop skills in the design and use of workforce analytics. Some of these competencies will need to be resident in the firm's IT function, including data acquisition and management, data storage and auditing, data access for analytics team, data analysis, data visualization, and communication. But many new skills will be needed to help the leadership team capitalize on the opportunities afforded by workforce analytics.

In The "HR Scorecard,"[3] we focused on the competencies needed in HR leaders to design and execute effective workforce analytics systems. We termed this competency "strategic HR performance management," which we subdivided into four dimensions:

1. *Critical causal thinking* – As its core, designing and implementing an effective workforce management system requires managers to think strategically about "what causes what" in their organizations. Because there is often a long lag between investments in talent and the reflection of these investments in firm performance, it is especially important to be able to show the causal path that reflects how improvement in talent and employee behavior affect important organizational outcomes. Many firms have successfully used strategy maps to describe this process, which can become effective teaching tools to help the workforce understand what is expected of them and where to focus their improvement efforts.

2. *Understanding the principles of good measurement* – A second capability has to do with the ability to clearly define what we mean by each dimension of "performance" and the subsequent ability to develop metrics for those constructs. Not all metrics are created equal, and there can be substantial differences in the reliability and validity of workforce measures. Good metrics will not only exhibit reliability but also provide an adequate representation of the underlying construct that they are intended to assess.

3. *Estimating causal relationships* – Once you have developed a series of hypotheses about "what causes what" in your firm and have developed reliable and valid measures of workforce success, you are ready to begin to connect your workforce measures (independent variables) to unit- or organizational-level outcomes (dependent measures). These measures can be either quantitative or qualitative, but in either case the statistical tools can help managers "connect the dots" between an investment in talent and subsequent job performance. In most organizations there are two broad levels of this competency: the ability to conduct the analyses (needed by relatively few employees); and the ability to understand and act on the implications of the results (needed by many more managers).

4. *Communicating HR strategic performance results to senior line managers* – Finally, we have argued that measures are answers to questions, and these questions should be focused on the processes through which talent helps to execute strategy. Measures need to be communicated and well understood to drive effective decision-making. Many new tools are available to HR executives

to facilitate this process, and the ability to leverage these tools is reflected in the final component of strategic HR performance management.

IN SUMMARY

The challenges and opportunities associated with managing a workforce and workplace strategically are greater than ever. A key component of this process is enhancing managerial accountability for talent. An important step is to design and implement systems of workforce metrics and analytics that help managers ask and answer the key questions about the workforce—and then act on these insights!

About Mark Huselid

Mark Huselid is a distinguished professor of workforce analytics and director of the Center for Workforce Analytics at the D'Amore-McKim School of Business at Northeastern University. Prior to joining Northeastern, Huselid was a distinguished professor of HR strategy in the School of Management and Labor Relations at Rutgers University. His current academic research and consulting activities focus on the linkages between HR management systems, corporate strategy, and firm performance. He also has an active research and consulting program focused on the development of balanced measurement systems to reflect the contribution of the workforce, workforce management systems, and the HR management function to business success. Huselid was editor of the Human Resource Management Journal from 2000 to 2004 and is a current or former member of numerous professional and academic boards. A frequent speaker and writer, he has delivered more than 500 presentations throughout the United States, Europe, Asia, and Africa and has written several books, including "The HR Scorecard: Linking People, Strategy, and Performance" (with Brian Becker and Dave Ulrich, Harvard Business Press, 2001), which was translated into 10 languages and was an international bestseller. His newest book, "Disrupting Workforce Competition: Executing Strategy Through Strategic Work, Workforce Differentiation, and Workforce Analytics," is currently in development.

1   Brian E. Becker, Mark A. Huselid, and Richard W. Beatty, The Differentiated Workforce: Transforming Talent into Strategic Impact (Cambridge, MA: Harvard Business Press, 2009).
2   Dave Ulrich, Wayne Brockbank, Jon Younger, and Mike Ulrich, Global HR Competencies: Mastering Competitive Value from the Outside In (New York: McGraw Hill, 2012).
3   Brian E. Becker, Mark A. Huselid, and Dave Ulrich, The HR Scorecard: Linking People, Strategy, and Performance (Cambridge, MA: Harvard Business Press, 2001).

DON'T FORGET ABOUT THE MACHINERY

Mark James

While there are many books written on leadership, most of them focus on charisma and motivating people. In my view, there are three important areas leaders need to focus on and get right:

1. ***Pick the right strategy.*** This is important, because otherwise you can motivate your organization to follow you in the wrong direction. Sometimes it isn't clear if you picked the right strategy until years have passed.
2. ***Motivate people to pursue your strategy.*** Picking the right strategy isn't enough if you can't motivate anyone to pursue it. This is the most visible aspect of leadership, and it gets plenty of attention.
3. ***Understand how the machinery works.*** This area gets very little attention and yet is arguably the most important of the three. If you don't understand how the machinery works, it doesn't matter that you picked the right strategy and motivated people to pursue it—you will be continually disappointed with the results and wonder why your strategy isn't working like it should. You may decide you haven't motivated people sufficiently and put all your effort there, only to get the same disappointing results.

Understanding how the machinery works means using business acumen to know how all the pieces fit together and how you can maximize results by leveraging the machinery. You have to know which levers to pull and what happens when you pull them. You have to understand how things actually happen in the organization, where the levers are and how they work—and make sure they have been pulled instead of trusting what people tell you without verification.

How do you learn about the machinery? Put in the time and effort. Go see how widgets are made and how the process works so that you thoroughly understand it instead of just saying, "I am strategic and don't get involved in tactical things." If you don't understand how things work and how people think, you will continually be confused as to why they won't execute your strategy effectively despite all of your motivational attempts to get them to do it. You have to understand how things happen in the organization, including human nature and the effect of culture.

In addition, you need a strong management operating system (MOS) to ensure you know whether things are getting done the way you expect them to be done. One of the primary reasons leaders fail is lack of a strong MOS. Your MOS will ensure you know exactly what is going on and how it is going. It will help you verify that work is being completed—and in the right way. The earlier you identify any issues, the easier it is to make a course correction. Making adjustments later takes a lot more time, energy, and money. Without a MOS, people are going to deliver negative surprises.

One of the ways I know what's happening in my organization is through an annual "Voice of the Customer" survey. This year, more than 3,400 managers around the world responded to our seventh annual survey, providing feedback that helps us ensure the work we're doing aligns with business priorities and indicates areas where we need to improve. One of the areas we receive feedback on is our speed of service. In an effort to continuously improve, we have implemented and executed an action plan. The entire HR organization completed a self-assessment related to speed, and those results were analyzed and compared to our survey results to identify critical gaps. In addition, all HR employees were required to attend a specially designed training that provided strategies for improving speed and responsiveness.

ONE HONEYWELL

I also have been asked how culture is created and sustained within a large, diversified global company like Honeywell. It starts at the top. I have been fortunate to work for Dave Cote, a chairman and CEO who has successfully transformed and led the company for more than a decade. That strong, consistent leadership goes a long way. He picks the right strategies, motivates people to achieve them, and truly understands how the machinery works.

We also have a robust "One Honeywell" culture that allows us to do amazing things. We stay focused on great positions in good industries, and drive our "Five Initiatives" (Growth, Productivity, Cash, People, and our Enablers, which are critical business initiatives) and our "12 Behaviors"—one of which is leadership impact—to succeed globally in a competitive world. Culture is a big part of our business model and really does make a difference. Our pay-for-performance culture creates differentiation— in our technologies, from our competitors, and among our employees—that drives growth. Ours is a culture of adaptability. Everything around you is always evolving, and if you're not evolving faster, you are falling behind. We strive to continually do two seemingly competing things well. We aim to achieve the flexibility of a small company along with the efficiency of strong common processes and deep technical expertise.

Over the last six years, more than 85 percent of our top 700 management hires have come from within. We provide opportunities that span businesses, functions, and geographies. This helps drive One Honeywell. Because we're multi-industry and a big global company in more than 100 different countries, we are in a unique position to promote from within. We can shift talent between groups, giving our leaders more breadth, depth, and experience that can only be gained by working in different businesses and geographies. There is little downside to this—we gain different viewpoints and insight, without losing our top talent. In addition, by hiring from within we are able to ensure a culture fit, which is always a risk when hiring externally.

BE A SELF-AWARE LEARNER

As a leader, self-awareness and being a good learner go hand-in-hand. The more you know and understand about a wide variety of topics, the more effective you can be. I have found that the best ideas can come from outside your area of expertise. In HR, I've lifted best practices from integrated supply chain, engineering, and general managers to improve our HR organization, as opposed to getting those ideas from other HR organizations. Having the ability to recognize something that works really well in a group not related to your team—spotting the pattern that makes it successful—and applying it to your area can be a tremendous competitive advantage. That thinking should never stop.

Being a self-aware learner in HR means keeping an open mind and going to meetings that aren't just HR meetings. If you ask questions about things outside your area, eventually you're able to solve more problems for people because you've been able to broaden your knowledge. You need to stay in learner mode and help people solve the things that keep them awake at night, not the things that you think they should do.

Being self-aware means knowing what are you good at—and, conversely, what are you not good at. What tendencies do you have? Once you know what your own strengths and weaknesses are, you need to figure out how to improve your weak areas and surround yourself with people who have offsetting strengths, while making sure that you give them the opportunity to weigh in on different decisions.

About Mark James

Mark James is Honeywell's senior vice president of human resources, procurement, and communications, a position he was appointed to in 2007. Honeywell is a $40 billion diversified technology and manufacturing company serving customers in the aerospace, automation control, automotive, and chemical industries. A member of Honeywell's senior leadership team, James is responsible for leading global human resources strategy and programs for the company's 140,000 employees in more than 100 countries. This includes organization and talent development, staffing, learning, compensation and benefits, labor and employee relations, HR services, and the Six Sigma training organization. His role also includes leading the company's procurement, communications, and aviation functions. Prior to this position, James served as vice president of HR and communications for Honeywell Aerospace, vice president of HR for Aerospace Electronic Systems, and director of HR for Federal Manufacturing

& Technologies. Prior to Honeywell, James held a variety of HR positions with Iomega, JM Family Enterprises (Toyota distributor), AT&T, and Lockheed Martin. He is a designated Senior Professional in Human Resources (SPHR), a Certified Compensation Professional (CCP), a Certified Benefits Professional (CBP), and a certified Six Sigma Leadership Black Belt. In 2013, he was named "HR Executive of the Year" by HR Executive magazine. James holds a master's degree in public administration from the University of Utah and a business administration degree in personnel and industrial relations from Utah State University.

DEVELOPING AN EVIDENCE-BASED HRM THROUGH THE CONSCIENTIOUS RELIANCE ON EVIDENCE, SOUND DECISION PROCESS, AND STAKEHOLDERS PERSPECTIVES

Denise M. Rousseau

I am going to make a case for the future of human resource management (HRM) as an evidence-based practice. As applied in fields as diverse as medicine, criminology, and education, evidence-based practice means the conscientious use of scientific knowledge, organizational facts, valid decision processes, and judgment honed through reflection and experience, with attention to stakeholder concerns in the decisions made.

In effect, this means that the HRM of the future will be conducted increasingly by practitioners who act as professionals. To be professional in one's work is to rely on specialized knowledge acquired through education and lifelong learning, to reflectively develop over time the ability to make well-informed judgments, and to adhere to a code of ethics.

MANY FLAVORS OF HRM
Still, HRM is no monolith. Like a lot of organizational endeavors, HRM practice today is a mixed bag. Some of its practitioners have considerable professional education in the domain. Others have very little. Some are up-to-date in the

psychology of human development, selection, and assessment; know the works of Wayne F. Cascio or Dave Ulrich cold; and do statistical analyses with ease. Others lack a technical background in HR and are afraid of numbers.

Some folks act as partners, proactively developing, evaluating, and redesigning HRM programs to better support their organization and its members. Others are compliantly bureaucratic, letting the legal department and company custom drive their practice. Many more practice HRM somewhere in the middle. HRM practitioners in big organizations and small, public and private, and in the Americas, Asia, and Europe do a lot of things differently. But evidence-based practice is adaptable by all.

INNOVATORS AND EARLY ADOPTERS ON THE LEADING EDGE OF HRM

When we talk about the future of HRM, we are looking ahead to those firms whose HRM practitioners make the acquisition, development, and use of knowledge the cornerstone of their strategic and professional practice. These savvy (defined as well-informed and perceptive) organizations can be corporations as varied as the Gap and the Royal Bank of Canada and nonprofits as varied as DonorsChoose and the United States Army. These sentinel organizations use scientific principles in selecting and developing talented people (and in many more HRM activities) and systematically gather organizational data to assess the results. Along the way, their practitioners are redefining what it means to be an HRM professional.

SO WHAT IS IT THAT EVIDENCE-BASED HRM PRACTITIONERS (WILL) DO?

Evidence-based HRM (EBHRM) practitioners know that tradition, authority, and taken-for-granted assumptions about what works (and what doesn't) just won't cut it in a more complicated world. They know that "shiny object syndrome"—that is, chasing the latest hot new fad in HRM—is likely to be a waste of time. (Engagement, anyone?) They know it takes conscientious and cumulative effort to bring greater value to the organization and its members in the way work gets done. To effectively organize people and work in complex organizations requires a bundle of mutually reinforcing practices and systems. Developing these requires sound knowledge of both science and the local setting.

EBHRM practitioners understand they cannot know everything upfront that sound decisions require. But they do know how to *identify the questions that need answers* in order to make a good decision or resolve a problem—or to advise others in doing so. Asking the right questions is a matter of critical thinking, to get beyond assumptions and old habits in order to identify potential drivers of good decisions. A big issue here is to go beyond the easily available data from last quarter's financials or the most recent glitch everybody is talking about. Organizations are full of mysteries! An EBHRM practitioner is part scientist and part detective. Are ethics complaints going up from year to year? OK, so what questions might we need to answer? (Hmm, do these complaints continue despite the ethics program every new manager attends?)

Of course, EBHRM practitioners also *know how to get answers* to those questions. This means being able to search the scientific research related to their questions (www.googlescholar; www.CEBMa.org). They are able to appraise the relevance and value of the research they find. But they also realize that their own organization is a source of important evidence. (It might be worthwhile to read that stack of ethics complaints to see if any patterns exist. An EBHRM practitioner did just that and found that most came from employees complaining of mistreatment by their boss.) Obtaining, analyzing, and interpreting organizational evidence related to important practice questions are ongoing activities for EBHRM practitioners.

EBHRM practitioners know how to run experiments to figure out what decision or solution might work in their organization. Looking to resolve the ethics issues employees were raising, that conscientious EBHRM practitioner identified the business units with the highest rates of complaints and, after further inquiry, began developing a training program targeting improved procedural justice and managerial trustworthiness. The training was rolled out in a way that randomized participation over several waves, allowing managers trained later to serve as controls for those trained earlier.

Doing experiments to test out ideas is likely to become increasingly important in the future. Experiments are key when situations arise for which there is no precedent (that is, no research, no existing data, and no relevant prior experience). In truly novel circumstances, the only way forward is to learning by doing. Little wonder that the US Army systematically used after-action reviews to figure out what worked and what didn't when confronted with a challenge few armies had ever successfully dealt with before—peacekeeping in Haiti, Bosnia, and elsewhere.

Evidence-based HRM practitioners know how to *bring the array of stakeholders together* to integrate their perspectives into the decision process. Part of being evidence-based is recognizing that human judgment is fundamentally fallible. Decisions often have implications invisible to the decision-maker, a particular problem in companies where pressures can narrow the alternatives considered and limit the evidence weighed. Matters blocked out of by one decision-maker's mindset can create real trouble when the decision is carried out. Getting input from employees and managers at different levels, community members, and clients can help balance out immediate situational pressures and the narrowing of judgment for decision-makers under stress.

A given decision can involve multiple objectives, leading to tradeoffs between cost and human well-being and between short- and long-term goals. Its increasingly part of evidence-based practice to pay explicit attention to multiple objectives when framing decisions in order to help resolve ambiguities that decision-makers routinely face. This consideration of diverse interests and potential tradeoffs often leads to the use of higher-quality evidence. A key idea here is that attention to diverse stakeholder concerns can help address the ethical issues associated with HRM decisions, where harm that might otherwise be done can be prevented by deliberately reaching out to stakeholders with a different vantage point.

Last, evidence-based HRM practitioners don't just make better decisions—they *manage their decisions better*. They know when to use systematic—that is, slow and careful— decision-making processes, especially when critical information is widely distributed across sources and stakeholders (where to locate a new facility, how to reconcile the different HRM systems of newly merged business units, etc.). They know when fast decision-making can yield good outcomes.

This is the case where strong evidence already exists about what works. In these familiar situations, EBHRM practitioners recognize the value of developing and implementing routines and checklists around repeat activities such as how to run a meeting, develop a training program, give feedback, or make a change in HRM policy. They also know how to deal with truly novel situations where no good information exists in the organization or in science—learning by doing, evaluating the results, and adapting as you go.

MADAM ZAZA PREDICTS THE FUTURE

Just so you know, I am not pulling these notions out of my hat. I meet such HRM practitioners regularly through a variety of EBHRM communities in North America and Europe. These communities have formed around the use of data analytics, rapid evidence reviews, and decision support tools in order to improve the quality of HRM-related decisions and practices—all under the umbrella of evidence-based practice.

In truth, I may manifest the availability bias that Daniel Kahneman describes in "Thinking Fast and Slow." But as is the case with many innovative trends that have historical forces behind them—from automation to globalization—the signs of their trajectory can be visible years before. The force for greater evidence use in professional practice is observable in the evidence-based practice movement that began in medicine in the late 1980s. It has joined with another escalating force promoting access to scientific and other evidence (and a lot else)—that is to say, the internet.

And last but not least, these forces reinforce and are supported in turn by yet another trend toward demanding increasing accountability: the expectation that decisions, corporate as well as public, should be justifiable, fact-based, and transparent. (Of course, one hazard of trends is mimicry and cheap knockoffs, so I am not too disturbed by ads touting "evidence-based fitness!") Thus, I suggest that the way forward for HRM will be led by the professional HRM practitioner—an innovator, adopter, and community member in evidence-based practice.

About Denise M. Rousseau

Denise M. Rousseau is the H.J. Heinz II University Professor of Organizational Behavior and Public Policy at Carnegie Mellon University's Heinz College and Tepper School of Business. She is also the faculty director of the Institute for Social Innovation and chair of the Health Care Policy and Management Program. She served as president of the Academy of Management from 2004 to 2005 and editor-in-chief of the Journal of Organizational Behavior from 1998 to 2007. In 2007, she founded the

Evidence-Based Management Collaborative, a network of scholars, consultants, and practicing managers that promotes evidence-informed organizational practices and managerial decision-making; its outreach today operates as the Center for Evidence-Based Management. Rousseau is also editor of the Oxford Handbook of Evidence-Based Management (2012) and the recipient of numerous awards, including AOM's Career Service Award, two George Terry Awards for best management book, the OB Division's Lifetime Achievement Award, and the Practice Theme Committee's Impact Award. Her teaching and research focus on evidence-based management and positive organizational practices in managing people and change. She received her bachelor's degree, master's degree, and PhD from the University of California at Berkeley and holds several honorary doctorates.

OPTIMIZING TALENT: HR'S KEY ROLE FOR TOMORROW

William A. Schiemann

As a good researcher, I began to answer the question posed to all the contributors— "What do HR professionals need to know or do to be effective in today's and tomorrow's business world?"—by polling my colleagues in the field. I received a wide variety of suggestions that I will share in this piece.

But before I do that, I stepped back to ask the question: "How is HR different from other functions, and how does that difference help the enterprise succeed?" Perhaps the obvious answer is that HR focuses on people—the life blood of organizational success—rather than materials, customers, finances, technology, and so forth. Finance is trying to optimize capital in one way or another. Marketing is trying to optimize the market or desired customer segments, while sales is focused on optimizing the buyer. In parallel, HR's unique contribution is *optimizing people or talent investments*, including leadership. This is not the only thing that HR does, but it carries a huge responsibility, given the impact of people on organizational success.

Two terms need definition. By *talent*, I am referring to the skills, abilities, interests, knowledge, and behaviors of the people (employees or other forms of labor) that enable the organization to pursue its vision and strategy. To *optimize* implies that a resource is utilized to the best of its potential. For capital, are we getting the highest ROI on money invested? For marketing, are we getting the most return from investments in market intelligence, segmentation, branding, and so forth?

HR professionals have the unique role to help the organization obtain the highest results that can be achieved through people—high productivity and quality, satisfied customers, low accidents, and the creation of proprietary knowledge. HR can help achieve these goals through great sourcing of talent, creating high-performance cultures, and developing great leaders. The other side of the optimization coin is mitigating risk—for example, by reducing employee turnover to create more cost savings and higher knowledge retention. In sum, HR professionals help organizations achieve their goals and strategies with the most effective use of talent.

OPTIMIZING TALENT AND ORGANIZATIONAL VALUE

For HR, trying to demonstrate how human capital investments produce value for the organization has been a historical struggle. Is that leader development program adding value—and if so, how much? Are we providing the optimal level of benefits or flexibility?

My team at the Metrus Institute began to examine this issue more than a decade ago. How can we connect people investments to business or organizational results, and what is optimal in terms of overall workforce investments? After reviewing hundreds of research articles, scouring our own databases, and conducting targeted research in this area, we identified three factors that we think serve as a good surrogate for talent optimization.[1]

These factors transcend industry uniqueness, stage of organizational lifecycle, or region. The three factors are:

- *Alignment* – The extent to which individual or team goals line up within and across interdependent departments and the organization
- *Capabilities* – The extent to which people in the organization have the necessary competencies, information, and resources to meet customer expectations
- *Engagement* – The extent to which people are not only satisfied or committed to the organization but also advocates for the organization

Collectively, we call these three factors "People Equity."[2] While People Equity is not an ROI measure per se, it is a strategic indicator of how well our talent investments are paying off. All three are necessary and crucial factors to organizational success.[3] While none of these terms are brand new, the way in which they are defined, interact, and are measured provide unique insights into how people or talent investments yield valuable organizational results.

For example, in a study of more than 2,000 organizations, we learned that organizations with high People Equity financially outperform low People Equity organizations and have about half the employee turnover. We went on to show that People Equity is also related to productivity and customer satisfaction or retention, among other important outcomes.[4] While crudely measured at first through audits, we have refined the three constructs so they can be measured on a common scale and compared using survey methods. Furthermore, we have also spent many years identifying the drivers of Alignment, Capabilities, and Engagement so that it is possible to take actions to improve one or more of these factors. The drivers are controllable—and many of them relate to the processes, structures, competencies, leader behaviors, and cultural elements that HR controls or influences. For example, effective training and teamwork are frequent drivers of Capabilities, while recognition and career growth are common drivers of Engagement.

WHAT ARE THE IMPLICATIONS FOR HR PROFESSIONALS?

If we start with the premise that we want to achieve the highest Alignment (A), Capabilities (C), and Engagement (E) for each unit of invested capital, then we can use A, C, and E as success criteria to evaluate the many talent investments that we are making in our organizations. When we invest in training, we should see changes in Capabilities. When we invest in performance management, we should expect to see higher Alignment. When we invest in recruiting and selection tools and processes, we should expect to hire people not only with the right competencies, but also with high potential to be aligned and engaged in the culture of the organization—that is, "good fit." When we invest in leader development, we help leaders create more aligned, capable, and engaged teams, leading to faster and better results.

HOW WELL IS HR DOING?

While some organizations have a high percentage of optimized units—high A, C, and E units—most organizations have a blend ranging from severely challenged to mid-range. About 25 percent of organizations that we track in our database are what we would consider "high ACE." The rest have considerable room to improve.

HR can, and should, play a crucial role in ensuring that talent investments are not squandered.

HOW CAN HR INFLUENCE PEOPLE EQUITY IN A POSITIVE DIRECTION?

There are many ways for an organization to improve its ACE factors, beginning with the following:

Measure People Equity to obtain a baseline of where you are today. This can be easily done using employee survey methods complemented by focus groups and interviews. If you are already doing an Engagement survey, you can either enhance it or conduct separate Alignment and Capabilities assessments.

1. *Connect ACE to your business strategy and then validate how ACE factors connect to organizational goals.* Organizations such as Jack in the Box know that high ACE restaurants have 10 percent higher revenue and 30 percent higher profit—and they know which drivers of ACE have the most leverage for improving business results.[5] You can predict 50 percent of turnover just by knowing your ACE score.

2. *Develop leaders who can optimize People Equity.* Managers are a key leverage point for Alignment, Capabilities, and Engagement. Strong People Equity managers should be duly recognized, rewarded, and served up as role models. Conversely, managers who cannot create high ACE among their people need to be moved out of people-intensive roles. They are sub-optimizing—essentially, wasting—the organization's human investments.

3. *Focus on the ACE drivers of People Equity.* HR professionals should have a clear understanding of how they influence Alignment, Capabilities, and Engagement in the organization. One pharmaceutical firm used the ACE framework to recast many processes that it manages and were pleasantly surprised to find that most of them support one or more of the ACE factors.

Below is a short list of the ways that HR can influence and increase each of the ACE factors:

Alignment Drivers
- Be strategic by developing talent strategies that enable execution of the business strategy and having an HR plan that is connected to the business and talent strategies.

- Have a strong talent scorecard that helps evaluate how well talent investments are doing.
- Manage the employer brand. Often underutilized, a good talent value proposition (or EVP) is a critical Alignment tool that HR can use to help the organization translate the business and talent strategy into a talent brand that connects stages of the talent lifecycle—identification, acquisition, development, performance optimization, and retention. A highly effective brand is one where recruiters, potential job candidates, new hires, veteran employees, and former employees describe the organization in similar terms.
- Ensure that metrics, especially people metrics, are driving the right behaviors.
- Design and execute performance management systems (goal setting, feedback, coaching, and rewards) that align with company goals and target/scorecard metrics.
- Hire people who will fit the culture.
- Break down silos. Silos are one of the top three complaints and weaknesses of most organizations today. Indeed, they can debilitate organizations. HR can play a key role in coaching top leaders and redesigning structures to break down silos. But HR must also break down its own silos as well.
- Measure HR's value to key stakeholders—funders and users. Value is in the eye of the beholder. Don't be afraid to get feedback! Take time to calculate how HR produces value to the business and develop good analytical skills to understand and link what HR does to organizational outcomes. In studies we have conducted with the American Society for Quality (ASQ) across more than 30 functions and sub-functions, value gaps are usually due to A, C or E issues: HR does not understand or is not aligned with a business unit (A); HR is missing some key skills (C); or HR has people who are not taking the extra effort to help solve a problem (E).

Capabilities drivers

- Measure skill and behavioral changes resulting from leader development and coaching. Most organizations cannot tell you the ROI on these efforts!
- Enable innovation. Help translate organizational strategies and ambitions into more innovative skills and processes and shape reward structures to balance risk and innovation.
- Ensure that great competencies are not suppressed because of lack of information and resources. Why have great talent using "stone age" tools?

- Master the business. Pretend it is a startup—what would you be doing? This recommendation incorporates the need for business, industry, market, technology, and financial acumen. Suggestions for mastering the business also include taking a line position and not staying solely in HR; becoming a generalist in HR and not staying in a functional HR silo (such as benefits or OD) for your entire career; and learning how your business makes money.
- Stop worrying so much about benchmarking HR processes. When you benchmark, it will only help you catch up to the pack. Bring innovative ideas to HR processes that are tailor-made to your organization's unique strategy—the factors that make it different from competitors.

Engagement drivers

- Build recognition competencies. Recognition continues to be one of the lowest-cost investments with high Engagement return. HR can help managers become far better than what we measure today.
- Create growth opportunities—an essential for Millennials entering the workforce but also for Gen Xers and Baby Boomers. They too want to grow, but often in different ways. Start mass customizing your organizations to individual differences just as you do for customers.

One final piece of advice: Create a "high ACE" HR team within your organization. Often, HR is like the shoemaker's children—threadbare in keeping their own competencies state-of-the-art, and in maximizing Alignment and Engagement within their own team.

If HR professionals can make giant strides in these areas, they will be both leading and serving their organization well.

About William A. Schiemann

William A. Schiemann, PhD, GPHR, is founder and CEO of Metrus Group, specializing in strategic performance measurement, organizational change, and employee alignment. He and his firm are known for their pioneering work in the creation of the People Equity (ACE) talent optimization framework, strategic performance metrics, and balanced scorecards. Schiemann has consulted extensively with corporations on the development and implementation of business and people strategies; HR measurement; strategic employee surveys; internal value assessments; and creating high-performance cultures. He also founded the Metrus Institute, which supports research and publications in the human capital arena. Schiemann is a thought leader in the human resources field, having written scores of articles and six books in the human capital area, most recently the SHRM-published book, "Hidden Drivers of Success: Leveraging Employee Insights for Strategic Advantage" (2013). He currently serves on the board of directors of the HR Certification Institute (HRCI) and is the past chair of the SHRM Foundation board of directors. He has been named a Fellow and Scholar by the Society of Industrial and Organizational Psychology.

---

[1] See William A. Schiemann, "Reinventing Talent Management: How to Maximize Performance in the New Marketplace" (Hoboken, NJ: John Wiley & Sons, 2009).

[2] Schiemann, W.A. (2006). "People Equity: A New Paradigm for Measuring and Managing Human Capital," Human Resource Planning, 29.1, April 2006.

[3] Schiemann, W.A. & Seibert, J.H. (2013). "Optimizing Human Capital: Moving Beyond Engagement," People & Strategy, Volume 36/Issue 1.

[4] Seibert, J.H. & Schiemann, W.A. (2010). "Power to the People," Quality Progress, April 2010.

[5] Blankenship, M. & Schiemann, W.A. (2012). "How Jack in the Box Optimizes Its Talent," QSR Magazine, September 2012.

6 HR GOVERNANCE

HR GOVERNANCE

Introduction

When we think and talk about HR governance, we have historically focused on how HR is organized and led, where we fit into our organizations, and how we get our work done. For some, we might be referring to policies, processes, and roles within the organization; for others, the focus may be on structure, key relationships with stakeholders inside and outside the organization, centers of excellence or expertise, analytics and monitoring, cross-organizational communications and work channels, corporate culture, or employer brand.

In this section, 12 authors give their points of view related to where HR is now and where we are going with specific views on how we must change the way we get our work done. The essays look at what HR needs to shed and where we need to focus to add value to our organizations. Most agree that we are at a crossroads and our organizations require many more competencies and skills from HR—all of it coming about within the evolving business context and environment described by several as our VUCA (volatile, uncertain, complex, ambiguous) world.

BUSINESS AND ENVIRONMENTAL CONTEXT

Essays in all sections of this book describe the context of our current reality. As Peter Cheese of the Chartered Institute of Personnel and Development (CIPD) describes it, we have seen seismic shifts in the political, economic, and social environment in which we all operate. Research presented by John W. Boudreau from the Center for Effective Organizations (CEO) suggests that the current role that HR leaders play in their organizations is less than ideal. In CEO's study, HR leaders identified nine emerging trends that are pushing HR to new heights: globalization, generational diversity, sustainability, social media, personal technology, mass customization, open innovation, big data, and gamification. Ron Mester of ERE Media, Inc. describes massive changes that have big implications for the HR leader and for the relationship workers have with employers. He adds to the list volatility and transparency.

These shifts are bringing about big changes for workers and our work. Workers are less and less dependent on the organization. Where once clustered in workplaces, they are now distributed geographically and can work from anywhere. The focus on work-life balance has moved to a focus on integrating work and life. According to Mester, this all makes it much more difficult for us to account for work activity and puts more responsibility on the workers themselves to honor their commitments.

WHAT DOES THIS MEAN FOR THE HR LEADER?

We need new skills and expertise. Peter Cheese states that we must move to new behaviors in business, including agility, adaptability, and resilience. Anthony Nyberg and Mike Ulrich of the University of South Carolina's Darla Moore School of Business encourage wider and deeper expertise across many roles: strategist, analyst, ethicist, psychologist, coach, business expert, economist, marketer, operations expert, lawyer, teacher, and professional.

Our authors believe that while some have criticized HR for lacking the skills and competencies to take the lead in the context of all of this change, HR is poised to step up and take the lead if we can adopt new thinking, skills, and competencies and shed some of our portfolio that is no longer relevant to the business. Nyberg and M. Ulrich refer to "Renaissance HR," meaning that HR needs to both broaden and deepen our skill sets. According to John W. Boudreau, It is time to retool HR and build a profession that is flexible, permeable, and grows quickly by applying the best ideas from other disciplines.

Peter Cheese advocates for a change in the HR mindset to focus outward and on delivering value. David Kryscynski of BYU's Marriott School and Mike Ulrich believe that HR is becoming the cultivator or organizational paradoxes—for example, we need to lead change while maintaining stability, lead global and local businesses, and run centralized HR and localized HR. We are entering "the age of HR," which will require rearranging HR's DNA, according to Mester. Paul Sparrow of the Lancaster University Management School argues that HR needs to be repositioned to deliver value through more network-based arrangements, pursue horizontal solutions through more cross-functional work, and shift our attention from process to outcomes.

NEW FRAMEWORKS FOR HR

Several authors describe the need for new frameworks for HR. Mark Blankenship of Jack In the Box Inc. shares some headlines from what has worked for his organization. It starts with a global framework in which HR can contextualize their organizations, their role, and how they add value. Lorraine Murphy shares the opportunity she had to rebuild HR from the ground up at Air New Zealand, working closely with a newly appointed CEO. As part of this work, the airline needed to get a people framework established to focus on the core HR strategies. She began by focusing on the customer and answering key questions to identify levers to move the needle.

Matt Schuyler shares lessons learned at Hilton as they moved through an IPO back to a public company. He describes how HR was able to recast its strategy and rebuild itself to enable the alignment of the Hilton culture across the world. Mester gives examples of long-held HR assumptions that need to be reexamined. For example, talent now includes sources outside of the organization and encompasses more than just employees, so it make sense that we need to rethink talent and related programming.

Jorge Jauregui Morales, president of the World Federation of People Management Associations, examines frameworks for small and medium-sized enterprises (SMEs) and family-owned businesses (FOBs). He points out that these organizations represent 70 percent of employment across the globe. The model for these organizations calls for relying on organization leaders to perform some traditional HR activities. SMEs and FOBs need to adopt best practices—particularly in talent management—and move toward a more holistic deliver of HR within their organizations.

Blankenship encourages HR to move away from measurements that track people and organizational data to measure administrative excellence to new measurement frameworks that are more relevant to the business. At his organization they use an ACE (Alignment, Capabilities, Engagement) framework that links to business performance from the return on investment in talent. Schuyler's HR team enabled a massive shift in culture for Hilton by establishing a values framework, based on the vision defined by Conrad Hilton, that would resonate with team members across the globe. Today, according to Cheese, HR needs to take a lead in the real value drivers of business. Thus we need to share definitions of terms and frameworks with other business leaders, functions, and our boards.

WHAT WE CAN SHED FROM THE HR PORTFOLIO

Low Peck Kim, chief HR officer for the Singapore government's Public Service Division, puts it in a way that many of us can relate to: HR simply needs to go on a diet, to trim the fat and build the right muscles. She urges HR to shed complexity and focus on what is most relevant to business and customers. One example is performance management that adds more complexity for leaders and may not be adding value. It's time to move away from old models of "command and control" to an ecosystem in which HR manages polarities. Throw out the rules, urges Sparrow.

Boudreau advises HR to avoid territorialism and extend our competency set to embrace frameworks from other established disciplines. Mester adds that we need to move away from HR as a support function for line operations to organizing around project work. In a project-driven world, workers are a shared resource. That kind of thinking is reminiscent of the IT "cloud." Rather than one company or one business line within an organization owning the talent, now talent and workers can be shared inside an organization or brought in for projects or specific work. Sparrow encourages HR to move away from managing the employment relationships in owned entities to managing risk, governance, and capability across what is now a whole network of parties being brought together. Organizations are beginning to "de-functionalize," and HR can take on the intellectual leadership of this shift.

HOW HR WINS

HR wins by creating value. Talent drives value in this VUCA world, so HR needs to be able to capitalize on the opportunities and adapt to many new variables coming our way. Cheese reminds us that 70 percent or more of the total value in an organization is intangible. Value is driven not just from people and talent, but also from organization, capability, and leadership. These drivers are the outcomes of HR practices, but we need to move away from focus on cost to value.

Various perspectives on how HR can build high-performing cultures are offered in this and other sections in this book. According to Nyberg and M. Ulrich, HR must focus on the organization's strategy by identifying the right talent to achieve the organization's goals and inspire talent to maximize performance. Jauregui Morales agrees, and adds that SMEs and FOBs would do best by keeping their focus on attracting, acquiring, engaging, aligning, and empowering the core talent for their businesses.

At Air New Zealand, Murphy inventoried top leaders to establish a high-performance ethos in the organization. Blankenship created a mindset within Jack In the Box Inc. known as "head, heart, and hands" to align, engage, and build capabilities in leaders. Schuyler recognized the importance of winning the hearts and minds of Hilton's people, so his group formed "culture committees" around the world and kicked off town hall meetings each quarter with the CEO. Kryscinski and M. Ulrich discuss how HR can add value by cultivating tensions within the business and facilitating decisions that balance these tensions. Several authors describe how the integration of various talent resources inside and outside of organizations is quickly becoming a new way to capitalize on talent and add value.

GOVERNANCE

These essays offer perspective on HR governance now and in the future. Several authors see cultural alignment as an overlying theme. For Blankenship, a well-crafted culture can create alignment between governing values and beliefs and generate an organization that is more than the sum of its parts. Cheese sees that organizations must be clear about their greater purpose, so governance needs to move away from controlling and toward enablement and empowerment. How we build value is more important than how we organize.

As previously mentioned, several authors see that HR needs to not only embrace the competencies of other business disciplines but also reach inside and outside the organization for talent and other resources. This requires replacing old roles and rules with collaboration and culture. Governance in an HR world now requires talent optimization (discussed in another section), fiduciary responsibility over investments in talent (including compensation and benefits), and mitigating risk related to talent. It includes abandoning old tools and mindsets for new ways to enable work to be done efficiently so that we can focus on building talent capability to drive strategic initiatives now and for the future.

PROFESSIONALISM AND CERTIFICATION

All of this brings about opportunities for our profession and argues for developing new competencies, knowledge, and skills. But Boudreau warns against falling into the "profession trap." He means that we should resist the urge to develop an exclusive professional boundary that does not allow for working across disciplines. Cheese believes that the evolution of standards, codes of conduct, and professional certifications can build confidence and help define what it is to be a professional, and that we need to work more collaboratively across the globe to better define common understandings of HR competencies, skills, standards, and recognition.

The Human Resource Competency Study (HRCS) shared by Kryscynski and M. Ulrich has been framing competencies and agendas for HR since 1987 and identifies major trends. New competencies emerging in this global business context are the ability to innovate and adapt HR practices and the ability to design strategically relevant organizational culture. One of the emergent themes from HRCS is that competencies are becoming more complex as HR needs to work within competing paradoxes.

Blankenship cites RBL institute's competency-based framework to enable HR to understand how to deliver in a way that adds value to the enterprise. This is not about a license or certificate but about being able to ensure that the organization maximizes strategy creation and activation. He sees that outside of the HR function, this framework allows for alignment of expectations with business leaders.

SUMMARY

This is a turbulent time for business as our organizations struggle to address our VUCA world, driving many to rethink business models and transform their capabilities. HR can take the lead if we can transform how we think about our profession and function. We are certainly at the cusp of a revolution in how organizations are governed. Where HR has historically focused on employees, permanent assignments, ongoing tasks, and defined jobs, we are now looking at work organized around projects with extensive collaboration inside and outside of our organizations. We are thinking less about how to achieve operational or administrative excellence inside our companies and more about how we deliver products and services to a more demanding customer in the most effective and efficient way. It is time to reinvent HR as we reinvent our organizations.

THE FUTURE OF HR: WILL YOU BE READY, WILLING AND ABLE TO LEAD?

Mark Blankenship

In thinking about what we need to know or do as human resources professionals to be effective in the business environment of today and tomorrow, I chose a holistic perspective on an architecture that incorporates all of the aspects of life as a person, professional, and member of an organization. This perspective has been informed by 30 years of practice—including many failures and successes—in HR and business, and has been significantly influenced by colleagues, academics, and consultants alike. The following seven headlines best represent my universal view, or thinking, of what HR can and should do within our respective organizations.

1. *Have an organizational framework.* The starting place for HR professionals is to have a global framework under which they contextualize their organization(s), their role, and how they add value. The framework should capture not only what HR is directly responsible for but the entire organization's ecosystem, from strategy to stakeholders. This allows the HR professional to understand the intended and unintended consequences/outcomes of organizational decisions. A favorite of mine is Jay Galbraith's Star Model[1] of strategy, structure, process, people, and rewards, wherein each piece must

fit together to ensure alignment, both internally and externally. Business leaders often wonder why great strategies, structures, plans, programs, and the like don't achieve the full intended results they were designed to, and much has been written about why. A good starting place for today's HR professional is to take responsibility for ensuring that their organization sees and understands the interplay between the components of the Star Model. It doesn't matter if you are the CHRO or an aspiring HR specialist: using this framework with your business partners will result in better decisions, alignment, and outcomes.

2. *Understand the power of culture: Is yours lubricant or tar?* Closely tied to the organizational framework is organizational culture. While we don't have time to discuss the chicken or egg relationship between culture as an outcome or culture as part of organizational design, it's fair to say that all organizations have a culture (and even subcultures) that is either by design or default. A well-crafted culture (norms, values, and beliefs) creates alignment between espoused and governing values/beliefs and serves as lubrication for an operationalized, productive Star Model. It generates a whole organization that is more than the sum of its parts. Accidental or misaligned cultures often act as tar, slowing change and in the worst cases sabotaging strategy execution. We've all heard that culture eats strategy for lunch. The HR professional must have a keen sense of cultural alignment within his or her organization to help accelerate business agility/outcomes.[2] This is especially true as globalization has a greater impact on more organizations and the VUCA environment in which we live continues to accelerate (taken from the military acronym for volatility, uncertainty, complexity, and ambiguity).

3. *Have a professional competency/role framework.* For the past 25 years, Dave Ulrich and his colleagues at the RBL Institute have developed and refined a competency-based framework for HR and HR professionals.[3] Their data-driven model has evolved with changing global, business, and environmental factors, allowing the modern HR practitioner to understand how they can not only deliver "what they own," but do it in a way that adds value to the enterprise—a true strategic positioner role. The framework connects HR to the business and provides the connective tissue/context for adding value for key stakeholders (e.g., customers, employees, shareholders, etc.).

This framework also allows HR professionals to develop their teams on a common platform, supporting talent management within the function across strategic and tactical competencies. The framework is not about a license or certificate—it's about being able to ensure that the organization maximizes strategy creation and activation. I'll revisit this crucial pairing later. Outside of the HR function, I find that the framework allows me to align expectations with internal business partners when I share it with them. This is an important step. While the roles of other executive functions are more widely established and accepted (CFO, CLO, CEO, and brand president, for example), the broader role of HR is not. Therefore HR professionals must educate their business partners on their role—and then consistently deliver on those expectations to ensure personal credibility.

4. *Understand the role and leverage of leadership.* Within the tapestry of any organization, leadership represents the weave that either creates or diminishes value. Okay, maybe that's a bit strong, but more organizational value is created through people than through what organizations make or do.[4] The key of what leaders do is to drive alignment, capabilities, and engagement (ACE).[5]

  – *Alignment* has to do with the rational or intellectual piece of the business. What are we doing? Why we are doing it? What is your role (the employee, department, business unit) in helping us achieve our bigger mission? What is our customer value proposition? Etc.
  – *Capabilities* are what employees need to do their jobs: the knowledge, skills, abilities, tools, information, processes, training, teammates, etc.
  – *Engagement* is the emotional attachment to role and organization: it's the part that captures discretionary effort, pride in the organization, commitment, etc.

The *what* of leadership must fit with the *how* of leadership. Beyond the cultural alignment of how, the organization (primarily through the HR function) must build, deliver, and sustain a common framework or understanding (mindset or brand as Ulrich and Smallwood[6] would say) of leadership.

At Jack in the Box Inc., this framework or mindset is known as "head, heart, and hands." It is easy to see the connection between ACE and this framework: *head* is alignment, *heart* is engagement, and *hands* means capabilities. Organizations with a shared/common understanding of leadership (what and how) that is aligned to strategy and culture are often recognized for their agility, differentiation, competitive advantage, and market performance.

By definition the HR professional owns the design, build, and execution of an organization's leadership framework/brand. The implications are clear: HR professionals must know how leadership impacts an organization's performance (more in the next section) and they must own the process of creating and sustaining a winning leadership brand that aligns with organizational strategy.

5. *Have a measurement framework.* HR functions often track lots of people and organizational data: time-to-hire, turnover, career pathing, employee engagement, cost of people-related activities, etc. When used to justify budgets, provide leadership with feedback about their operations, or benchmark with "best in class," HR achieves administrative excellence but fails to demonstrate strategic value add. The HR professional of today and tomorrow must ensure that their measurement framework not only captures what is important to stakeholders but also demonstrates how the information connects to critical people and business performance. As John Wells would ask: "Do you have a strategic model of success that anyone in the firm can explain to a stranger in two minutes? Is the logic well understood? The metrics clear? The key assumptions identified? If not, your firm is in grave danger."[7]

A specific example of how HR does this at Jack in the Box Inc. is to connect the leadership framework (head, heart, and hands via ACE) to business performance.[8] With more than a decade of data collection and results, the organization understands the business connection and imperative behind strategic intent, leadership, culture, and stakeholder (customers, employees, and shareholders) expectations.

Without debating causation versus correlation, the results are consistent and clear: restaurants with higher ACE scores outperform restaurants with lower ACE scores on virtually every operational and financial measure the company captures (employee satisfaction and retention, guest satisfaction, food and labor costs, sales and profit).[9] For example, when comparing the performance of optimized versus sub-optimized restaurants based on ACE scores (optimized is score-carded "green" across all three ACE dimensions, while sub-optimized is "red" on each dimension), optimized restaurants experience 21 percent less turnover and 10 percent higher productivity (in correlation terms, ACE accounts for 51 percent of the variance in turnover and 26 percent of the variance in productivity).

When translated into dollars, this amounts to $27,000 in reduced turnover costs (cost-to-hire and train) and $72,000 in increased profits (which includes lower labor costs as a percentage of sales) per restaurant per year. That amounts to about 5.5 percent of average unit volume sales. The bottom line is that optimized restaurants have 10 percent higher sales and 30 percent higher profitability than sub-optimized restaurants on average. When those numbers are multiplied across the entire restaurant chain, the total is in the millions of dollars of real impact!

While most of the variance within ACE scores is attributable to leadership behaviors, some is related to systems or processes at the organizational level. Building and aligning a measurement framework (scorecard) to your organization, culture, and leadership frameworks and meaningful business outcomes is a critical role for the HR professional. Understanding the return on people investment is as important as knowing your return on invested capital. Said differently, if not HR, then who will take ownership for such systems of measurement?

6. ***Create and activate strategy.*** In all of my years as an HR professional, this area is where most of the discontent arises from CHROs. Those who cannot connect strategic creation with activation are relegated to an activation role. This is where HR has been struggling to gain a seat at the table. On the other hand, CHROs who can utilize and take advantage of the frameworks and systems described above transform the role of HR to strategy partner or leader. If this is the case, then what stands or gets in the way of today's HR professional from crossing that line? It starts with the role of HR—the competency framework that outlines the expectations and deliverables from key business partners and stakeholders. It then layers on the organization, culture, leadership, and measurement frameworks. When HR can say that it either owns or plays a key leadership role across all five elements of the Star Model, we will achieve what is necessary to earn a true seat at the table.

Lastly, at any given time, parts of the organization live in yesterday, today, and tomorrow. The HR professionals of today and tomorrow must use their role and their frameworks to help the organization minimize the distance between yesterday (old culture, old structure, old processes), today (in-the-moment change management to improve alignment and move forward), and tomorrow (those who have already broken the bonds of today's resistance and are aligned with strategy and execution objectives). HR must take the lead on painting a picture of the organization— through frameworks or shared mental models[10]—so that better decisions can be made about how to continually create sustainable competitive advantage.

7. *Have fun.* My last bit of advice is to have fun. The work of today is dynamic and challenging—and it's accelerating. Walk the talk by loving what you do and how you do it. Arrive at work each day excited, knowing that you (HR) are responsible for the success of each employee and the organization. Why not have that as a personal affirmation? What is more fulfilling than serving others and finding reward in those moments when you've helped unleash the true potential in others' lives? Celebrate all wins, small and big. Enjoy the journey, for we trade one day of our lives at a time for it.

About Mark Blankenship

Mark Blankenship, PhD, is executive vice president and chief people, culture, and corporate strategy officer for Jack in the Box Inc., where he is responsible for the company's human resources, compensation and benefits, Jack's University, training and development, consumer intelligence and analytics, internal brand communications, and corporate strategy functions. He also serves on the board of The Jack in the Box Foundation, a nonprofit organization that focuses the company's charitable donations to make a difference in communities where employees, franchisees, and guests of Jack in the Box restaurants work and live. Blankenship joined the company in 1997 and has held roles as division vice president of training, development, and field human resources; vice president of human resources; and senior vice president and chief administrative officer. He was promoted to his current position in November 2013. Prior to joining Jack in the Box, he was vice president of human resources for Mitchell International, a San Diego-based company that provides information products, software, and e-business solutions to the insurance industry. Blankenship holds a doctorate and a master's degree in industrial organizational psychology from the California School of Professional Psychology in San Diego and a bachelor's degree in psychology from California State University, Sacramento.

---

[1] Jay Galbraith, Designing Organizations: An Executive Briefing on Strategy, Structure, and Process (San Francisco: Jossey-Bass, 1995).

[2] For more on driving business outcomes by aligning experiences, beliefs, actions, and results, see Roger Connors and Tom Smith's Change the Culture, Change the Game: The Breakthrough Strategy for Energizing Your Organization and Creating Accountability for Results (New York: Penguin, 2011).

[3] Dave Ulrich, Jon Younger, Wayne Brockbank, and Mike Ulrich, HR from the Outside In: Six Competencies for the Future of Human Resources (New York: McGraw-Hill, 2012).

[4] Dave Ulrich and Norm Smallwood, Why the Bottom Line Isn't! How to Build Value through People and Organization (New Jersey: John Wiley & Sons, 2003).

[5] William A. Schiemann, The ACE Advantage: How Smart Companies Unleash Talent for Optimal Performance (Metrus Group, 2012).

[6] Dave Ulrich and Norm Smallwood, Leadership Brand: Developing Customer-Focused Leaders to Drive Performance and Build Lasting Value (Boston: Harvard Publishing, 2007).

[7] John Wells, Strategic IQ: Creating Smarter Corporations (New Jersey: John Wiley & Sons, 2012), page 15.

[8] Mark Blankenship, "Happier Employees + Happier Customers = More Profit," HR Magazine, Society for Human Resource Management, July 2012.

[9] William A. Schiemann, Reinventing Talent Management: How to Maximize Performance in the New Marketplace (Hoboken, NJ: John Wiley & Sons; Alexandria, VA: SHRM, 2009).

[10] John W. Boudreau, "Will HR's Grasp Match Its Reach? An Estimable Profession Grown Complacent and Outpaced," Organizational Dynamics, Vol 43, Issue 3, pages 189–196.

AVOIDING THE "PROFESSION" TRAP BY REACHING OUT AND RETOOLING HR

John W. Boudreau

HR's capability can meet its opportunity only through retooling and reaching out to other disciplines, and not being too rigid about its professional boundary.

Can any human do human resource management? That's what HR constituents and clients sometimes seem to believe—especially when leadership teams admonish their HR leaders to adopt practices such as "rank and yank" performance systems simply because they read about them in a book about Jack Welch and GE, or when they appoint leaders with little professional HR training to top HR roles. Although these practices do have value, they can also seem to dilute the profession's stature by implying that professional HR qualifications are unnecessary.

HR professionals and professional associations work hard to banish the idea that HR is just common sense, and to establish valid professional standards for HR professional status and practice. As the historical development of the medical profession in the nineteenth century shows, emerging professions strive to establish common qualifications, adjudicate professional practice, establish a monopoly on professional practice among members, and carry out science to build knowledge and inform practice.

There are promising efforts to establish HR as a proper profession, including proposed standards for human capital reporting, several efforts to set HR standards with the ISO and others, renewed attention to certification by SHRM and HRCI, and an increasingly clear and independent role within organizational leadership teams and boards.

In an effort to protect the HR profession, it is tempting to draw a line and say, "You cannot practice unless you meet these standards." Indeed, sociology research shows that placing such limits is one of several paths to transforming an occupation into a profession. Though tempting, it is important that HR not fall into the "profession trap" by using exclusion to define its professional boundary. Evidence from our work on the future of HR at the Center for Effective Organizations (CEO) suggests a more inclusive approach—one that properly welcomes the contributions of disciplines beyond HR while advancing the profession's stature and evidence-based platform.

"Ah, but a man's reach should exceed his grasp, Or what's a heaven for?" The Robert Browning poem that contains those lines, "Andrea del Sarto," makes me think of challenges facing many HR departments today. In the poem, del Sarto, a sixteenth-century painter, describes his love for his wife but laments that he is limited by the mundane duties of earning money and supporting her, while his more famous (and unmarried) contemporaries da Vinci, Michelangelo, and Rafael live for their work with greater passion and spirit. Similarly, the demands of day-to-day HR may crowd out the focus, passion, and spirit that are necessary if the function is to take a leading role.

Our research suggests that HR's grasp falls well short of its reach, or its aspirations. The current roles that HR leaders play are far smaller than the roles they believe they should ideally play.

CEO convened a consortium of 11 leading companies, each of which nominated about 20 HR leaders to respond to surveys on the following nine emerging trends:

- *Globalization* – Integrating world economies through the exchange of goods, services, and capital
- *Generational diversity* – The presence of many different age groups among workers, citizens, and consumers

- *Sustainability* – Meeting the needs of the present without compromising the ability of future generations to meet their needs
- *Social media* – Online networks and two-way communication channels that connect users in the virtual world, establishing new relationships that expand users' networks and facilitate user participation in interactions and exchanges
- *Personal technology* – Mobile platforms such as smartphones, laptops, and tablets; future technology such as wrist devices and Google Glass; and the apps that support them, seamlessly and constantly connecting people and web-based content
- *Mass customization* – Combining mass production with customization for specific individual consumers or groups, in order to meet people's needs with the effectiveness and efficiency of mass production
- *Open innovation* – The inflow and outflow of knowledge to increase innovation, including user innovation, innovation ecosystems, codevelopment, innovation contests, and crowdsourcing
- *Big data* – Data that is too big, too unstructured, or too diverse to be stored and analyzed by conventional means, processes, or tools
- *Gamification* – Applying game mechanics to non-game situations to motivate or change behavior

Our work uncovered isolated examples of groundbreaking HR innovations, but the responses from hundreds of HR leaders painted a picture of a profession with lofty ambitions but a less-elevated reality. For every trend, HR leaders believed they should be providing primary input or acting as a key leader. Yet for none of the trends is that the case. Even for gamification, where HR is now playing at best an occasional role, our sample felt it should play a primary input role.

What's the best way to close the gap? Our data suggest an answer: HR leaders must avoid the temptation to be too territorial, particularly in the early stages of emerging trends, and extend their competency set to embrace frameworks from other established disciplines.

The evidence for this conclusion emerged when we created an index of forward-thinking HR. We had HR leaders rate how much their organization embraces advanced HR practices (such as customized employment value proposition, use of analytics, crowdsourcing, and social media) and nontraditional disciplines (such as consumer behavior, engineering, storytelling, finance, and marketing).

We correlated that index with answers to the question, "To what extent do other functions take the lead in applying this trend inside of HR?"

For more established trends, forward-thinking HR organizations are less likely to have other disciplines take the lead. For the emergent trends, forward-thinking HR organizations are more likely to have other disciplines take the lead. Forward-thinking HR organizations choose their leadership arenas carefully, letting others take the lead when trends are new to HR, and taking a leadership role as HR becomes more involved.

This has implications for how HR defines its profession. One approach would be for HR to avoid involving other disciplines, or restrict their HR role, as a way to preserve the purity of the function and reduce the impression that "just anyone" can do HR. Follow that path, and HR leaders must wait to address emerging trends until the profession develops the internal expertise. In a world of rapid change, that will take too long. Our data suggest that a better approach is for HR to be inclusive, incorporating other disciplines and encouraging them to take leadership where they have expertise. As they educate HR leaders, HR will eventually be prepared to take the lead.

Ian Ziskin and I have suggested that the future of the HR profession must involve "reaching out" by infusing HR with talent from other disciplines such as marketing, finance, logistics, and engineering. It must involve bringing those disciplines to bear on HR issues such as the employment value proposition, leadership development, talent supply chains, and performance management. The evidence suggests that this is just what future-focused HR organizations do.

This requires skills that are not always common among HR professionals. It means gaining credibility with functional partners from other disciplines so that they welcome the involvement of HR in their domain and are willing to help translate and apply their expertise to HR issues. How can HR leaders accomplish this? Does it mean filling top HR positions with marketers, operations engineers, finance professionals, or lawyers? Does it mean splitting up HR functions and tucking the parts within more strategically powerful functions such as operations and finance?

There is a more nuanced approach that I call "retooling HR"—adapting financial and other management frameworks to HR and talent decisions. Examples include:

- Retooling leadership development using options theory and portfolio risk optimization
- Retooling talent development using a supply-chain framework to optimize talent flows, as IBM has done
- Retooling performance management using engineering frameworks to optimize the return on improved performance (ROIP), as Unilever has done
- Retooling total rewards using product design and market segmentation to optimize the "deal" and balance customization and standardization, as Starbucks and 3M have done
- Retooling employee turnover analytics by using inventory management frameworks that integrate employee acquisition, development, and separation, as McDonald's has done

Retooling HR invites an organization's leaders to be smarter about HR by applying frameworks where they are already sophisticated—such as finance, engineering, operations, and marketing—to HR and talent decisions. The resulting retooled frameworks and tools do not abdicate HR's professional stature. Indeed, the hybrid combinations of management frameworks and HR principles create new and more powerful professional models.

Reaching out and retooling HR is the way to build a profession that is flexible, permeable, and able to grow quickly by applying the best ideas from other disciplines.

About John. W. Boudreau

John W. Boudreau is a professor and research director at the University of Southern California's Marshall School of Business and Center for Effective Organizations (CEO). Widely recognized for his breakthrough research on the bridge between superior human capital, talent, and sustainable competitive advantage, he consults and conducts executive development with companies worldwide that seek to maximize their employees' effectiveness by discovering the specific strategic bottom-line impact of superior people and human capital strategies. A prolific thinker and writer, Boudreau has published more than 100 books, chapters, and articles, including in

Management Science, Academy of Management Executive, Journal of Applied Psychology, Personnel Psychology, Asia-Pacific Human Resource Management, Human Resource Management, Journal of Vocational Behavior, Human Relations, and Industrial Relations, with features in Harvard Business Review, The Wall Street Journal, Fortune, Fast Company, and BusinessWeek. His books include "Beyond HR" (with Pete Ramstad, Harvard Business Publishing, 2007); "Investing in People" (with Wayne F. Cascio, Pearson, 2008); "Achieving Strategic Excellence in Human Resource Management" (with Edward Lawler, Stanford University Press, 2009); "Retooling HR" (Harvard Business Publishing, 2010), and "Transformative HR" (Wiley Publishing, 2011). Boudreau holds a BBA from New Mexico State University, and both a master's degree in management and a PhD in industrial relations from Purdue University's Krannert School of Management.

THE FUTURE OF HR: A CONTEXT OF CHANGE AND OPPORTUNITY

Peter Cheese

The last few years have seen seismic shifts in political, economic, and social terms. The VUCA world we live in—characterized by volatility, uncertainty, complexity, and ambiguity—looks set for the longer term. This creates a context where the new watchwords of business are agility, adaptability, and resilience. But it has also raised many questions about the real nature and fundamentals of business, including business behaviors and cultures and how to build long-term sustainable and socially responsible businesses with high trust and ethics.

New digital technologies and social media are also huge game-changers. They are greatly impacting our profession and our areas of focus, from the nature of our jobs and the skills needed to perform them to the nature of organizations and how we work, recruit, communicate, and learn. Some estimate that as many as 50 percent of jobs will change in next five to 10 years and as many as one in three jobs will be automated or robotized, impacting not just low-skill but also higher-skill jobs.[1]

Our workforces are increasingly diverse and working in more and more diverse ways. In many countries, the most significant job growth of the last few years has been among self-employed or contract workers. We talk now of a "life of jobs" instead of a "job for life." The younger generations have quite different expectations about work. The workplace is becoming more virtual and the boundaries between work and life more blurred. More networked forms of organization are appearing everywhere, and what we expect of good leaders is more about authenticity and people management skills than just about technical competence. At the same time, we have seen a systemic shift in the growth of youth unemployment and under-employment; challenging debates about productivity growth and wages; and growing gaps between education and the world of work.

These hugely significant contextual shifts create an opportunity for HR to really grasp and secure its place. It is the purpose of HR to help build more agile, adaptive, and resilient organizations, and to enable the workforce to perform and grow. So this is our space and our time, but we need to step up.

As business leaders and even governments and regulators acknowledge these shifts, they are looking toward HR for more insight, more innovative thinking, more strategic abilities to connect to and influence business strategy. However, business leaders are still not fully confident in HR's ability to play a bigger role. A recent survey by Deloitte showed that 42 percent of business leaders believe their HR teams are underperforming or just getting by, compared to the 27 percent who rate HR as excellent or good when assessing HR and talent programs. Some even call for splitting off the more strategic aspects of HR from the transactional domain that many see as HR's core focus and capability.

SHOW ME THE VALUE

These shifts in the nature of the workforce and the workplace are creating big changes in the nature of enterprise value. Seventy percent or more of a business's total value is now "intangible"—accounting speak for not measured—and the biggest elements relate to human capital (people) and social capital (organization). Talent (skills and competencies), capability (connections, engagement, culture), and leadership (team level to organization level) are the critical drivers of this value.

These are the outcomes of HR and what we do—but historically we've been too focused on costs and inputs, struggling to measure and properly understand these values and value drivers and to build analytics-based insight. Examples include a focus on the costs of recruitment versus the value of the right hire, or the costs of staff training versus the benefits of learning (improved performance, retention, and engagement).

A recent KPMG survey showed that as few as 15 percent of business leaders think that HR provides insightful analytics. Or as was recently said to me by a business leader, "We want HR to bring less PowerPoint and more Excel." But this isn't easy. It was Albert Einstein who observed that "not everything that's counted counts, and not everything that counts is counted." We need to ensure we are measuring the right things, and not just the things that are simple to measure. This is true for business in general but particularly true for HR.

Today, the need to understand the real value drivers of business is not just an issue for HR, but it is vital that HR takes a lead. Given the context discussed earlier, business leaders, boards, the finance function, the risk function, and many external stakeholders all are asking more questions about the people side of business—and this demands that we have better measures and insights. We need to start by creating common definitions of terms and frameworks, and then make sure that other key stakeholders—particularly our colleagues in the finance world—share these definitions.

The evolution of standards can certainly help. We need to start with some of the basics, like headcount. For example, do individual contractors count? Quite literally, if we are not counting them, then they probably don't count. We don't engage them, align them, and train them—yet today, in most businesses, contractors of all forms are performing vital and often frontline functions. So even the most basic people metrics impact our thinking and prove the old adage of "what gets measured gets done."

Evolving more common frameworks and exemplars of good people and organizational metrics is something we all need—and something we are actively working on in the UK. We need to develop a business language for HR before we can become fully fluent in the language of business. We need to be able to use people data and analytics to drive new insights, such as predictive analytics that help us understand where key people risks might lie—people who may be likely to leave, or where behavioral risks are emerging. And we should look to other sources of expertise within our organizations, such as taking the analytics from our marketing teams that have given us so many new insights on our customers and applying them to our workforces.

BACK TO THE SCIENCE OF HR

Better data and analytics are fundamental to helping put more "science" into the art of HR and giving us a stronger base and ability to engage fully with business at all levels. However, there are some even more fundamental sciences that we need to better embrace as part of building HR for the future.

At its heart, HR is about understanding people and understanding organizations—how people learn, how to understand their competencies and capabilities, why people behave as they do, what motivates and engages them, how teams and leaders work, and how networks and organizations work and behave. The interventions, investments, and processes we create through the HR function should be built around these fundamental understandings.

Yet we have lost sight of much of this in recent years as we have pursued other agendas around process efficiency, policies, and systems. We still reference models of motivation from the 1940s (Maslow, anyone?), learning models from the 1950s (Kirkpatrick), and change models from the 1960s (Kubler-Ross). While these models benefit from being memorable and relatively simple, we now have a much deeper understanding of how the brain works through neuroscience and of behavior and behavioral change through positive psychology and behavioral science. We have different ways of understanding the interactions of the many dynamics and variables that affect organizations through fields like systems thinking. Behavioral science and behavioral economics can now teach us a lot more about how to drive behavioral change than anything we have tried to adapt from the very negative paradigm of bereavement as a model of change.

We need this stronger base of science, not only to rethink some of HR's processes to drive greater impact and value, but also to help business leaders and managers better understand how and why they need to change. Science that shows how the brain reacts under stress or threat or how we don't learn or engage gives us a stronger basis of argument to take to managers often brought up in a world that favors status over power, control over empowerment, and threat over encouragement.

HR AS A FUNCTION AND AS A MINDSET

Which then brings us to what HR is really about. What is our purpose? Surely our wider purpose is to build better businesses and business success and to support and enable people to have fulfilling working lives.

In today's context, we need organizations that are fit for purpose, but also clear on what that purpose is. That means also designing organizations and jobs that have meaning, that are of themselves purposeful, and not letting automation and technology let our people become cogs in the machine. It means creating more opportunities for more people to add value and to feel of value. It means creating environments where diversity in all its forms thrives. And it means creating flexi-work options that enable many more people to balance their lives and responsibilities.

This requires an outward-looking focus and value-based mindset. It also requires us to think of our role primarily as enabling versus controlling. We must enable and support the workforce, including the team leaders and managers who manage people; build engagement; live the organization's values; create an organization and culture that drive success; and be adaptive and responsive to change.

Building leadership capabilities at all levels therefore is vital. Most recognize now that qualities and capabilities such as resilience and emotional intelligence are just as important as technical competence and intellect. All the research on trust shows that benevolence and integrity often rate higher than competence or predictability (e.g., Kennexa's Work Trends Report 2013) in terms of what motivates and drives trust. We must focus much more on developing and recognizing these aspects of people management capabilities.

We need to think about changing HR policies that are based only on a mindset of control rather than empowerment, and therefore often frustrate and do not signal trust. The widely reported approaches being taken at organizations like Netflix or the Virgin Group, where they are letting employees determine their own time off, are interesting examples of empowered thinking and trusting people to do the right thing.

This applies to our processes as well. Let's take performance management, one of the least popular but critically important processes, the purpose of which should be to improve performance and focus on how managers provide regular feedback, coaching, and support. The typical emphasis on documentation and formal performance review meetings appears to be designed more for managing the risks associated with addressing the minority of low performers than enabling higher performance from the majority.

So how we *organize* the HR function is less the issue now than how we *build value and focus on the right things.* The reality is that there are many different operating models for HR and they should reflect the operating models of the businesses they serve. We want to be efficient just as any business function should be, but the real value comes from being effective. A continued focus on trying to take cost out of HR, when as a function the total cost is usually in the range of 1 percent to 2 percent of the total cost of the business, misses the point that the value we can add hugely exceeds the cost.

BUILDING THE PROFESSION OF THE FUTURE

In a world of increasing change and complexity, we have a lot to think about as we develop the future for HR. But we also have a great opportunity to position HR at the heart of business, rising to our role in building organizations that are more agile and adaptive, more diverse, more responsible and sustainable, and that drive greater value.

To get there, we also need to invest more in ourselves. We are too often the cobbler's children, focused on building the capabilities of others but not our own. CPD, professional accreditation, and codes of conduct are all part of what it means to be a professional and to build confidence, and we are not at the same level in these areas as our colleagues in functions like finance. It is important for the future of the profession that the international HR professional bodies and institutes work more collaboratively to better define common understandings of HR competencies and skills, standards and recognition.

About Peter Cheese

Peter Cheese is chief executive of the Chartered Institute of Personnel and Development, where he is leading a significant change agenda for the CIPD and for the future of the HR and learning professions. Before joining CIPD in 2012 he had a long career at Accenture, holding various leadership positions before serving a seven-year spell as global managing director, leading the firm's human capital and organization consulting and services practice. After leaving Accenture in 2009 and before joining the CIPD, Cheese became chairman of the Institute of Leadership and Management, was an Executive Fellow at London Business School, and continued with some consulting as well as teaching and writing. He is a member of the advisory board of the Open University Business School, a member of the board at BPP University, and a member of the Council of City&Guilds. He has authored numerous articles, speaks on many platforms, and has authored a book on globalization and the trends in organizations and people management called "The Talent-Powered Organisation." He holds an honorary doctorate from Kingston University, is a Fellow of CIPD and the Australian HR Institute (AHRI), and a Companion of the Institute of Leadership and Management.

---

[1] Carl Benedikt Frey and Michael A. Osborne, "The Future of Employment: How Susceptible Are Jobs to Computerisation?" University of Oxford, September 2013.

HR CHALLENGES AND SOLUTIONS FOR SMALL, MEDIUM-SIZED AND FAMILY-OWNED BUSINESSES

Jorge Jauregui Morales

There are many definitions of small and medium-sized enterprises (SMEs). Nevertheless, one commonly accepted characteristic of a small business is that the number of employees is fewer than 100 (for goods-producing businesses) or 50 (for service-based businesses). Any business with fewer than 500 employees is generally considered a medium-sized business. Many of them are family-owned businesses (FOBs).

In general terms, more than 50 percent of the world's GDP is generated by SMEs, and they represent about 70 percent of the world's formal employment. Therefore, having best HR practices inside these companies and positively impacting their respective organizations is relevant to the societies in which they operate and their countries' economies.

Some of the main characteristics of SMEs include:

- Scarcity of talent at most levels of the organization
- Relatively low level of access to formal credit lines

- Middle to low level of financial resources dedicated to training and development
- Management mostly focused on the short term
- Continually dealing with more uncertainty than their larger peers

The fact that most of the recruiting, hiring, and other key HR processes within the majority of the world's economies are done by SMEs and FOBs—and not by the largest companies—generates a significant challenge to effectively sharing world-class human resources practices and success stories. In addition, SMEs and FOBs, which are often not able to afford a full HR organizational structure, rely more on line managers for HR activities.

ATTRACTING TALENT TO SMES AND FOBS

One of the most challenging HR aspects for SMEs and FOBs is obtaining the proper talent to satisfy their current and future needs. This problematic situation can encourage SMEs and FOBs to apply bold and innovative practices. These practices might include contacting technical schools and universities to find students willing to work part time during their education, rather than pursuing the traditional recruiting practices of their larger counterparts.

SMEs and FOBs also rely more on referrals by current employees, and they incorporate a higher percentage of younger talent (such as interns) or older talent (such as senior citizens who have retired from larger companies but still have valuable technical or managerial expertise). Another practice that is probably used more often in these types of organizations is to gather names of potential candidates from trust-based, closed groups of recruiting managers. These groups meet periodically in person or virtually to confidentially exchange candidates' information and fill specific job openings.

The talent attraction processes in SMEs and FOBs normally come to life to respond quickly to a company's urgent need, and not because of a well-structured HR planning process—in other words, with a significant level of improvisation, and generally in a reactive, rather than proactive, way. In attracting talent to SMEs and FOBs, the focus should be on defining clearly how to properly sell the employer brand in the right recruitment channels in order to get competent candidates.

DEVELOPING TALENT IN SMES AND FOBS

SMEs and FOBs normally present fewer traditional promotion opportunities than their larger or multinational counterparts. Nevertheless, to take a broader interpretation of human development, SMEs and FOBs offer more chances for employees to consistently wear more hats, or have broader roles, partly because the roles of middle and senior managers are more versatile and not as specialized as they are at larger organizations.

One practice of SMEs and FOBs that can be used more frequently is the "helicoidal" development model. This model, instead of focusing on developing competencies for the position immediately above an employee, provides development opportunities for lateral jobs, allowing employees to lead projects or fulfill temporary assignments outside the normal scope of their current position before getting a fully vertical promotion.

To develop talent, SMEs and FOBs should identify "high potentials" and key employees, and provide them with challenging development opportunities earlier than a larger company would.

RETAINING TALENT IN SMES AND FOBS

With fewer resources for obtaining and retaining employees, SMEs and FOBs can face difficulty in the so-called war for talent. The scarcity of qualified talent is a day-to-day reality for these organizations. Therefore, most small and medium-sized companies choose to hire from other companies, rather than design and implement a succession-planning strategy to develop talent.

Some measures that SMEs and FOBs have taken or are considering in this extremely competitive environment include:

- Offering broader and more frequent chances for employees to apply their competencies and initiatives (within a less specialized and sometimes less structured environment than in larger companies)
- Designing and implementing retention packages for key employees
- Partially or fully financing education opportunities—including MBA programs or other specialized courses—for key employees

To retain talent, SMEs and FOBs should identify key employees and learn about their primary sources of motivation, professional goals, or interests, and then provide them with a personalized retention plan.

ENGAGEMENT CHALLENGES FOR SMES AND FOBS

Due to a relatively scarce talent pool, engagement practices can be one of the most important and complex processes, whether it's performed by HR or a line manager. Smaller organizations face the challenge of motivating a workforce dealing with all kinds of limited resources. This sets the stage for HR professionals to continuously reinforce engagement practices, using every single opportunity to do so.

The capacity of a SME or FOB to operate and grow within this framework depends greatly on whether its internal HR professionals, company leaders, and line managers are capable of achieving sustainable levels of employee engagement to the company's vision, mission, values, and strategies.

Some companies might create continuously refreshed engagement activities, beginning with the orientation processes and continuing with solid messages that include real business cases or stories and lessons on how to deal with challenges successfully. It is also useful to show living examples in which popular company leaders and employees of different organizational levels share success stories and reinforce key messages.

A solid, sound engagement program is always useful and can lead to better employee alignment, lower turnover, and a more feasible way of achieving expected results. This is true for all companies, regardless of size, but is even more relevant and appreciated by employees in SMEs and FOBs.

To engage employees, businesses should focus on monitoring data related to losses of key employees and high potentials, clearly identifying the real causes for their departures, and implementing activities that allow SMEs and FOBs to create or reinforce a positive image. An organizational climate survey, taken periodically by an independent entity, might help calibrate the effectiveness of engagement activities.

GENERAL CONCLUSIONS

Small, medium-sized, and family-owned businesses face more complex challenges and have significant fewer financial resources than their larger counterparts.

- Because they operate with higher levels of uncertainty and lack easily available financial and human resources, SMEs and FOBs need to focus on innovation, flexibility, decision-making speed, and creativity to successfully deal with challenges.
- Within SMEs and FOBs, one of the main challenges for HR is how to adapt world-class human capital practices in combination with their companies' capabilities to create practical and strategic solutions that are in line with their own culture and support growth for their organizations and for their people.
- We might consider human resources in a holistic way—not simply as adding names to a company's payroll, but rather as the multiplication of resources belonging to any human being, including cumulative experience, creativity, personal will to continuously improve, and many others. This concept could be equally applied by SMEs, FOBs, or larger companies.
- Both types of organizations can mutually benefit from each other. Large companies—with their generally more rigorous design and planning and systematic approach to HR strategies—and SMEs and FOBs—with a more dynamic and flexible way of operating—can be open to learn from each other and profit from that learning. Regardless of an organization's size, HR professionals can share challenges as well as relevant and creative useful solutions.

About Jorge Jauregui Morales

Jorge Jauregui Morales is the current president of the WFPMA; the immediate past president of NAHRMA (North American Human Resources Management Association); and a past president and current board member of AMEDIRH (Mexican Human Resources Executives Association). In his career, he has worked for Unilever, Bristol Myers-Squibb, Bestfoods, USA, Corn Products Corporation, and DESC Industrial Group. He has been involved in labor arbitration as the technical advisor of the Mexican Employers Delegation to ILO (International Labor Organization) in Geneva, Switzerland, and the employers' representative at the Federal Arbitration Labor Board of the State of Mexico. He's also been an independent consultant focusing on various areas, including human capital, productivity, and corporate governance in several countries in Latin America. Jauregui Morales studied organizational development at the Ibero-American University in Mexico and achieved HRMP certification from the HR Certification Institute in the United States.

HR AS THE CULTIVATOR OF ORGANIZATIONAL PARADOXES

David Kryscynski and Mike Ulrich

What do HR professionals need to know, do, and be in order to drive business results? The Human Resource Competency Study (HRCS) has been working to answer this question since 1987. Now preparing for the seventh round (beginning global data collection in 2015), the study has tracked the increasing complexity in the HR profession for more than 25 years.

One of the most significant findings over time is that the required HR competencies are becoming more comprehensive as business challenges become more complex. While HR once needed some business acumen, culture management, and change management competencies, HR now needs a comprehensive understanding of the global business context, the ability to innovate and adapt HR practices, the ability to design strategically relevant organizational cultures, and so forth. But, in addition to learning more about the breadth of required HR competencies, the HRCS also reveals an unsettling truth about the future: HR is becoming the cultivator of "organizational paradoxes."

Organizational paradoxes are seemingly conflicting imperatives that organizations face in their efforts to perform. Consider, for example, the simultaneous need within organizations for change and stability. The constant shifts in technology, global economic trends, political landscapes, and so forth require organizations to continually adapt their strategies and operations. Such drastic changes also require HR to prepare and facilitate adaptations in the workforce. At the same time, however, organizations require some measure of stability in order to prevent the challenges associated with constantly moving targets and employee burnout.

The simultaneous challenges associated with change and stability seem contradictory and/or mutually exclusive. Many may claim that maintaining both change and stability is an impossible pipe dream. Yet this is one of several paradoxes that HR professionals face every day in their efforts to create and support a productive workforce. For example, a long-standing goal of HR is to reduce voluntary turnover in an effort to improve the stability of the workforce, which has been shown to improve productivity and firm performance. However, a rapidly changing business environment may require new employees with new skills and abilities. In other words, the new external environment may require turnover.

Should the modern HR professional ignore, resolve, or cultivate paradox? Much has been written about the value of paradox in managing organizations.[1] Ignoring paradoxes can prevent opportunities for organizational learning and growth, while attempting to resolve paradoxes can create oversimplifications that lead organizations to favor one side of a paradox at the expense of its opposing side. But cultivating paradoxes leads to learning, growth, and innovation. Cultivating paradoxes challenges existing dogmas, leading to new ideas, new solutions, and new opportunities. Thus, paradoxes create opportunities for innovation and business growth. We argue that one of the critical ways that HR will add value to organizations moving forward is by embracing and cultivating paradoxes.

In the table below, we briefly highlight a few key paradoxes that we see emerging in the HR profession and offer a few examples that show how embracing these paradoxes can lead to organizational learning and growth.

BUSINESS PARADOXES: Paradoxes that arise at the level of the organization

---

Globalization: Pressure to generalize business offerings to the global marketplace	**VS.**	**Localization:** Pressure to customize business offerings to local demands

---

Centralized HR: Central corporate control over HR policies and practices to increase equality and efficiency	**VS.**	**Localized HR:** Customized HR policies and practices that are unique to local workforce preferences and demands

---

Change: Rapidly shifting external environments requiring organizations to continuously adjust and change	**VS.**	**Stability:** Organizations must have stable internal operations in order to deliver consistent value to core customers

---

Employee advocate: HR must protect the interest of the employee and ensure legal compliance, respectful treatment, equity, etc.	**VS.**	**Strategic Partner:** HR must adjust policies and practices in ways that deliver the right employees at the right times with the right skills

---

ANALYTICAL PARADOXES: Paradoxes that arise in analyzing and interpreting data for decision-making

---

Accurate decision-making: Business decisions require intense data analysis and interpretation	**VS.**	**Timely decision-making:** Business decisions may not be able to wait for full data analysis and gathering additional information

---

Structured Information: Increasing access to data and information allows organizations to develop algorithms to automate the interpretation of structured information	**VS.**	**Unstructured Information:** Information in multiple formats from multiple sources may provide the key insights needed for decisions, but structured data algorithms cannot help provide such insights

---

TALENT PARADOXES: Paradoxes that arise in analyzing and interpreting data for decision-making

---

Internal talent development: Organizations must develop talent internally to ensure a robust leadership pipeline	**VS.**	**External talent acquisition:** Organizations must constantly scan the external labor market to identify talent that can provide new and useful leadership

---

Tight managerial control: Tight managerial control can ensure efficient delivery of customer value by keeping all employees pointed in the same direction	**VS.**	**Employee autonomy:** On-the-job freedom and autonomy creates higher individual development and fosters greater creativity at work

---

Investing in employee development: Organizations must increasingly develop their talent so that there is a pipeline of employees who are prepared to step into critical roles	**VS.**	**Cutting operational costs:** HR is continually pressured to participate in cost reductions, including headcount reductions and reduced training budgets

---

HISTORY OF THE HUMAN RESOURCE COMPETENCY STUDY

Since 1987, the Human Resource Competency Study (HRCS) has provided a fundamental framing of the competencies and agendas for HR resource professionals. The study tracks the major trends in the field of human resource management and helps HR professionals and departments add greater value to their businesses.

The HRCS began with two simple questions. First, what do HR professionals need to do to deliver greater value for the business? Second, how can the HR function deliver value for the business? To further understand these questions, in the 2015 HRCS (results to be published 2015-16) we recruited leading universities and HR organizations throughout the world, representing every continent and more than 30 countries. These partners spent three to four months conducting focus groups with leading business and HR leaders in their respective regions.

During these focus groups, our partners sought to understand the major business trends and challenges facing organizations and what role HR might play in providing value-adding solutions to these challenges. One of the major emergent themes from these focus groups was the prevalence of seemingly contradictory issues within organizations that have clear implications for HR professionals—in other words, the increasingly important role of HR professionals in cultivating organizational paradoxes.

HR AS CULTIVATOR OF ORGANIZATIONAL PARADOXES

Organizational paradoxes represent sources of stress and tension as well as opportunities for organizational growth. They are sources of great tension because they require HR professionals to simultaneously attend to multiple conflicting demands. Consider, for example, a recent push for greater customization in the individual employment contract—that is, customizing the perks, benefits, rewards, work responsibilities, and so forth, for each individual employee. Scholars have shown that these individualized employment contracts can have powerful benefits for the individual and the organization. At the same time, however, managing and administering such customized relationships can be very costly, very complicated, and exactly opposite the pressure for greater equality in the workforce.

Thus, while HR professionals have an opportunity to increase customization in order to more carefully meet the needs of individual employees, HR also feels strong pressure to ensure that equality guides the principles underlying these deals. If, for some reason, women prefer flexibility over wage and men prefer wage over flexibility, then increased customization may prevent the closure of the gender-wage gap in business. Which pressure becomes more dominant as the HR professional and HR departments make decisions about how to run the organization? Do they err on the side of specialization or do they err on the side of standardization?

The tension between these two competing imperatives may be quite stressful for HR professionals because there is no clearly right approach. In any situation HR professionals face, they likely have to balance conflicting and competing demands. A clear-cut policy for wage equality may stand in the way of customizing work arrangements and restrict the organization's ability to retain key talent. At the same time, allowing managers tremendous flexibility in assigning wages may perpetuate unethical inequalities between different demographic groups.

A simple policy cannot be sufficient for all situations. Do we adopt a local talent strategy or a global talent strategy? Do we develop corporate HR practices and policies or local/specialized HR practices and policies? Do we emphasize interpretation of structured or unstructured information? Do we focus on internal or external business stakeholders? Does management or does HR own the talent agenda? The answer to all of these situations is probably both—but with different emphasis at different times and places.

But there is also great beauty, opportunity, and growth in managing paradox. In the absence of a universal set of correct guiding principles that fit every situation, the HR professional must carefully consider each situation and find ways to balance the competing demands of the paradoxes in play. Openly discussing and exploring these paradoxes can allow HR professionals to help managers and other stakeholders better understand and embrace the conflicting demands that make organizations so complex.

HR professionals who become dogmatically committed to one side of a paradoxical dilemma (e.g., who become purely the compliance police or purely the business advocate) create HR as a dogmatic and inflexible profession, unable to balance the demands of complex business environments. In contrast, HR professionals who embrace paradoxes and use them to generate insight and discussion with business leaders will help those leaders to feel and experience the deep complexities that ultimately lead to opportunities.

As we consider the paradoxes we have heard from HR and business leaders, we see three key themes emerging (summarized with examples in the table above):

1. ***Business paradoxes*** are those that are embedded in the organization's efforts to compete effectively in the changing external environment. As shown in the table above, these include the tensions between global and local issues, outside and inside, and so forth.
2. ***Analytical paradoxes*** are those related to the management and interpretation of information.[2] These include managing the tension between descriptive and prescriptive interpretations, structured and unstructured information, and so forth.
3. ***Talent paradoxes*** are those embedded within the traditional realm of HR practices and policies around hiring, developing, and retaining talent. These paradoxes capture tensions such as the need for outside perspectives, the need to develop and promote internally, the challenges of having both global and local workforces, and the tension between customization and standardization of HR policies and practices.

While we are sure that our short list of paradoxes is incomplete, we are also sure that the need to balance these tensions is an ever-increasing challenge for modern HR. Thus, as business becomes more complicated and paradoxes become more commonplace, we propose that HR has an opportunity to step into a mature but potentially critical role as the "cultivator of paradoxes." HR's unique position within the business—spanning across functions and business units—and its responsibility for the businesses talent positions HR to be an ideal manager of paradox.

As HR raises these tensions and helps decision-makers understand the complexities of each situation, they will also help managers see the need for innovation and new solutions. Managing paradoxes is challenging, and businesses that effectively do so will have unique opportunities and advantages over competitors who can't. Thus, HR professionals can leverage their seat at the table by bringing paradoxes to the forefront of the business discussion and helping leaders find ways to manage the organization through these tumultuous but exciting times.

In summary, then, we do not suggest that paradoxes represent problems for HR to resolve, but rather tensions for HR to cultivate. Cultivating critical business tensions and facilitating business decisions that balance these tensions will allow HR to continue to add value to the business.

About David Kryscynski

David Kryscynski is an assistant professor of organizational leadership and strategy at Brigham Young University's Marriot School of Business. His research and consulting focus on developing and implementing sustainable human capital strategies and sustaining competitive advantages through investments in human capital. Kryscynski spent several years as a process engineer while leading several strategic HR taskforces for Holcim (US) Inc. His consulting experience has focused on strategic HR alignment and cultural capabilities in the Middle East as well as strategic incentive systems for a number of US-based firms in the software industry. He has also consulted with leading firms in the Middle East on major survey interventions and provided strategic guidance to several large and mid-sized US companies in the banking and manufacturing industries. Kryscynski received his BSE from the University of Michigan and his PhD in business strategy from Emory University.

About Mike Ulrich

Mike Ulrich is co-director of the Human Resource Competency Study, the world's largest study of HR competencies. He is also a PhD candidate at the University of South Carolina's Moore School of Business, where he studies international human resources. Prior to starting his doctoral program, Ulrich was a research associate with the RBL Group. He holds a master's degree in statistics from Brigham Young University.

---

[1] See, for example, Kim S. Cameron and Robert E. Quinn, eds., Paradox and Transformation: Toward a Theory of Change in Organization and Management (New York: Ballinger Publishing Co/Harper & Row Publishers, 1988); and Marianne W. Lewis, "Exploring Paradox: Toward a More Comprehensive Guide," The Academy of Management Review, Vol 25, No 4, October 2000, pages 760–776.

[2] As a side note, the importance of information management on its own is another critical theme that has emerged in our global focus groups in preparation for round seven of the HRCS.

THE HR LEADERSHIP DIET: TRIMMING THE FAT AND BUILDING UP MUSCLE FOR A SUSTAINABLE FUTURE-READY WORKFORCE

Low Peck Kem

HR has come a long way over the last 30 years, shifting from struggling to be a value-adding part of the organization to being a valued strategic business partner to the organization. I have been privileged to experience the evolution of HR while working in large multinational corporations in Asia (Tandon, Western Digital, Hewlett Packard, Agilent Technologies, Avago Technologies), an NGO based in Switzerland (Global Alliance for Improved Nutrition), and the government of Singapore (Ministry of Manpower and Prime Minister's Office—Public Service Division). HR has evolved in all three sectors.

Part of this evolution has been an HR diet where HR trims fat and builds muscle to create a sustainable and future-ready workforce.

There is a "trim and fit" HR leader within all of us, waiting to come out and be a valued partner to the business. We just need to have the will, discipline, desire, and supportive environment to stick to the right diet plan for the long run. Today's VUCA business environment demands that HR professionals continuously stay agile, innovative, and relevant. With these skills, HR professionals will have the courage and foresight to look at where and what to trim (the fat) and where to build (the muscle), so that, on the whole, the organization, environment, and society grow better for all.

There are four key ingredients to the HR diet, which is essential for HR professionals to stay relevant and be highly valued in the business world. Each is explored below.

STRATEGIC WORKFORCE PLAN (THE DIET)

A strategic workforce plan (SWP) is a continuous business planning process that involves shaping and structuring the workforce to ensure there is sufficient and sustainable capability and capacity to deliver organizational objectives, now and in the future.

A good SWP goes beyond just bringing in the right people at the right time and price. HR needs to be more confident and proactive in planning for the right mix of talents. The goal is not just to address immediate demand but to design for a future-ready organization.

HR needs to take the lead in orchestrating the senior management team—including line managers, strategic planners, CFOs, and OD heads—to work in partnership to develop an SWP. A well-thought-through SWP is usually drafted with much foresight and insight gleaned from a range of colleagues. Collaboration between HR, strategic planning, OD, and the line is thus critical to enabling effective SWP to take place.

More and more, we are recognizing that the various manpower challenges today— including demographic shifts and pressure to contain headcounts; the changing mindsets of the new generation of workers; and shifts in the external governance context necessitating new skills and capabilities—will require us to put together a long-term SWP in terms of capability development, headcount management, organizational development, capacity building, leadership, and succession plans.

At an organizational level, SWP will allow organizations to draw a sharper alignment between strategic objectives and workforce strategies by: (1) looking at long-term manpower demand and putting in place timely interventions to source, equip, and retain such talent; (2) reviewing workforce needs to ensure that identified new capabilities and priority areas can be resourced adequately; (3) enabling organizations to develop deeper insights into our workforce risk areas such as staff retention, attractiveness of careers, skill gaps, leadership, and succession pipeline; and (4) assessing if the organization has the capacity (or the stomach) to implement the plans. Is there the right culture, leadership, and grit within the organization?

At a national level, having a strong understanding of the country's plans will allow the government to better develop a coherent and comprehensive national SWP. Not only can we proactively identify and respond swiftly to common workforce challenges, but we will be able to aggregate demands, facilitate cross-organizational partnerships and synergy, and intervene directly in areas where there are gaps or duplications. In this way, we can ensure optimum allocation of limited manpower and talent resources across the country by deploying talent to areas of strategic importance. The government can then plan ahead to ensure that the education system churns out industry-ready graduates at a right time, right price, and right quality and quantity to support national objectives and goals.

STAYING RELEVANT TO THE BUSINESS AND OUR CUSTOMERS (BUILDING THE MUSCLES)
In today's highly interconnected world, it is no longer adequate for HR to work alone. The kind of skills required of HR today are more about networking, building communities, building organizational resilience, and tapping into the wisdom of the crowd than being the "know all" in HR. HR needs to relentlessly learn, unlearn, and relearn in order to stay agile, relevant, and value adding to the business and our customers. We need to build the right set of muscles to serve the needs of the organization.

The HR structure has evolved over the years from one based on hierarchy, power, and control to an ecosystem based on managing polarities, as show in **Table 1**.

TABLE 1. THE EVOLUTION OF HR

STATE OF HR	SKILLS/MUSCLE REQUIRED
Hierarchal	— Command and control — Information is power
Service Centric	— Business partnerships
Highly Networked	— Influence — Relational
Community Building	— Collaboration
Constellation Of Communities	— Ecosystem — Managing polarities

HR professionals need to acquire the skills to manage this evolution. Using Singapore as an example, in the past 50 years, Singapore's government has successfully managed the country with a public service that is known to be highly efficient and effective. From the immigration counters at our airport to public housing to ease of doing business to efficient public transportation systems, Singapore today is one of the most livable countries in the world. For a country that has zero natural resources apart from her people, it is crucial for Singapore's government to have a SWP to ensure the survival of Singapore and her relevance in the world. Our people are not just our key resource and source of competitive advantage—they are our only resource! Not surprisingly, senior government officials take our SWP very seriously.

Fifty years ago, when Singapore was still trying to prove her worth and learn how to contribute to the world, hierarchical HR structures worked very well. As a young country, we took very well to the "command and control" structure.

As the country progressed and competition intensified from neighboring countries for lower costs, higher productivity, more customization, more customer satisfaction, and higher quality, we invested heavily in automation, technology, productivity, and customer-focused initiatives. The valued HR capabilities of power and control shifted to strategic business partnerships, speaking our customers' language, and managing outsourcing and shared services to enhance productivity and efficiency. Very often, these were all done without letting go of some of the power of command and control, especially in the remuneration and headcount controls.

But HR cannot fight against the trend of exploding transparency and widely available HR solutions. Instead of trying to hold on to power and control, HR has to learn to tap the wisdom of the crowd and work with key stakeholders to share accountability and ownership by co-creating solutions. We also need to tap into the power of technology and social media to help HR and the management team get connected with employees and end customers—and learn to touch hearts and minds. Being logical and making business sense is not good enough. Employees want to know and feel that they are doing meaningful work and that they are valued by their employer.

Fundamentally, HR professionals require the muscles to be agile and resilient, to understand the pulse of the business and the people, and to be change agents. They also need the courage to call out the gorilla in the room when nobody else dares to, simply because it is the right thing to do.

KISSES—KEEPING IT (HR) SIMPLE, SWEET, ENJOYABLE AND SUSTAINABLE (*TRIMMING THE FAT*)

HR is most valued when we make lives easier for our customers such that they become less dependent on HR intervention. As such, we must continuously evaluate how we can make HR more "dispensable."

Over the years, HR has developed performance management systems, ranking and promotion processes, learning and development interventions, succession planning templates, employee engagement surveys, recruitment and retention processes, etc. We make our customers fill out form after form, and force them to have structured conversations and go through hours of training to learn how to fill out our HR forms and be better managers or more engaged employees. Very seldom do we take stock and ask fundamental questions like:

- How has your performance management system improved performance in your organization?
- How has your employee engagement survey helped improve your employees' engagement? Are you getting the ROI to conduct this regular survey?

- Is anybody going to miss HR if the HR department disappears tomorrow?
- How might we make lives easier and more pleasant for our businesses and customers?
- How might we be so much a part of the ecosystem that HR work is not HR for the sake of HR—it is part of doing business and it is a joy to deal with HR?

We have been adding more and more HR work to our managers' plates—but we have not trimmed the fat. We can only achieve partnership when we consciously keep HR simple, easy to understand, and easy to implement, and allow managers to exercise autonomy and good judgment to win the hearts and minds of their employees. It must always be an enjoyable experience to deal with HR. For an organization to be an employer of choice, the managers have to be effective leaders, facilitated by simple and effective HR practices.

THE COURAGE AND WILL TO MAKE CHANGES (*REGULAR EXERCISE*)

Over the years, HR has build up the competencies and skills (muscles) to run HR departments in support of the business needs. As we adapt and pick up new skills and capabilities to meet changing needs, it will take courage and perseverance to cull the things (fat) that may no longer be relevant. This is where HR needs a regular exercise regime.

Many organizations set up a sizable compensation and benefits department, conducting market surveys to benchmark salaries, total remuneration, competitive benefits, etc. Now faced with a Millennial generation for whom money is not the main motivator, should HR continue to pay survey companies to do our annual benchmarking surveys? Should we continue to invest days and months of HR resources—as well as employees' and managers' resources—to do relative performance ranking and salary administration? If we can have a simple enough performance management system or employee engagement system that cuts down work (and headcount) by 50 percent, are we prepared to make that change?

So, it all boils down to my final point: Does HR have the courage and will to make those changes? Do our organizations have the capacity to allow us to cut out what we think we should from the HR system?

CONCLUSION

HR has come a long way indeed. It is the oldest function in almost any organization. Whether we call it human resources, personnel, people matters, or the administration department, it is always the first and last function needed in any organization. As the oldest function, we have adapted, we have changed, we have contributed, and we have made business and the work environment what it is today.

I am very confident that HR, or whatever name it may evolve into in the future, will continue to be a highly valued function in the business world because of our ability to evolve and change. We may have embarked on some yo-yo "dieting plans" in the past, but with new agility and resilience, we can create a sustainable plan to build the HR muscles necessary to develop a future-ready organization.

About Low Peck Kem

Low Peck Kem is CHRO and senior director of business partnerships for the Public Service Division of the Singapore Prime Minister's Office. Her responsibilities include overseeing the development of public sector HR capability; providing professional leadership to the HR community across public agencies; and professionalizing HR in Singapore's public sector. Previously, she served as senior director for HR and organizational development at the Global Alliance for Improved Nutrition (GAIN), a nonprofit based in Geneva, and played a range of roles—from quality engineer to manufacturing manager to VP of HR—in the private sector, including at Tandon, Western Digital, Hewlett-Packard, Agilent Technologies, and Avago Technologies. She also served for five years as a divisional director to the CHRO of the Singapore Ministry of Manpower, where she headed the National Human Capital Office, which has the mandate to uplift HR capabilities throughout Singapore. She also initiated and established the Human Capital Leadership Institute, the annual Singapore Human Capital Summit, and the Asian Human Capital Award.

HR: THINK BIG AND BOLD

Brigette McInnis-Day

It's a new world with new rules! Be bold, take risks, and challenge the status quo.

HR professionals need to think differently. We need to shift our mindset from back office to front office by setting strategy, leading transformations, and running with our businesses. We are at a critical point where we need to change our brand and purpose. We know that accelerating talent development, designing simple organizations, and amazing leadership are key to an organization's success. It's our time to adjust to be in front of this evolution and drive impact in this new world.

I have held diverse HR roles in high-tech software and professional consulting organizations, from startups to large global organizations. In this essay, I share my beliefs, my experiences, and the changes I see in our global economy that are creating a new type of demand for us as HR professionals.

BACKGROUND FOR CHANGE

We all know that "change is constant." When we look at how the business world will evolve over the next five years, this cliché becomes a reality. Just look at the changing demographics. We now have five generations working together. By 2025, it is predicted that Millennials will be 75 percent of the workforce, requiring us to prepare differently for developing and retaining this new generation of talent. In addition, the business landscape is now digital and operates at the speed of light, and people can do business anywhere and everywhere. This constant accessibility of the workforce requires people to be "always on."

Given these changes, HR professionals have an opportunity to create new ways of adding value to our businesses. We know what people want and have the ability to couple this desire with achieving business objectives while creating higher engagement and productivity. We need to create more sustainable initiatives with clear outcomes tied to business success. People bring their best selves to work if they are fundamentally committed to their organization's mission.

In 2014 we partnered with Oxford Economics to study the 2020 Workforce. Our research found people are happier and more productive if they have meaningful work or work that "makes a difference," and this is true for every generation. This changing expectation forces companies to reflect on how their mission and purpose inspire teams to be impactful. At SAP, our new hires indicate that this is a differentiator and a main reason why they joined our company. SAP's mission is to improve people's lives and help the world run better. We evaluate the cultural fit of a new hire and assess how their contribution and style will align with our ability to do that. We have programs for motivating and retaining employees that stand out in the market, such as our social sabbaticals, fellowships, month of community service, and gift matching.

Employees want to communicate quickly, share information, provide input into decisions, interact through collaborative tools, and get frequent feedback from all levels of management. They desire to operate in flat structures with fewer layers. Employees also want to be accessible to one another and exchange a quick text rather than attend a two-hour team meeting.

Teams want to see one another virtually on FaceTime or Skype to build virtual relationships. They also want to learn from others' experiences. When employees vote for the most-liked training course, rate their leaders' effectiveness, or vote for the best solution, this type of instant feedback in turn shapes how we do business. At SAP, our employees have smartphones and iPads and work in a variety of environments—including at home and in "open air spaces." It is normal at SAP to communicate via text, instant messaging, video conferencing, Telepresence, and FaceTime. This constant interaction ensures that no boundaries inhibit relationships or the ability to execute.

Meanwhile, we need to consider people in the workforce who aren't part of our current employee picture yet. Studies indicate that 35 percent of workers in the US are contingent or temporary workers, and that number will continues to rise. In our study with Oxford Economics, 83 percent of the 2,700 executives surveyed expected an increase in temporary workers and consultants in the next three years. This is creating a network-based economy of human talent that will change how we train, retain, and invest in people. Workers will be their own agents and feel increased pressure to keep their skills to date or risk becoming obsolete.

STRONG HR LEADERSHIP AND SETTING BIG, BOLD GOALS

So what do you need to change in HR to adjust to this new world? The key is that we need HR professionals who are agile and have the ability to adapt and lead change. We risk our skills becoming outdated if we do not invest in learning new technologies—and keeping on top of an evolving market that is growing faster than our people can develop. Our people and organizational strategies can strengthen leaders, transform organizational structures, and ignite a culture of learning.

It all starts with leaders. Amazing leaders are self-aware, own all aspects of people development, build high-performing sustainable teams, and execute against their strategic plan. They need to make people feel that they are essential to achieving the business strategy to get the very best out of their team. I agree with Jim Collins' mantra of leadership taking their teams from "good" to "great"!

To begin, leaders need to articulate a clear vision and business strategy and tie individuals' roles to achieving this strategy. Involving team members in defining what success is and how they can accomplish their goals builds buy in and helps them understand how they fit into the overall grand strategy of the company. I find that setting big, bold goals helps people think differently and challenge the current structures and policies that can hold companies back from innovating.

I have an example I love to share that illustrates setting big goals. We started a sales graduate program in the US and the team was trying to establish goals (not targets—don't get excited) for diversity. Everyone came with a conservative plan using trends and previous statistics, pointing out all of the risks, and suggested a "careful" target. I challenged the team to think big and differently and reach for a target of 70 percent diversity. Everyone laughed, scoffed at the idea, and told me, "No way!" But I held firm on what I knew we could achieve—and we nailed it. We beat our goal by reaching 72 percent. The lead early talent recruiter said to me, "If you did not put that big goal in my head, I would never have strived for it. Once I believed, it was easy!" Even better, it turned the nonbelievers into believers and they changed their hiring approach going forward.

Leaders need to ask themselves, "Do I inspire and reward innovation and big, bold thinking? Do I remove obstacles and support and reward my people?" We all know the right things we need leaders to do. But somehow, we all get pulled in different directions and lose the personal touch. When leaders know their leadership point of view and communicate objectives consistently with their team and support them, new ideas, new energy, and better results emerge.

At SAP, we tackle this from different angles, testing innovative approaches to develop amazing leaders—including peer learning, encouraging direct reports to assess leaders, robust mentoring (and reverse mentoring), and shadowing. Our responsibility in HR is to invest in and enable aspiring leaders and continue to coach more seasoned leaders to develop their people. We can easily evaluate how leaders are building talent through quarterly talent roundtables, employee engagement scores, and assessing if direct reports recommend their leader as someone they trust. Leadership trust scores are the currency at SAP to assess and grow amazing leaders. If employees feel their leader is someone they trust, the business results are endless.

SIMPLE ORGANIZATIONS

If we have the right leaders in place, with clearly established business goals, we also need to ensure the organizational structure is built for success. The term "organizational structure" can be misleading, as organizations are becoming less hierarchical and more flexible. HR can add value by taking a strategy, linking it to every employee's goals or work to be done, and organizing the work in a simple, flexible way based on the needs of customers and employees. Building an organization on people alone may mean you will be reorganizing quite a bit. To do this, you need to be well versed in the business, the needs of the customers, and interdependencies across organizations or lines of business.

For example, building an entire organization around a leader to "manage" their career and aspirations may introduce complexity, duplication of roles, and lack of ownership and trust, as it may not be what is right for customers and not aligned to the overall mission/vision of the company. On the flip side, giving people "stretch" roles, creating new organizations based on business need, and moving talent to lead these new organizations is a stealth way to accelerate talent and build trust within an organization. We can add significant value in coaching leaders to eliminate duplication, make tough business decisions, and have meaningful conversations that may be uncomfortable but will achieve the right results for customers and for the company. You add value by linking goals to your strategy; delivering enablement to build amazing leaders; building simple, agile structures; and influencing stakeholders based on strong business acumen.

TALENT CURIOUS TO LEARN

Now you have leaders and structures in place to inspire individuals to achieve business goals. So what's left? We have a responsibility to foster a culture of continual learning. It is my fear that employees will not have the both the hard and the soft skills needed in the future to meet business demands. You see the dynamics of change that are shaping this new world. To get ready for this change, we have an obligation to put systems in place that perpetuate learning. It isn't good enough to simply eliminate roles that the business doesn't need and potentially neglect the human element of transformation. While we don't have a crystal ball to predict the future, we can learn what key skills are needed in the future—especially the soft skills.

For example, the Millennial generation has a need for soft skills, including all types related to communication and executive presence. Millennials grew up in a technical age where communication is parsed into short texts and posts on social media. They may have relied on information at their fingertips and may not have developed the critical thinking or research ability to solve complex problems. Knowing the profiles of the five generations in our workforce and how they learn is critical. Creating a learning strategy that blends a variety of delivery mechanisms for formal training or on-the-job experiential assignments is essential. We understand that the majority of learning occurs on the job.

It is our job to create these opportunities for learning. Consider the following big, bold goals that challenge the status quo:

1. Encourage team members to take social sabbaticals.
2. Shadow senior talent within the organization.
3. Host fellowships to exchange talent.
4. Create peer exchange forums.
5. Target specific skill development like presenting to the board or driving strategic transformations.
6. Reinforce the importance of soft skills. When done well, verbal conversations delivering tough messages to peers, employees, customers, and bosses win trust.

The time is here for change, and your people are demanding it. Be bold in providing new solutions that challenge the status quo by being a trusted advisor, driving change, and running with the business—not behind it. You can respond to change and prepare for the future by accelerating talent and leadership, creating simple organizations, and igniting a love of learning. If we don't focus and try to do it all, we risk becoming obsolete as a function. Our time is now. Let's take it!

About Brigette Mcinnis-Day

Brigette McInnis-Day is the executive vice president of human resources at SAP, an organization with more than 30,000 people worldwide. In her role, she oversees the Office of the CEO, led by Bill McDermott, and SAP's largest organizational unit, Global Customer Operations (GCO), led by president and executive board member Robert Enslin. GCO encompasses the company's global license sales teams, consulting delivery and sales organizations, ecosystem and channels, platform solutions, strategic industry go-to-market teams, industry business solutions, and all supporting operational business areas that contribute to GCO success. In addition to her primary responsibilities, McInnis-Day has made it her personal passion to uniquely amplify SAP's culture and behaviors through employee-centric programs. To this end, she has successfully piloted and executed initiatives such as Build your Brand, LEAP (Leadership Excellence Acceleration Program), Talent Roundtables, and People Communities. These programs contribute to employees having a voice as it relates to corporate direction and delivering business-focused solutions. Prior to her current role, McInnis-Day served as vice president of human resources for North America GCO. She also held leadership positions abroad, spending four years as HR director at SAP's global headquarters in Walldorf, Germany, working as a member of the global HR board management team. She has also led across various functions of HR, having served as director of Total Rewards for North America.

TO USHER IN THE AGE OF HR, WE NEED TO START BY TEARING IT APART

Ron Mester

We are at the dawn of the Age of Talent. But will this also be the Age of HR?

I believe the answer can and *should* be yes. Organizations, workers, and even the broader economy will be better off if the answer is yes. But, it's an open question.

The power to make the answer "yes" lies with HR leaders—but exercising that power will be very difficult and likely very painful as well. It will require challenging and uprooting some of the longest-held assumptions about the human resource function, including assumptions about the focus on employees, the definition of "HR expertise," HR's status as a "support function," and the very competencies it takes to be an effective human resource professional.

In short, making this the Age of HR requires that HR leaders do nothing less than rearrange the HR function's DNA—and quickly. It's the ultimate version of HR transformation, well beyond reengineering HR processes or creating centers of excellence.

If this seems a little overdramatic, consider this: Our business environment is radically changing. The way people work is radically changing. And, as many others have pointed out (and something I won't belabor), we're in the Age of Talent, where people's impact on organizations is at unprecedented levels.

These radical changes are fundamentally altering the relationships between work activities, people, and organizations. Given this, it's nearly impossible to imagine that HR can be effective, much less bring about the Age of HR, under the same basic assumptions and DNA largely formed more than 50 years ago.

THE RADICALLY CHANGING BUSINESS ENVIRONMENT

The context in which all of us do business is undergoing massive change. We all know this. But I'd like to highlight a few examples (not an exhaustive list) that have big implications for the relationship between work activities, people, and organizations.

- *From stability to volatility.* We used to talk about five- and 10-year business plans, but rarely do anymore. That's because almost every element of the business world has shifted from largely stable to consistently volatile. New competitors rise and fall in months, sometimes weeks. New products are released and promoted or killed in quick bursts. Customer spending and needs are harder than ever to forecast. All of this means that predicting the work that will need to be done next quarter (much less next year), and the type of talent needed to do it, is impossible—or at least increasingly complex. It's not surprising that we're seeing a shift from organizing work around "jobs" to "projects."
- *From confidentiality to transparency.* It's becoming easier to learn just about anything about organizations and individuals, even (or perhaps especially!) about information that used to be considered "private" or "confidential." Not only is technology creating and forcing transparency, but being transparent is increasingly viewed as a desirable characteristic. This means companies can learn almost anything they want about workers, *and vice versa.* And workers can also learn much about their fellow workers. As formerly private and confidential information becomes readily available, this new knowledge will change relationships between people and organizations, and workers and their colleagues.
- *From standardization to mass customization.* Just as the Industrial Revolution brought us standardization to drive down costs and make more products accessible to more people, our current technology revolution is bringing us

mass customization. More now than even five or 10 years ago, consumers expect websites, products, and services to be tailored to their specific and individual wants and needs. It's also reasonable to assume that we'll see this expectation carry over to the world of work, meaning that people will increasingly expect their work to be tailored to their personal wants and needs. These new expectations could impact every aspect of work—hours, schedule, job location, pay, benefits, reporting relationships, professional development, tenure, title, work assignments, etc.

THE RADICAL CHANGES IN HOW PEOPLE WORK

Of course, our work environments are also changing radically. Again, I'd like to share few examples that are fundamentally altering the relationship between work activities, people, and organizations. You can undoubtedly think of many more.

- *From dependent employees to independent talent.* Until very recently, employees were largely dependent on companies to do their work. Organizations provided not only the jobs but also the space, tools, knowledge, and colleagues to do the job—not to mention the compensation. But today, more people than ever can do their work without much (if any) help from a company. They can contract themselves out, in whole or in part. They can work from home or from the local Starbucks. For little or no money, they can access the tools and information they need to do their work. They can easily build their own network of colleagues and mentors. In short, more than ever, workers are independent. And with that independence comes an increasing ability—even desire—for people to view employment or work, for any given company, as a "gig" more than a career.

- *From clustered workers to distributed workers.* The Industrial Revolution brought us not only standardization but also clustering. For more than 100 years we've been clustering people in factories and offices, often making people move or commute great distances so they can work next to their colleagues. But for many different reasons, we are rapidly moving to a more distributed model of work. As companies have become more globally integrated, teams within companies have become more globally integrated, and companies have had to let go of the requirement that teams must be clustered.

As companies look to reduce costs to stay competitive, they've looked for ways to reduce office requirements and have become more willing to let employees work from home. As hard-to-retain workers seek ways to balance their work and personal lives, they're increasingly demanding the ability to work virtually, and more companies are listening. Technology makes distributed workers much more possible. And yet, a distributed work environment changes the relationship between work activities, people, and organizations. Even basic tasks like managing and communicating must be done in very different ways.

- *From work/life balance to work/life integration.* The idea of balancing one's work life and personal life starts with an assumption that time spent on one is largely independent from the other. Increasingly, this isn't true or even necessary. People willingly work in the evenings, weekends, and even while on "vacation." And people need or want time during the day to take care of personal errands or to enjoy watching their child play soccer. More people are wanting— and more companies are enabling—the integration of work and personal lives. This makes it more difficult for companies to "track" work activity, and puts more responsibility on individuals to effectively address all of their commitments.

USHERING IN THE AGE OF HR

People who talk and write about the "Age of Talent" don't always agree on what that means, but in broad terms they agree that, more than ever, workers make or break organizational success. Talent has become (or is fast becoming) the most important source of competitive differentiation, at least for many organizations. It stands to reason, therefore, that HR should be the most strategic, most centric, and most impactful function in a company. Forget the whole discussion about HR getting a seat at the table. Maybe the advent of the Age of Talent means it should *be* HR's table. In short, for the Age of Talent to reach its full potential, it must accompanied by the Age of HR.

But given the radical changes afoot in our business environment and the way people work, and the monumental implications for the relationships between work activities, people, and organizations, ushering in the Age of HR requires HR leaders to reexamine every assumption about HR's role, how it does its work, and how it creates value. This goes far beyond putting HR technology in the cloud, or leveraging big data to drive HR decisions, or changing employee-related policies to account for the rise of social media, or any of a number of other worthy changes to consider. Instead, it's time for HR leaders to look at HR's DNA itself—the function's fundamental building blocks—and rearrange it to address the emerging new realities of our business environment and the way we work.

Here are three examples of long-held assumptions about HR that deserve reexamination. I hope this provokes you into identifying and challenging other core HR assumptions, because that's how we'll truly usher in the Age of HR.

1. ***The focus on employees.*** At its core, HR has always been (and still is) about employees—finding them, compensating them, training them, motivating them. Virtually every HR program is designed around employees. But we're not talking about the Age of Employees—it's the Age of Talent. And talent comes to organizations in many forms—temporaries, independent contractors, outsourced services, professional services, volunteers, partners, and more. In fact, largely as a result of the changes in the business environment and how people work, organizations are relying on *non*-employee talent more than ever before, and that's likely to keep increasing. What happens if we discard the assumption that HR is about employees, and that instead, HR is about talent of every type and source? If two programmers are sitting next to each other, and one is an employee and the other is a contractor, do we only want the employee programmer to be engaged and well trained? How would we rethink every aspect of HR and HR programs if the focus was on talent rather than employees?

2. ***HR expertise.*** HR departments are organized in many different ways. But underlying the structure of just about every HR function is the assumption that HR expertise is developed through its disciplines—recruiting, compensation, benefits, training, labor relations, and so on. But this method of classifying expertise is fundamentally "industrial"—internally driven to promote assembly-line-like efficiency. Imagine if, instead, HR expertise were developed around generations (Baby Boomers, Gen X), or talent sources (temps, independent contractors, services), or skill sets (engineers, marketers), or internal stakeholders (finance department, operations). Could a change in the way HR thinks about "expertise" better position HR to address the changing business environment and the way people work?

3. ***Support function.*** We simply assume that, along with functions like finance and IT, HR provides support to an organization's "line" operations. By and large we define line operations as the part of the company that directly hires and manages people. But what happens when we increasingly organize work

around projects rather than jobs? A project manager manages people during the weeks/months of the project, but who has overall responsibility for ensuring that the company has the right number/type of workers on hand to support all the projects, and that those people are being managed and developed properly? In a project-driven world, are workers a shared resource? In that case, is it possible that HR should manage that shared resource, thereby becoming, in essence, a "line" operation?

CHALLENGE, PAIN, AND REWARD

Challenging assumptions is hard. Sometimes those assumptions are so deeply ingrained that we don't even realize they are assumptions anymore. Instead, we mistake them for "laws of the universe" that can't be tampered with. Moreover, altering those assumptions and changing DNA is not only hard but painful. People in HR will rebel. Employees may rebel. HR's internal customers will likely rebel. Many current HR professionals may not have the right skills to be effective in the Age of HR.

But isn't this *exactly* the work that leaders are meant to do? And specifically, that HR leaders are meant to do? The reward for doing this work well is ensuring that talent rules and that the organizations we serve are very successful. As HR leaders, we can't ask for much more than that.

About Ron Mester

Ron Mester is president and CEO of ERE Media, Inc., which, through its four brands (TLNT, ERE, SourceCon, and The Fordyce Letter), is the preeminent source for information about talent acquisition and talent management. Most of his career has been focused on human capital-related information, research, and strategy. He spent 11 years with Towers Perrin (now Towers Watson)—including five years as a partner—where he advised Fortune 1000 companies in more than a dozen industries on human capital strategy, organizational effectiveness, and overall business strategy. He was also extensively involved in the development of Towers Perrin's "People Strategy" framework for how to make talent a source of sustainable competitive advantage. More recently, Mester served for eight years as president and CEO of Staffing Industry Analysts (SIA), transforming the company into the premier research and analysis firm covering the contingent workforce. He also served as an executive at two venture-backed startups in the research/business intelligence space and earned a patent for Zoomerang, which became one of the world's top online survey tools (before being acquired in 2012 by SurveyMonkey). He holds an MBA from the Wharton School of the University of Pennsylvania and a BA from the University of California, Berkeley.

BALANCING RESPECT AND OPPORTUNITY: WHEN IS IT TIME TO PRESS THE RESET BUTTON?

Lorraine Murphy

What if you had the chance to press the reset button and build HR from the ground up—if you could take the best and revamp the rest?

This was the opportunity I had when I joined Air New Zealand under newly appointed CEO Christopher Luxon, who said, "Let's build the company we have always wanted to work for." I was very fortunate to be given this mandate, which was effectively a blank sheet of paper.

Air New Zealand is a domestic and international airline with 11,000 staff members who fly more than 13 million passengers per year—that's 40,000 people a day. We have six flights per day to the United States or Canada and also fly to London, Shanghai, Tokyo, Singapore, Australia, and the Pacific Islands, as well as domestically throughout New Zealand. Each year, we receive more than 50,000 employment applications from candidates all over the world for about 1,000 positions. We were listed on the New Zealand Stock Exchange (AIR) 25 years ago but have been operating for 75 years as the national carrier of New Zealand.

What do you do when faced with an opportunity like this? Something I liken to changing the tires on the bus while driving it!

First and foremost, we needed to retain and respect Air New Zealand's remarkable legacy. It was hugely exciting to recognize the opportunity to take the airline from good to great. There was so much I wanted to do, but I knew I had to have realistic expectations, especially because our workforce is both experienced (45 percent of our staff have more than 10 years of service) and highly unionized (around 70 percent). For me, it has been about being patient, setting very clear priorities and not swaying from them, and having a resolute focus on what really matters—all while keeping things simple and clear. The company did not need any more complexity.

Second, I considered my experience in industrials and fast-moving consumer goods and focused on bringing the very best from those worlds into the aviation environment—in a way that complemented and enhanced Air New Zealand's unique culture. One thing I was clear about: A few things mattered a lot, and a lot of things mattered a little. Christopher and I agreed that we needed to establish a new "people framework" quickly—within the first two years—before we lost momentum. Then the next three years would be focused on quality execution. We also agreed to start at the top, with the executive and senior leadership team, and arm them with the tools to lead change through the organization.

Third, the people framework helped me to focus on which core HR strategies would have the maximum impact. Simplicity is key, and I believe HR teams often lose their way amid complexity and perfectionism when they try to progress on too many fronts. I have learned this through bitter experience.

To make progress, I asked four critical questions:

- What do we keep?
- What needs to change?
- What can we do that will make the biggest difference?
- How can we build it quickly, cleanly, and simply—and get it to stick?

By answering these questions from the customer perspective (or "outside in"), we built the internal mechanisms to deliver the desired customer experience. As we know, the culture that employees experience inside the company is reflected in their interactions with external customers. In an increasingly commoditized industry that commonly lacks the past's "wow" factor, our only differentiating factor is our customer service—from booking, to check-in, to lounge and airport experiences, to being on board, to delivering luggage. To survive and thrive, we need to be a seamlessly customer-focused machine.

As we went through these steps and questions, we identified six HR levers that would help us build a high-performance culture and deliver on customer expectations.

1. FOCUS ON TALENT

As strategic partners to the business, we ask questions that focus on talent:

- Where is our company heading?
- Where is our industry heading?
- What does the future state look like, and what does that mean for our people?
- Do we have the talent for the organization now and in the future?
- Can we "make" it or do we need to "buy" it?

The aviation industry is moving from a service-based to a retail-based industry, where it's no longer solely about getting people on planes. We're now selling new and different propositions to our customers, including Airpoints and credit cards. This means we need new knowledge and expertise if we want to truly stay ahead of this new game. We need to be prepared to adapt to the ever-changing needs of our customers, which means building and bringing in capability for our current and future needs. We are continually looking forward two, three, five, and even 10 years.

We have completed a comprehensive talent inventory of our top 400 senior leaders, which involved 360-degree assessments of each leader; implementing accelerated development centers for our "high potentials"; succession planning to build our "bench strength"; and reporting back to individuals with full transparency on our view of their potential, which we then reported to the board. These talent conversations were difficult for many, but people now know where they stand, and the process set the tone for our high-performance ethos.

2. DEFINE AND DELIVER HIGH PERFORMANCE

I saw the words "high-performance organization" all over our previous business strategy, but there was no clear view of what that meant. We've set out to instill a true performance ethic by articulating exactly what we mean by high performance and reinforcing that by differentiating between our high and low performers financially.

We took the existing performance cycle that was in place for our top 3,000 leaders and reengineered it. My experience has shown me that employees who understand how their role contributes to an organization's strategy—and who are rewarded and recognized appropriately—will deliver stronger performances, leading to stronger company performance. It is key to take into account not only *what* people achieve but also *how* they go about doing it. We reoriented our performance cycle by implementing:

- Three to five transformation objectives per leader (instead of a long list restating their job description)
- A "how" behavioral framework
- A simple and clear rating system with a new short-term incentive system; the bottom 5 percent of performers receive no bonus, and the top 5 percent get a 200 percent bonus (This was very tough to implement in a year where the company achieved record profits and the bonus was significant.)
- Formal, monthly one-on-one conversations with a focus on honesty and transparency
- A designated Development Month, when we form and discuss development plans and have a number of development events

3. ENSURE STRONG TECHNICAL AND ORGANIZATION-WIDE CAPABILITY

Keeping in mind where we were heading, my team completed an audit of the current employee base's competencies and any gaps. We are now setting up a framework to address organization-wide and function-specific capability. Organization-wide capability is owned by the CEO and the executive team and addresses core capabilities that all Air New Zealanders need—including leadership, innovation, business acumen, and collaboration. Function-wide capability is owned by function leaders and rolled through the organization across all geographies. For example, we were not capitalizing on building our sales capability. Given that the sales team is responsible for around 85 percent of our revenue per year, it's a priority to rectify this.

Our approach is not to simply throw money at this. Instead, we use the 10/20/70 model of capability building—10 percent formal training, 20 percent coaching, 70 percent on-the-job experience—which gives ownership to leaders and individuals themselves (with the support of HR).

4. PROVIDE LEADERSHIP AT ALL LEVELS OF THE ORGANIZATION

We have around 11,000 people, and 1,000 are leaders of people. That's 1,000 people who can play a huge role in our company culture and directly impact employee performance. At a very basic level, great leaders hire great people, enable high performance, and coach and develop their teams to perform. We need them all to be thinking, feeling, and acting in ways that support the direction of the company.

As a start, we made it clear to leaders what we expected. We used a couple of 360-degree tools to give our leaders insight into their current leadership style and help them form a plan for their development. We are currently rolling out leadership training programs targeting front-line managers, middle management, and senior leaders. Our front-line program, called Leadership Everyday, focuses on the fundamentals of good day-to-day leadership. It is made up of four modules over 18 months, with coaching and practice in between.

To hold leaders accountable, we will repeat the leadership styles survey every 12 to 18 months, and we have included leadership effectiveness questions in our company-wide engagement survey.

5. CREATE A STRONG CULTURE WITH HIGH ENGAGEMENT

The model is clear: A great culture leads to engaged employees who throw all of their effort into company performance. We see culture and engagement as business imperatives, not HR "kumbaya," and we believe we will act our way into the culture we deserve. So we're setting out to build an organization where our leadership behaviors, our systems and processes, and our reward, recognition, selection, and promotion systems are aligned toward building the culture that will deliver business performance.

As a starting point, we identified the culture that would set Air New Zealand apart for both customers and staff. We want to retain and restore the magic of air travel, which means our customer experience must liberate our customers from the ordinary. We are uniquely "Kiwi"—it's in our name—which means our culture must reflect the style and attitude of being Kiwi whether you are in Shanghai, Los Angeles, or Auckland.

We also want to be ambitious in how we run the business, which means everything needs to align with these principles, including who we recruit, how we reward, and the goals we set. We want our staff and customers to know we love them, which means allowing staff to be themselves, solving problems for customers, treating staff and customers as friends, and sharing our love of New Zealand. We also need to be easy to do business with, which means breaking down silos and bureaucracies and simplifying our processes.

There is no silver bullet or "culture campaign" that will magically get us there. Instead, we are making sure that any shifts in systems, processes, and behaviors across the organization are aligned to moving forward toward a truly high-performing culture.

Some of the tangible things we've done to drive our culture forward include:

- *Aligning our people around our new strategy.* We built a strong understanding of our five-year strategy, "Go Beyond," so that people in every position, function, and location can describe in broad terms what we're trying to achieve, how we'll get there, and how we're tracking.
- *Building better collaboration between functions, between leaders and their people, and between the company and our unions.* We have worked in partnership with our continuous improvement team and used various problem-solving techniques to acknowledge the abilities and roles of our workforce and involve them in shaping the future of our business. We believe the historical model of making decisions on issues, then inflicting them on employees, does not lead to long-term sustainable solutions. We're committed to not working in this way.

6. ALIGN REWARD AND RECOGNITION PROGRAMS TOWARD THE DESIRED CULTURE

It goes to the absolute basics of human nature that in order to drive performance you must reward and recognize people appropriately. A program that is aligned to performance and your desired culture in a meaningful way—that is, where people genuinely see value in what you are offering—will go a long way toward driving the discretionary effort that all companies so desperately desire. We consciously review and adjust our "give/get" model to ensure employees who give the most also get the most.

INTEGRATING THE LEVERS

These six levers are all intertwined, and any one of them can unravel you if you're not careful. Part of our role has been to manage the interdependencies between them, continually audit how they are tracking, and maintain focus on those that make the biggest impact. It's easy to get bogged down in day-to-day tactical matters, but keep your eyes on the prize and don't lose sight of your key strategic priorities. If it's not adding value, trash it!

We are two years into a five-year journey, but early results are promising:

- We are delivering record profits.
- Our share prices have risen from $0.80 in June 2012 to $2.60 in January 2015.
- We are one of only four investment-grade airlines in the world.
- We are growing at 5 percent and have invested $2.2 billion in new planes.

Don't hesitate to press the reset button. This liberating process can help you, your team, and your organization focus on the few things that make the biggest difference.

About Lorraine Murphy

Lorraine Murphy is chief people officer at Air New Zealand, a global airline employing more than 11,000 staff and based in Auckland, New Zealand. Prior to joining Air New Zealand in 2013, she was vice president of human resources, international/corporate for Campbell Soup Company, based in the United States, where she provided leadership across the global Campbell footprint and in key geographic locations such as Asia, Europe, and Latin America. Her extensive international career in human resource leadership also includes senior human resources roles with Lion Nathan Australia, the Australian Gas Light Company, and global chemical company ICI. Murpy has a bachelor's degree in education from La Trobe University in Melbourne, Australia, and an MBA from Monash University in Melbourne, Australia.

RENAISSANCE HR

Anthony Nyberg and Mike Ulrich

Everyone who is serious about doing or studying HR understands that the HR field is constantly evolving. As competitive pressures force organizations to better leverage all their resources, HR increasingly provides strategies and solutions to better align the most important resource—human capital—with the organization's goals. Such evolution requires HR professionals to have broader and deeper skills. We refer to these new skills as "Renaissance HR."

What do we mean by Renaissance HR? Someone who once worked with Bill Gates referred to him as a true Renaissance man. He described Bill Gates as having expert knowledge in at least 10 areas as great as most other experts have in only one area.

We do not expect anyone to develop such deep knowledge across so many areas. But based on HR's responsibilities, it is clear that HR professionals must develop both wider and deeper skills across many roles. Below we provide 13 examples.

STRATEGIST

In the early days of HR, professionals only needed to react and follow standard operating procedures. They rarely even needed to develop the procedures. Today, HR professionals must have deep knowledge of the organization's goals and business strategies in order to develop corresponding talent and HR strategies to support the business. This requires proactive, forward-thinking, integrated HR plans that fit and support the larger business plan.

ANALYST
Today's HR professional must be analytical. HR functions increasingly need to use data and make evidence-based decisions, including capitalizing on the power of "big data." This requires statistical and analytical skills not previously seen in the HR function. These skills are sometimes feared by those who joined the function because they "like people and hate math." However, a less tangible and less quantitative side of analysis also exists. HR executives must also be able to spot problems, factually determine their root causes, and logically produce solutions to those problems.

ETHICIST
Many refer to HR as the "conscience" of the organization, meaning that HR professionals are responsible for ensuring high ethical standards across the organization. While not agreeing completely (ethics is everyone's responsibility!), we note that HR does share ownership of this responsibility. This requires that HR professionals understand ethical frameworks and common ethical standards across many dimensions (integrity in behavior, ethical treatment of employees, corporate social responsibility, etc.) and contexts (national cultures have varying ethical standards that HR needs to understand and harmonize).

PSYCHOLOGIST
HR professionals often act as psychologists. They comfort hurting employees, calm angry employees, and mediate employee conflicts. However, they also must act as industrial/organizational psychologists, knowing how to select, motivate, develop, and retain employees. This requires technical knowledge about how to best assess skills and behaviors, and how to develop the most effective total reward portfolios.

SOCIOLOGIST
As organizations increasingly seek to leverage culture as a competitive tool, HR professionals must also act as sociologists. They must understand how communities form, grow, maintain, or deteriorate based on the communities' norms and values. They must also understand how cultural values develop, as well as how and under what circumstances those values effectively guide individual behavior.

COACH

Even the greatest business minds may be lacking in some areas of leadership. Despite the ability to sense an industry's future, anticipate changing customer needs, or visualize the next great technology, these business minds may not always connect with their teams or employees. If they are to lead with maximal effectiveness, they need someone to help them sense interpersonal dynamics, craft impactful messages, and provide feedback on both their strengths and weaknesses. HR leaders must often serve as the coach who provides such guidance to increase the effectiveness of the business leader.

BUSINESS EXPERT

We often hear that HR professionals need to "understand the business." However, few articulate what that means. Often, people assume it means knowing accounting and finance—and these areas are clearly important. If one does not understand how the business makes money, one cannot truly understand the business. However, understanding the business requires much more. It also entails understanding your customers and competitors, as well as how these competitors seek to steal your customers. It requires a clear understanding of the organizational capabilities necessary to deliver value in a way that competitors cannot. It also involves understanding the rhythm of the business in terms of the regularity of the processes and/or the regularity of the fluctuations in demand for the company's products and services. HR's position—often spanning departments, functions, geographies, and business units—places it in a unique position to not only understand the business but see how disparate areas fit together to create greater firm value.

ECONOMIST

While business experts understand the details of the business, all businesses are subject to larger economic forces. As the most recent recession revealed, these forces may be at a macro level, affecting all industries at the same time. However, forces within an industry (ala Porter's Five Forces framework) can make some industries more or less susceptible. HR professionals must understand how these forces affect their business, how to respond effectively to better position the firm to compete, and how to predict macroeconomic trends that will affect the business.

MARKETER

Customers are the focus of marketers. Marketers must understand who their customers are, what their customers need, how their organization can meet those needs, and how to communicate this with customers. HR must act similarly. HR serves a number of internal customers, and must be able to effectively identify their needs and communicate how the tools, processes, and programs HR offers can meet those needs. HR must also understand outside customers in order to know how best to develop the personnel to meet those customers' needs.

OPERATIONS EXPERT

CHROs often speak about the need to be operationally focused. While HR executives need to be strategically skilled, such as thinking through strategic developments, they must also be operationally capable—able to do the hard work of execution. This operational focus must traverse both the HR and the business function.

LAWYER

Employment law seems to be one of the fastest growing and changing areas of law. As new laws proliferate and new causes of action emerge, HR professionals must develop a deep knowledge of the legal environment in which HR operates. They must know how new regulations (e.g., the Affordable Care Act) affect their firm, and be able to develop strategies for dealing with these new requirements.

TEACHER

The upheaval in today's environment is ubiquitous, and the only constant is that change is imminent. Micro and macro factors morph the competitive landscape, and competitors arise seemingly overnight. In such an environment, the HR professional must recognize new challenges and teach others to address these challenges. This includes both creating a culture of adaptation and continually learning about and teaching others to deal with the newest threats and opportunities. This requires mastering communication skills and understanding how to design the best learning techniques and processes.

PROFESSIONAL

The role of the HR leader incorporates aspects from each of the skillsets described. A modern HR professional must: focus on the organization's strategy while protecting the employees within it; identify the right people to achieve the organization's goals and then motivate those employees to maximize performance; support business leaders while being an expert on the business and broader economic factors; understand the organization's customers and the customers of the HR function while being able to operationalize plans that affect each; and understand the legal environment while being able to masterfully communicate and educate. HR professionals must also uphold standards of training, expertise, knowledge, and skills, and act as scientists when dealing with and presenting sound analytically derived facts. Ultimately, HR leaders must be professional in all of their activities.

RENAISSANCE HR—OR PURPLE UNICORN?

HR professionals are increasingly required to both deepen and broaden their knowledge base. In an ideal world, the perfect HR professional would be a master of finance, economics, psychology, law, and more. However, in the real world, such a profile resembles what recruiters jokingly refer to as a "purple unicorn"—a job profile that no one individual could ever fill.

We do not intend to suggest that such a profile is necessary or even possible. However, we do believe that all HR professionals need to manage the paradox of both broadening and deepening their knowledge across a wide range of knowledge and skills. The lesson is that the required knowledge base of HR today is different from that of yesterday and will be different from that of tomorrow. Those who feel satisfied with their current skills will soon find them outdated.

About Anthony Nyberg

Anthony Nyberg is an associate professor at the Moore School of Business at the University of South Carolina, where he teaches course in negotiations, compensation, and strategic human resources. His research focuses on human capital, primarily within strategic human resource management. Nyberg has received numerous awards for his teaching and research and has been selected as a featured scholar and a "Breakthrough Rising Star" by the University of South Carolina. His research has been highlighted in major international media outlets, including BusinessWeek, Time Magazine, National Public Radio, US News & World Report, Harvard Business Review, and CNBC. His work has been published in the Academy of Management Journal, the Academy of Management Review, the Journal of Applied Psychology, the Journal of Management, and Harvard Business Review, among others. Nyberg serves on the editorial board of the Academy of Management Journal, the Journal of Applied Psychology, and the Journal of Management. Earlier in his career, he served for nine years as managing partner for an international financial services firm based in Northern California, was a licensed mediator, and served as an arbitrator for the National Association of Securities Dealers. He holds a BA in philosophy and mathematics from St. John's College, an MBA from Tulane University, and a PhD in management and human resources from the University of Wisconsin-Madison.

About Mike Ulrich

Mike Ulrich is co-director of the Human Resource Competency Study, the world's largest study of HR competencies. He is also a PhD candidate at the University of South Carolina's Moore School of Business, where he studies international human resources. Prior to starting his doctoral program, Ulrich was a research associate with the RBL Group. He holds a master's degree in statistics from Brigham Young University.

HILTON WORLDWIDE: CHRO LESSONS LEARNED FROM OUR IPO JOURNEY

Matt Schuyler

IPOs involve an incredible amount of focus and work. In hindsight, the 2013 IPO of Hilton Worldwide was driven by an intense amount of leadership alignment and a relentless focus on human resources. We learned many enduring lessons during our journey to once again becoming a public company.

In 2008, Hilton was purchased by the Blackstone Group, ending a nearly 80-year run as a public company. Though destiny would restore the company to a publicly traded enterprise, there would be many years of work ahead before this outcome. At the time of privatization, there was no cohesive strategy and no uniform mission or vision; each brand and corporate office had its own set of values and business priorities. Most importantly, there was little collaboration and few shared efficiencies across the company. Our people were working hard, but not toward a uniform set of goals. Developing a new pathway started with a revamped people strategy.

Over the next six years, we recast our HR strategy and rebuilt our department. We did so in a way that was deliberate, strategic, and at times controversial. There were several key themes, or lessons, that were critical to our journey and highlight areas that HR professionals should be fluent in:

1. It all starts with a strategic assessment of HR.
2. Understanding the business is critical.
3. Technology, digitalization, and speed lead to great results.
4. People analytics is no longer optional.
5. We need to win both the minds and hearts of team members.

STRATEGIC ASSESSMENT OF HR—AND LITERALLY THROWING OUT THE RULES

When Hilton was taken private in 2008, the company was functionally and regionally fragmented, operating in silos with minimal integration. HR was no different—and it had a very "rules-based" approach to managing talent. In fact, the new HR team looked around and discovered there were more than 320 HR policies, including one that did not allow team members to have a Hilton Honors card. It is hard to imagine not letting your team members participate in your signature company programs, yet we were doing so. We knew then we needed to make big changes, starting with our headquarters.

In 2009, we moved our global headquarters from Beverly Hills, California, to McLean, Virginia. At the same time, we replaced 75 percent of the senior leadership team. We rebuilt our executive committee with a new CEO and several industry veterans and forward-thinking leaders. We brought 90 team members with us from Beverly Hills and hired 600 more in McLean over the next five years. Such a large-scale transition required patience and active communications. Only after many years of active change management are we starting to see the benefits. And those HR policies? Instead of 320, we now have three: joining Hilton, working at Hilton, and leaving Hilton.

Similarly, our HR team rebuilt the HR function, enabling the company to establish a fresh start with a new culture. The HR team needed to not only support our leaders in defining the vision for the company, but also define a strategy for ourselves. Our vision was to evolve HR from a personnel function to a strategic, consultative, and innovative partner to the business. This strategy called for three stages: (1) building a solid foundation, (2) delivering practical results, and (3) staying on the cutting edge. In other words, we needed to change from a tactical department into a strategic one.

The skills required from our HR team in this work were similar to those of a strategy consultant, including the ability to define competitive advantage, identify sources of leverage, communicate effectively, and organize an approach into a framework. This type of work is most often expected at senior leadership levels, but should be utilized by program owners and people managers as well to enable better socialization, decision-making, and focus across organizational levels.

UNDERSTANDING THE BUSINESS

At the heart of our corporate strategic goals was aligning our culture around the world. To do this, we had to lead with a set of values that could support the vision defined by our founder, Conrad Hilton: "It is our goal to fill the earth with the light and warmth of hospitality."

In 2009, we established our organizational values in a simple framework that would resonate with team members around the world.

HOSPITALITY	We're passionate about delivering exceptional guest experiences.
INTEGRITY	We do the right thing, all the time.
LEADERSHIP	We're leaders in our industry and in our communities.
TEAMWORK	We're team players in everything we do.
OWNERSHIP	We're the owners of our actions and decisions.
NOW	We operate with a sense of urgency and discipline.

Because culture starts at the top of an organization, our leaders committed to living these values. We began measuring how they lived them as part of our performance management cycle. We also ask team members annually how they feel about the values, and we measure leader performance in this dimension as well.

Beyond enabling a strong cultural foundation, knowing the business is critical for any HR professional. The obvious homework involved in garnering this knowledge includes understanding competitors, anticipating future disruptors, following quarterly performance results, and internalizing analyst and stakeholder feedback. In addition, knowing what type of talent to attract and where to find it, creating incentive plans, tailoring learning to critical business needs, and understanding how to effectively develop predictive workforce plans all require nuanced and up-to-date knowledge of how your company operates. At Hilton, we established many best practices for our HR professionals. Examples include team members joining quarterly earnings call for context, sharing analyst reports on our industry, providing cascading newsfeeds to help team members stay up-to-date on industry chatter and intelligence, and holding monthly breakfasts where our team hears company updates and priorities directly from HR and business leaders. Context is key to understanding the business, and we emphasized sharing context as a way to improve our performance.

Beyond staying up to speed on the financials and living our values, our leaders also needed to fully understand the business day in and day out, and to experience working in our hotels. At the request of the CEO, one of the first programs that HR put in place to enable this was a business immersion for senior executives. During their immersion, leaders spend three days at one of our properties, working alongside hourly employees, making beds, cleaning bathrooms, and welcoming guests at the front desk. By serving our customers and working with our team members, these executives experience firsthand the pride and challenges associated with line jobs. They hear direct feedback on our culture and products. This program pays off in spades with a true sense of teamwork, connectivity, and respect for the work that our properties deliver.

TECHNOLOGY, DIGITALIZATION, AND SPEED

Technology is changing every aspect of how we live, buy, learn, and socialize. Yet many HR programs and tools are still delivered in archaic, paper-based formats. At Hilton, we looked to modernize our entire suite of HR programs as we rebuilt our function. We started by collecting feedback from our employees. Participants in our business immersion program wanted to share their ideas and experiences with us, so we needed a mechanism by which to scale that dialogue. Within 60 days of deciding to conduct a global survey, we launched our first-ever Global Team Member Survey (GTMS) in more than 40 languages across 80 countries. To our surprise, more than 70 percent of GTMS participants in that first year responded to the survey electronically. We had underestimated our team's abilities to leverage technology and realized that we had to continue meeting their digital needs.

We continue to learn key lessons from our survey, now in its sixth year with a 93 percent participation rate, all through digital means. We learned that team members want quick, on-the-go access to learning and leadership development, and that they want real-time professional development delivered in digital format. In response, we built Hilton Worldwide University, an online learning platform filled with asynchronous courses tailored to all functional areas. Our latest launch effort is a new internal careers website that lets team members participate in a live virtual worldwide career marketplace directly from their mobile devices. One of our most popular digital products is "Leadership in Three Minutes or Less," a monthly digital newsletter that collects video insights from internal and external leaders. Relevant, easily digestible, and mobile-enabled content is our biggest area of growth as we move toward our vision of a paperless department at headquarters and on property.

The team member population (inclusive of franchise employees) has grown by 55,000 in the last six years to 325,000 around the world, with a hotel pipeline that has shifted to growth outside the United States. This scale and focus on emerging markets has clear ramifications on our HR model: We need to be globally relevant and digitally connected. Our investments in more and better technology bring speed of information and consistency in data, and ultimately allow for unprecedented ability to drive timely action in response to feedback.

PEOPLE ANALYTICS

Historically, the HR departments of most companies have operated as personnel and compliance functions. Over the last few years, however, this has begun to shift. Today, there are countless articles about using "big data" in HR. Yet the vast majority of HR teams still don't know how to leverage the ever-increasing amounts of people data at their fingertips.

At Hilton, private-equity ownership meant that our HR and workforce updates required the same analytical rigor as our financial statements: We had to infuse all people decision-making with sound data. By leveraging a system of record for people information, our global survey scores, and data from our newly established performance management program, we could capture metrics on several types of trends: demographic (gender, age), attitudinal (survey scores), and behavioral (performance scores, promotions, attrition). These metrics helped us establish correlations and drivers of employee success.

We started small: How many employees do we have around the world? Who are the general managers (GMs) at our hotels? Implementing a GM Excellence Program and performance management cycle gave us insight into how we stacked up against the rapid expansion of our hotel pipeline. We began collecting data on leader profiles, performance ratings, and movement in order to identify potential successors for key roles and organizational gaps.

We then focused on consolidating data and reporting, and began to uncover insights about our people, such as drivers of attrition and correlations between promotions and performance. Our People Analytics team now publishes a quarterly Workforce Dashboard to monitor headcount, recruitment volume and cycle time, performance, diversity, and attrition trends. We are using this data for crucial workforce tasks, such as coaching or exiting our lowest-performing leaders, strengthening our diversity pipeline, and leveraging our recruitment efforts with highest ROI talent sources. Our work in this space is picking up speed and momentum as the business clamors for more data and insights. Our vision is to expand our predictive analytics work and connect it with powerful storytelling to drive innovation and growth.

WINNING THE HEARTS AND MINDS OF OUR PEOPLE

Ultimately, people want and need to be inspired at work to deliver their best effort. We knew we could not achieve our objective of an effective IPO without motivating our talent to stay and work hard. We examined our approach to career management and made necessary changes. For example, we removed time-in-role requirements for moves and promotions. We built culture committees around the world and kicked off quarterly town halls with our CEO for all team members. The response from team members has been overwhelming: We had 97 percent recognition of and agreement with our values within two years, and our trust scores have steadily risen to 80 percent.

Our vision is still to empower leaders and our HR team to use their own judgment rather than rely on policies or follow a rulebook. We would rather have people make mistakes when applying judgment than follow limiting rules. Today, we are on a continued journey to capture team members' hearts with a renewed employment value proposition. Our goal is for team members to understand that they are a part of something bigger. Our messaging to employees is anchored in both our rich legacy and our expansive future. We have centered our theme of this value proposition with a simple statement: "We are Hilton."

On our journey we have learned that to be successful, today's HR professionals must wear many hats: business expert, workforce strategist, data analyst, digital disrupter, and inspirational leader. This opens up the door to many nontraditional backgrounds and offers unlimited opportunity for sourcing and growth of our function's future leaders. Today, human resources is at the heart of all business decisions. With the right talent and skills, we can define strategies for future generations and global markets in a more powerful way than ever before.

About Matt Schuyler

Matt Schuyler is the chief human resources officer for Hilton Worldwide and leads the company's global human resources organization. Before joining Hilton Worldwide in 2008, he was CHRO at Capital One Financial Corporation; served as a vice president of human resources with Cisco Systems Inc.; and was a partner with PricewaterhouseCoopers in its Global Human Resources Group. Schuyler serves on the board of directors for the Make-A-Wish Foundation of America and is a member of the Penn State University Business School's board of visitors and the advisory board of Penn State's College of Information Sciences and Technology. He holds an MBA from the University of Michigan and a BS in business administration from Penn State University.

WHAT DO HR DEPARTMENTS NEED TO KNOW IN THE FUTURE?

Paul Sparrow

I argue in this thought piece that HR needs to be repositioned as a consequence of two developments:

1. The growing importance of external interdependence and partnership across organizations—what I call "network HR."
2. Internal organizational design pressures resulting from complex business models.

Given these developments, a picture of a new HR is emerging—and HR will need to make choices to deliver three performance outcomes:

1. ***Proximal performance outcomes*** – An employee's or team's immediate task performance and contextual performance (well-being)
2. ***Intermediate performance outcomes essential to the delivery of business strategy*** – Customer orientation or delivery of a brand's value proposition, innovative behavior, or an understanding of the factors that shape the efficiency and effectiveness associated with an organization's broader business model and performance context

3. *Distal or organizational performance outcomes associated with financial performance* – The typical business unit dashboard measures of quality or financial performance that form part of the organization's service-profit chain

I believe that HR should shift its focus to the second (intermediate) level of business outcomes. This means delivering HR through more network-based arrangements, pursuing horizontal solutions through more cross-functional work, and shifting attention from process to intermediate performance outcomes. Below I will expand on these three requirements, then raise critical questions about our future HR delivery systems and some risks in this delivery that we need to manage.

NETWORK HR

Under the drive of competitive pressure, the need to differentiate services, and the development of more complex financial offerings, organizations now operate increasingly as part of a highly integrated network economy. They are merging ideas about many-to-many market relationships, servitization, customer-centric through-life cost models, network resource management, and lean consumption. They are also widening their business models to co-fund and co-create value not only with customers and suppliers but also with competitors, intermediaries, governments, and customer-to-customer networks.

This has been called a value-creating network economy. In this economy, the value chain is best thought of as a value system, as it may extend beyond a firm and across whole supply chains, distribution networks, and even previously distinct industrial sectors. There is a need to coordinate the reputational and technical risks, governance arrangements, and network-wide capability across a whole range of collaborative settings. Multiple stakeholders are often brought together to solve problems by a mandate from funders. This in turn requires collaborative information sharing and decisions over resource allocation. Such developments are not restricted to complex and capital-intensive industries or sectors reliant on open innovation systems. Network HR is needed within collaborative business models, outsourcing arrangements, joint ventures, strategic alliances, joint R&D, collaborative manufacturing, supply chains, public-private partnerships, social partnerships, multi-employer networks, and in multi-organizational or agency projects and response operations.

Network HR requires that HR be brought together both within and across organizations to solve the problems of risk and reputation, governance, and network capability that arise from this interdependency. Implicitly, HR needs to move from managing the employment relationship within the owned entities where the function historically belonged to managing risk, governance, and capability across what is now a network of parties. HR will be moving into a world where organizations—much like the new breed of industry regulators—will search for powerful players inside the organization to help oversee all parties and partners involved in people-related aspects of their business model, regulating both internal and external HR systems and ensuring they perform in line with the overall goals of the broader collaboration.

HORIZONTAL SOLUTIONS THROUGH CROSS-FUNCTIONAL WORK

Regardless of the level of inter-organizational collaboration, business outcomes now require far more cross-disciplinary insight. For example, many organizations have begun to recognize the limitations of their existing corporate social responsibility (CSR) strategies. Despite good intentions and significant investments in marketing, branding, product development, the supply chain, culture, and the employer brand, they often end up with incoherent strategies, narrow activities that are not integrated across functions, and inefficient investments. But such piecemeal solutions are not sustainable.

The CSR debate is informed by several viewpoints, including reputational capital, eco-social entrepreneurship, and legal rights. Each suggests different shifts in focus for internal resources, such as redirecting investments from marketing to product development. CEOs are listening to people telling them to push more resources into important horizontal and nonfunctional activities, or to redistribute resources either from one function to another or from vertical functions into the new horizontal strategic units and activity streams. Piecemeal functional work will not deliver integrated strategy solutions.

The (non-HR) literature on a range of intermediate strategic outcomes—such as innovation, customer centricity, lean management, and collaborative business models—shows that academics in strategy, marketing, operations management, and technology management are drawing attention to people and organizational behavior issues. These intermediate performance outcomes represent "horizontal" problems, and their solutions sit "above" the traditional functions. Delivering organizational capabilities requires cross-functional collaboration, which in turn requires better coordination beyond the organization among partners, supply chains, and governments.

SHIFTING ATTENTION FROM PROCESS TO INTERMEDIATE PERFORMANCE OUTCOMES

HR needs to address a range of performance outcomes:

- *Productivity* – Investments should be coordinated at national and institutional levels, and this should be coupled with changes inside organizations that combine technology, space and design, knowledge, and people in new ways. This draws upon know-how from technology management, R&D, economics, and organizational behavior.
- *Innovation* – This requires similar joined-up thinking, combining ideas from strategy, business model change, organizational design, and work psychology.
- *Lean management* – A more intelligent approach to lean management combines operations management with organizational behavior.
- *Customer-centric organizations* – The topic of customer centricity crosses marketing, consumer behavior, organizational design, and IT.

A CHALLENGE TO OUR DELIVERY MODELS: SOME CRITICAL REFLECTIONS

There are critical questions we should ask of our future HR delivery systems and risks that we need to manage. Successfully delivering on business strategies now requires a shift in perspective, with far less focus on functional agendas. This is also changing the pattern of demand for professional knowledge inside organizations. HR will not be immune from this. I have long been an advocate of HR and am always wary of claims about its imminent demise. But a constellation of forces are now at play that may lead to such an outcome.

HR is at a crossroads: It will either go to more traditional (administrative) work or to more people-centric but cross-disciplinary work. Organizations are beginning to de-functionalize themselves, and HR has a great opportunity to take on intellectual leadership in this process. But to do so, it needs to establish a new HR syllabus. It is not just HR's knowledge base that is being reengineered. If HR is to become cross-functional, other functions must also change.

A hidden consequence of the trend toward horizontal and cross-functional work is that HR knowledge risks becoming commoditized. In other words, HR's proprietary expertise is now becoming generic. We may see a new breed of non-HR professionals who are educated and equipped with more holistic skillsets and networked into much broader professional communities. If HR cannot lay claim to such people, work may move away from HR and further fragment what remains of the function.

This would be disastrous for HR and its talent, but also for the wisdom and quality of the organization's strategies, and for its employees, customers, and society. People management and organizational behavior issues have never been more central for organizations, but that is not enough. To avoid becoming isolated, HR needs to gain experience and analyze cross-business division experience. Even the best business-embedded HR directors and business partners risk becoming too narrowly focused with many other "people-savvy" business leaders (and academic departments) now plying our trade.

The business outcomes I have discussed need more collaboration in three areas:

- Between centers of expertise (COEs) within the HR function
- Across the traditional functions within the organization as a whole
- Between and across organizations

This creates many questions. How might HR align its centers of expertise against these intermediate performance outcomes? Are good HR centers organizing holistically around client solutions? What essential input can HR provide about these issues?

Traditional centers risk being seen as over-siloed, too process-driven, and unable to contribute the generic business-model acumen being asked of them. Each performance outcome has implications for rewards, engagement, talent, or organizational development, but each needs different combinations of expertise. As we shift from HR process to performance outcome knowledge, there is a risk that we prematurely "hollow out" the HR function. In other words, as budget pressures make it hard for HR directors to balance the "strategic upskilling" they want to engineer, a lack of demand for the HR process knowledge around which many traditional centers are built makes it difficult for internal HR functions to keep the current expertise in house.

Two things are happening in the short term. HR is learning how to "mix and match" its traditional centers of expertise much more flexibly to meet demand (but this changes both the importance of our traditional centers in the pecking order and the power relationships within the HR delivery model). Organizations are also informally building small groups of multi-skilled and cross-business educated professionals who can be attached to the various business outcomes outlined above (but often in an ad hoc or project-by-project way). COEs tend to fragment—not integrate—the HR solutions required for more complex business.

I argue below for more HR generalists, but accept that there is a paradox of HR becoming more specialized, with increased theory and research on specific HR tools (including compensation, training, and staffing) while also needing to offer integrated business solutions.

THE DEBATE THAT WILL FOLLOW

In the long term, I think we will see HR professionals return to their core intellectual identities and skills and market the strategic value of these skills for solving problems of organizational effectiveness. But they will be combining this core intellectual insight with an education base that also incorporates multiple functional insights and modes of understanding. This type of knowledge will not easily equate to the internal centers of expertise traditionally aligned to existing (internal) HR processes.

HR will need to initiate external centers of excellence, accessing insight without owning it. It needs to embed its own professionals in think tanks and networks that can manage the proprietary HR expertise necessary for long-term performance-driving processes. It will need to pool HR resources across partners to lessen the "collaborative burden" faced by each organization, developing project management structures to support strategic, cross-organization work; partitioning the HR function into inward- and outward-facing structures; and creating strategic integrator roles that operate across internal and external businesses and bring together dedicated expertise under its leadership.

Should HR also try to clone broader business acumen and have its own specialists in productivity or innovation, knowing that other functions such as operations, marketing, IT, or finance might have such individuals? In a lean-managed world, HR departments might feel they have neither the resources nor the expertise to develop their own new centers of excellence. Certainly, the people in these units would need to be a shared resource, and their role, as far as the organization is concerned, would need to be impartial and horizontal.

Or should organizations begin to move this knowledge out from all of the functions, building new policy and project directorates above them (and indeed across organizations) and stripping out their need for each to replicate it? In enabling new, performance-linked expertise in the function, and ceding these people to strategic units that sit above the function, it is hoped that these newly empowered strategic leaders will be able to fight their corner and persuade other (less functional but also other-functional) experts to invest in the people aspects of the performance project.

Politics are at play across functions, and most top teams have enough on their own plates before they purposefully fillet their own functions. But new horizontal management strategies and resource allocations are inevitable. HR has some time to establish an intellectual lead, but it must act now. It needs to build up its cross-functional skills and expertise in performance outcomes, ready the people who will need to fight for it, and lay out a vision that explains the future it will fight for.

About Paul Sparrow

Paul Sparrow is the director of the Centre for Performance-Led HR and professor of international human resource management at Lancaster University Management School. His research interests include cross-cultural and international HRM, HR strategy, and changes in the employment relationship. His research at the Centre focuses on eight areas: the nature of strategic competence; HR leadership and boardroom engagement; performance drivers such as innovation, customer service, and globalization; business model change; the employee engagement-performance link; talent management; evaluating the ways in which people improve the capital of an organization; and future HR trajectories. Sparrow has consulted with major multinationals, public-sector organizations, and inter-governmental agencies. He is regularly ranked among the world's "most influential HR thinkers" by Human Resources Magazine; in 2014, he made the top 10. His latest books are "Strategic Talent Management" and "Do We Need HR?"

7 HR PROFESSIONALS

HR PROFESSIONALS

Introduction

Other sections have reviewed how HR professionals should understand context, manage organization, source and optimize talent, use information and analytics, and build a strong HR function. The essays in this section describe the personal knowledge, skills, and abilities of effective HR professionals. This introduction overviews HR competencies and highlights how these essays advance this dialogue.

The discussion of personal competencies for HR professionals is an extension of the competency based approach to building leaders overall. One of the first large-scale applications of competency to the work environment occurred during World War II; the U.S. Army Air Corps applied competency logic in selecting and training fighter pilots. Following the war, a central figure in the air force's task force, John Flanagan, applied this approach on a large scale at the Delco-Remy division of General Motors[1]. This approach was advanced by David McClelland in 1973 in "Testing for Competencies," then developed by Richard Boyatzis then of the McBer consulting firm in his work "The Competent Manager."[2]

Personal competencies for HR professionals began across organizations in the 1970's with work through American Society for Training and Development where Patricia McLagan documented the variety of possible roles for HR professionals and examined the detailed competencies of those involved in human resource development (coordinated integration of training, development, organization development, and career development).[3] Since her work, a number of efforts have been pursued to define competencies for HR professionals as summarized below.

SPONSOR, YET	SAMPLE	MAJOR FINDING
Towers Perrin with IBM, 1991[4]	Interviewed 3,000 line managers, consultants, HR managers	Line wanted HR more computer literate; Consultants predict change HR influence line managers
University of Michigan and RBL group (Dave Ulrich and Wayne Brockbank)[5]	Six rounds of HR competency studies from data by HR and line (sample size): 1987: 10,291 1992: 4,556 1997: 3,229 2002: 7,082 (with SHRM) 2007: 10,063 (with SHRM) 2012: 20,103	Most recent round (2012) should competencies that predict personal effectiveness and business results in six areas: − Strategic positioner − Credible activist − Capability builder − Change champion − HR innovator and integrator − Information (technology) proponent
Arthur Yeung and California strategic HR partnership, 1996	Interviews of senior HR leaders in 10 companies	Leadership, HR expertise, Consulting, Core competencies
Pat Wright and colleagues, with HR Policy Association	CHRO focus: 2009: 56 CHROs 2010: 72 CHROs 2011: 172 CHROs 2012: 143 CHROs 2014: 213 CHROs	CHRO's need skills in: − Managing talent − Cost − Succession − Culture Also defined 8 roles for HR
Center for Effective Organization (Ed Lawler and John W. Boudreau)[6]	Have done six rounds of study to show evolution of HR function over 15 years (starting in 1996).[7]	Highlight how HR leaders use time and trends in HR overall more than specific competencies Hero Leadership to Collective Leadership − Intellectual Property to Agile Co-Creativity − Employment Value Proposition to Personal Value Proposition − Sameness to Segmentation − Fatigue to Sustainability − Persuasion to Education

Boston consulting group with World federation of people management[8]	Conduct studies every few years on HR trends, particularly in Europe. 2011: 2,039 executives	Four critical topics: managing talent, improving leadership, transforming HR, strategic workforce planning
		Five critical HR skills: HR business partner, HR processes, recruiting, restructuring organization, and leadership development
Deloitte[9]	40 colleagues within Deloitte	Business: commercial awareness, business acumen
		HR: employee relations, HR expertise, Consulting: trusted advisor, influence
SHRM[10]	1989: ASPA build learning system with Golle and Holmes[11]	This was the foundation of the learning system for HR professionals.
	1990: Tom Lawson[12] 20 CEO and 50 HR interviews	Building management abilities in leadership, influence, business, and technology
	1998: Steve Schoonover 300 interviews in 21 companies	Core competencies Level specific competencies Role specific competencies
	2002-2007: Partnered with the Michigan/RBL group	Worked as partner on 2 rounds of the Michigan study and published books and workbooks on the competencies
	2013-current: did 111 focus groups, surveyed 640 CHROs and SHRM members	Identified 9 competencies
CIPD professional map[13]	Generated after an in-depth investigation involving detailed interviews with HR directors across all main economic sectors and scores of senior professionals and academics.	Identified 10 professional areas and 4 bands for HR's professional map: organization design, organization development, resourcing and talent planning, learning and talent development, performance and rewards, employee engagement, employee relations, service delivery, and information

Clearly a lot of work has been done on HR competencies. We can say with some certainty that HR competency work requires that the HR competencies be tied to personal and business outcomes, that data be collected from observers of HR professionals not just self-report, that data competencies be granular to vary by situation (globalization, level, role, experience), and that competencies become the basis for HR certification and improvement.

MESSAGES OF ESSAYS IN THIS SECTION

The essays in this section move the personal HR competency discussion forward in some very valuable ways. Most authors have over 30 years of experience in doing, observing, and leading HR work. Each author synthesizes those experiences into specific lessons for the next generation. Collectively, these essays capture the wisdom of senior HR leaders as they envision a future. While this wisdom may not be rooted in large scale research, these authors capture the themes that future research may study.

IDENTIFY BASELINE COMPETENCIES

Looking forward, HR professionals must master some baseline competencies to be effective. Antoine, with a unique history as CHRO and CEO of NAHR, suggests the importance of credibility with line leaders, solutions, counsel, and change agent as the basis for HR's influence. May's 30 years of experience in increasing senior HR responsibilities has enabled him to identify six personal behaviors that should be required for highly successful HR leaders: Intellectual Curiosity, Simplicity, Empathy, Courage, Dynamic Range and Grit. Oldham, with senior HR experience in many companies, drives home the importance of knowing the business. She offers very specific guidelines on how to become business literate when entering a new role or company. Smart, former CHRO for Accenture and now CEO of NAHR, reinforces the need to know the business through strategic relationships, training business acumen throughout, varied job experiences for HR professionals, mentoring, reading and listening, seeking opportunities. Collectively, these ideas help HR professionals be fluent in the language of the business. Westerdahl, CHRO at Oracle, advocates that HR professionals follow the path of marketing staff by building business acumen, having a data driven mindset in all decisions, making the right technology choices for the business, and leveraging ideas to move faster.

TAILOR COMPETENCIES TO BUSINESS REQUIREMENTS

In addition to master new basic competencies, HR professionals will need to tailor their competencies to the requirements of their business. Hartman, the Chief Operating Officer of AMEDIRH (Mexico's leading HR association), reports on research from 100 companies about requirements for HR in the Mexican culture. They find 3 categories and 8 competencies: intelligence to solve problems (self awareness, synthesis, formulation), innovation management (collaboration, knowledge management, coaching), and innovative organization culture (innovation and integration of innovation to vision).

Ridge (CEO) and Sewitch (head of organization development) offer unique insights about HR from a business leader's perspective. They encourage HR to know their stuff (including business and HR), earn role of trusted advisor, support decisions fully, be business psychologists, and teach people to take action.

HIGHLIGHT THE FUTURE

Some of the essay look forward and project what HR professionals might need to know and do in the future. Foulkes, a leading professor in the field, offers six caveats about CHRO failures as a way to help CHROs prepare for and succeed in the job (overwhelmed, board confidence, management identification, missing signals, business acumen, relationship with all c-suite executives). In the future, by providing real leadership, CHROs can become valued partners of CEOs. McKee, an HR senior statesman for decades, does a marvelous job synthesizing the history of HR competencies and comparing 1989 to 2013 work. She then encourages aspiring HR professionals to pay attention to the diversity of HR competency models, to learn the business from customer point of view, and to not wait to be asked to act.

Morris, CHRO at Adobe, offers an optimistic view of HR professionals who embrace the numbers, innovate and adapt, drive employee experience, leverage technology, and think global and act local. Salisbury, with 45 plus years in senior HR advisory roles most recently in employee benefits, encourages helping workers get their work done through global sourcing, employer flexibility and capped liabilities, managing personal and society risk with government models, and offering a mix of flexibility and security for aging employees.

DEAL WITH CERTIFICATION

Competencies enable certification. Certification has clearly become a major topic for HR associations about the world. Clearly, certification has different meanings based on career stage. For early HR entrants, certification is like a license that validates their ability to practice the craft (like an attorney passing the bar or psychologist being licensed). But the licensing does not ensure quality of the practicing profession. This proficiency certification indicates the quality of HR professionals in being able to do the jobs they are assigned. This certification is being proposed by SHRM through situational judgment tests.[14] Proficiency is also assessed for the professional through granular assessments of which HR competencies apply in which setting (size of company, level of HR, role of HR, experience in HR, business strategy, organization culture, and so forth). Agrawal, head of NHRDN in India, discusses the Indian business context, then shows how the NHRDN competency work will lead to an Indian national HR competency model (HRSCAPE) with 8 functional competencies at 4 levels (basic, competent, advanced, expert). Finally at the mastery level, HR competencies define someone who is a "Fellow" or truly advanced in his or her career. Wilson, CEO of AHRI, reviews the importance of differentiating competencies by career level and shows how AHRI validates competency master for very seasoned and senior HR leaders.

Collectively, these essays offer a wonderful template for future HR competency work. As HR professionals want to know what they should know and do to be effective, there are some insights that should be recognized:

- Focus less on HR competencies and more on how HR competencies drive both personal effectiveness and business results;
- Emphasize less self report on what HR people think they should know and do and more about how they are see by others;
- Recognize both base competencies for HR professionals and granularity for how competencies vary by career stage, geography, strategy, role, and other factors.
- Anticipate future HR value added more than past activities.

The answer to the appropriate question, "what do I have to be, know, and do to be an effective HR professional" is much more than asking HR professionals what they think. It requires partnership of HR professional associations around the world, focusing on outcomes of HR skills, aligning competencies to current and future business conditions, tailoring competencies to specific situations and identifying the competencies that matter most for business performance.

---

[1] Christie, M. & Young, R. (1995). "Critical Incidents in Vocational Teaching." Darwin: Northern Territory University Press.

[2] Kamoche, K. (1999). Strategic human resource management within a resource-capability view of the firm. In R. Schuler & S. Jackson. "Strategic Human Resource Management," Britain: Blackwell Publishers Ltd; Catano, V. (2001). "Empirically supported interventions and HR practice." HRM Research Quarterly, 5 (1).

[3] McLagan, P. & Bedrick, D. (1983). "Models for excellence: The results of the ASTD training and development study." Training and Development Journal, 37 (6), 10-20.

[4] Brockbank, W., Ulrich, D. & Beatty, R. (1999) "HR professional development: Creating the future creators at the University of Michigan Business School." Human Resource Management, 38 (2), 111-118.

[5] Dave Ulrich, Jon Younger, Wayne Brockbank, and Michael Ulrich. 2012. "HR From the Outside In: Six Competencies for the Future of Human Resources." McGraw-Hill Publishing Company.
Dave Ulrich, Wayne Brockbank, Jon Younger, & Michael Ulrich, M. 2012. "Global HR Competencies: Mastering Competitive Value from the Outside-In." McGraw-Hill Publishing Company.
Dave Ulrich, Justin Allen, Wayne Brockbank, Jon Younger, Mark Nyman. 2009. "HR Transformation: Building Human Resources from the Outside In. McGraw Hill Publishing Company."
Dave Ulrich, Wayne Brockbank, Dani Johnson, Kurt Sandholtz, Jon Younger. 2008. "HR Competencies: Mastery at the intersection of people and business." SHRM.

[6] The work by Center for Effective Organizations (CEO) can be referenced on their web site Edward Lawler and John W. Boudreau. 2009. "Achieving Excellence In Human Resources Management: An Assessment of Human Resource Functions." Stanford, CA: Stanford University Press.
Edward Lawler, III, 2012. "Effective Human Resource Management: A Global Analysis." Stanford, CA: Stanford University Press.
John W. Boudreau and Ian Ziskin. 2011. "The Future of HR and Effective Organizations." CEO. To appear in Organization Dynamics.

[7] Edward E. Lawler III and John W. Boudreau. "Effective Human Resource Management: A Global Analysis." Stanford University Press, 2012.

[8] Boston Consulting Group. "Creating People Advantage 2009 and 2011: Time to Act: HR Certainties in Uncertain Times."

[9] Deloitte. 2011. "Business Driven HR: Unlock the Value of HR Business Partners."

[10] Lawson, T. (1990). "The Competency Initiative: Standards of Excellence for Human Resource Executives." The Society for Human Resource Management.

[11] "A History of Human Resources: SHRM's 60 year history." 2009. Published by SHRM.

[12] Lawson, T. (1990). "The Competency Initiative: Standards of Excellence for Human Resource Executives." The Society for Human Resource Management.

[13] The CIPD professional map can be found on their website: http://www.cipd.co.uk/cipd-hr-profession/hr-profession-map/professional-areas/

[14] Situational Judgement tests are elegantly summarized as a way to ascribe confidence in individuals being able to do specific jobs: Michael Campion, Robert Ployhart, and William MacKenzie, JR. "The state of research on situational judgment tests: A content analysis and directions for future research." Human Performance. 27:4, 283-310.

DEVELOPING HUMAN RESOURCE PROFESSIONALS IN INDIA

Arvind N. Agrawal

The Indian economy, as measured in gross domestic product (GDP), continues to record an impressive growth at the rate of roughly 5 percent annually despite turmoil across the globe on the economic as well as political front. Economic pundits and business czars have predicted that infrastructure will be the engine of growth in the years ahead. This presents a huge opportunity in India for infrastructure players to meet the growing aspirations of the country's 1.2 billion citizens. What will further propel the India growth story is the rising purchasing power of its vast population and the fact that India's huge domestic market is bigger than the whole of Europe for the entire range of products and services.

Indian enterprises are globally linked in terms of exports, imports, and transfer of technology, and management talent from India competes well in global companies around the world. Indira Nooyi (PepsiCo), Sateyn Nadela (Microsoft), Rajiv Suri (Nokia), and Nitin Nohria (Harvard Business School) are examples of such talents from India who now lead global organizations. Back home, several Indian institutes—such as the Indian Institute of Management, the Indian School of Business, and the Indian Institute of Technology—are temples of modern education and learning systems and widely considered at par with educational institutions in the developed world.

Over the past six decades, India has successfully practiced a democratic form of government. In the recent national elections in 2013, BJP, led by Prime Minister Narendra Modi, got an overwhelming majority of the vote on a platform of development and growth. We have also witnessed a gradual positive change in investor perceptions and business sentiment toward India. The global business community strongly believes that India can well achieve a sustainable annual growth rate of 8 to 9 percent. Ironically, India also has the largest proportion of poor of the world. Hence development strategy in India must be inclusive—that is, it must include the poor in a manner that helps alleviate poverty from the nation.

This is precisely where human resource professionals in the country have a role to play. As business partners, they need to make the organizations globally competitive. They need to equip the vast talent pool with skills and opportunities to fuel the economic engines of business as well as meet the rising aspirations of its young workforce.

INDIA'S BUSINESS LANDSCAPE

Today, India boasts several Indian multinational corporations (MNCs) with global footprints. Tata, Mahindra, Aditya Birla Group, Reliance Industries, Godrej, Larsen & Toubro, Murugappa, and RPG are all examples of large Indian enterprises that have global presence. These professionally run organizations are entrepreneurial in their outlook, nimble-footed, and quick in capitalizing opportunities in India and across the globe. With an appetite for high risk, these organizations are progressively becoming more global, growing organically as well as through acquisitions. They are also early adapters of contemporary management practices and creators of innovative and new management practices.

There are also large numbers of non-Indian multinational corporations that are successfully competing in the Indian market. Unilever, GE, Siemens, Procter & Gamble, Toyota, Bosch, Abbott, IBM, PepsiCo, and Coca Cola are examples of MNCs that are thriving in the Indian marketplace. These MNCs bring in cutting-edge management practices, are quick to adapt to Indian market conditions, and are often a benchmark for Indian companies for global best practices.

The Indian growth story would be incomplete without mention of the strong presence and contribution of public sector companies. Steel Authority of India, Bharat

Heavy Electricals, National Thermal Power Corporation, Indian Oil Corporation, Oil & Natural Gas Corporation, and the State Bank of India are examples of highly successful enterprises in the public sector run by senior management teams appointed by the Indian government. These public-sector companies are complex and mammoth organizations operating successfully despite having their hands tied behind their backs as they go about fulfilling the "socialist agenda" of providing employment. Despite a remuneration structure that is far lower than the private sector, these enterprises are magnets for high-quality talent.

Over the years, the work environment at Indian companies, both in the public and private sectors, is constantly improving—and even becoming comparable to global enterprises. The human resource management practices in these companies are also quite evolved and compare well with global benchmarks.

FIVE HR OPPORTUNITIES AND CHALLENGES IN INDIA

In the context of these tremendous opportunities both at home and overseas, Indian organizations still face several challenges.

1. India continues to be a high inflation economy where the cost of production is constantly increasing. This is compounded by rising wages, low productivity, and inadequate infrastructure. Our wages, at all levels, are lower then global averages, although they are rising faster then anywhere else in the world. As the country progresses, wages are bound to go up. An increase in GDP will be reflected by an increase in per capita GDP, implying higher wages—and higher earnings at the individual level is an indicator of national prosperity.

In this context, it is key that human resource professionals should not be myopic by fighting the wage increase battle. Instead, the focus needs to be on productivity improvement. Until now, the HR focus in India has been on controlling costs through effective wage negotiation. Going forward, it needs to shift to negotiation for increased productivity. Low skill levels, lack of discipline to follow laid-down processes, poor infrastructure, and a low level of empowerment are all factors leading to lower productivity in India—and this is true across levels in all types of organizations. By increasing productivity, HR can make significant positive impact.

2. *Indian organizations face growing globalization.* Whether Indian companies are going to global markets or competing with global companies in the domestic market, competition is still global. To succeed in such conditions, Indian companies need to meet world-class product and services standards. This will require many Indian companies to shift their mindset and foster a culture of innovation, operational efficiency, and customer orientation. Thus, building a globally competitive culture in the company is another important area of focus for HR practitioners.

3. *Organizations need to redesign themselves for scale and complexity to compete in the globalized world.* New and emerging opportunities will need to be pursued aggressively lest those opportunities are lost to the competition. Over the years, Indian companies have grown bigger and more complex, with operations in different continents, widely varying cultures, and varied industry segments. This complexity is relatively new to the Indian corporate sector. HR has an opportunity to design appropriate organizational structure, processes, and managerial skills and style to adapt and compete globally. Integrating people across nationalities and cultures is another challenge that falls on the shoulders of HR practitioners.

4. *HR needs to ensure the availability of trained and talented manpower at all levels to meet the growing and changing needs of business.* Despite having one of the largest pools of young workers in the world, there is a severe skills deficit in India. Workforce planning, recruitment, training, and talent retention will continue to be challenges that HR needs to address. This will also include encouraging government and business collaboration around the education of future talent.

5. *There is a need to manage India's vast workforce in ways that are inclusive, innovative, and socially responsible.* Indian businesses cannot afford to blindly embrace the policy of "hire and fire." Rather, they need to take responsibility for nurturing employees and treating them well. The Indian economy should not grow at the expense of people. The growth agenda also has to be inclusive of the people coming from the lowest economic strata of the country—they need to be beneficiaries of the country's development and growth. Employees and the community within which an enterprise operates also need to be treated as equal stakeholders.

TOWARD A NATIONAL HR COMPETENCY MODEL

India boasts several large and successful organizations where the HR function continues to successfully deal with these challenges. In general, HR professionals in the country display a great sense of openness to learn from industry peers. To that end, the National HRD Network (NHRDN) in India has played a pivotal role in developing a vibrant community of competent human resource professionals. Further, trade unions in the country, led by experienced senior leaders, have also initiated many forward-looking initiatives to build competitive organizations that serve the long-term interests of the workforce and build world-class organizations at the same time.

For a vast and rapidly growing economy like India, responding to the five challenges mentioned above remains a huge responsibility for human resource professionals. Throughout India, there is growing realization of the immense shortage of trained human resource talent with the requisite competence, commitment, and credibility to help lead organizations through these challenges.

Recognizing this need, NHRDN launched HRSCAPE—a nationwide certification and development program for HR professionals. The program was developed by a team of senior HR leaders, with the active involvement of academics, HR professionals, thought leaders, subject matter experts, and business leaders from across the country and abroad. To develop a competency model, NHRDN appointed a committee consisting of senior HR leaders in the country. The committee created a draft document after very intense discussions lasting nearly 100 days. During these deliberations, the team also looked at existing competency models elsewhere in the world, held focus group discussions across India with a cross-section of HR professionals, and conducted one-on-one interviews with senior HR leaders, subject matter experts, thought leaders, and business leaders.

In these interviews, opinions were obtained as to what competencies have been demonstrated by successful HR professionals and what competencies will be needed in the future. These were then incorporated into the model. For instance, the senior business leaders who were interviewed were unanimous that the credibility of HR professionals is more important than their functional competency. This led us to include "credible champion" as one of the behavioral competencies required of HR professionals.

HRSCAPE (see **Figure 1**) consists of eight functional competencies (as shown in the outer periphery) and four behavioral competencies (shown in the inner circle). Each also has sub-competencies. For instance, strategic HRM has four sub-competencies: understanding the business context, HR strategy, aligning HR architecture, and contribution in business strategy. The competency framework provides for assessment at four levels: basic, competent, advanced, and expert.

At the basic and competent levels, assessment is envisaged to be done through online tests that will include a knowledge test as well as caselets and 360° feedback. In addition, there will also be an assessment center to assess HR skill levels. At the advanced and expert levels, certification will be based on evidence of work done, the presentation of projects on themes directly related to competencies, 360° feedback, and a freewheeling dialogue with a jury panel.

FIGURE 1: HRSCAPE

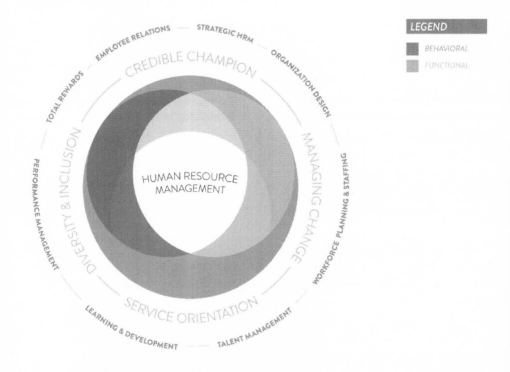

We believe that this initiative to certify HR professionals through HRSCAPE will help Indian organizations re-profile their HR function. We also hope that the country's educational institutions will align their course curriculum with this competency model to develop high-quality human resource professionals.

We are in the process of developing the assessment tools and hope to make the model available for use by June 2015. Our intention is to help HR professionals re-profile themselves—thus giving credence to the growing importance of the function—and for HR to play the role of a partner in their organization and in the nation-building process.

About Arvind N. Agrawal

Arvind N. Agrawal has served since 1999 as president of corporate development and group human resources for RPG Group. His current responsibilities at RPG comprise HR and total quality management (TQM). The first 12 years of his working life were spent in the HR function in companies such as Escorts and Modi Xerox. Thereafter, he assumed additional responsibilities for TQM in Modi Xerox, a move that brought him closer to the business environment and business issues. The exposure gained in TQM equipped him to take on the role of leading corporate strategy and marketing at Modi Xerox itself. From 1994 to 1999, Agrawal was chief executive at Escorts, responsible for its construction equipment business companies. He is a 1992 recipient of the National HRD Award and served as the national president of the National HRD Network from 2000 to 2002. He was also qualified as a professional certified coach (PCC) by the International Coach Federation. On the professional front, Agrawal continues to be active in management and HR forums in the country. He is an alumnus of IIT (Kharagpur), IIM (Ahmadabad), and IIT (Bombay), where he completed his PhD in strategic leadership in 2010.

ALWAYS GLOBAL, ALWAYS DIGITAL!

Pranesh Anthapur

My unique perspective on HR comes from my global and digital business background. I began my HR career in my home country of India, but immigrated to the United States 20 years ago. I landed in Silicon Valley just as dot-com businesses started booming. During my time with Yahoo! and other organizations, I traveled all over the world overseeing HR functions in Asia and Europe. Eventually Yahoo! offered me a role in business operations back in Bangalore, where I spent a few years seeing HR from the perspective of a customer.

I have worked in several organizations—all innovators in their industry. My multi-company, global experience has put me inside the creative ecosystem in Silicon Valley, in the middle of an emerging market, deep inside HR, and deep inside the business. This experience has shaped my perspectives on what HR needs to know and do, now and in the future, to be effective.

HR GOES DIGITAL

Many of the skills and experience that will be needed from HR talent in the workplaces and workspaces of the future are obvious. The world will be even more digital and even more mobile. Technology will permeate every aspect of the job. Predictive intelligence will be required of most jobs, as data mining and "user behavior match" replace good old intuition in most areas. The customers of tomorrow will want companies to know them and their tastes and preferences, so sellers, manufacturers, content providers, and service providers will all have to develop the capabilities in their organizations to satisfy this demand. Organizations that do business in the older ways, without predictive and data capabilities, will decline.

Now add in the future workforce, which will be dominated by Millennials and digital natives who seek more wholesome life experiences from the workplace than their predecessors. Asian and other emerging markets will participate even more in the global economy, both as consumers and as workforce talent. Organizations will see much more diversity in all aspects—age, ethnicity, nationality, gender.

HR professionals will need the capabilities and skills to be more data and analytics driven. HR also has to take the lead in creating organizational environments where work and life can come together more seamlessly using people analytics and "big data." An equally important trend will be that HR professionals will need to think and apply more strategic thinking at all layers—not just at the top. Algorithms will do much of what people do today, leaving strategy to be done by professionals.

GLOBAL BUSINESS EXPERIENCE

In an effort to enrich myself and my career, I stepped away from HR and moved into operations. I worked as a line executive for almost six years (three years in Asia and three years in the United States) before coming back to a full-time HR role a few years ago. Yahoo! was looking to solve the complex India puzzle—how to set up in that country, how to leverage the local market, and how to build local talent for global initiatives.

With active support from my manager and the team at the top, I relocated to Bangalore as Yahoo!'s chief operating officer for India. My role was to define the charter for India to support our global business—and furiously scale up business in India. I was also involved in overseeing parts of our operations in Asia. It was a fabulous experience. There were many eye openers for me as I sat on the other side of table and became an executive client of HR.

LESSONS LEARNED IN OPERATIONS

The operations role taught me several things. Fundamentally, I learned to bring strategic thinking to all aspects of my work. I quickly learned to look at business situations with the "customer first" view. I saw the need to act with agility even when I didn't have all the data or the answers. I also learned how to take risks. There is no greater lesson in accountability than visiting a company, shaking hands with its CEO, promising to deliver, then getting back to the office and wondering, "How the heck am I going to do it?" I quickly learned that as a business leader, you need to pull different small teams together and make them a larger unified team with a common mission to solve customer problems. A business role teaches you how to define a mission and align the entire company to rally behind a shared goal. That was one of my biggest learnings.

I also developed empathy for the line managers and the challenge of implementing everything we in HR ask them to do. I saw the futility of some HR tools and some policies and programs that were irrelevant in the field. I learned to recruit top talent and to talk about rewards and motivation without the HR jargon of fiftieth percentiles, compa ratios, and complex OD terminology. I learned that you need keep your language very simple or it doesn't reach the masses.

As a business leader, I experienced that the buck stopped with me. I had the responsibility to motivate and manage a large number of employees, stakeholders, customers, and key vendors—which required me to take decision-making to a whole new level. I also learned how critical the external branding of the company is and how important it is to represent your organization at key events. PR provided me with training to handle the rather aggressive media. I also worked closely with my finance colleagues to learn the nuances of forecasting and budgeting and the "art of money management."

Upon my return to the US, I handled several other business roles, including global expansion for the company, running offshore shared services centers, large-scale program management, and real estate. I learned that organizations need not just specialists but generalists who can quickly own problems and solve them by working with a diverse set of teams.

COMBING HR AND BUSINESS SKILLS: THE LESSON OF OUTSOURCING

In my operations role, I also gained a much deeper understanding of outsourcing—and when and why it does and doesn't work. Yahoo! had outsourced significant work to various vendors in India and Beijing as it grew rapidly. When I got to Bangalore, I analyzed all the major business indices—including cost of operations, dollar spend in resolving customer issues, our own capital assets, and the tax incentives provided by the local government—and compared them to the cost of outsourcing. It became apparent to me that certain areas of support need to work closely with R&D—and that they should be grown organically, in-house. We had excellent recruiting talent who knew how to aggressively recruit, but we were not fully utilizing their skills.

Indeed, bringing these responsibilities in-house meant a huge change in our strategy. I had to sell this concept to our corporate and regional leadership in order to get their buy-in. I had to explain, in business terms, the benefit of in-house versus outsource. It was not easy proposition, as we were an unproven business. I had to use all my persuasive and sales skills—and then some.

So I adopted a very transparent business process and designed a dashboard that was accessible to all at all times (which vendors couldn't do). Leaders could see the dollars saved and service level agreements (SLAs) accomplished on a daily basis. This became a win-win for all, and the company grew rapidly after that. But making the business transparent was a significant change.

Throughout this effort, I deployed all the change management skills I had learned in HR. One was constantly combining my EQ and IQ skills. Another was quantifying *everything*. Once the pilot proved successful, the word spread and I had people knocking on my door. Looking back, I wonder if I would have developed the initiative at all had I not worked in HR. Would I have been as confident in hiring the resources we needed? Likewise, if had not been exposed to the business, would my eyes have opened up to potential cost savings of millions of dollars for the company?

This is not to say that outsourcing can't be effective. In fact, for certain parts of the business, based on similar analysis, I advocated outsourcing as a strategy because I realized that we wouldn't have been able to hire all the talent we needed and that we had to tap into talent in the vendor ecosystem. Again, my combined experience in HR and business helped me balance those tradeoffs effectively.

TAKING IT BACK TO HR

People often ask me why I moved back into HR after six years as an operator. The answer is simple. It all boils down to passion. I enjoyed my stint in business and learned a lot. My passion is not just to frenetically execute but also to coach and mentor leaders. HR provides the perfect platform where I can do both. As I explained earlier, strategic and commercial acumen is being demanded of HR leaders from all industries. Even startups and venture capitalists have begun hiring HR leaders much earlier compared to a few years ago. Applying the business skills I learned to my role in HR means keeping my language simple—even though I speak the language of tradeoffs and SLAs. I groom program management talent in HR. I also tap into product management and design teams to create HR initiatives. I work closely with marketing to create a seamless internal branding experience aligned to our external branding promise. I constantly quantify and speak the language of ROI. And above all I create various dashboards and help businesses understand and follow patterns.

All things considered, running an HR department is no different than running a business. You have limited resources and there are business problems to solve. You codify the problems as data sets, look for patterns, develop a strategy, deploy your resources, course correct, adapt, and evolve. Sounds like business, right?

ONE LAST LESSON: DEVELOP A GLOBAL MINDSET

If you have a global role or are drafted into one, it is good to prepare as much as possible. There are many online resources these days that will teach you the basics about doing business in another country. I would also encourage you to undertake a day or two of cultural assimilation training, which helps develop empathy.

In today's global world, HR professionals need to be global in their thinking. You might be called upon to work on acquiring a company based in Malaysia or Israel or Brazil. Even if your organization doesn't have any global offices or international employees, you could be called on to inspect working conditions in vendor organizations based in Bangladesh or Vietnam or Egypt. You may have to work on your logo with marketing or design teams from Seoul or Beijing or Zurich. You may need to increase your talent pipeline from several countries or relocate a workforce from one country to another.

In any of these situations, your ability to understand and deliver global initiatives matters a great deal to the success of your organization's people programs. To that end, I would encourage the HR professionals of tomorrow to do two things if they can:

1. Take on an assignment abroad for any length of time—even just for a few months.
2. Do a stint outside of HR in any line role, or rotate through different functions such as marketing, IT, finance, sales, or engineering. (You don't have to be an engineer to work in the technology department!)

Doing these two things helped me a lot. I hope it helps you, too.

Aboout Pranesh Anthapur

Pranesh Anthapur is a 20-year global human resources executive for Fortune 100 companies, with additional experience in line management functions. He currently serves as chief people officer at Nutanix Inc., an industry leader in the converged infrastructure space. As a member of the senior executive team, he leads all aspects of HR for one of the world's fastest-growing companies. Prior to joining Nutanix, he was vice president of HR at Walmart Global eCommerce, where he oversaw the company's "People and Places" function; built out Walmart labs and other commercial functions; and helped Walmart scale as a multibillion-dollar e-commerce leader. Prior to Walmart, Pranesh spent more than 13 years at Yahoo! Inc., eventually taking on the role as chief operating officer for India. In that role, he was responsible for providing operational leadership to various businesses, and scaled Yahoo! India to more than 2,000 employees. He also served as Yahoo!'s vice president of Global Business Solutions, overseeing all of the company's offshore shared services centers and managing more than 1,500 employees worldwide. Earlier in his career, he held various HR executive roles at Hewlett Packard, VeriFone, and Wipro GE Medical Systems in Asia and the US. He holds a BS in engineering, an MA in personnel management, and an IR degree from Tata Institute of Social Sciences, Mumbai, India.

HR AS BUSINESS PARTNER

Richard L. Antoine

In the summer of 2014, Ram Charan published an article in Harvard Business Review titled "It's Time to Split HR." Even though Ram is a respected colleague and a friend, I wrote a rebuttal (as did several of our other colleagues) taking exception to his proposed solution to split HR. However, I very much concurred with Ram on his basic premise—*more HR leaders need to be better business partners.*

Whether they are at for-profit companies, academic institutions or nonprofit organizations, business leaders need HR leaders who are functionally knowledgeable and understand the business. HR leaders will be viewed as strategic partners who can help solve real problems if they:

- Use the business or entity strategy to drive HR activities.
- Understand the business and financial model.
- Know what drives success for the business. Does business success depend on innovation, capital utilization, customer connectivity, service excellence?
- Understand the business metrics (such as profit, margin, ROI, free cash flow productivity) and what drives them. For example, if your company uses Total Shareholder Return (TSR) as a key performance metric, the HR leader should know the specific metrics that drive TSR.

- Determine the skills and capabilities that are needed to deliver the business strategies.
- Identify the top talent and match them to business-critical roles.
- Determine the organizational risks that could jeopardize the company's business success.
- Design organizations that deliver outstanding business results.

HR leaders who consistently demonstrate these behaviors will be sought for their expertise, included in critical discussions, and used as a sounding board for difficult business decisions. In other words, they will be valued business partners.

If the behaviors above demonstrate effective business focus, then what are the characteristics that HR leaders must possess to be seen as valued business partners instead of HR caretakers?

First is *credibility* with line leaders. The leaders who run the business want HR leaders who understand the business, who know the pressures they face to deliver results, and who provide practical organizational solutions. The best way to obtain this credibility is through "line experience." Some managers work their way up through various line positions and then transfer to HR. Or HR professionals are moved into a line role for a two- or three-year assignment. I spent 25 years in Proctor & Gamble's supply chain before becoming the global HR officer. "Walking in their shoes" gives an HR professional maximum credibility.

If line experience or a line assignment is not possible, then the HR professional needs to become a student of the business. Learn everything you can about the business strategy, financial model, and business terminology (including the items listed at the beginning of this article). The great chief human resources officers (CHROs) I know are all great students and observers of the businesses in their companies. They listen, seek understanding, and learn from the best line leaders. At Procter & Gamble we developed a course called MBA (Managing Business Accounts), where top professionals from finance, strategy, supply chain, business services, and other functions taught our HR professionals about the business so they could be good business partners.

Second, HR leaders need to offer solutions to business problems. Business leaders don't want to hear what they can't do. (One caveat: The planned solution or the business leader's behaviors cannot violate the ethics of the company or the laws of the country.) Business leaders want thoughtful, sound, and creative solutions to problems. If HR leaders combine their knowledge of the business with their understanding of the human capital that drives the business, new approaches and solutions can be presented.

Third, business leaders need and value HR partners who can provide advice and counsel. Everyone needs a sounding board—someone who can be trusted to provide impartial, confidential advice. As business leaders rise higher in the organization, they have a greater need for a counselor. And who is better qualified than the HR leader, a person who understands the pressures and challenges of the business leader, a neutral observer who is trained as a coach?

Regarding the last point (being a neutral observer), I believe it is important that the HR leader is not in the succession plan for the business. If the HR leader is a top succession candidate, he or she is no longer a neutral observer. How can the business leader rely on the advice and counsel of a person who may have career goals to replace them? This conflict of interest is why I am not a fan of rotating line leaders through the CHRO role. It deprives the CEO of a valued coach and advisor who has no agenda other than what's best for the company.

Finally, valued HR business partners need to be *change agents*. In the physical world of energy, there is no such thing as stability. The same is true in business; things either get better or worse. Of course, business leaders want better results, which usually result from change. Changing the strategy, changing the business model, changing the culture, and introducing innovation are all methods for changing the trajectory of the business. All require making significant changes to the talent or organizational design in some or all parts of the organization, and the HR leader is the one best qualified to help the business leader with the change. It is most useful if the HR leader has a model or framework for change. My favorite is the Kotter model, but there are several that work equally well.

One of the many challenges I faced as the CHRO of a major company was rotating the HR business leaders (VPs of HR for multibillion-dollar businesses). If the VP of HR exhibited the four characteristics enumerated previously, I had a very difficult time trying to convince the business leader of the need for a different HR partner.

That's one way of measuring the importance of a HR leader as business partner—the business leader is reluctant to give up their HR leader.

Business leaders, from CEOs to division heads, need strong, smart, and capable HR leaders that are true business partners. If that HR leader has credibility, provides solutions, assists with neutral counsel, and leads change, then the business leader has a valued HR partner.

About Richard L. Antoine

Richard L. Antoine is president of AO Consulting, a human resources consulting firm working with CEOs and chief human resources officers on leadership, talent development, and HR strategy. He also serves as president of the National Academy of Human Resources (NAHR). In 2008, Antoine retired from Procter & Gamble after a 39-year career in supply chain and HR. For 10 of those years, he served as P&G's global HR officer, reporting to CEO AG Lafley. During his P&G career, he lived in several US locations and Kobe, Japan. Currently, Antoine chairs the board of the University of Wisconsin Foundation and serves on the boards of Northlich Advertising and IRC (Industrial Resources Counselors). He is also on the advisory boards of the University of Wisconsin Engineering School and the Center for Brand and Product Management. He was elected an NAHR Fellow and is a member of two professional HR organizations (PRT and HRPI). Antoine has a degree in chemical engineering from the University of Wisconsin and an MBA from the University of Chicago.

SUCCEEDING AS A CHRO: ADVICE FROM AN OBSERVER

Fred K. Foulkes

In talking to dozens of CHROs and CEOs over the years, as well as being a judge for the HR Executive of the Year for many years, I have come to some conclusions about what makes for the success or failure of a CHRO. This brief paper summarizes where I come out based on my experiences and observations.

WHAT MAKES A SUCCESSFUL OR UNSUCCESSFUL CHRO?

To begin, it is important to start this discussion listing a number of reasons why the top person in HR loses or keeps his or her job. Some factors are totally out of the incumbent's control, while others are based on his or her performance. Reasons that are beyond the incumbent's control include, but are not limited to, the following:

- A new CEO, especially from the outside, may simply want his or her own person. The list is relatively short of those CHROs who survive a CEO change.
- A new CEO from the inside senses that the incumbent HR person was too closely identified with his or her rival for the CEO position to be a valuable and loyal partner going forward.
- There is a merger and the CHRO from the acquiring company takes the top job in the merged organization.

- The CHRO becomes aware of ethical or values differences that he or she cannot influence.
- There is a dramatic shift in the business and the future requirements for the CHRO job have significantly changed. Perhaps labor relations competences that were once very important are now not as important as the emphasis has shifted to talent and succession planning.

But of more significance to the reader is why HR leaders fail when it is not due to reasons beyond their control. From my observations and interviews with CHROs and CEOs, I think there are six major reasons.

They are:

1. The new responsibilities and required competencies of the top HR job simply overwhelm the CHRO. As one CEO told me: "Dave was a star in the division HR role, but he could not think multi-business in the corporate job. Division presidents kept coming to me with HR problems that Dave was unable to handle. We did not realize when we selected him that the job would be over his head."
2. Some CHROs get in trouble with the CEO when they get in trouble with either the board or the compensation committee. If, because of frequent and extended contact, board members lose confidence in the CHRO, his or her days at the company will be numbered.
3. Some CHROs develop an insufficient identification with management and an over-identification with employees, especially in non-union companies. One CEO told me that he heard that his CHRO was saying at employee meetings that he had argued for higher merit increases than the company adopted. One can and should have an opinion, but once the decision is made, it is time to close ranks and support that decision. It has been said that the CHRO is the hand of the employee and the arm of management, and the proper balance must be found. There are also some CHROs who have gotten into trouble when they were too closely identified with the CEO and CFO and forgot about the human in HR.
4. The CHRO needs to be sensitive to signals and be clear that his or her actions are in alignment with the HR agenda of the top of the house. In one case, reflecting on why the top HR person was let go, the company's COO said, "Mary did not

pick up on signals and she had an agenda that was not the agenda of the CEO."

5. Sometimes CHROs get into major difficulties because of decisions made that conflict with the needs of the business. In an organization that had systemically eliminated cost of living in its labor contracts, the CHRO gave such a clause to the union to avoid a strike without telling the CEO in advance.

6. Another reason is over-identification with the CEO to the detriment of his or her relationships with peers in the executive suite. If you are the CEO's golfing or hunting buddy or bag carrier, peers may not trust you. And if the CEO steps down, you may be the next to depart. Again, one has to strike the right balance in identifying with the CEO, the board, peers, and direct reports, as well as with outsiders to the corporation.

CHRO SUCCESS IN THE EYES OF THE CEO

Nominations for the HR Executive of the Year come from many sources: subordinates, bosses, peers, as well as consultants. Evidence-based, thoughtful letters from CEOs about the contributions of the CHRO are always impressive. When it is clear how the CHRO's leadership in the HR area has contributed to the success of the business, one takes note. Consider the following actual quotes from CEO letters, with the names of course disguised.

On Cost Savings

- "The new health plan will generate savings with its focus on wellness and preventive care and provide financial incentives for employees to actively engage in decisions about their medical care. This consumer-driven health care plan is moving the company forward in controlling its spiraling multibillion annual health care costs."

- "Our CHRO had a vision to revolutionize the employee experience and drive significant cost out of the HR business. The result was HROneStop—an online resource. The savings generated by HROneStop is significant."

- "The CHRO also implemented a process to match employees in overstaffed organizations with job openings in other segments of the business...saving approximately $20 million in management severance costs."

On Leadership

- "Our CHRO has the unique ability to balance bottom-line business requirements with utmost compassion and concern. She oversees more than 1,500 employees in the HR function alone and has gained the respect and trust of employees through her ability to balance the needs of the business with the needs of the employees."

- "Through Bob's efforts, HR leaders at the company are on an equal footing with CFOs. The HR leader needs to be as strong in their stewardship role as the CFO is in his controlling role. The thing that I really like about Bob is that in addition to being my strategic business partner and trusted confidant, he is also First Friend to all of our business leaders on the executive committee."

- "Under Susan's leadership, employee engagement was elevated to a strategic level. The entire HR function was redesigned and all processes changed to support a 'culture of excellence,' with a strategic focus on patient-centered care and the 3Cs (clinical excellence, customers and service excellence, and corporate effectiveness). Service excellence standards were integrated into the entire employee 'life cycle,' beginning with the employee selection process, orientation and training, and the annual performance review process. Under her leadership, employee turnover has steadily decreased, with its current rate well below the national industry average."

- "Bill performs his job masterfully, as a true expert in the discipline of HR and as an astute business person who understands how to position our company for success in the dynamic environment of 21st century health care delivery. A true champion for our employees, Bill is leading out renewed commitment to develop capable leaders throughout our company. Bill's leadership has been and continues to be crucial to the success of our company, not only within the confines of managing the HR function, but more broadly in the overall strategic trajectory of our business."

- "Jason has been instrumental in getting the company to focus on leaders and HR strategy. His HR leadership practices fully align with the company values and business objectives. He has successfully created and advanced a new HR operating model, defined a multiyear HR strategic plan, and set our strategy priorities to set us up for continued success in the future. Jason is a trusted and admired individual who leads by example, serving as a role model for other HR and business leaders."

- "I value Bill's integral involvement in both routine HR matters and high-profile company initiatives on a regular basis. Bill is not only a genuine expert within the field of HR but is also a highly capable business person who contributes substantially to the strategic success of the company."

So, what constitutes success in the eyes of the CEO? CEOs want a true business partner who can build the HR vision and strategy around business models. They want someone who can talk candidly and competently about talent, succession, compensation, change management, and company culture. They also, of course, want someone they can trust will "tell it like it is," even if it is not what the CEO always wants to hear. In an interview in The Wall Street Journal, Gary Burnison, CEO of Korn Ferry International, the world's largest executive search firm, said: "The strategic partner to the CEO should be the CHRO in almost any organization. It shouldn't be the CFO. The person that is responsible for people should be the biggest lever that a CEO can pull. Too often, it's not."

Following the advice offered here, CHROs will become the strategic partners that most CEOs want on their team.

About Fred K. Foulkes

Fred K. Foulkes is a professor of organizational behavior at Boston University's School of Management and founder and director of the Human Resources Policy Institute, a partnership between School of Management faculty and more than 45 senior human resources executives. A prolific writer on subjects related to human resources, his principal publications include "Creating More Meaningful Work" (The American Management Association); "Personnel Policies in Large Nonunion Companies" (Prentice-Hall); and "Human Resources Management: Cases and Text" (with E.R. Livernash, Prentice-Hall). He has also written numerous articles, including five published in Harvard Business Review, and developed more than 160 case studies. Recipient of the Employment Management Association Award and the Five Star Achievement Award from the Northeast Human Resources Association, Foulkes was named a Fellow of the National Academy of Human Resources (NAHR), the human resources profession's highest honor for outstanding achievement. Currently, he serves as a director of Panera Bread and is a member of the High Roads advisory board and the NAHR Foundation board. A former board member of the HR Planning Society and of both the Society for Human Resources Management (SHRM) and the SHRM Foundation, he is a senior advisor to the Northeast Human Resources

Association (NEHRA) and leader of its Senior Executive HR Forum. He holds an AB from Princeton University and MBA and DBA degrees from Harvard Business School.

---

[1] Lauren Weber, "Here's What Boards Want in Executives," The Wall Street Journal, 10 December 2014.

CREATIVITY, INNOVATION, AND LEADERSHIP AS KEY FACTORS IN HR'S FUTURE

Pedro Borda Hartmann

In the structure of the global market, organizations face an imperative to be innovative and achieve both productivity and profitability. Capabilities such as effectiveness and adaptability are critical in this regard, as extinction is the fate of those who fail to assimilate. Creativity and innovation are also key factors—as is the role of HR leaders. A culture of leadership and innovation is built on the ability of a company's talent to reach a high performance level.

MEXICO'S HR COMMUNITY

Since its founding 68 years ago, the Mexican Association for Human Resources Management (AMEDIRH) has maintained a vision for developing the country's HR executives. During that time, AMEDIRH has witnessed the gradual transformation of HR professionals from operators to strategists. HR professionals have moved from a paradigm of operational efficiency and goals-meeting to one of integrating market values and operating in a knowledge society.

In Mexico today, the workers we help to recruit and to grow are respected and appreciated as valuable by employers around the world. However, there is much more that HR professional can do to identify and develop the nation's talent. Indeed, both specialized research and empirical evidence reveal that there is a gap, or mismatch, between what HR professionals in Mexico are currently contributing to their organizations and the kinds of leadership they need to demonstrate in order to ensure the kinds of innovation and creativity that today's companies demand.

After organizing 49 editions of the International Human Resources Congress and establishing the first Center for Talent Development in the country, AMEDIRH launched a research study to identify the key leadership competencies that HR professionals in Mexico need to possess. This article presents some of this study's preliminary findings.

AMEDIRH'S RESEARCH STUDY

The goal of the study was to identify the main gaps or mismatches between what HR executives are currently contributing to the leadership and development of their organizations and the contributions they need to make in order to ensure their organizations' productivity, profitability, and long-term competitiveness.

The first stage of research—which was conducted in 2014—focused on senior executives who are leading the HR function in their organizations. The sample included HR executives from 100 of the 900 companies affiliated with AMEDIRH. All were medium- and large-size enterprises with at least one person responsible for the HR function.

The first part of the study was qualitative; focus groups and ethnographic research were conducted within the 100 organizations that participated. A second phase— to be conducted in 2015—will be quantitative. Overall, the main assumption guiding the study is that the ability of HR executives to create an environment for creativity and innovation and a culture of talent throughout the organization has a multidimensional impact on employees, customers, and the company's ability to be profitable.

The study had four research objectives: (1) to characterize the behavior of senior management and management leaders regarding the creative abilities of employees; (2) to identify the variables at work in organizational systems related to the development of individual and group skills to solve problems; (3) to analyze the structure and behavior of processes for managing innovation; and (4) to resize the gap in the leadership relationship between HR executives and senior management in innovation.

PRELIMINARY FINDINGS

Preliminary findings reveal that there is a direct relationship between the integration of innovation into the business vision and the capacity of senior management leaders and HR to manage innovation. **Table 1** provides a breakdown of the competencies that senior HR leaders need in order to create cultures of innovation within their organizations.

TABLE 1. INNOVATIVE LEADERSHIP COMPETENCIES[1]

CATEGORIES	COMPETENCIES
Intelligence to solve problems	− Self-awareness and competence − Synthesis − Formulation
Innovation management	− Collaboration − Knowledge management − Coaching
Innovative organizational culture	− Knowledge for innovation − Integration of innovation to the business vision

During the second stage of the research project, we will quantitatively measure the correlations between these variables. Ultimately, we seek to discover further information about the relationship between senior management in innovation and HR executives, and how any mismatch or misalignment between their skills and capabilities can be managed.

WHAT DO HR PROFESSIONALS NEED TO KNOW OR DO TO BE EFFECTIVE?

Five years ago, the conventional wisdom was that in order to be effective in their role, what HR executives needed to know to be effective mainly pertained to a combination of domain function and deep knowledge of the processes that give meaning and life to the business. However, this has taken a dramatic turn. At least in Mexico, with the sample of companies analyzed, there is a semantic gap between

HR executives and other leaders within the organization that is preventing a shared understanding of organizational goals, market needs, and users. Not all executives within an organization use the same language—therefore, the cultural meanings are not shared and this affects how they act and respond as leaders.

At first we assumed this was because HR executives had a poor understanding of metrics—that they lacked the language, methodologies, and competencies needed for analysis and measurement. But the bigger problem was a lack of understanding about the kinds of processes and culture that needed to be created in order to spark innovation throughout the organization.

While the findings of the research developed by AMEDIRH are still preliminary, we identified a clear pattern whereby leaders largely distrusted the creative skills of their employees, which in turn suppressed and censored their desire to contribute to the organization's problem-solving. In other words, this distrust of talent had a negative impact on the organization's capacity to innovate.

Additionally, a lack of clearly defined processes for managing innovation makes it difficult to implement divergent and convergent tools that ensure innovative idea generation. In summary, mutual mistrust between senior management and human resources leaders has a direct impact on an organization's ability to be innovative and to compete in the marketplace.

CONCLUSION

A culture of innovation leadership is defined as "the process of creating contexts for innovation to happen...[and] creating and implementing roles for active contributors to the subject as well as structures for decision-making, appropriate spaces to detonate creativity, human networks that facilitate the development of innovative intelligence, and equipment that will support the generation and testing of ideas."[2]

In that regard, the international literature is consistent when it states that businesses must embrace a culture of innovation in order to survive.[3] AMEDIRH believes that human resources executives are the best-positioned leaders to take on the role of transforming organizations and creating innovative cultures in the twenty-first century.

About Pedro Borda Hartmann

Since 2006, Pedro Borda Hartmann has served as executive director of the Mexican Association for Human Resources (AMEDIRH). Formerly in the administration of President Vicente Fox, he was executive director of the National Institute for the Elderly. He has also served as CEO of the National Chamber of the Rubber Industry and director of public relations, human resources, exhibitions, and conventions and private secretary to the chairman of the World Trade Center in Mexico City. He has also worked for a range of companies—including Grupo Accor, Warner Lambert, Gillette de México, Laboratorios Syntex, and Cementos Tolteca—and has given speeches in Argentina, Venezuela, Thailand, Brazil, Japan, Canada, Chile, and Puerto Rico, among other countries. On October 2012, he received the George's Petipas award at the World Congress of HR in Australia. This recognition was approved by members of the five continents that make up the World Federation. He holds a degree in industrial relations from the Universidad Iberoamericana.

---

[1] Kathy Malloch, "Creating the Organizational Context for Innovation," in Tim Porter-O'Grady and Kathy Malloch, "Innovation leadership: Creating the Landscape of Healthcare" (Sudbury, MA: Jones and Bartlett Publishers, 2010), pages 33–57.

[2] Ibid.

[3] M. S. Basadur, "Organizational Development Interventions for Enhancing Creativity in the Workplace," Journal of Creative Behavior, 31(1), 1997, pages 59–72; Richard Florida and J. Goodnight, "Managing for Creativity," Harvard Business Review, 83(7), 2005, pages 125–131.

BEHAVIORAL CHARACTERISTICS OF HIGHLY SUCCESSFUL HR LEADERS: A SUBJECTIVE VIEW

Alan R. May

The academic and popular management literature is replete with observations on leadership competencies. However, there are few references to the personal behaviors associated with success within any particular functional discipline. Indeed, we typically encounter a fixed (and often long) list of behavioral attributes that, in total, define "leadership" in the view of the author.

As HR practitioners, we tend to apply leadership behavioral definitions at either a broad organizational or specific job level. Across large, complex organizations, we use these lists to select a subset of attributes that define preferred leadership behaviors. In turn, the HR function will infuse these behavioral attributes into the selection, training, development, and assessment systems throughout an organization as a means to define and align a corporate culture. At a job level, it is also common to find a set of "leadership competencies" advanced as predictive of success in a given role. HR functions will often apply competency assessments in the selection process to increase the odds that a candidate will experience success in their new assignment.

Within the HR functional discipline, many organizations maintain "HR competencies" that are applied at all levels of HR functional practice. A number of HR professional associations, including SHRM, HRCI and CIPD, are refining HR competency models to include personal behaviors in the mix of success elements for HR practitioners. Ask any chief human resources officer—and even many CEOs—and you will hear about the requirements of knowing the business, delivering HR service excellence, and change management as descriptors of HR excellence. However, far fewer organizations have defined the distinctive *personal behaviors* that are indicative of highly successful HR practitioners. I would like to advance an admittedly subjective list of personal attributes that may be of value to organizations as they evolve their HR competency models or to aspiring HR professionals as they develop their careers.

My experience and observations over 30 years of HR practice suggest that there are six discernible behavioral traits of successful HR leaders. Across a career that began with an HR internship in state government and continued to a CHRO role and beyond, I have held HR generalist and specialist assignments at every organizational level. I have also had the privilege of leading HR teams ranging from a personal assistant sitting outside my office to hundreds of HR professionals deployed globally.

Moreover, my professional experiences to date have enabled me to work with perhaps more than 1,000 business leaders—from front-line supervisors to CEOs—across numerous industries, including manufacturing, consumer products, and financial services. Therefore, the recognition of these six behavioral attributes has been informed by the views of countless business professionals across industrial categories, functional disciplines, and organizational hierarchy.

In my experience, the following six personal characteristics are resident within highly successful HR leaders: intellectual curiosity, simplicity, empathy, courage, dynamic range, and grit. While one might argue that most, if not all, of these characteristics are essential in any leader, I have seen these six in combination differentiate true excellence from mere competency in the HR practitioner. Furthermore, I have witnessed that these personal traits are evident despite the strong forces that corporate culture tends to impose on defining preferred behaviors in any given organization. Let me take a moment to define each, as applied to the unique role HR plays within an organization and the impact the function can have on both the enterprise and individuals.

INTELLECTUAL CURIOSITY

This personal characteristic can be seen as an obvious prerequisite for success in just about anything in life. While that might be true, intellectual curiosity is also the spark that drives an HR professional to both know the business cold and develop effective relationships. The intellectually curious HR professional asks the second or third question to explore core assumptions, proposes alternatives or new models in decision-making discussions, and helps others connect the dots between objective facts and behavioral observations.

A highly inquisitive mind enables an HR professional, especially in a generalist role, to explore all facets of the value chain within an enterprise. In turn, the insights developed in an unrelenting quest to understand a given business model are applied in the form of HR expertise and recommendations that transform organizational performance. In addition, this behavioral trait is the basis for developing deep interpersonal relationships within the workplace. Through intellect and genuine interest in others, outstanding HR professionals also develop an expanding network of enduring and reciprocal relationships that allow them to get complex work "done done" through others.

SIMPLICITY

Most "customers" of HR services—line managers, individual employees, corporate directors, or third parties such as unions or regulators—are so engaged in their day jobs that they have a limited share of mind for HR processes, procedures, policies, or practices. Human resources is a highly complex field of practice; ask any line leader about three months after they have accepted an HR position as a supposed developmental assignment!

A highly successful HR leader makes the complex simple, without compromising functional integrity or organizational impact. Simplicity in HR practice is one hallmark of functional excellence. As Albert Einstein so eloquently stated, "If you can't explain it simply, you don't understand it well enough." This is as true for an HR generalist coaching a first-level supervisor as for a benefits director explaining the operational dynamics and financial implications of a pension plan. The demonstration of simplicity is not about "dumbing down" the function; it is about capturing the essence of what an end-user really needs from HR to meet a specific organizational or individual need.

EMPATHY

Several years ago, I worked with a mid-level executive in a large consumer products company who was seeking a new HR manager from a number of highly qualified internal candidates. As the head of the function, I knew all of the candidates and suspected that we would face a difficult choice to select the best individual for a role that supported hundreds of front-line employees.

As we prepared to conduct our interviews, I asked the executive what would be the most heavily weighted criteria among several I had advanced to guide the process. He responded that all those criteria were important, but that I had missed a key behavioral attribute which, in his experience, enabled HR professionals to excel within his business unit: empathy. His logic was simple: "Leaders come to work each day and spend their time with either people or things. Great leaders spend the majority of their time with people because people get things done. Without this investment of time—the most precious of all resources in an organization—a leader will never develop the empathy for those he or she leads."

He was particularly insistent about the demonstration of empathy in an HR leader. "It's not enough to get the fundamentals and transactions correct and to have a foundation in behavioral science. I expect my HR leader to provide genuine insights regarding every individual within the organization I lead," he told me. Exceptional HR professionals at all levels go beyond expertise in behavioral sciences. They demonstrate empathy as they inform and inspire others to provide individual support, align teams, manage conflict, and lead change.

Let me provide a simple example of the power of empathy. Early in my career I was an HR generalist in a large, unionized distribution facility. Frankly, morale in the plant was very low and the HR team at times seemed to thrive on creating an adversarial relationship with the union and, by extension, with the workforce at large.

One day a front-line employee who had worked at the site for more than 40 years walked into the HR office seeking help in understanding her retirement options.

This employee was well known to all throughout the site for being highly vocal in her negative opinions regarding management practices. One of the HR representatives offered to spend a few minutes with her to explain the nuances of the pension plan. Minutes soon turned into a few hours, subsequent one-on-one meetings, and ultimately a joint visit to the local Social Security Administration office to resolve some paperwork issues as the HR representative assisted her with an application for federal benefits.

Despite the fact that this was one HR professional working with a lone employee among hundreds at the site, the empathy demonstrated in support of a long-service employee "went viral" well before the era of social media. In fact, the HR team was so inspired by its representative's demonstration of empathy that the team decided to change its employee support processes from more "high tech" to much more "high touch." This was just one of many changes inspired by this empathetic behavior that, over time, not only improved morale (as reflected in employee surveys) but led to greater workforce productivity and more amicable relationships with the union.

COURAGE

Even the most open and progressive organization can be a tough place to work as an HR professional. Whether they are navigating interpersonal conflicts, team dynamics, ethical dilemmas, a union negotiation, or a workplace crisis, HR professionals often must demonstrate courage to be successful. At its best, courage in this context goes beyond merely expressing a dissenting view at a business meeting or confronting the dysfunctional behavior of an executive, manager, or employee. It is the personal conviction to say and do what you believe is right—adopting a fact-based, objective demeanor in the heat of battle.

Courage in an HR role can be as seemingly trivial as insisting that a manager continue to search for a better candidate rather than accepting an average candidate just to get the job filled quickly. Or it can be as profound as overtly opposing a short-term tactic, like forcing high levels of overtime, that will inevitably sap morale and actually reduce productivity in the long term. In extreme instances, a courageous position can cost an HR leader their job. However, in most instances it inspires others to advance the debate on a given issue and ultimately to make a balanced decision.

DYNAMIC RANGE

Life within a large, complex organization can be a bit like theater. There are moments when the script calls for gravitas and others that may invite levity—all in the same day. HR professionals may be called upon to inspire thousands of employees with their passion and creativity while delivering what may be a relatively dry topic. At the same time, HR professionals need to master the art of the "quiet conversation" as they coach, cajole, or otherwise guide superiors, peers, and subordinates through matters that are often quite personal.

My experience suggests that the extent of this range needs to be as broad among CHROs as entry-level HR representatives. Ultimately the personal expression of a broad dynamic range is all about having the desired impact on groups or individuals in a fast-paced workplace where most communication is conducted via email and social media. The expression of a broad dynamic range is not manipulative if done in a genuine manner. Highly effective HR leaders can flex their emotions across a continuum of situational, cross-cultural, or topical variations.

GRIT

Success often comes from doing the same mundane things longer and better than anyone else, well after others have lost patience or given up in frustration. Perhaps the best example of this behavior among HR professionals is in the area of driving long-term organizational change. Within HR, we often get excited about particular "change models" or methodologies for aligning organizations against a given business strategy. While many business leaders across all functions seem to enjoy defining these strategies and formulating plans, more often than not these leaders stray from the intended course not too long after an exhilarating offsite or dynamic board review.

Great HR leaders recognize that it takes months if not years to produce sustainable business results within an enterprise. This is a matter of functional discipline that at times can get labeled as overly bureaucratic or process-driven. However, it takes grit to stay the course, remind the team of the required actions, and drive the communications and processes necessary to achieve the economic or organizational strategic intent.

Another example of grit in the HR profession is the tenacity of holding to a vital policy objective or management principle. Often HR leaders are called upon to sustain strategic distinctions in policy or practice despite intense pressure to do otherwise. Examples of "HR grit" can be found when organizations conduct mergers, acquisitions, or divestitures, during collective bargaining negotiations, or in the annual review of compensation and benefits levels.

IN CONCLUSION

There may be other behavioral attributes that can be observed across a broad population of highly successful HR professionals. And any personal qualities brought to the role must augment the core requirements of HR functional depth, business savvy, and analytical skills to ensure success. However, I have found that exercising intellectual curiosity, simplicity, empathy, courage, dynamic range, and grit in the workplace will differentiate the truly great from the merely adequate among HR professionals.

I readily admit that I have struggled with demonstrating each of these behavioral markers throughout every aspect of my career. However, I find the list useful in self-assessment, often as I debrief a given situation, interaction, or initiative. And I would invite leaders to reexamine the HR competencies within their organizations and consider adding the six behavioral elements that ultimately define excellence within the function. Further, I would challenge those aspiring to a long-term career as an HR professional to assess their behavioral strengths against this list and to seek opportunities to demonstrate these traits as they maximize the impact of HR within their organizations.

Alan R. May

Alan R. May is vice president of Boeing Commercial Airplanes' human resources organization. Previously, he served as vice president of HR for Boeing Defense, Space & Security and as vice president of strategy, compensation, and benefits for the Boeing Company. In this capacity, he directed HR strategy, executive and enterprise compensation, health care policy, and retirement benefits for the company. Prior to joining Boeing, May served as chief talent and HR officer for Cerberus Capital Management, a leading private equity firm based in New York, and held a number of global HR and business integration roles during a 15-year career at PepsiCo, culminating with an assignment as senior vice president of HR for the rapidly growing Quaker, Tropicana, and Gatorade division. Prior to PepsiCo, May held HR and general management roles at Caterpillar and TRW. May serves as a trustee of the Ravinia Festival and the Chicago Symphony Orchestra Association, and sits on the corporate advisory board for the Marshall School of Business at the University of Southern California. He also is a member of the Economic Club of Chicago, the Human Resources Policy Association, and the University of Illinois Foundation. May holds a bachelor's degree in economics and a master's degree in labor and industrial relations from the University of Illinois.

HOW DO WE GET THERE FROM HERE?

Kathryn McKee

In 1997, I wrote an article titled "The Human Resource Profession: Insurrection or Resurrection?" published in Human Resource Management. It told the story of the profession and how it changed decade by decade. *In 1997 I said:* "HR can gain a place at the leadership table with full membership; a true strategic partner—reporting to the CEO, and interacting with the board of directors. It is virtually impossible for an organization to achieve any organizational torqueing without involving HR in the strategizing, plan development, and execution.... HR has the opportunity to throw off the mantle of command and control. HR can be a shaper of destiny, providing ideas that are efficient and cost-effective.... [HR] can be profit-oriented and HR can lead by example."

Seventeen years later, HR—in many (or most?) cases—*is* at the table and is the full strategic partner. Between then and now, the "C-suite" terminology came into being, and consequently many of us are the CHRO along with the CFO, CEO, CMO, CTO, and so forth. The Society for Human Resource Management says they are now using the term chief HR executive (CHRE).

Now I'm asking: What's happened in the meantime? In re-reading that article from years ago, it is highly disappointing to realize the same concerns raised then about the ineffectiveness of the HR profession still exist. If we needed to be able to perform competently *then* to be effective, what was in the way of keeping us from getting there by *now*?

Is this a question of competencies? Maybe. Is it a question of time? Maybe. Is it a question of curiosity, drive, and ambition to reach for greater things? Absolutely.

SHRM has had a series of competency models since 1989, when they retained Golle and Holmes to develop a senior-level competency model. Over the years, SHRM developed four additional models: Rothwell's in 1996 in cooperation with CCH; Dr. Steven Schoonover's in 1997 and 1998; and SHRM's model in 2012. Dave Ulrich and Wayne Brockbank, who have been studying HR competencies since 1987, began a partnership with SHRM on competencies in 2002, which ended in 2007 when SHRM decided to go its own way.[1]

The first call to develop attributes, skills, knowledge, abilities, and observable behaviors to be competent HR practitioners occurred 25 years ago. While the words have changed—and new attributes, skills, knowledge, abilities, and observable behaviors have been added—much is the same.

So have HR practitioners kept up with this? Maybe. Why has there been such difficulty achieving individual success in acquiring the skills, knowledge, and behavioral attributes that experts say we need in the 21st century? Is it due to lack of time to enhance one's own performance and scope of responsibility, or apathy? Is it waiting to be asked? Or is it a matter of stepping out and exercising the initiative to broaden one's understanding of the world today and what it takes to be stellar at what you do?

What we needed then and what we need now: Below is a rough comparison of the original SHRM competency model from 1989 and the 2013 SHRM competency model. It is difficult to do a total apples-to-apples comparison because the sorting and terminology are different. Some match, and some do not. Those that have remained constant are italicized, and those that are new are in boldface.

SHRM'S ORIGINAL COMPETENCY MODEL (1989)	SHRM'S NEW COMPETENCY MODEL (2013)
Goal and Action Management: Efficient use of time and resources; initiating activity to head off problems; concern with impact and sensitivity about own and department image internally and externally; exercising judgment and making effective and timely decisions	
Leadership: Identifying staff development needs; formulating development plans; assessing impact of programs on organization results and line-staff relationships; using group process skills to accomplish organizationally driven and team-oriented tasks; marketing HR's role/services capabilities to strengthen and position the department's charter and mission; leading/mobilizing others with the vision of possible and probable direction for HR; instilling trust and respect of others by being open and candid, keeping things confidential, behaving fair and ethically toward others, and demonstrating a sense of corporate responsibility	**Leadership and Navigation:** Transformational and functional leadership; results and goal-oriented; resource management; succession planning; project management; mission-driven; **change management**; politically savvy; able to influence; consensus-builder
Influence Management: Approaching problems with a clear perception of organization and political reality; working effectively with others in organization/utilizing contacts to build and strengthen an internal support base; communicating intended or desired information through the appropriate organizational channels; effective written, verbal, and nonverbal communications and cues; recognizing confrontational situations appropriate to negotiation, persuading others to change positions, and facilitating win-wins	
Business Knowledge: Strategic focus; awareness of external/internal forces that will impact the future effectiveness/efficiency of the organization; understanding business operation, how organization competes, what current and future issues are and their impact on the organization, short and long-term plans, and cultural value systems impacting organizational effectiveness; understanding the industry, including suppliers, product/service substitutes, buyers, and potential entrants; adding value by perceiving opportunities for HR to deliver value-added services and programs to the business; possessing strong knowledge of the functional areas of the business	**Business Acumen:** Strategic agility; knowledge of the business; systems thinking; economic awareness; effective administration; knowledge of finance and accounting; sales and marketing; technology; labor markets; business operation/**logistics**; government and regulatory guidelines; **HR and organizational metrics/analytics/business indicators**

HR Technical Proficiency: HR planning, selection, and placement; training/development; employee/labor relations; compensation and benefits; health, safety, and security; organizational development; HRIS

HR Expertise: Strategic business management; workforce planning and employment; HR development; compensation and benefits; **risk management**; employee and labor relations; HR technology; **global/international HR capabilities; talent management; change management**

SHRM 2013 MODEL

SHRM 2013 MODEL

Relationship Management: Business networking expertise; **visibility; customer service, internal and external**; people management; advocacy; negotiation and conflict management; credibility; **community relations; transparency**; proactivity; responsiveness; **mentorship**; influence; **employee engagement**; teamwork; mutual respect

Consultation: Coaching; project management; **analytic reasoning**; problem-solving; **inquisitiveness**; creativity and innovation; flexibility; respected business partner; career pathing; **talent management**/people management; time management

Communication: Verbal and written communication skills; presentation skills; persuasion; **diplomacy**; perceptual objectivity; **active listening; effective timely feedback; facilitation skills; meeting effectiveness**; social **technology and social media savvy; public relations**

Global and Cultural Effectiveness: Global perspective; diversity perspective; openness to various perspectives; empathy; openness to experience; tolerance for ambiguity; adaptability; cultural awareness and respect

Ethical Practice: Rapport-building; trust building; personal, professional, and behavioral integrity; professionalism; credibility; personal and professional courage

Critical Evaluation: Measurement and assessment skills; objectivity; **critical thinking**; problem-solving; **curiosity and inquisitiveness; research methodology**; decision-making; **auditing skills; knowledge management**

What the SHRM model reveals is the change in global behavior and the technical change in the profession. However, Ulrich and Brockbank earlier identified these items over several years of studying the HR profession and the competencies necessary to be successful.

Today there are dramatic new requirements for HR professionals to be successful.

Just look at what's happened since 1989:

DATA	– Big data
	– Predictive analytics
	– Trending

CULTURE	– Organizational and national cultures
	– Doing business globally
	– World issues and their impact on your organization
	– More constant organizational change
	– Understanding the importance of value systems and value propositions

YOUR BUSINESS	– Impact of the local and national economy and Wall Street on your business
	– Trade flows and capital flows
	– The Industry you are in and where your organization fits in that industry
	– Your product/services cycle
	– Entrepreneurship mindset
	– Corporate social responsibility

THE WORKFORCE	– Five generations in the workplace and their impact on one another
	– How prepared you are for Millennials to become a major part of your organization's workforce, and planning ahead for Generation 2020 or whatever it will be called
	– The Labor markets, skills gaps, and reasonable accommodation
	– Sensitivity to family needs
	– Workplace violence
	– Sexual harassment and bullying
	– Executive coaching

HR PRESSURES	– The constant changes in local, state, and federal labor laws and their impact on your business
	– Small company vs. large company needs and demands on the HR function
	– The personnel police vs. problem-solving
	– "Talent management"
	– Automated recruitment processes

FAIRNESS	– Justice: organizational, procedural, and interactional
	– Performance management—making it real and meaningful to employer and employee
	– Paying people properly
	– Micro-discrimination
	– Violence in the workplace
	– Sexual harassment and bullying

Given the changes in the model, and the issues that today's HR professionals face, how then *do* we get from *there* to *here* and from *then* to *now*?

We need to do three things:

1. Understand what it takes to be competent by studying HR competency models—there are several (see endnote).
2. Learn what your business is—from the creation of the idea to stuff in a box or an email delivered to the client or customer.
3. Do not wait to be asked to take a leadership role.

Where do you begin? Here are stories from two role models:

Wanda Lee, SPHR, retired from her role as senior vice president of HR for 5,000-employee PacifiCare before it was acquired by United Health Care. Where did she start her career? As a buyer in the purchasing department of a manufacturer. As she describes it, she had a natural curiosity about how things worked and why they needed the materials. This led to a very strong understanding of how the business worked. She asked lots of questions and found better ways to do things without being asked. Then she was bored.

This led to an opportunity in another company to take over the "personnel" function. A single parent with all the responsibilities of raising two children, Lee went to night school and finished her bachelor's degree—and then her master's degree—in business. And thus began her HR career. Along the way, her education, curiosity, and inquisitiveness led her to a very strong understanding of business strategy and all the things that go into developing the strategic initiatives that drive the business. Since she was not a shy and retiring person, she began asking tough questions of the senior teams in the companies where she worked, and that led to the top-level job at PacifiCare as strategic partner, with all the joy and agony that comes from being visible and an influential member of the senior team.

Lee became a certified coach, and used these skills to guide and support her CEO, peers. and staff. She also became active externally, serving on boards and in the community, bringing back to PacifiCare an enhanced knowledge of their external stakeholders. When she started there was no competency model that could serve as a pathway; she just figured it out on her own. She honed her leadership skills through involvement in the SHRM chapters in Southern California, leading to her chairmanship of SHRM.

Deb Horne, SPHR, director of HR at CMC Rescue in Santa Barbara, California, has had a slightly different career path. She started her business career as a simultaneous franchisee of Jazzercise and co-owner of a restaurant.

After a few years in those businesses, she was asked to be employee number five of a startup R&D/manufacturer of infrared cameras. Her job? Everything necessary to run the business. Horne acted as a "Jill of all trades" until the company had around 25 employees and planned to double its workforce. That's when she decided to specialize in HR.

When asked what helped her in obtaining her current role as CHRO of CMC Rescue, she answered "business acumen, finance, and strategic planning." She also went back to school, earning her master's degree in organizational management at night, and enhanced her leadership skills by serving as president of the local SHRM chapter and playing national roles for SHRM. She gained her competencies through education, watching, doing, stepping up, and pointing the strategic way for her leadership team.

Horne calls herself a "credible activist" and refuses to be an HR person who hides behind laws, processes, and procedures. She also used the word "curiosity" and went on to say: "Persuasion requires credibility so you can be influential.... One gains trust through that credibility, your expertise, your actions, and your results... and this applies to a department of one or 10,000."

How do you get from **there** *to* **here?** Exercise the initiative to learn, watch, take moderate risks, understand the business, develop leadership and influence skills by assuming leadership roles in volunteer organizations where it is a safe place to fail, pick yourself up, learn from your mistakes, and do not wait to be asked. Do I have hope for our profession? Indeed I do! We just have to step up and into competency, leadership, and understanding the wondrous opportunities open to us to make a difference.

About Kathryn McKee

Kathryn McKee, SPHR, is retired senior vice president and HR director, the Americas, for Standard Chartered Bank, having joined them when they acquired parts of First Interstate Bank Ltd. McKee has honed her leadership skills through her experiences as national president of NHRA, chair of HRCI, chair of the SHRM Foundation, and national chair of SHRM and several other boards. She learned about the business of business at Mattel Toys, Twentieth-Century Fox Film Corp., First Interstate Bancorp and First Interstate Bank, where she served as CHRO. She is an author, speaker, and instructor in a variety of HR-related courses offered by UC Santa Barbara Extension. McKee started her career in "personnel" behind a typewriter in spite of her BA degree. She went back and graduated from the Executive Program in UCLA's Anderson School. She also did not wait to be asked.

---

[1] See the following references on competency models: William J. Rothwell, PhD, "HR's Survival Depends on Developing Competencies to Manage Future Issues," CCH, Issue 382, June 1996; Tom E. Lawson and Vaughan Limbrick, "Critical Competencies and Developmental Experiences for Top HR Executives," Human Resource Management, Spring 1996, Vol 35, Number 1, pages 67–85; Steven Schoonover, MD, "New Skills Needed for a New Work Environment," Employment Relations Today, 1997, 24(3), pages 21–32; Dave Ulrich, Wayne Brockbank, Dani Johnson, Kurt Sandholtz, and Jon Younger, "HR Competencies: Mastery at the Intersection of People and Business," SHRM, 2008.

LEVERAGING EMPLOYER BRANDING AS A KEY BUSINESS STRATEGY

Tresha Moreland

"It's my hospital," a group of employees said to me after a leadership team presentation explained the great recession's dire impact on the hospital. The employees' voices and teary eyes expressed sincerity, determination, and a sense of deep ownership of a hospital they had great pride in. This touching exchange with employees compelled me to find out more about the hospital's employer branding strategy.

I have found that if an organization has the ability to earn the hearts and minds of its people, there is nothing it can't accomplish. That complex quest can be achieved through leveraging employer branding as a key business strategy.

Why should we discuss the need to attract talent when there are so many people looking for work? After all, we have just gone through a major recessionary period with a slow recovery. There are more than 9 million people unemployed and 7 million people underemployed.

Here's why.

THE GREAT SKILLS DIVIDE

Unsettling concerns about talent scarcity are on the rise. PricewaterhouseCoopers reports that 63 percent of CEOs say a top concern is finding key skills. This result is up sharply from 46 percent in 2009.[1] Not only has the talent shortage not been resolved, but there are also anxieties that the skills gap will worsen. Forty-six percent of human resource managers surveyed by Robert Half anticipate that hard-to-fill positions will remain open for more than three months.[2]

To further complicate matters, according to the Labor Department, 2.8 million people quit their jobs in September 2014. That is up nearly 10 percent from August 2014.[3] These statistics may be a sign of a recovering economy. However, they are bad news for those who wish to retain skilled talent. And I haven't even touched the concern of future increasing retirement numbers among baby boomers.

What can we do about a skills shortage in our organizations?

AN INFLUENTIAL SOLUTION: THE EMPLOYER BRAND PROPOSITION

In their efforts to retain and attract skilled talent, one of the most influential areas that too many organizations currently overlook is employer brand as a key business strategy. Organizations often get buried in other priorities, or feel that there is nothing wrong with the status quo. But in my experience, making a good business case for an employer brand strategy is what helps overcome these challenges. It starts with understanding the concept and benefits of an employer brand strategy.

Employer branding is "a targeted, long-term strategy to manage the awareness and perceptions of employees, potential employees, and related stakeholders with regards to a particular organization."[4] In essence, employer branding is how we tell the world, "People want to work for us, and here's why." It's ultimately earning the hearts and minds of people and having the ability to communicate your story in a way that compels people to learn more.

But the employer brand has grown into much more than how customers and employees view an organization. It has become a business imperative that directly impactsthe bottom line. A 2011 study by TMP Worldwide found that of those organizations leveraging employer branding, 35 percent feel it has been a significant contributor to reduced turnover and 45 percent have found it leads to increased engagement.[5]

The ability to attract and engage skilled talent depends on a strong employer brand, as people's perceptions of "what it is like to work at a company" are becoming increasingly important in their "buying decision." The link between shareholder value and people is also evident: motivated people improve your ability to drive value.

Apple leveraged a brand concept that successfully created worldwide appeal. In his biography of Steve Jobs, Walter Isaacson quoted the Apple co-founder as saying, "We at Apple had forgotten who we were. One way to remember who you are is to remember who your heroes are."[6] This was the basis for Apple's "Think Different" brand campaign. The Apple commercial that started out as part of a consumer brand strategy expanded rapidly to its employer brand as well:

"Here's to the crazy ones. The misfits. The rebels. The troublemakers. The round pegs in square holes. The ones who see things differently. They're not fond of rules. And they have no respect for the status quo. You can quote them, disagree with them, glorify them, or villify them. About the only thing you can't do is ignore them. Because they change things. They push the human race forward. And while some may see them as the crazy ones, we see genius. Because the people who are crazy enough to think they can change the world are the ones who do."

STEP AWAY FROM THE BOUNDARIES: HR AND MARKETING ALIGNMENT

Effective employer brand strategies compel HR and marketing to step out of their functional boundaries (called silos) and collaborate. Both functions have a common link—earning the hearts and minds of people. Both functions must influence and motivate people.

I have been able to write the most compelling recruitment and internal communication messages when collaborating with marketing. For example, when working for a small independent hospital in Northern California, I was able to recruit hard-to-find skilled nurses away from beaches and city life to work for smaller employers in rural areas. This started with partnering with a marketing firm and building our message with our key audience—skilled talent—in mind. Together, we brainstormed different messages until we came upon a compelling message that we knew would resonate with our target audience. As soon as our campaign launched, calls from prospective nurses started to come in.

Each function can bring to the equation a unique set of skills.

Marketing can:

- Define an organization's key differentiation—what makes it special over its competitors
- Create a brand promise
- Optimize technology to connect with people
- Leverage group segmentation to personalize the message

HR can:

- Create, reward, and communicate values and mission
- Convert a brand promise into brand behavior
- Recruit employees to be brand advocates
- Develop leaders to reinforce the brand message

Together, HR and marketing minds can learn from each other, resulting in magical strategies that propel an organization to new heights. Ultimately, by silo busting, an organization can achieve a spectacular value proposition.

Forming collaborative partnerships can strengthen an organization's success. In larger organizations, I've reached out to the marketing department and requested assistance. I've also worked for smaller organizations that didn't have a marketing department, in which case I've been able to partner with an external marketing firm. From there I've begun to build a strategy with our end audience in mind.

THE POWER OF SOCIAL MEDIA

Before social media, organizations could almost fully control their reputation. However, social media, through public opinion, can make or break an organization's reputation overnight. In developing a social media strategy, I again have found it helpful to partner with marketing. Together, we could think about how to develop an online presence in areas where our ideal talent hangs out.

We also had videos made of those same employees who said, "It's my hospital," talking about why they love working there. When I watched video after video, I realized our top talent is our brand. Through social media, hearing and seeing employees relay their compelling story tugs at the hearts and minds of others.

WHY HAVING A BRAND STRATEGY DOESN'T MEAN WE ARE FINISHED

A successful strategy today may fail tomorrow. Consumer tastes change, markets shifts, disruptive innovations occur, and leaders leave. Each of these factors influences consumer and employee impressions, ultimately impacting short- and long-term directions.

We looked at Apple earlier as a prime example of an effective employer brand strategy. However, since Steve Jobs passed away, investors are questioning whether Apple has lost its sparkle. An organization that once was known for delivering radical, innovative products is now seen as delivering incremental changes to existing products. What was once considered a "cool" place to work may not be seen that way now.

It is easy to create a strategy and forget about it. It's like taking a pair of comfortable shoes for granted. But over time the soles wear out and the shoes becomes useless. An employer's brand strategy is not something that is ever done and forgotten about. An effective employer brand strategy is not a flavor of the month program that fades over time. It is an ever-evolving target that requires a flexible and responsive mindset.

A successful employer brand is not necessarily what you do, but it defines who you are. Defining who you are and communicating a compelling message will help earn people's hearts and minds. Ultimately, an effective employer brand strategy will compel skilled talent to come to you.

About Tresha Moreland

Tresha Moreland is an executive leader in human resource management. Her most recent role is as vice president of human resources for the Dameron Hospital Association. For more than 20 years, she has held key human resource leadership roles in multiple industries, including manufacturing, distribution, retail, hospitality, media, and health care. Moreland is the founder and publisher of HR C-Suite (www.hrcsuite.com), a results-based HR strategy publishing resource dedicated to connecting HR with business results. She served on the SHRM chapter board for four years, receiving a Superior Chapter Award under her leadership as chapter president, and on the CHA HR Advisory Council. She writes on relevant workplace and career topics and received the ASHHRA Communication Award for an article entitled, "Leveraging Human Resources During Times of Uncertainty." Moreland holds an MS in human resource management and an MBA. She has also earned a Senior Professional in Human Resources (SPHR) certification.

---

[1] PricewaterhouseCoopers, "Fit for the Future: 17th Annual Global CEO Survey," 2014, page 18. (http://www.pwc.com/gx/en/ceo-survey/2014/assets/pwc-17th-annual-global-ceo-survey-jan-2014.pdf)

[2] Robert Half, "The Demand for Skilled Talent," 2014, page 2. (http://www.scribd.com/doc/236089704/Demand-for-Skilled-Talent-US-2014)

[3] Bureau of Labor Statistics, "Job Openings and Labor Turnover Survey Highlights," September 2014, page 6. (http://www.bls.gov/web/jolts/jlt_labstatgraphs.pdf)

[4] John Sullivan, "The 8 Elements of a Successful Employment Brand," ERE.net, 2004. (http://www.ere.net/2004/02/23/the-8-elements-of-a-successful-employment-brand/)

[5] TMP Worldwide, "The Value of a Managed Employer Brand in an Increasing Competitive Landscape," 2011, page 3. (http://www.slideshare.net/hrtecheurope/employer-branding-whitepaper-tmp-worldwide)

[6] Walter Isaacson, Steve Jobs (New York: Simon & Schuster, 2011), page 657.

THE STATUS QUO IS YOUR BIGGEST THREAT

Donna C. Morris

We have entered the next generation of HR. To help propel people and business forward in today's competitive environment, the HR function requires increased discipline, agility, and constant adaptation. The ultimate threat to our function is not recognizing that change is required. This essay highlights five key practices that HR leaders must adopt in order to become strategic partners within their organizations—and shares how we have applied them in my own organization.

EMBRACE THE BUSINESS AND ITS NUMBERS

The HR function requires a blend of strong business, analytical, interpersonal, and communications skills. What was once viewed as a function to support the people of the business has now become a strategic driver for the business. This subtle but important shift requires HR leaders to have the strong business acumen and analytical skills to address important strategic questions about cost management, growth trajectories, risk analysis, mergers and acquisitions, and other key issues that have a direct impact on both the organization's people and its bottom line. Deloitte Consulting reports that companies that go through the process of "datafying" their HR function are seeing results that are two to three times better in terms of quality of hire, leadership pipelines, and employee turnover.

In most Fortune 500 companies, the total cost of the workforce represents nearly 70 percent of operating expenses. This further demonstrates the direct correlation between financial performance and people practices. The dashboard of people measures and metrics varies by company, but there is a requirement for the HR function to work toward tracking, evaluating, and linking company financial performance with people practices. This requires a solid understanding of the business, financials, and people.

Having a strong business orientation within the HR team has helped Adobe execute successful mergers and acquisitions. For example, with the strategic Omniture acquisition in 2009, my team and I worked closely with the finance team to assess how best to integrate the extended team to catapult Adobe into a new market—digital marketing solutions. This required understanding Adobe's growth goals in this new market and how best to align our workforce to meet our business goals.

INNOVATE AND ADAPT

As business leaders we need to constantly reevaluate our processes and have the courage to disrupt those that may no longer provide value to our people or to the company. The annual performance review is potentially one such process. According to Mercer's 2013 Global Performance Management Survey, only 3 percent of organizations say their performance management system delivers exceptional value, while almost half (48 percent) say their overall approach to performance management needs work.

In 2012 we made the decision at Adobe to abolish our annual performance review and introduce what we call "Check-in." Check-in was designed to make our performance management more agile and innovative. It aims to establish clear expectations and goals between the manager and employee and facilitate frequent feedback based on expectations. Check-in provides a disciplined framework for managers and employees to continuously share genuine feedback, while being flexible enough that people can tailor it based on their roles, expectations, and feedback preferences. Through this tool, we have effectively eliminated obstacles—like rigorous processes and forms—that inhibit continuous feedback. Ultimately, this change was designed to reflect our broader business transformation and product innovation, underscoring that people processes can also be innovative.

HR professionals have the opportunity to role model continuous improvement, innovation, and adaptation. Indeed, the HR function can set the tone in an organization that change is important and vital to organizational success.

DRIVE THE EXPERIENCE

At Adobe our employees are our core business asset and drive our innovation and creativity. Providing a superior employee experience is not an option—it's integral to our success. At Adobe and elsewhere, the HR function has evolved to take on more roles and include elements that touch directly upon employee experience. While it is dependent on the company strategy, the HR function is broadening its responsibility to oversee functions (e.g., real estate strategy, operations and security, employee communications, brand communications) that connect to the employee experience, workforce strategy, and organizational success.

This was evident at Adobe when we shifted our business to the cloud in order to be more innovative and nimble with the solutions we offer customers. To align with this business transformation, we took a holistic look at how to evolve our culture. We responded to employee requests to foster ongoing creativity and collaboration by renovating our workspaces around the globe to be open and community-oriented. This change was driven by the goal to provide exceptional employee experiences while helping to propel our business forward.

LEVERAGE TECHNOLOGY FOR IMPACT

HR technology is a growing and disruptive element for everyone in our function. As Josh Bersin, founder of Bersin by Deloitte, has said, "Ignore technology at your peril."

Today HR organizations are leveraging technology across key functional domains, not just to administer but more importantly to gain key insights and analytics related to both people and the business. The use of technology is changing how we recruit and develop talent, and it is also making us more "green" in the process. Think about how we recruited and sourced talent in the pre-internet and pre-LinkedIn days. Our approach has been completely transformed. Stacks of resumes and offer letters and hallways of file cabinets have been replaced by digital signatures (e.g., Adobe EchoSign) and stored electronic employee files.

At Adobe we have simplified our HR management systems (HRMS) as we take advantage of the host of cloud software providers who are eager to support the function. In 2015, we will launch a new HR system leveraging Workday's cloud-based applications. Gone are the days of complex, hard-to-use, proprietary systems. We are moving to a self-service model where ease of use is an expectation among employees and applications are used on a daily basis to update profiles, find benefits information, locate experts across the organization, set and monitor goals, and more.

We are also engaging with current and prospective employees through social applications—including social media and collaboration tools. At Adobe we have had great success amplifying our culture through our Adobe Life blog and #AdobeLife on Twitter and Facebook. We are also taking advantage of web-based collaboration solutions, like Adobe Connect, to foster employee interaction and build communities at a global scale.

THINK LOCAL AND GLOBAL

Literally every sector has experienced significant disruption and change as a result of continued globalization and technology advancements. Our industry's workforces are more global than ever and the boundary for many businesses has expanded. However, cultures within countries are still very distinct and need to be taken into consideration when engaging with employees worldwide. Organizations must build strategies to engage with their people globally and at scale to maintain efficiencies while also respecting the cultural nuances where their employees are based. It's a lot to consider, but it is imperative for engaging with people in compelling and relevant ways.

At Adobe we have implemented a web-based New Employee Success orientation program that has replaced our constrained "in room" orientation sessions. The new virtual orientation leverages technology and social platforms to bring together distributed and geographically dispersed employees. Through online, interactive sessions, we are able to interface with hundreds of new employees in each region while also building a global community among our employees. We tailor the orientation sessions for each geographical region to ensure cultural relevancy. As our company continues to grow, this is the right scalable solution for introducing new employees around the world to Adobe and sets the tone for their professional growth. As HR professionals, we must be able to think local and consider the broader global context on our people and our business.

OPPORTUNITIES AHEAD

I am energized by the next generation of HR, where leaders are focused on the intersection of business and people and are positioned as strategic partners to drive the business. With this evolution, we must consider the adaptations, agility, and skills needed to contribute to business and employee success.

Having a strong acumen in business and metrics is essential to correlating company financial performance with people practices. We must consistently find ways to innovate and iterate, and in some cases disrupt when a process no longer aligns with the goals of the organization. Taking a holistic approach to the employee experience enables leaders to cultivate superior experiences—from the workplace environment, to rewards and benefits, to the programs that help employees grow professionally—with the understanding that people are critical to organizational success. As global workforces continue to grow, we need to be thoughtful in how we engage with employees at a local level but also foster an inclusive global community. And a key lever in achieving this is the use of technology platforms that give us the ability to be even more impactful, efficient, and nimble. It is evident that the HR function is constantly evolving and change must be embraced.

I look forward to collaborating with our community of HR and business leaders to continue to share knowledge and best practices that will help our function have even more impact. It is a very exciting time to be in the function that provides for people and business results.

About Donna C. Morris

As Adobe's senior vice president of Global People and Places, Donna C. Morris leads an organization focused on driving the company's workforce strategy—including talent acquisition, development, rewards, and workplace experience—for more than 12,000 employees worldwide. During her career, Morris has led both generalist and specialist human resources functions in the high technology, communications, and government fields. Prior to becoming senior vice president in 2007, she held several other management positions at Adobe, providing leadership to the company's global organizational and people activities. Before joining Adobe, she was vice president of human resources and learning at Accelio Corporation, a Canadian software company acquired by Adobe in 2002. Morris has earned several industry honors, including Human Resources Professional of the Year in Ottawa, Canada, and the Silicon Valley YWCA's Tribute to Women (TWIN) Award. She is currently on the board of directors for the Adobe Foundation and was formerly a board member for Second Harvest Food Bank of Santa Clara and San Mateo Counties in California. Additionally, she is on the Foothill-DeAnza Community College Industry Advisory Council, and a mentor with C100, a nonprofit that supports Canadian technology entrepreneurship. Donna has a bachelor's degree from Carleton University, Ottawa, Canada, and holds the Senior HR Professional (SHRP) and Canadian Certified Human Resources Professional (CHRP) designations.

FROM BANKING TO BERRIES: ACQUIRING BUSINESS KNOWLEDGE ALL OVER AGAIN TO CREATE IMPACT

Lynne Oldham

After spending more than a decade in banking in various HR leadership roles, I recently moved as far from the banking industry as you can get—to the agriculture sector. I took the position of chief human resources officer with global oversight at Driscoll's, a privately held berry company. While the idea of making a dramatic shift in industries was attractive, my first real concern was how I would begin to understand a vastly different business. How could I affect change without possessing a deep knowledge of the berry business? Naively, I wondered how hard it could be to plant a seed, grow a plant, harvest delicious berries, and get them to market. I quickly learned the answer: Very hard!

Upon onboarding I learned just how much I underestimated the complexity of growing the right berry, in the right climates, with the right partners, and with the right speed to market on six continents. In my early days I spent 50 percent of my time walking berry fields, visiting the test plots and coolers, and (what I liked best) tasting fruit. I spent half of my time in the "field," listening, and half the time asking questions like "How much does an acre yield? How do we motivate our growers to grow the most delightful fruit? What are our challenges to moving the fruit to market? How do we choose our proprietary varieties?" I needed to discover everything I could about the berry business, knowing that understanding the context was critical to my efficacy. What was equally critical was believing that I am always a businessperson first and an HR professional second. Experience running my own HR outsourcing business grounded me in that core perspective and has helped me transition from financial services to Driscoll's.

 For as long as I have been a human resources professional, business acumen has been identified as a necessary competency in our field. HR people everywhere, especially those who have "grown up" in the field, have been trying to acquire the holy grail of mastering business fundamentals. Unfortunately, what we have failed to realize as a profession is that business acumen and HR are not separately sought-after competencies but one and the same. The sooner we consider ourselves business professionals first and HR specialists second, the sooner we will attain the nirvana we strive for.

What is business acumen anyway? It's an innate understanding of how your company makes money, which includes knowing what drives profitability, being able to take a market-focused look at the business, and having a big-picture awareness of the business and its context.

HR professionals have been talking about this need for a long time, so what stands in the way of our having the business acumen necessary to be the best HR professionals we can be?

Let me pose a few questions that HR professionals should ask themselves:

- Did I get into this field primarily because I like people? Do I have an aptitude for numbers or a head for business?
- Do I let my mind wander during business discussions or executive meetings?
- Does the financial review seem like a foreign language, as if the CFO is speaking Greek?
- Do I truly understand how my company makes money? Do I understand the business challenges in our industry?
- Do I comment during business meetings only when the topic is people-related?

Now, consider this: Everything that concerns the people in your organization has context—the competitive landscape for talent, the political environment, geographies, culture, unions, and other factors. Without knowledge or understanding of those contexts, you would be unable to do your job. The business that you find yourself in is just another contextual element—and a necessary one. Your job depends on intimately knowing the business that you serve. Without the big-picture context, you risk delivering HR results that do not add value to the bottom line.

Let's face it, we've all heard anti-HR sentiments and read the recent musings of Ram Charan in Harvard Business Review, where he suggested eliminating the CHRO role and relegating HR types to transactional work so that the real talent work goes to non-HR "high-potential" leaders. How did HR get to be thought of as so dysfunctional and ineffective that we would draw such criticism? I think the answer lies within us. We, as HR professionals, have to be fearless about "upping our game" with respect to business acuity. Baseline financial skills are critical; industry know-how and understanding of investor relations are essential. We have to know customers, the supply chain, and our competitors so that we can position our firm to win in the industry. Strategic savvy and overall agility are also requirements of the HR function. Again, HR professionals should think of themselves as businesspeople first and HR people second.

How do you acquire business skills and practice them regularly? Here are some of the many things you can do for yourself and the HR team:

1. *Understand your customers.* Spend a day with a customer. Tag along to sales meetings. We have an in-store training program at Driscoll's, originally created for sales and marketing, where employees spend a week working for one of our retail customers. We now regularly send HR people to this training. Customer perspective helps the HR professional gain an "outside-in" view.
2. *Create routines around constantly learning the business.* Treat this as any other task you have to do, and set aside several days a month. Review the business strategy. What are the critical jobs to the overall success of the organization? Shadow the people in those jobs one day a month. For example, because Driscoll's is known for premium berries, I wanted to understand what that label truly meant to the market. So last month I spent an afternoon with a quality

assurance professional, inspecting berries as they came out of the field, one by one by one. I have also shadowed agronomists (a job I did not comprehend until I spent the day with one of them) and production personnel. These experiences have been invaluable to raising my level of insight of our business.

3. *Read, read, and read some more*—anything related to business or the industry. Review strategic business plans. It is critical to understand how the company creates strategic value. If you do, you can translate that into how HR can help the business achieve results. Study the financials. Highlight them, write your questions in the margins, and find a business buddy who doesn't mind spending time to educate you. Trade time—help him or her understand some HR concepts. If you are in a public company, listen to analyst calls.

4. *Volunteer to be part of a business project* playing a non-traditional, non-HR role. Once I led a group of high-potential employees from all parts of the business who were looking at how to increase collaboration in the workplace.

5. *Take a line assignment.* There is really no better way to get a deep understanding of a business than to spend a few years in a line job.

6. *Don't neglect your own team.* You may need to reexamine and/or reskill your HR team to ensure its relevancy. "Good with people" may have been what attracted people to the field in the past, but today, HR people need to know how to effectively use the "people" lever to achieve intended business results. HR professionals are often very good at helping business leaders look at their teams, but they must also turn this skill inward. We also need to be deliberate in designing and executing development plans to help HR professionals obtain or improve a wide range of sophisticated skills, including ones related to how the business works, makes money, and competes. Admittedly, this one has been challenging for me in my new role. Culturally, we are a 100-year-old company that has not made this part of our regular practices—in HR or any department. So my changes within the HR team were frightening to team members, despite my best efforts to help them understand the business rationale for them.

7. *Demonstrate your own understanding of the numbers* and hire more "quant-like" people into the HR team. HR leaders have traditionally been more concerned with qualitative metrics and have stayed away from quantitative analytics. This just can't continue. HR should strive to get the decision-makers the data and analytics that help them make better decisions for the business. The use of metrics to drive, create, support, and stimulate the strategic agenda

will give new credibility to the HR function. In addition, HR should complete return-on-investment (ROI) calculations for its own HR activities.

8. *Finally, speak up on business-related issues* even if they don't involve people. So what if you're wrong? The majority of the time when I do this, I get "Good point" or "Didn't think about that" from my colleagues. You have fresh eyes, so don't be afraid to question something that appears unusual to you.

The list is obviously not exhaustive, but it's a start. If you try some of these things and don't succeed at first, just keep trying. Determination is key.

Don't let yourself or HR be marginalized or pigeonholed. Your job and the value you bring to your organization can be greatly enhanced by expanding your business knowledge base. You, your company, and the HR community would be well served if you are a businessperson who happens to also be an expert in human capital. I like to say that my job is to make my business "hum" through its people. This requires me to thoroughly understand the business so I can apply the appropriate talent interventions to reach business outcomes. When I was hired at Driscoll's, I was exhilarated to learn that the talent agenda was mission critical for Driscoll's and its CEO—and many other businesses and CEOs feel the same way.

To put an end to our naysayers, we need to use this serious and top-of-mind business agenda item as our rallying cry. I implore you to step up with increased industry knowledge and context that will enable us to better solve important business issues. This is the approach that I have taken as I've started in a very new and different business and industry. I spent nearly the first six months just learning, and I still have so much more to learn. But I am zealous in my desire to know more, hoping someday very soon to call myself a berry business expert and not a banker.

About Lynne Oldham

Lynne Oldham is CHRO for Driscoll's, the global market leader in fresh berries. During her more than 25 years in the HR profession, she has practiced business-centric HR in a variety of industries. Prior to Driscoll's, she served in progressive HR roles at BNP Paribas, a European bank, culminating in her role as regional

CHRO for the Americas. During her time at BNP, she had opportunities to work in numerous areas of HR and multiple countries, including the UK and France. Lynne holds a BS in business and finance from State University of New York at New Paltz and a JD from Seton Hall School of Law.

HOW HR CAN GET THE SQUEAKS OUT OF AN ORGANIZATION

Garry Ridge and Stan Sewitch

HR has long sought its rightful place at the table of senior leadership. This is not the case for professions like sales, finance, operations, product development, legal, and others. These fields are unequivocally recognized as essential to strategic thinking in the business. Why does HR have to bang on the conference room door when others are already inside?

To be a business partner in today's and tomorrow's world of business, HR must recognize that it is not a decision-making function in terms of how the business is run. Its role is to provide the best advice possible to leaders who must make decisions about strategy, sales, operations, hiring, promotions, separations, job structure, and succession. It's an advisory function for 99 percent of its activities. HR strays afield of its role when it behaves otherwise.

Many HR departments try to take on the role of enforcer of the rules. This places the HR professional in the impossible position of identifying infractions and attempting to initiate corrective action involving employees who do not report to HR. The employees themselves, along with their leadership chain, often do not appreciate what is perceived as intervention.

Another behavioral impediment to business contribution by HR is when the function acts like the caring parent, looking for ways to take the pain, suffering, and difficulty out of workers' lives, or by adding so much support around them that they come to expect someone else will solve their work-life problems for them.

A third fatal flaw of HR is attempting to influence business decisions outside of our expertise. Even if we may not be trying to assume a decision-making role, HR can be tempted to have opinions and make statements about areas of the business where we have no experience. Such expressions ensure that no line manager or functional leader will come to us for any opinion, even when we might be qualified to offer one.

Another source of dysfunction, or at least reduced contribution, is when other leaders attempt to delegate their authority to HR, usually in cases of difficult employee interactions and decisions. Since most HR professionals do want to assist leaders, we can take the invitation as a vote of confidence for our skills and an opportunity to meaningfully contribute. But accepting this delegated authority only undermines the leader's ability to learn and grow.

At WD-40 Company, we strive mightily to avoid these pitfalls and to construct a role for HR that it can truly deliver upon. We've approached the design of the function in the same manner as a top-level consulting firm would. This approach has resulted in higher accountability in the company, more capable leaders, and an unambiguously valuable contribution from the HR function. Below are the principles that we strive to follow.

1. KNOW OUR STUFF

Peter Block wrote the classic consultants' bible, "Flawless Consulting," about 30 years ago. It is still a relevant work today, and it starts with this admonition to the aspiring consultant: Know your stuff. It means that before anything else, the HR professional has to be competent in the field or specialty in which he or she practices. The corollary to this principle is that we also need to know what we don't know, and not attempt to sound knowledgeable in order to make a good impression. "I don't know" is a powerful trust-building response to a question.

In addition to knowing our HR stuff, we also need to know the business, and not just at the 30,000-foot level. If HR doesn't understand how the business creates and sells its products or services, it cannot provide truly relevant advice. Without in-depth knowledge of the business model, HR advice and input tends to be overly general or misses the mark because it does not take into account the realities of the business. We encourage our HR professionals to take on cross-functional projects to increase our understanding of the business. We sometimes go on sales calls. We join our leaders and go into the markets. We participate in product education training. We visit our production partners to learn about supply chain processes and challenges.

HR is also expected to be familiar with the variety of cultures in which we operate. We have employees in 14 countries, all of whom have both similar and unique characteristics. The only way to gain that knowledge is by going there.

Ideally, HR professionals should get some non-HR experience in a business somewhere along their career path. It may be only projects, but it would be best to spend a year or more performing roles in other departments. The HR people who actually do this have the unique opportunity of viewing HR like everyone else in the company does. Sometimes the view is flattering. Sometimes it's not.

2. EARN THE ROLE OF TRUSTED ADVISOR

Advisors hold themselves accountable for the quality of their advice, and have deep motivation to provide solutions for problems. But the advice does no good if it's not accepted and acted upon.

To earn that trusted role, HR applies the consultant's mantra: Go where you are invited. You don't have to wait for an invitation to ask for one, either. The simple query "May I offer an idea for you to consider?" is appreciated. It shows respect and acknowledges who is accountable for the decision or action. It seldom receives a "no."

If your advice is good, and you recognize who really is the decision-maker on a given subject, you will be invited back over and over.

3. SUPPORT THE DECISION FULLY

We have spirited debates in our company. There are no shortages of opinions or passionate advocates. Our Tribe, as we call ourselves, is deeply committed to our values, our company, and our direction. That means when we disagree, all that positive emotion is brought to bear by all our "Tribe" members who take personal responsibility for our collective success. (We call ourselves a Tribe because we are more than a team of people, and less than blood relatives. We share culture, traditions, a warrior spirit, and our life lessons as we join together to create an enduring organization that we'd be proud to pass on to others.)

In debates that involve HR-related matters, the passion and dedication is no less. But at our company, we often ask the question: "Whose decision is it?" Outside of matters that relate to the HR function itself, the answer is almost never HR. The exceptions relate to issues involving legal, ethical, or policy factors as primary ingredients.

So once a decision is made by the person who has the authority to make it, HR's role is to fully support it, just as any other function or leader should. We might disagree with what the manager wishes to do, but if it's not contrary to policy, law, or ethics, it's not our call.

4. BE BUSINESS PSYCHOLOGISTS

People go to HR for solutions that involve knowledge and skills that are outside of their professional span or current capability. HR solves human challenges in the context of business. HR needs to apply the principles of human behavior to do so.

One key area of behavioral principles relates to adult learning methods. We teach these methods in our Leadership Laboratory, a 16-course curriculum open to all employees. Embedded in those methods is the concept that mistakes are moments of learning to be treasured for the education that they provide. Learning moments are a welcome part of our path toward continual improvement.

Therefore, all HR professionals must be students of human behavior and strive to understand, as deeply as we can, the basic principles of that behavior. This goes beyond reading the latest popular book, listening to the most recent conference speakers' addresses, or conferring with other HR professionals. HR needs to study psychology on an ongoing basis—and that study should be of research that follows the scientific method.

A fair amount of what is called "research" would not satisfy the proven methods of scientific inquiry that can offer predictive validity. We focus on these scientific principles in every aspect of our HR services.

5. TEACH PEOPLE HOW TO TAKE ACTION

This is a key function of HR at our company. HR strives to help people solve their own problems, rather than doing it for them. If someone has a conflict with a supervisor and wants help, we teach them the principles of human conflict resolution in a business, and then coach them through the steps.

HR can often become a cul-de-sac where people take their problems and HR then attempts to intervene, playing peacemaker. As anyone who has experienced marital difficulties will tell you, unless both parties want mediation, nothing good comes from interloping.

HR doesn't advocate for a given employee's needs, except that we advocate the "Maniac Pledge," which states: *"I am responsible for taking action, asking questions, getting answers and making decisions. I won't wait for someone to tell me. If I need to know, I am responsible for asking. I have no right to be offended that I didn't 'get this sooner.' If I am doing something others should know about, I am responsible for telling them."* We call this the Maniac Pledge, because one definition of the word maniac is "an obsessive enthusiast."

We look for ways to make HR non-essential to critical business processes and decisions, except as an available advisor. When HR doesn't need to monitor decision flows, then it has succeeded in creating better leaders.

SUMMARY

We believe that HR makes the biggest contribution toward an engaged workforce by acting as an expert advisor to leaders who are committed to following our values and are motivated by the rewards that come from servant leadership. "Servant," in the context of leadership, does not mean "subservient." Rather, it describes an attitude of devotion to the role of serving the needs of our three constituent groups: our customers and end-users, our shareholders, and our Tribe.

If you'll forgive the self-serving analogy, we believe that the proper role of HR in a business is to act in the same fashion as our WD-40 multipurpose product. HR exists to eliminate the human friction that every organization faces. Our employee engagement scores and our company performance over time determine whether we are succeeding.

About Garry Ridge

As chief executive officer and a member of the board of directors of WD-40 Company, Garry Ridge is responsible for developing and implementing high-level strategies, all operations, and the oversight of all relationships and partnerships for the company. Ridge joined WD-40 Company in 1987 and has held various management positions in the company—including executive vice president, chief operating officer, and vice president of international—and has worked directly with WD-40 Company in more than 50 countries. A native of Australia, Ridge served in advisory roles for the Australian Marketing Institute and the Australian Automotive Aftermarket Association. Currently, he serves as a member of the board of governors of The San Diego Foundation and on the advisory boards of TrendSource Inc. and The Ken Blanchard Companies. He sits on the University of San Diego's School of Business Administration board of advisors and is also an adjunct professor at the university, where he teaches leadership development, talent management, and succession planning in the executive leadership graduate program. In 2009, he co-authored a book with Ken Blanchard titled, "Helping People Win at Work: A Business Philosophy Called 'Don't Mark My Paper, Help Me Get an A.'" Ridge holds a diploma in retail and wholesale distribution from Sydney Technical College and an MS in executive leadership from the University of San Diego.

About Stan Sewitch

Stan Sewitch is vice president of global organization development at WD-40 Corporation, where his chief role is to catalyze the organizational evolution of the company, preparing it for its second 60 years. He is also responsible for leadership of the global human resources function, with employees spanning 14 countries across three trading blocs. Sewitch joined WD-40 in 2012 but served the company for 12 years prior through his consulting firm HRG Inc., at one time the largest broad-service organizational consulting company in the San Diego region. HRG served more than 1,200 clients during his 23-year tenure as its founder and CEO; he now sits on its board. Sewitch also founded three other companies—Emlyn Systems, Chromagen Corporation, and KI Investment Holdings LLC—and currently serves as a director of KI, Sabia Inc., and Ridge Diagnostics. An avid contributor to his profession, Sewitch has been a weekly columnist for the San Diego Daily Transcript for more than 10 years, writing about business, strategy, and people. In 2005 he published "Notes from the Corporate Underground," a collection of essays on humanistic capitalism, and is currently completing a second volume. Sewitch holds a bachelor's degree in psychology from San Diego State University and a master's degree in organizational psychology from California State University at Long Beach.

HEALTH AND FINANCIAL WELLNESS AS KEYS TO PRODUCTIVITY

Dallas L. Salisbury

HR professionals must embrace the importance of supporting employee health and financial wellness through a variety of means. Organization that want employees who can focus on getting the job done without being distracted by their own financial and health distress will favor safety nets. They should lead their employers away from decisions based upon the ideology that "there should be no social insurance" and all should be left to the individual. An employer that wants to operate within a growing economy fueled by a well-prepared workforce should want the government to do all it can to facilitate health and financial wellness at the lowest possible cost to the employer and the worker, while providing the employer with the maximum flexibility to survive and prosper.

When it comes to programs that are essential to citizen well-being—such as education, health care, and sufficient income to survive and thus to consume—employers that are focused on the bottom line and/or shareholder satisfaction should be happy to outsource nonessential functions to the government (Social Security, unemployment compensation, a structure for indigent health services, etc.) rather than providing nonessential programs that eat up the limited time the enterprise has to excel at its core functions.

During my 45 adult and professional years, I have been surrounded by the consolidation of enterprises, the creation of new enterprises, the disappearance of those that fell behind, and more and more focus on "keeping the owner/shareholder happy." The growing role of chief financial officers in HR and employee benefit decisions, and the focus of M&As on employee benefit programs and liabilities, have served to underline focus on the future of the "enterprise." More and more often in this age of "private equity," the enterprise is being prepared for sale or resale or re-resale, as opposed to the "good old days" of "this is our families business."

THE MOVE FROM LOCAL TO GLOBAL SOURCING AND SELLING

Governments and employers around the world spent recent decades adapting to the normalization of relations between democracies and communist nations; the embrace of capitalism by democracies, dictatorships, communists, and socialists; and world shrinkage in time and travel brought about by technological innovation and the spread of advanced education in developed and developing nations around the world. Work can now truly follow the sun around the globe, creating true 24/7 organizations and services sourced from anywhere.

THE BENEFITS OF UNIVERSAL PROGRAMS THAT ARE ESSENTIAL FOR WORKERS BUT NON-CORE FOR EMPLOYERS

As US employers have embraced "ERISA Preemption of State Laws" in order to provide common employee benefit programs to all of their workers across many states, the absence of *global* preemption may actually mean that companies that have employees in many nations should simply allow workers to have what makes sense in that nation (as determined by the government of that nation), while allowing globally mobile employees to maintain accounts and "return rights" in their home nation. This may mean embracing the payment of very high payroll taxes and provision of no supplemental benefits for employees in Sweden or Canada, if that allows the hiring and retention of needed employees; a blended approach in the US; and something quite different in China or Russia.

WORKER SECURITY AND CHOICE WITH EMPLOYER FLEXIBILITY AND CAPPED LIABILITIES

Because employers now find it possible to market product worldwide, to place the production crew wherever it is needed, and to have pieces of work done in far-flung nations prior to assembly, the HR objective should be focused on attraction, retention while needed, and limited programs that make employee departure complicated or difficult. For many employers, social insurance or national exchanges might be superior to approaches that have been more common in the post-WWII period.

Many companies formed since the mid-'70s have embraced limiting employer liabilities by embracing employee choice as the best route to worker security and employer flexibility over paternalism. Much has been written about the way in which communications, technology, internet, and information companies such as Apple have owned in-house design, creativity, and sales while subcontracting out almost all of the functions of manufacturing, packaging, shipping, etc. In the process of creating for themselves the ability to change direction quickly, subcontractors have been left to deal with many of the human resources implications for large numbers of employees that are theirs, not Apples'.

Other companies founded in the '70s such as Microsoft and Starbucks—and more recently founded companies such as Yahoo!, Amazon, and Facebook—never embraced the paternalism of defined benefit pension plans with life income annuities, or their companion retiree medical benefits. Instead, these employers have stressed communicating total compensation and total rewards, with a heavy emphasis on incentive compensation, stock ownership, and individual choice. Microsoft, for example, has publically noted that they do not have auto-enrollment in their 401(k) plan, as it would be too "paternalistic" to even provide a default with opt-out under their employment philosophy.

Companies that have "reinvented" themselves in order to compete with the newer breed of firm have ended their fixed-benefit promises and embraced higher current cost and greater employee choice in order to control future liabilities, move to a more performance-based workforce, and increase the ease of worker mobility.

LOWER CORPORATE RISK WITH INCREASED INDIVIDUAL AND SOCIETAL RISK

More to the point, this highly dynamic "one-world" view of work placement and who "owns" responsibility for the workers carries with it significant risk. Employers continue the march toward more and more individual responsibility for decisions related to savings, lifelong planning, health care, disability protections, etc.—and away from employer provision and funding and employer decision-making on behalf of the worker. This includes a mandate for taking a life income annuity (the rule prior to the late 1970s), the single option or encouragement of single-sum distributions in "retirement" programs, and moving from comprehensive full pay medical programs to high-deductibles, health savings accounts, and bonuses/penalties for behaviors that might drive up the cost of health care.

GOVERNMENTS HAVE FREQUENTLY BEEN AT THE CUTTING EDGE OF RISK REALLOCATION

The US government was one of the first large employers in the nation to replace its extremely generous defined benefit pension plan for new workers in the 1980s with one worth about 40 percent as much, supplemented by Social Security and a 401(k) type plan—again, limiting the hard-to-predict liabilities of the rich, defined benefit plan with the more knowable current cost of defined contribution. A move to choice in health plans was taken by the US in the 1960s, and it is one of the largest employers to have offered high-deductible health plans early in their life. Congressman Paul Ryan, incoming chair of the House Ways and Means Committee, last year proposed that that lesser defined benefit plan be closed to new entrants, and that all future hires have only the defined contribution plan. The final budget action of the US Congress in 2014 included amendments to ERISA that will allow certain multi-employer private pension plans to reduce future benefits if required to avoid insolvency. Again, limiting liabilities that are hard to estimate takes precedence over certainty for the worker or retiree—a trend that continues to spread across industries and sectors.

Single "site" employers such as US states—at least for their direct employees, as opposed to contractors—have still held more firmly to the "older" and "more paternalistic" retirement and health program designs, including more comprehensive health insurance and life income annuities. But that is slowly changing as well, as the size of their "supplemental" defined contribution programs grows and as some move all new workers to defined contribution or hybrid plans only.

THESE TRENDS ARE GLOBAL

Around the world, governments are acting to deemphasize defined benefit plans and mandatory life income annuities and reducing the role of employers in health care decisions while increasing the role of individuals—continuing a march toward universal health care financing and availability, and reinforcement/strengthening their social insurance safety nets to provide a floor of income and services for those that would otherwise be incapable of supporting life, but moving away from seeking to have those programs provide for "adequacy." However, some of the nations that were viewed as "socialist," like Sweden and the Netherlands, have been revising those social insurance programs to provide less, and to specifically allow for reductions in benefits if it becomes necessary to ensure future solvency. In fact, these nations' actions were used as a model in the recent multi-employer pension "reforms" here in the US.

HR professionals around the world need to anticipate, incorporate, and then accommodate changes in employee benefits being driven by competition, technology, economic uncertainty, loss of employee trust in institutions, and the resulting willingness of workers to look more to the government for certainty and protections, wrapped in a blanket of increased flexibility and choice.

THE SPIN OF CHANGE WILL NOT SLOW AS THE SEARCH CONTINUES FOR THE RIGHT BLEND OF FLEXIBILITY AND SECURITY

The US political system continues to rock back and forth on whether programs should be voluntary or mandatory and whether they should be tied to the government, the employer, or the individual. There is variation state by state, region by region, economic class by economic class, and ideology by ideology. The same variations can be seen in other nations, as those like England move to a mandatory automatic enrollment defined contribution program in order to deemphasize both social insurance and employer-provided benefit plans—and, as I previously noted, to expand employee choice by changing the law to require that individuals have the option of a single sum instead of only life income, in spite of the knowledge that this will decrease the likelihood of post-retirement adequacy for many citizens, even as it increases it for those who experience superior investment returns and do not spend the money prior to retirement, or too quickly.

Should HR professionals and their employers push themselves into the middle of such debates, or should they do what meets their workforce needs and let others worry about retirement security and the long-term economy? After all, given the global age of enterprise consolidation that marches forward, should an enterprise assume that it will still be around (or, more particularly, with the current managers involved in decisions, as opposed to those that came with the acquirer)? Or should it instead put full energy and focus into being the best that it can be in terms of growth and profitability, now?

CONSOLIDATION AND SHRINKING OF OUR WORLDS HAS DEFINED OUR HISTORY

I grew up in a town of about 50,000. During those years there was a First National Bank of Everett. By my college years in Seattle it had become part of Seattle First National Bank. Today, both are part of Bank of America, which, other than in name, is actually Nations Bank. In other words, it evolved from a local "powerhouse" to a local branch of a global powerhouse, taking on a different role in my home community with a totally different view of its obligations to that community—and to the employees in that community. As those wheels turn at every level, as US firms become British or Chinese or German or Japanese firms, would workers be better off with national benefits that can survive all that rolling M&A turmoil? Would their employers be better off as well?

WHAT IT MEANS FOR HR PROFESSIONALS

I do not have the answer to these questions. Like individual health and financial well-being, the answer tends to vary as you move beyond basic needs. HR professionals, to be effective in today's and tomorrow's business world, need to throw aside ideology and compel their enterprises to consider these issues. What approach will provide the greatest probability of business success? What approach will give the enterprise the greatest ability to be agile and to make necessary changes in structure, employment, location, and product/service mix today, tomorrow, and every period ahead? And if the day comes when a sale or merger is on the table, how will the enterprise provide the best options and the best outcomes?

In sum, the HR professional must be open-minded, non-ideological, flexible, and innovative. HR must focus on enhancing employee productivity through a focus on—and delivery of services that provide for or lead to—health and financial well-being. The choice of how and by whom they are provided should be cost/benefit/results driven, with openness to public or private or voluntary or mandatory, whatever produces the best outcomes for the enterprise. HR must embrace the best approaches from around the world for providing the population with basic health and financial security, including retirement security, in order to ensure social stability and economic success for the world and its citizens.

Dallas L. Salisbury

Dallas L. Salisbury is president and CEO of the Employee Benefit Research Institute (EBRI), which he joined at its founding in 1978. He currently serves as an appointee of President Obama on the PBGC Advisory Committee (having served in the late 1980s as an appointee of President H. W. Bush; an appointee of the comptroller general of the United States to his board of advisors; a member of the Financial Security Commission; and commissioner of the Bipartisan Policy Center's Commission on Personal Savings. A Fellow of the National Academy of Human Resources, Salisbury has been honored with the Award for Professional Excellence from the Society for Human Resource Management, the Plan Sponsor Lifetime Achievement Award, the Keystone Award of WorldatWork, and the Public Service Award of the International Foundation of Employee Benefit Plans. In 2007, he accepted a National Emmy Award for Savingsman™ and the Choose to Save® public education program. Salisbury has written and lectured extensively on economic security topics and is author of numerous books. Prior to joining EBRI, he held full-time positions with the Washington State Legislature, the US Department of Justice, the Employee Benefits Security Administration of the US Department of Labor, and the Pension Benefit Guaranty Corporation (PBGC). He holds a BA from the University of Washington and an MA from the Maxwell School of Citizenship and Public Affairs.

SPEAK THE LANGUAGE!

Jill B. Smart

You might be asking, "Well, what language is that?" Business language, of course! Every human resources professional needs to be first and foremost a business professional. Yes, even before being a human resources professional. You might have two reactions to that statement:

- *First reaction:* "Of course I need to look at my HR role from the perspective of a business person." This might even seem very obvious. But I do not believe all of us in HR live up to that standard.
- *Second reaction:* "Okay, literally taken, are you saying that as an HR professional I need to 'grow up in the business'—meaning work outside of HR in some other part of the business—and then move over to HR as my second profession?" No, that is not what I mean.

I believe that no matter what your background is, whether you grew up in HR or grew up "in the business" and moved to HR, you need to do your HR job from the perspective of a business person. That is always first and foremost. But HR professionals don't do that often enough. All HR professionals need to be business people, not just senior HR leaders.

So how do you become a business person first and foremost? Some of the ideas shared below may seem obvious, but don't walk past them so fast. Sometimes we just don't make enough time to build our skills or the skills of our teams—but HR professionals, of all people, need to "walk the talk."

FORM STRATEGIC RELATIONSHIPS

No matter what your role is in HR, you need to understand your organization's overall business as well as the specific part of the business you personally support. You need to thoroughly understand the business strategy and be able to translate that into a talent strategy. Those in an HR "business partner" role should also be key members of the team that develops and evolves the business strategy. Every HR person needs to understand how their business makes money, what causes it to potentially lose money, how the organization innovates and invests in the future, and how it understands, anticipates, and meets client demand.

Business strategy and business results need to be kept in mind with everything you do. The key is to have relationships with people at all levels of the business—spending time with them, observing how they do their jobs, and asking them questions about strategies, processes, customers, and employees. And always have your "safe" contacts. It might be someone in finance you can call and ask anything—even questions that you should already know the answers to.

BOTTOM LINE: HR cannot be a function performed solely from behind a desk. You need to be out in the field with business leaders and employees, at least periodically, to really understand the business.

PURSUE TRAINING

Many of us work in organizations where we have a number of internal and external training courses for employees—yet HR professionals might not be required to take them. Look at all the training courses available in your organization that will help the individuals on your HR team be better business professionals, and create a mandatory HR business acumen curriculum. This curriculum can include courses from finance, marketing, legal, or other parts of your business.

Additionally, make sure your HR professionals understand the specific part of the business they support. Include required electives that are specific to the industry and segments within that industry that they support, as well as the functional or technology segments they support. HR professionals do not have to become experts in these areas, but they do need to understand the functions, marketplace, competitive landscape, and regulatory environment of the business they support.

BOTTOM LINE: Using what you have available, create a business acumen curriculum for your HR people—and actually have them take the courses!

ROTATE JOBS

We don't move enough high-performing employees from outside of HR into HR; we don't move enough high-performing HR professionals into roles outside of HR; and we don't move HR professionals to different jobs within HR nearly enough. Movement between functions, industries, clients, and geographies builds skills, perspectives, maturity, and engagement. But it can be painful. How can you replace a compensation expert that you move to finance for a year, or a recruiting expert you make a business partner for a year? It may be challenging, but when that recruiter comes back to recruiting after spending a year performing a different role, he or she will have a better understanding of the business and be a much better recruiter as a result.

BOTTOM LINE: Invest in job rotation for HR professionals early and often.

FIND A MENTOR

Mentoring in its best form is not a formal program but the result of a connection made through some source, whether formal or informal. Your mentor needs to be someone you can be vulnerable with but also someone you trust and admire as a great business person and leader. We all need many kinds of mentors throughout our careers. But it is particularly important to seek out a "business mentor" who understands your business more deeply and uniquely than you do. Don't be afraid to be the underdog. Connecting with someone who has worked in the business you are supporting is a good place to start.

BOTTOM LINE: A mentor is someone to whom you can show your gaps and insecurities but also reveal your beliefs and aspirations. Ultimately, a mentor can help you become a better business person.

READ AND LISTEN

HR professionals should read The Wall Street Journal, The New York Post, and their local newspapers every day. You should also listen to business news stations on the radio and on TV and be active in social media around your industry, your competitors, and your business landscape. In other words, you should be reading, listening to, and participating in what your business partners read, listen to, and participate in, whether it is general business information or something specific to the industry or geography you support.

You should also be reading HR magazines and periodicals such as Human Resources Executive magazine and Workforce Magazine. Remember, the HR function is a business in and of itself. We need to know what the best practices are, what the trends are, what others are doing, and what is being taught in academic institutions in our field. There are many good services that will summarize what's new and send links to key articles based on keywords. It is worth paying for these services for your HR team.

BOTTOM LINE: Spend the money to help your HR team stay current with the latest information from multiple sources, and make time to stay current yourself.

LEARN AND SHARE KNOWLEDGE

There are many outside learning, training, and certification opportunities that you may feel you don't have the time to take advantage of—but they are often worth the investment. The University of Illinois, the University of Michigan, Cornell University, the University of Southern California, the University of South Carolina, and others universities offer both HR degree programs and HR executive programs. The National Academy of Human Resources (NAHR), the Society of Human Resources Management (SHRM), the HR Policy Association (HRPA), the HR Certification Institute (HRCI), and many local and regional organizations also provide HR training, much of which can be done virtually and on your own time.

Additionally, there are many types of HR-related organizations where HR executives can speak, network, and share best practices while also learning from the knowledge capital shared by others. Many of us in HR leadership roles have a lot to share that is not proprietary or confidential and can help our overall profession. You should not underestimate the impact that one seasoned HR professional can have on you, nor the impact that you can have on your fellow HR professionals.

BOTTOM LINE: Get out there and listen and talk to others in the profession—and share your point of view!

STAY UPDATED ON YOUR BUSINESS

If you work for a publicly traded company, there is no better update on your business than your quarterly earnings call and earnings news release. Mandate that your HR team members listen to the call (preferably together in groups where they can have a dialogue about it), read the quarterly and annually filed SEC and other legally required documents, and consult someone in finance who can explain what impact HR had on the results and how HR can better help the organization realize its potential and achieve its forecasts.

BOTTOM LINE: Require your HR professionals to engage in your organization's business communications, which will better inform them about the business and help them improve the organization's performance in the future.

The *overall* bottom line is that we are in HR to help our organizations solve business problems, take advantage of business opportunities, and be catalysts for change. Talent is the best way to do that—which is why we need to know our businesses and our industries inside and out. We are "at the table"—so we had better have a point of view to contribute.

One last thought: "Speaking the language" of business doesn't mean you need to be 100 percent fluent. Most people who know a second language can understand and get by but may not be perfectly conversant. The same is true in HR and business. To be effective, HR professionals do not have to be qualified to be CFOs or COOs. But they do have to understand finance and operations. As one of my mentors once told me, each and every day you need to be a student of business—so get studying!

About Jill B. Smart

Jill B. Smart is president-elect for the National Academy of Human Resources (NAHR), which recognizes individuals and institutions of distinction in human resources by election as "Fellows of the NAHR." She retired from Accenture in 2014, after being with the organization for more than 33 years. She served as Accenture's chief human resources officer for almost 10 years, with overall responsibility for the full employee lifecycle of all Accenture people globally. She was also a member of Accenture's Global Management Committee. Under her leadership, Accenture's global headcount grew from 100,000 to 289,000, with offices and operations in more than 200 cities in 56 countries. Smart delivered for Accenture during periods of explosive growth, often hiring more than 5,000 people per month, and transformed the HR function while also reducing cost. Before being appointed CHRO in 2004, she held roles as the organization's managing director of HR delivery and head of its "People Enablement" business practice. Smart sits on the executive committee of the Personnel Roundtable and has been a director of the HR Policy Association and an active member of HR50 and the RBL Institute. She is very active at the University of Illinois, the Chicago Economic Club, and The Chicago Network, and is a trustee on the Executive Committee of Chicago's Goodman Theatre. She holds a bachelor's degree in business administration from the University of Illinois and a master's degree in business administration from the University of Chicago.

MARKETING, MEASUREMENT, AND MODERN HR

Joyce Westerdahl

Savvy HR professionals are studying the transition their marketing counterparts have made over the last decade in order to get a vision for what's coming and ideas for how to create a more strategic and modern HR for the future. Not that long ago, marketers were asking the question: "How do we get a seat at the business table?" Marketing professionals wanted to move past their perceived role as event planners, webpage builders, and brochure makers and gain a more equal standing as strategic business partners. They knew they had more to offer the business, but they had to get past outdated perceptions before their business counterparts could receive the value they had to give. And so it is with HR.

Underlying the ability to change perceptions and get to a position of business strategy setting rather than order filling is the capacity to effectively demonstrate and communicate value in quantifiable terms that matter to the business. No matter what functional area you're coming from, to do that successfully, you need to have the right measures—and the business acumen to know what those measures should be and how to get them.

For marketing, that meant moving from efficiency measures, such as click-through rates, to effectiveness measures, such as leads generated by marketing. But it wasn't until they started measuring impact in terms that mattered to the executive suite—namely, contribution to revenue—that they were able to shift perceptions and step up to a more strategic role within the business.

For HR, that means shifting from efficiency measures, such as time-to-hire, to business outcomes measures, such as the impact of hires on key business metrics, including customer satisfaction, revenue, and market value. That is a big shift and, as marketing knows, a difficult one to measure. However, getting there requires that HR professionals leverage their business acumen to better connect what they do with the business outcomes they drive.

BUILDING BUSINESS ACUMEN

Every HR professional needs to truly understand how the business operates and the HR levers that can be applied to impact key business metrics. What this really means is that HR people need to be business people first, with specialty expertise in HR second. It seems like a nuance, but people often gravitate to careers in HR because they "like working with people." These days, they need to really like (and understand) business, too. HR leaders can prioritize business acumen as an HR competency and build it into the fabric of the HR organization through objectives, development, and communications.

HR professionals should be expected to know the business they are covering and understand the numbers that drive that business. Everyone wants to have that key relationship with a business leader, but smart HR professionals will build relationships with key finance, marketing, sales, engineering, and operations contacts to really get to know what drives the business first.

They also need to be able to speak the language of the business they support and to translate HR speak into that language. For example, business-savvy HR professionals will be able to translate a business problem, such as being unable to effectively pursue a market opportunity, into associated HR-related issues and opportunities, then solve them with the right recruiting and talent strategy, organizational design, and development plans to drive better business outcomes in this area. The not-so-business-savvy HR person might miss the opportunity or even, more likely, wouldn't be in the conversation with the business to begin with.

Ultimately, the goal is to get to know the business so well that HR is able to proactively bring recommendations and business ideas to the table. The conversations expand from HR-focused incremental gains, such as improving time-to-hire or cost-per-hire, to business-focused gains such as improving the quality of customer interactions or decreasing the cost-per-interaction on service delivery, for example.

The "A" players can do this, but HR organizations need to put a focus on developing this competency in the rest of the organization before the entire function can rise to the level of strategic partner. One idea is to rotate HR people into the business so they can get experience in other functional areas such as finance, marketing, sales, customer support, and operations. Consider this a development approach for up-and-coming HR leaders. Besides helping to round out HR skills with business skills, it also builds important relationships inside the business.

Another idea is to hire people into HR from the business and surround them with HR professionals who have deep domain expertise in order to ground new ideas in practical application. Don't get stuck in a trap of thinking that only people with HR experience can work in HR or that the learning curve is too steep. There are many people in the business that can bring a fresh perspective to HR, including marketing people who can help us accelerate our transformation and do a better job of crafting and pitching our value proposition to the business.

HR touts diversity as a driver of innovation and creativity. One of the things that we need to do as a profession is move beyond incremental improvements to find opportunities for quantum leaps. We need to turn traditional thinking upside down. Diversifying the HR talent pool with employees that don't have an HR background can be a spark for new ways of thinking. It helps us integrate emerging trends that might not have been on our radar previously and draw on models from other disciplines to help us make new connections.

DATA-DRIVEN MINDSET

In addition to business acumen, a data-driven mindset needs to be pervasive throughout the HR organization. The evolving role that data is playing in measuring just about every human-powered process is opening up possibilities for gaining a deeper understanding of what really drives business outcomes. Access to the right data is the super-charger for business-oriented HR professionals. Being able to combine finance, operations, supply chain, and sales data with HR data is a force multiplier for HR effectiveness. Armed with the right data and a deep understanding of the business, HR professionals can draw new insights and bring new solutions to the business.

Data isn't really the issue, though. It is about access to the right data and the tools to help people make sense of the data within the context of the business—and ultimately, to make better business decisions. Both HR professionals and the business leaders they support need to be empowered with the reporting and analytics tools that help them make better decisions, answer complex workforce questions, and make comparisons to see how well their organizations are doing relative to other organizations. Easy-to-interpret dashboards built around the critical parameters for the business make data consumable and actionable. Predictive analytics and modeling help people identify and refine innovative ideas that will drive business success.

MAKING THE RIGHT TECHNOLOGY CHOICES FOR THE BUSINESS

The need for meaningful data analysis is insatiable—and so are the requests for technology to capture and manage that data. It is critical that HR prioritize technology implementations based on driving sustainable business advantage. Our HR organization at Oracle uses our own technology solutions, so we have access to an entire portfolio of world-class human capital management (HCM) solutions. Even with all of that technology available to us, we still have to focus our resources on enabling the right functionality at the right time to drive the most important business outcomes.

Once the technology decisions are made, start with good processes and don't underestimate the need for change management. Great technology cannot make up for poorly designed processes. If the process is broken, technology will not fix it. To achieve a seamless experience for users, take the time to get the underlying processes optimized end-to-end from the user perspective before layering in technology.

Likewise, do not underestimate the need for change management. Although some employee self-service solutions may require little to no training, business processes are not consumer processes. Business continuity matters and user adoption can be difficult even with the most well-designed technology. Change management skills are paramount for HR professionals so they can help people assimilate to new technology in order to avoid disruptions in the business and to gain the full benefits of the solutions.

LEVERAGING GOOD IDEAS TO MOVE FASTER

Looking ahead, HR can further accelerate the transformation to strategic business partner by collaborating with marketing and other key functional areas to leverage and build on their growing success.

For example, early in the advent of social media, marketers thought they could control perceptions of their brands until they realized that inauthentic efforts were met with social backlash that further eroded the brand. The extreme transparency of social media dictates that the ownership experience cannot be different from the brand promise for a product. It is the same with the employee experience and the employment brand. There is no way to mask it. Therefore, HR needs to shepherd the effort to be authentic and make improvements where needed to ensure that employees have the experience that is marketed to them.

Other examples include:

- *Audience segmentation and targeting.* For the most part, HR is still mass communicating with employees. But marketing has shown us a better way to engage people through creating one-to-one, highly personal, highly relevant relationships.
- *Keeping a pulse on the audience.* Constant sentiment monitoring instead of, or in addition to, employee surveys enables HR to know what is top of mind for employees, and act quickly as needed.
- *Getting closer to the customer.* Digital marketers are very close to the end customer and benefit from much more real-time feedback. HR needs to get closer to customers to understand what they need, so that HR can better enable the business to deliver on those needs.
- *Nurturing prospects.* Marketing has learned to meet prospects where they are and qualify them over time using behavioral cues to help them know what step to take next to move the relationship forward or when to redirect resources elsewhere. This is a shift from more direct, but less effective, cold calling and direct marketing techniques. As HR looks at how it recruits candidates and even

how it engages employees, marketing's nurturing approach can help us better engage with our targets by creating mutually beneficial relationships over time.

- *Leveraging marketing tools.* Sentiment monitoring, personas, and campaign management can help HR get to know its audiences better, accurately profile those who are likely to succeed, and use automation with integrated social capabilities to stay in touch.

HR can learn from other functions as well. For example, the rapid prototyping and constant revision processes in software development can help HR learn to move faster and be comfortable being in a constant state of change. Journey mapping from customer experience can help HR make sure we are delivering the optimal end-to-end employee experience. Just as marketers analyze where a customer is on the buyer's journey, HR must understand the employee and where they are in their career.

A MORE STRATEGIC HR FOR THE FUTURE

To be effective, HR has to be able to influence the business. The more we are seen as a strategic partner, the greater the business impact we will be able to drive. The challenge is overcoming perceptions that HR is a transactional support function and not strategic. This is not unlike the position our colleagues in marketing found themselves in just a few years ago. In changing the focus of how they measured themselves, they changed their role in the business and, subsequently, their ability to deliver greater business value.

HR has the same opportunity—and it starts with being able to demonstrate value in quantifiable terms that matter to the business. To do that, HR professionals need to deeply understand the business: how it operates, the market it competes in, the strategy, the key metrics, and the HR levers that can be applied to impact them. HR leaders need to prioritize business acumen as an HR competency and build it into the fabric of the HR organization.

In addition to business acumen, a data-driven mindset needs to be pervasive throughout the HR organization. The right technology projects need to be prioritized to help both HR people and the business people they support understand and use data to make better decisions. With the right data and a deep understanding of the business, HR professionals can draw new insights and bring new solutions to the business.

One of the most critical things that HR professionals need to do to be effective in tomorrow's business world is to take time today to reimagine HR. They can get a head start by learning from and collaborating with marketing and other key functional areas that have already created competencies, processes, and technologies that can be applied to HR. Looking outside of HR to integrate emerging trends and drawing on models from other disciplines help us make new connections, turn traditional constructs upside down, and make quantum leaps toward a more strategic and modern HR for the future.

About Joyce Westerdahl

Joyce Westerdahl is CHRO at Oracle, responsible for the company's global human resources practices, policies, and operations—and for ensuring that Oracle has the right talent strategy, performance-based culture, and human resources capabilities to support its goal of becoming the No. 1 cloud company in the world. She joined Oracle in 1990 and has held positions in both line and corporate HR. In 1999, she led the effort to convert HR management from manual processing to a web-based, self-service model. As CHRO, she has taken Oracle from multiple instances to a global, single instance of the HR information system (HRIS), which vastly streamlined HR processes and reporting and ensured the company could deliver on its robust acquisition strategy. Passionate about sharing best practices, Westerdahl frequently speaks with customers and partners about Oracle HR's journey and the results that transformed the HR organization and the business. She has participated for more than 15 years as a mentor for young women and contributes her time to helping students gain industry-relevant skills prior to entering the workforce through Oracle Academy and the Oracle Education Foundation. She is also the executive director for the Oracle Women's Leadership program (OWL).

TESTS AND TRIALS TO CERTIFY HUMAN RESOURCES PROFESSIONALS

Peter Wilson

A quiet debate is gathering momentum within certain developed nations, which have traditionally set trends and best practices for the global human resources profession. The country in which the greatest level of contention appears to be transpiring is also the most prominent international force in the HR profession.

In the middle of 2014, the US Society of Human Resource Management (SHRM), with 275,000 members worldwide, cut ties with the Human Resources Certification Institute (HRCI), which has its own 135,000 members. Approximately 70,000 of those members are common to both SHRM and HRCI. The very public announcement by SHRM that the two bodies were "going our separate ways" seemed principally about desires by SHRM not only to control certification of its own members, but also to streamline the number of certification levels applying to those members from six down to two. But the split has shone light on the process of certification, and in particular, the question of whether professional certification of "competence" can be determined solely by the results of an examination.

AHRI'S APPROACH TO PROFESSIONAL CERTIFICATION

As the single peak body for the HR profession in my country, the Australian Human Resources Institute (AHRI) respects these differences in the US landscape. AHRI itself discharges in Australia the equivalent certification functions of both SHRM and HRCI, which makes sense for a smaller professional association of 20,000 members. There is disapproval in some quarters about SHRM's decision to move itself to this independent state of sole certification control. That is not a view shared by AHRI, which has established its own set of "Chinese walls" to deliver integrity for its grading and certification roles by separating them from its general membership, commercial, and service functions.

To be more specific, AHRI employs "grading" to determine the primary professional classification of its members, reflecting knowledge and achieved career seniority. On the other hand, "certification" is a term we reserve to describe the professional practicing level reached by our members, in terms of not only their knowledge but also their demonstrated abilities to handle practical challenges and display mastery over applied case studies and projects.

However, to the extent that AHRI has a difference with SHRM, it is in the latter's belief that reliance can be placed in demonstrating competence through a single test, and a multiple-choice test at that.

AHRI's governing philosophical approach on this matter can therefore best be summarized in the following simple formula:

Competence = Knowledge + Skills

This formula seeks to articulate the difference between the two elements by distinguishing knowledge as representing "what you know" and skills as representing the application of this knowledge in workplace.

This year, AHRI has been updating its model of excellence (MoE). Informed over a number of years by a range of inputs—including the global data coming out of the RBL Group research findings by Dave Ulrich and his research partners—AHRI has made adjustments to those findings in transparent but useful ways that reflect our local business customs and parlance. "Think global but act local" is our guiding principle here.

The new 2014 AHRI model of excellence is succinctly depicted in the diagram[1] set out below:

FIGURE 1. AHRI MODEL OF EXCELLENCE

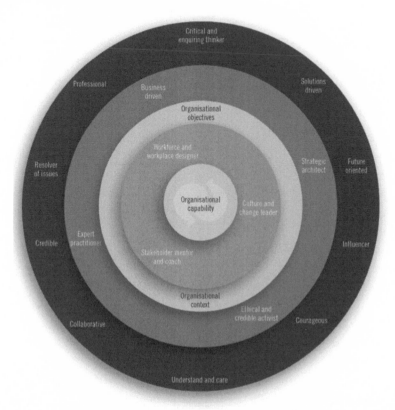

The AHRI model of excellence is now the focal point of a three-stage approach that integrates local survey data, development of intellectual property, and the initiating of a self-assessment tool that enables the determination of knowledge gaps. The aim of this approach is to arrive at a reliable and sustainable benchmark for primary HR accreditation, and also a baseline for subsequent certification.

During the early part of 2014, AHRI surveyed its member base with a questionnaire titled "What Is Good HR?" Respondents were treated anonymously and the findings were published in a discussion paper under the same title in October 2014.[2] This data was statistically significant, and further informed the AHRI Model of Excellence.[3]

The results referenced in the discussion paper are based on answers given by Australian HR practitioners to a number of probing questions about their own profession, including what it expects of practitioners entering the profession and continuing to practice within it.

The survey is the first of a two-part exercise, the second part being a survey of Australian chief executives planned for 2015. In setting the scene for "outside-in" responses from chief executives about what they want from their senior HR people, we will get a reality check on the way HR performs its function now as well as how it might inform adjustments to the MoE in the future.

We are conscious at AHRI that rapid developments in technology and communication have exposed Australian enterprises to competitive pressures on a global scale that are now reflected in how work is done, how workplaces operate, and how the workforce of the immediate future needs to adapt. As players with the potential to shape the way organizations position themselves with respect to changing rules of engagement, HR practitioners will need to ensure they possess the broader range of capabilities that business increasingly demands, and that they display the agility required to become the trustees of high people performance within organizations that contribute to competitive advantage and sustainability.

The Australian data coming out of the AHRI survey indicates plainly the behaviors rated highly by respondents, especially at the senior and executive level of the profession. More than 90 percent of respondents nominated testing qualities such as being decisive, following through on promises, and being skilled at managing priorities, in addition to less measurable behaviors such as being resilient, being approachable and open, and being personally credible.

Around a quarter of respondents indicated that they report to the CEO, and more than two-thirds operate as HR practitioners supported by either no reports at all or a maximum of two people, confirming that a great many Australian HR departments are running lean. That's a good thing, of course, as long as they have sufficient resources to make an impact. And impact is at the heart of our approach to "certification." What are the practices that HR practitioners regard as critical, and what do they believe are the expectations on the way they behave professionally in order to make an impact?

The expectations on new entrants to the profession list a number of transactional areas of practice but also list "workplace ethics and integrity." It was gratifying to see that quality highly rated by their peers at stage one of an HR career. It might well be something that is difficult to tune into later if it is not front-of-mind early. And it is not a characteristic that can be readily verified by a simple test.

It was also pleasing to note that entry-level practitioners are expected to be role models in behaviors that include being personally credible, taking responsibility for actions and decisions, and acknowledging errors. These are vital behaviors to internalize early because a failure to do so affects the regard in which the person is held as well as the profession to which she or he belongs. In turn, those behaviors affect the degree of influence that HR is able to exercise in the business.

A question was asked about ideal backgrounds for HR. I was interested to see that respondents tended to indicate disciplines such as organizational behavior, leadership, and psychology among the top items that they see as ideal. Without in any way denigrating the appropriateness of those fields of study, and being an economist with an accounting and mathematics background myself, I was somewhat disappointed to see that only 10 percent indicated a preference for economics or microeconomics as an ideal background for HR. As a profession that increasingly sees itself called upon to be credible, influential, and business driven, professional expertise outside the human sciences could well complement those disciplines and be a career plus.

Alongside the survey data, but also informed by it, has been the development of a four-unit AHRI Practising Certification Program. A distinguishing feature of the program is its work-integrated focus and practical application of learning in the organization. Undertaking the final capstone work-based project of this program enables participants to demonstrate their professional competency against the HR capabilities and behaviors outlined in the AHRI model of excellence.

Assessment of professional competence is determined by candidates' ability to demonstrate their advanced human resource management knowledge in HR strategy, organizational environment and workplace design, development, and performance, as well as showing evidence of the capacity to apply that knowledge in the workplace to contribute to the achievement of organizational objectives.

In order to embed the practices and behavior into the certification of practitioners, AHRI has invested in an easy-to-use HR training needs analysis self-assessment tool that enables practitioners to determine where they sit with respect to the AHRI model of excellence and to plan their further study accordingly on their pathway to final certification.

TRUST BUT VERIFY, MR. GORBACHEV!

Clearly, AHRI's activities reflect our belief that certification cannot be vested solely through a test that determines knowledge only, no matter how comprehensive that test may be. Further, our concerns extend to the type of test used to assess the "knowledge" component of professional competence, particularly when it is a multiple-choice format. Much of HR practice is concerned with business strategy and risk decisions for people, and these are often characterized by a combination of moral and commercial ambiguities. The risk entailed in using a multiple-choice test to bestow the judgment of competence on a candidate is that the most critical determinant for assigning that quality may be the very one answer that's left out.

In this context of establishing a judicious guideline for certification, I am reminded of former US President Ronald Reagan, who, in negotiations with then Soviet President Mikhail Gorbachev on the issue of validating arms control measures and ultimately ending the Cold War, uttered the memorable words: "Trust but verify, Mr. Gorbachev."

So it is with professional certification. As a national HR institute, we understand our members expect to pursue a lifelong journey of learning over 40 or more years of professional practice. AHRI believes a series of tests (not just one) can provide the necessary information for grading through accreditation of knowledge to a certain level of potential performance (for example, at graduate entry level, mid-range management level, and senior executive level) but that a further step is required to ensure that certification can be "entrusted" through reliance on demonstrated evidence of a candidate's skill in applied practice.

In contrast to universities and tertiary colleges, which play a basic role in teaching students to think well from first principles, AHRI sees a broader role for itself—to confirm not only that knowledge is assured, but also that the necessary practitioner skills are evident.

EXAMINATION TEST RELIANCE FOR PROFESSIONAL CERTIFICATION?

A simple example from my own life journey may illustrate the point further, and I suspect my adolescent experience at school is not atypical. The two standout students from my final high-school years were classmates by the respective names of Stanley and Gary. They often achieved perfect test scores, and both aspired to satisfy medical school entrance criteria, which they effortlessly attained. While they struggled with each other to take out the top percentile position at my high school, most of the rest of us just tried to do our best, and mainly succeeded in providing our examiners with an array of data to determine an exemplary curve fitting distribution of first, second, and third quartile test results.

As well as each of these two students exhibited brilliance in science and mathematics, Stanley was a gifted elite concert-level pianist and Gary was a first-rate team player at sports and military cadets. Onward to medical school each went, and we were encouraged to believe both would achieve the heights of professional distinction, not ruling out Nobel Prizes, with the addition of dazzling European concert tours for Stanley and likely Fortune 500 CEO stardom for Gary.

However, although both were unquestionably outstanding examination candidates, their scholastic scorecards were neither reliable predictors of their future career trajectories nor the resultant stratospheric career curve fitting predicted by their high-school educators. Stanley indeed qualified as a medical practitioner, but after graduation chose a mid-level academic career in order to free up his time to play piano exclusively for the enjoyment of his children. Gary also entered medical school, grew a Jimi Hendrix hairstyle, fell in love with a girl he thought would be the next Joan Baez, joined the protest movement, and dropped out of medicine in his second year to join the liberal arts faculty, where he applied himself to international studies and the vicissitudes of multilateral nongovernment organizations. After he completed university as an arts graduate, he also pursued a 40+ year career as an academic in the liberal arts field.

Back down in my high-school graduation class, and barely a decimal point above the median score, was Dave, who dropped out of the school military cadets because he found the discipline and dress all too much. His officers weren't sure if his style of dress was haplessly comedic or consciously rebellious. I don't think Dave quite knew either, but he surprised all of us after high school by achieving entry to the nation's top military academy at Duntroon—the Australian equivalent of West Point. After three years of exams and practical fieldwork assignments, Dave graduated with the rank of first lieutenant and finished second in his class list that year, just missing out on the prestigious Sword of Honour. Dave then went on to a decorated career of military leadership with responsibility for hundreds of soldiers in combat zones around the globe.

While each of my three former classmates may be enjoying lives they regard as personally satisfying and rewarding, their high-school test results were woefully inaccurate pointers to either their career aptitudes or prospects, and the inspired scholastic curve fitting of the time was the only real failure in these career life episodes.

THE FUTURE CHALLENGE FOR PROFESSIONAL HR ASSOCIATIONS

Certification of professional excellence cannot be reduced to exams alone. Tests and applied trials are both needed to certify a human resource professional. While SHRM's initial direct entry into the field of professional certification relies on an exam, based on the practices of other professional associations, this approach by SHRM may be reshaped over time by its interaction with the market it serves. Pathways need to be included that can help determine professional skill on the job. A core challenge for any professional HR institute is to construct those pathways for the optimum benefit of its members, and indeed the community those members are being prepared to serve.

About Peter Wilson

Peter Wilson is chairman of the Australian Human Resource Institute (AHRI), chairman of Yarra Valley Water, and a director and immediate past chair of Vision Super and the Vincent Fairfax Ethics in Leadership Foundation. He is also a director on the World HR Federation (WFPMA) and was elected as secretary-general in October 2014. Wilson led the Business Council's program to mentor senior executive women, is an advisory council member of Harvard Business Review, and is an adjunct professor in the School of Management at Monash University. Author of the 2012 book "Make Mentoring Work," he delivered the 2014 Kingsley Laffer Oration at Sydney University. Wilson held senior executive appointments at ANZ,

Amcor, and the Federal Treasury, was CEO of the Energy 21 Group, and held a range of senior board directorships. In 2005 he was made a Member of the Order of Australia for services to workplace relations and safety and community service, and was awarded a Centenary Medal in 2004.

---

[1] For a more detailed description of the model and its descriptors, see: https://www.ahri.com.au/__data/assets/pdf_file/0016/40255/MOE-layers.pdf.

[2] AHRI members can find the discussion paper (which is behind a firewall) at: https://www.ahri.com.au/resources/reports-and-white-papers/What-is-good-HR_report.pdf.

[3] https://www.ahri.com.au/about-us/model-of-excellence

CONCLUSION

NOW WHAT? IMPLICATIONS FOR THE PROFESSION AND FOR YOU, THE HR PROFESSIONAL

Dave Ulrich, William A. Schiemann and Libby Sartain

We began this volume by saying we are advocates for the HR profession. After reviewing these essays, we are even stronger advocates. Part of the vitality of a profession draws from the freshness of its ideas. We believe that these authors are indicative of innovative HR thinking and action.

Clearly, in a world filled with unprecedented change, HR professionals have greater opportunities than ever for influence. But to rise to those opportunities, they have to learn and do innovative things. They need to see the world from the outside in, deliver value through organization and talent, access and make decisions based on information and analytics, build the right HR organization, and develop personal competencies to receive respect and deliver business outcomes.

We are not the first, or last, group of HR observers to call for HR professionals to rise to the occasion. For decades, advocates and opponents of HR have ruminated that HR has not delivered more value to business results. We hope that this book models how to go from rhetoric to real progress. This progress will come not only from the content of HR, which includes the key issues HR professionals must address, but also from processes for how HR professionals go about dealing with these issues, how HR functions are organized, and how HR practices are redefined.

THE CONTENT OF HR

In terms of content, HR is increasingly less about HR and more about how HR delivers business results. Asking "What competencies do HR professionals need?" is the wrong leading question. It is time to ask "What do organizations need from HR professionals to be successful?" Or, "Which HR competencies best deliver business results?" HR is not a social agenda, dependent on the whims of socially conscious business leaders, but a business imperative. As a business imperative, HR outcomes (talent, leadership, and organization) are owned by line executives, with HR professionals being architects of how to deliver these outcomes.

The content of *value-added HR* is also woven throughout these essays. There is almost no discussion of specific HR tools (e.g., how to implement a nine-box performance review or how to manage career bands), but intense scrutiny of the outcomes of these tools. The outcomes of HR show up when organizations respond to external business drivers (e.g., global social, technological, economic, political, environmental, and demographic changes) and key external stakeholders such as investors, customers, and communities (see section on context to strategy). To deliver value to these stakeholders, HR professionals offer insight on talent (sections on sourcing and optimizing talent) and organization (section on organizational outcomes). To figure out how to prioritize HR investments, information and analytics have become de rigueur. While HR will continue to define problems through ideas, HR must solve problems through rigorous analytics that turns information into insight with impact.

This book also has content about how to govern HR. It is interesting that in the section on HR governance, few talked about the structure of an HR department (e.g., debating centers of expertise versus embedded HR). More HR governance issues are building the DNA or brand of HR, linking HR with other departments (e.g., marketing, finance, IT), helping HR departments create strategies that manage paradoxes, and managing the relationships within HR more than the roles of HR. Finally, we have exceptional content on what it means to be an effective HR professional. As debates continue about who, how, and when to certify HR professionals, this collection of essays may help highlight competencies required for value-added HR work.

The field of HR has rich content that will shape a positive future.

THE PROCESS OF HR

In the introduction, we called for a new way to think about improving the quality of HR through four criteria that define the process for doing HR. We hope that this volume models these criteria and establishes a pattern for how to move forward.

- *Collaboration* – In this volume, we have essays from academics, consultants, CHROs, and industry associations. Many of these authors compete with one another both directly and indirectly. By contributing to this volume, authors have agreed to share their best thinking with no financial remuneration. By openly sharing this volume with millions of HR and organizational leaders globally, we hope we have introduced both a new framework for learning and a spirit of cooperation and collaboration. Competition for ideas and services will continue, but we can also learn to respect and collaborate with one another.
- *Innovation* – In this volume, we have tried to report not on what has been done but on what *can be* done in the future. This means a little less focus on information that solves puzzles (traditional predictive analytics) than on ideas that shape mysteries (seeking answers to new questions) of what can be done. By aspiring to what can be, HR will continue to be vibrant and not get mired in tiresome and endless debates about what has been done.
- *Application* – The gap between theory, research, and practice gets mitigated when the focus is application. Application means that theory starts with a problem and works to find a solution that is theoretically robust and replicable. Research is not just about statistical elegance, but about getting data that leads to ideas with impact. Practice is not just solving a particular case study or situation, but building principles (theory) that endure. This virtuous cycle is evident over and over again in these essays. Traditional academics are offering insights that solve problems. Traditional HR leaders are generalizing from their personal experiences to a broader population. We hope these essays model ideas with impact that will stimulate the profession.
- *Globalization* – We are so pleased that we have essays from countries and thought leaders around the world (Asia, Australia, New Zealand, China, India, Europe, the Middle East, and North and South America). While generic principles of HR may traverse the globe, HR insights from around the world should be shared. The field of HR is far past the imperialistic days when ideas from one market were

imposed on others. As we share globally, we will learn that good HR ideas and practices exist throughout the world that can be shared.

In brief, we hope that the content of this work and the process of doing the work will increase the likelihood that the HR profession overall, HR departments, and HR professionals will make sustainable progress.

HR PROFESSION

The HR profession is vibrant and evolving. Drawing from research on committed relationships, we can identify four stages of the evolution of the HR profession:

- *Phase 1:Attraction/honeymoon* – The profession grew rapidly with the recognition that the ways people are treated shape organizational cultures and defines outcomes. Lots of innovative ideas earmark the enthusiasm for the HR profession.
- *Phase 2: Power struggle* – As a profession (or relationship) evolves, cliques emerge and groups who collaborate get testy with one another. Trust erodes and different groups claim to have more insight that someone else.
- *Phase 3: Withdrawal* – As a profession (or relationship) splinters, each group carves out its own niche and operates independently. The profession grows as independent and somewhat isolated thought leaders work to protect their turf.
- *Phase 4: Transcendence* – As a profession (or relationship) evolves, sometimes personal agendas are put aside for a broader good. Synergies and interdependencies occur as people with differences work together.

We envision a profession moving from a power struggle and withdrawal into a more transcendent state where new ideas are generated, experiments ensue, and debates occur, but in a broader context of looking forward to make progress. We hope that the HR profession can evolve to a transcendent state so that employees inside an organization and customers, investors, and communities outside are blessed by good HR work.

HR DEPARTMENTS

HR departments, or functions, are changing. Just like businesses have to remove barriers between themselves and others, HR departments need to learn to collaborate with other business groups. By collaborating with marketing, HR can access consumer and industry trends and make sure that customer criteria shape

HR investments. Marketing insights also can help HR build an HR, employer, and employee brand that distinguishes the HR department.

By collaborating with finance, HR can become more aggressive at measuring the impact of its work on business outcomes. By applying more rigorous analytics to HR investments, the return on HR activity becomes more clear. Financial collaboration can also connect HR to investors, either debt or equity, who may be interested in intangibles and leadership for deriving firm valuation.

By collaborating with IT, HR builds better systems to access information and accomplish work. Social media offers HR insights on how outside stakeholders view the firm. Technological platforms enable HR to more efficiently and effectively design and deliver HR services. Information more readily accessed through technology can also help organizations be more successful.

By collaborating with strategy, HR can learn to shape a mission, vision, and strategy for its function. This purpose-driven HR agenda will help HR operate like a business within a business, with clear goals, objectives, and outcomes.

As HR departments learn to collaborate with other functional departments, they are more able to offer integrated solutions to business problems.

The structure of an HR department will also evolve. The HR structure should match the business structure. Businesses that are centralized will likely have HR departments with enterprise-wide HR operations (e.g., staffing, training, compensation, benefits). Businesses that are decentralized and that operate as holding companies will likely have separate HR operations in each autonomous business unit. Businesses that are allied, conglomerate, or diversified, where the business operates as a matrix, will likely have HR operations that match this business structure.

HR PROFESSIONALS

We have coached many seasoned executives in and out of HR. In these coaching sessions, we often organize our conversations around three questions. These are the three questions that we hope HR professionals will ponder as they access the ideas in this book.

So, this final section is written to you, the aspiring HR professional, offering our coaching queries about how you will make use of the information in this book.

Question 1: What do you want?

Be clear. Probably the most critical question you will ask yourself for both your personal and professional pursuits is simply: "What do I want?" Knowing what you want captures your desires, clarifies your measures of success, focuses your attention, ensures that you have passion for what you do, and allows you to be resilient when challenges inevitably happen. As an HR professional, what do you most want from your career? Influence? Power? Status? Impact? Autonomy? Respect? Defining what you want starts with recognizing your strengths and passions by reflecting on some personal questions:

- What are my strengths? (Do a strengths test.)[1]
- What are my predispositions? (Do a personality test.)
- What challenges do I enjoy thinking about and solving? (Think about a time when you really enjoyed your work.)
- What comes naturally to me? (Reflect on tasks you look forward to doing.)
- What work would I choose to do? (Imagine you could pick any job or task. What would you do?)

It is amazing how otherwise thoughtful and directed people fall into their career by default, not intent. When you are clear about how your strengths will help you discover and solve problems you care about, you will have more enduring passion for what you do. You should be able to use HR competency models to benchmark yourself throughout your career.

Be realistic. Defining what you want requires a sense of realism. Are your passions consistent with your abilities? Do not run up sand dunes and pursue what does not work for you. One senior HR professional was frustrated that he was not getting the attention he felt he deserved for his ideas. As an HR professional, he spent time behind the scenes architecting business success. I suggested he change careers. A successful HR professional is more often a silent partner whose influence comes from ideas with impact more than a visible position with status. I often coach executives who say they want to lead, but are not comfortable or open to giving performance feedback. It is difficult to lead without being able to share feedback.

Show grit. Most people are pleased to know that IQ is not the biggest predictor of long-term leadership, career, or personal success. Nor is EQ. Resilience, learning agility, perseverance, determination—that is, grit—is a better predictor.[2] If you are doing work based on what you want, you are more likely to stick with it. Your resolve is increased if and when you value what you do. Doing work that others want you to do is not as sustainable as doing work that you want to do. Knowing what you want, acting on it, and being realistic increases your grittiness.

Question 2: Whom do you serve?

Sometimes brilliant leaders lack interpersonal savvy. They are lollipop leaders who have a great brain, but no heart. They have not recognized that learning to work with others is a foundation for both personal happiness and professional success. Research has shown that people who care about people are 60 percent more likely to be promoted. Economist Arthur Brooks also found that those who gave more and served more made more money, not less. Those who give to charity are 43 percent happier than those who do not give.[3] Volunteering and helping others promote emotional, physical, and economic well-being.

As an HR professional, repeatedly ask yourself the questions: Who can I help today? What can I do for someone else? How will the initiatives I craft affect others? Many days, nothing much comes to mind; other days, you may be reminded of opportunities to reach out and give to others. As you contemplate those you help, realize that the answer should be those inside the organization (employees, line managers) as well as those outside the organization (customers, investors, the broader community). When I ask HR professionals, "Who are your customers?" the best answers are the customers who buy products or services from the organization, investors who fund and profit from the organization, or the community who is nurtured by the organization. Think "outside in" to deliver long-term value to others.

When you focus on others, you turn your personal point of view into your personal brand. You use your strengths to strengthen others. When you perceive that your job as an HR professional is to make others better, you are less focused on who you are than on how you can improve others. You can model serving others by:

- Acknowledging others' efforts both privately and publicly. Be Teflon in success (share credit) and Velcro in failure (take responsibility).
- Expressing gratitude for what others do well. Research has shown that others improve when we have 3:1 (at work) and 5:1 (outside of work) positive to negative messages.
- Seeking others' opinions for how to improve. One of my favorite coaching questions is "What do you think?" asked before giving an answer to a question.
- Listening to understand why others are doing what they are doing. Learn to see their choices from their point of view.
- Offering candid encouragement for what they can improve. Learn to have positive accountability conversations.

As you serve others, you will ultimately build your personal well-being and a reservoir of good will. You will also become a role model for others about how to collaborate.

Question 3: How do you build?

Some go into HR because they "like people." While a good idea, it will likely limit your career because liking people may not create full value for the organizations where you work. Hopefully, you will not stop helping people, but increase your value by building organizations.

Your job is not to act as a lone wolf or independent contributor. Learn to work with others. Become a good team member. Be aware of how your personal work will be seen and used by others. Being part of a good HR team will outlast your personal presence.

In addition, institutionalize your ideas. Make sure that what you propose and sponsor is not tied to you or any other single individual. Create organizational systems or processes that capture your ideas. Work within the system to improve it. Iconoclasts do not last. Recognize that you want to build sustainable, lasting impact through the processes and systems you create.

There it is, our final mantra:

- Know yourself.
- Serve others.
- Build systems.

These are indeed great times for HR. The rising generation of HR leaders will not only help organizations compete economically, but become social and emotional reservoirs of goodwill and well-being. We wish you well in your personal journey.

---

[1] Martin Seligman and his colleagues offer an excellent strengths test: https://www.authentichappiness.sas.upenn.edu/user/login?destination=node/504

[2] A.L. Duckworth, C. Peterson, M.D. Matthews, and D.R. Kelly, "Grit: Perseverance and Passion for Long-Term Goals," Journal of Personality and Social Psychology, 92(6), 2007, pages 1087–1101.

[3] Arthur C. Brooks, "Who Really Cares: The Surprising Truth About Compassionate Conservatism"(New York: Basic Books, 2006).